DOUBLE

04

AYAKO NODA

TABLE OF CONTENTS

4

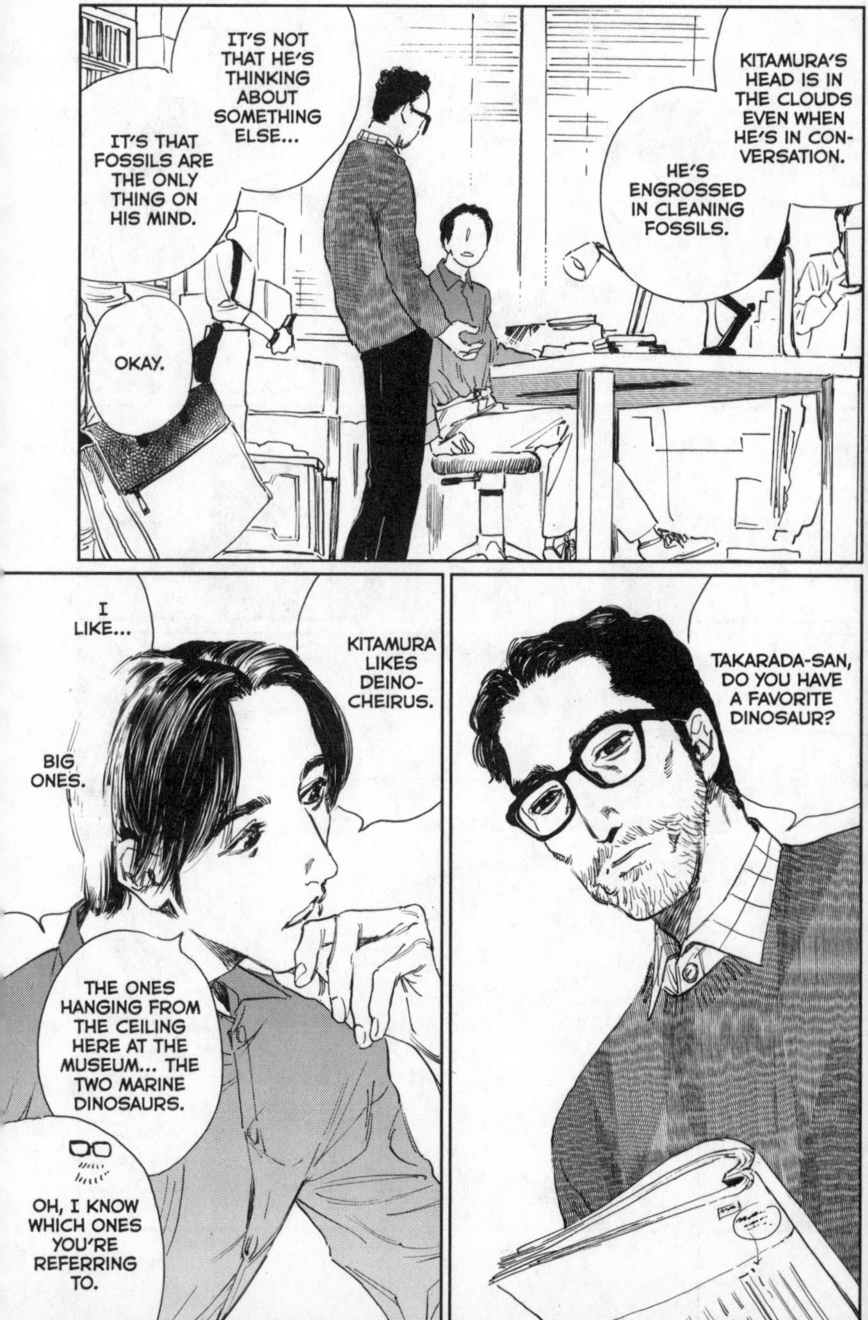
KITAMURA'S HEAD IS IN THE CLOUDS EVEN WHEN HE'S IN CONVERSATION.
HE'S ENGROSSED IN CLEANING FOSSILS.
IT'S NOT THAT HE'S THINKING ABOUT SOMETHING ELSE...
IT'S THAT FOSSILS ARE THE ONLY THING ON HIS MIND.
OKAY.
TAKARADA-SAN, DO YOU HAVE A FAVORITE DINOSAUR?
KITAMURA LIKES DEINOCHEIRUS.
I LIKE...
BIG ONES.
THE ONES HANGING FROM THE CEILING HERE AT THE MUSEUM... THE TWO MARINE DINOSAURS.
OH, I KNOW WHICH ONES YOU'RE REFERRING TO.

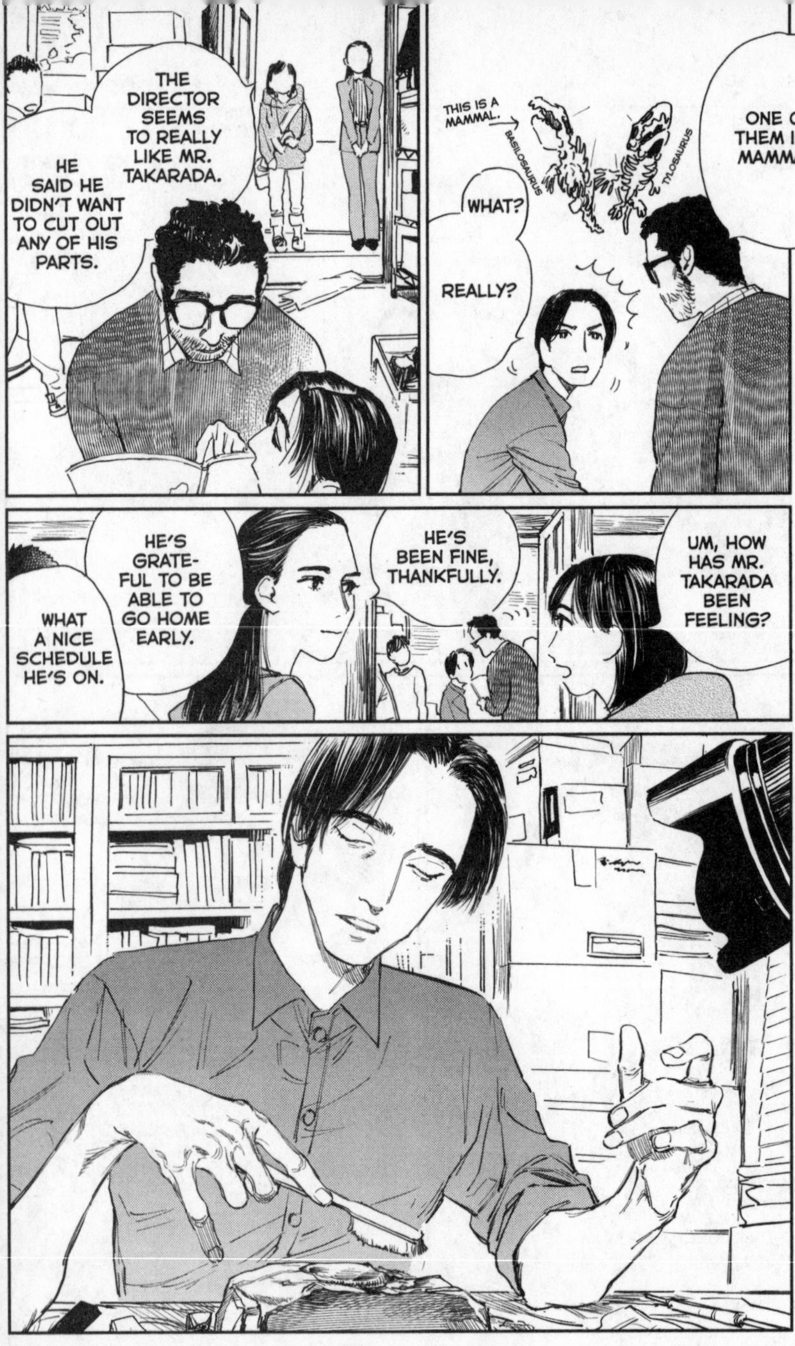
ONE OF THEM IS A MAMMAL.
THIS IS A MAMMAL.
BASILOSAURUS
TYLOSAURUS
WHAT?
REALLY?
THE DIRECTOR SEEMS TO REALLY LIKE MR. TAKARADA.
HE SAID HE DIDN'T WANT TO CUT OUT ANY OF HIS PARTS.
UM, HOW HAS MR. TAKARADA BEEN FEELING?
HE'S BEEN FINE, THANKFULLY.
HE'S GRATE-FUL TO BE ABLE TO GO HOME EARLY.
WHAT A NICE SCHEDULE HE'S ON.

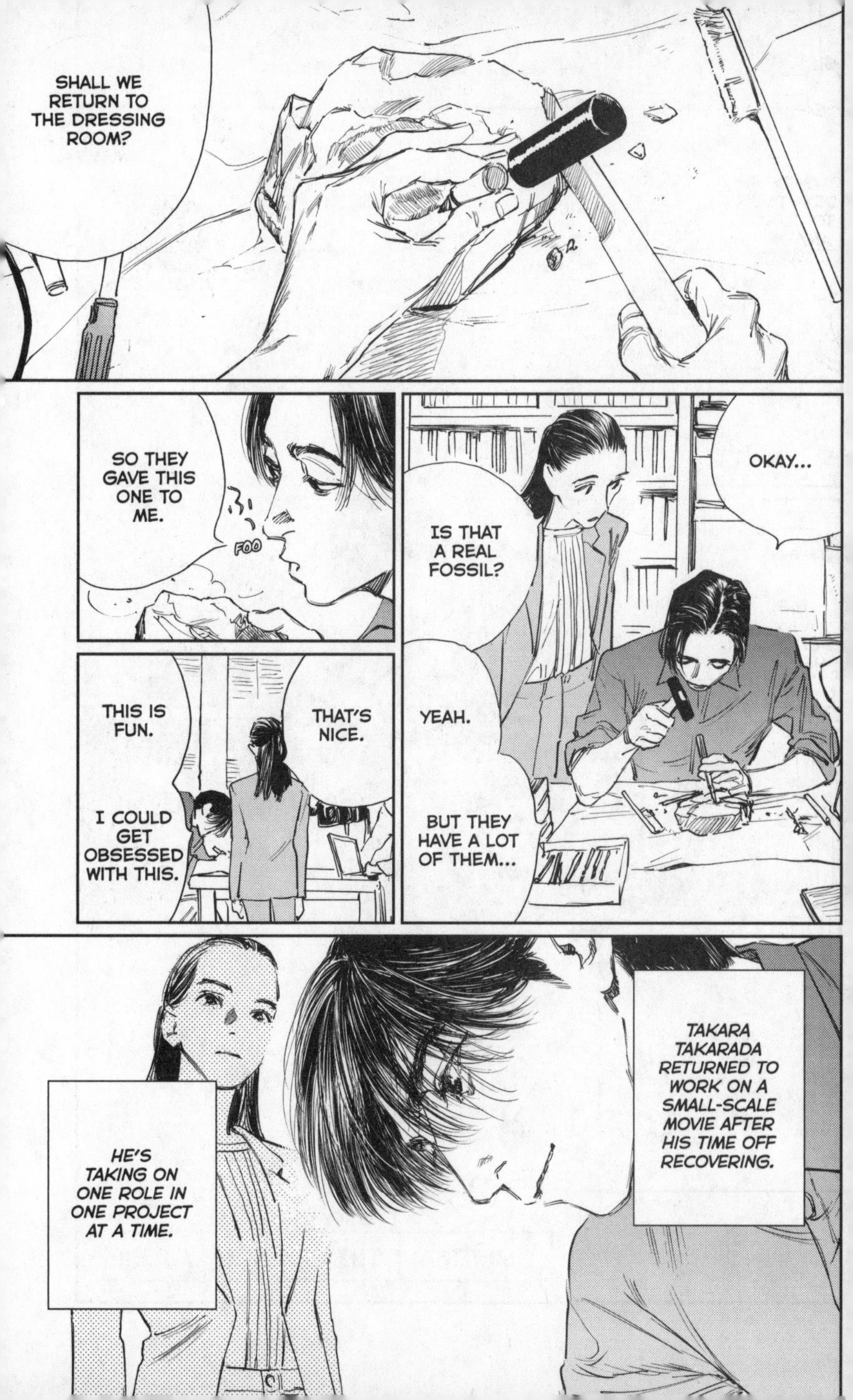
SHALL WE RETURN TO THE DRESSING ROOM?
OKAY...
IS THAT A REAL FOSSIL?
YEAH.
BUT THEY HAVE A LOT OF THEM...
SO THEY GAVE THIS ONE TO ME.
ふ
FOO
THAT'S NICE.
THIS IS FUN.
I COULD GET OBSESSED WITH THIS.
TAKARA TAKARADA RETURNED TO WORK ON A SMALL-SCALE MOVIE AFTER HIS TIME OFF RECOVERING.
HE'S TAKING ON ONE ROLE IN ONE PROJECT AT A TIME.

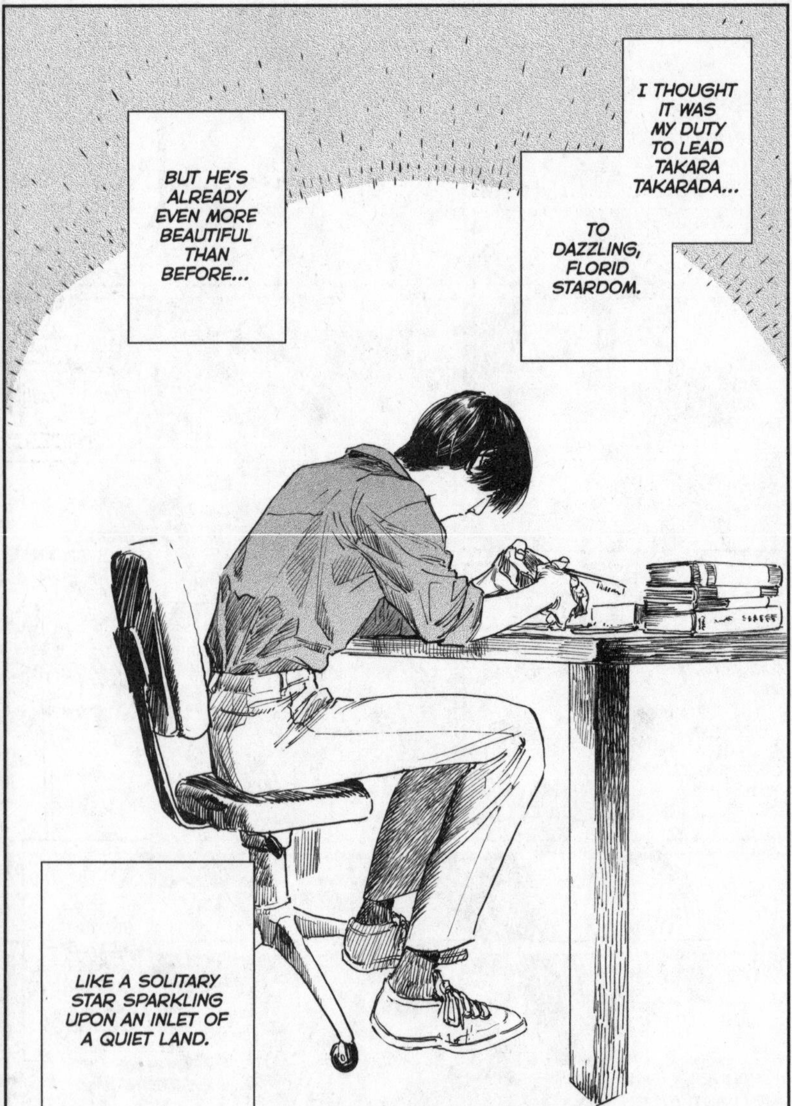
I THOUGHT IT WAS MY DUTY TO LEAD TAKARA TAKARADA...
TO DAZZLING, FLORID STARDOM.
BUT HE'S ALREADY EVEN MORE BEAUTIFUL THAN BEFORE...
LIKE A SOLITARY STAR SPARKLING UPON AN INLET OF A QUIET LAND.

CHAPTER 20 | THE GLASS MENAGERIE

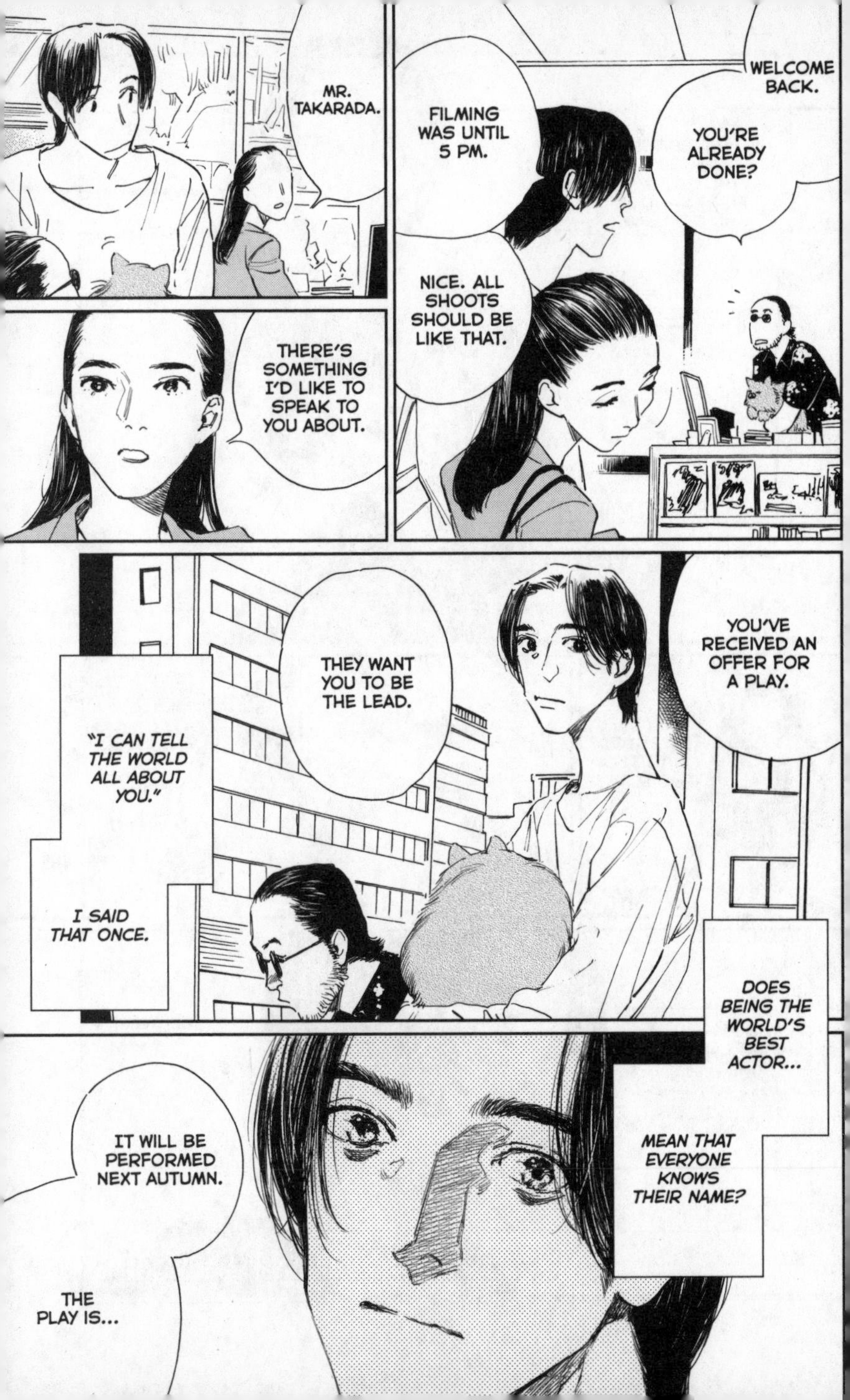
WELCOME BACK.
YOU'RE ALREADY DONE?
FILMING WAS UNTIL 5 PM.
NICE. ALL SHOOTS SHOULD BE LIKE THAT.
MR. TAKARADA.
THERE'S SOMETHING I'D LIKE TO SPEAK TO YOU ABOUT.
YOU'VE RECEIVED AN OFFER FOR A PLAY.
THEY WANT YOU TO BE THE LEAD.
"I CAN TELL THE WORLD ALL ABOUT YOU."
I SAID THAT ONCE.
DOES BEING THE WORLD'S BEST ACTOR...
MEAN THAT EVERYONE KNOWS THEIR NAME?
IT WILL BE PERFORMED NEXT AUTUMN.
THE PLAY IS...

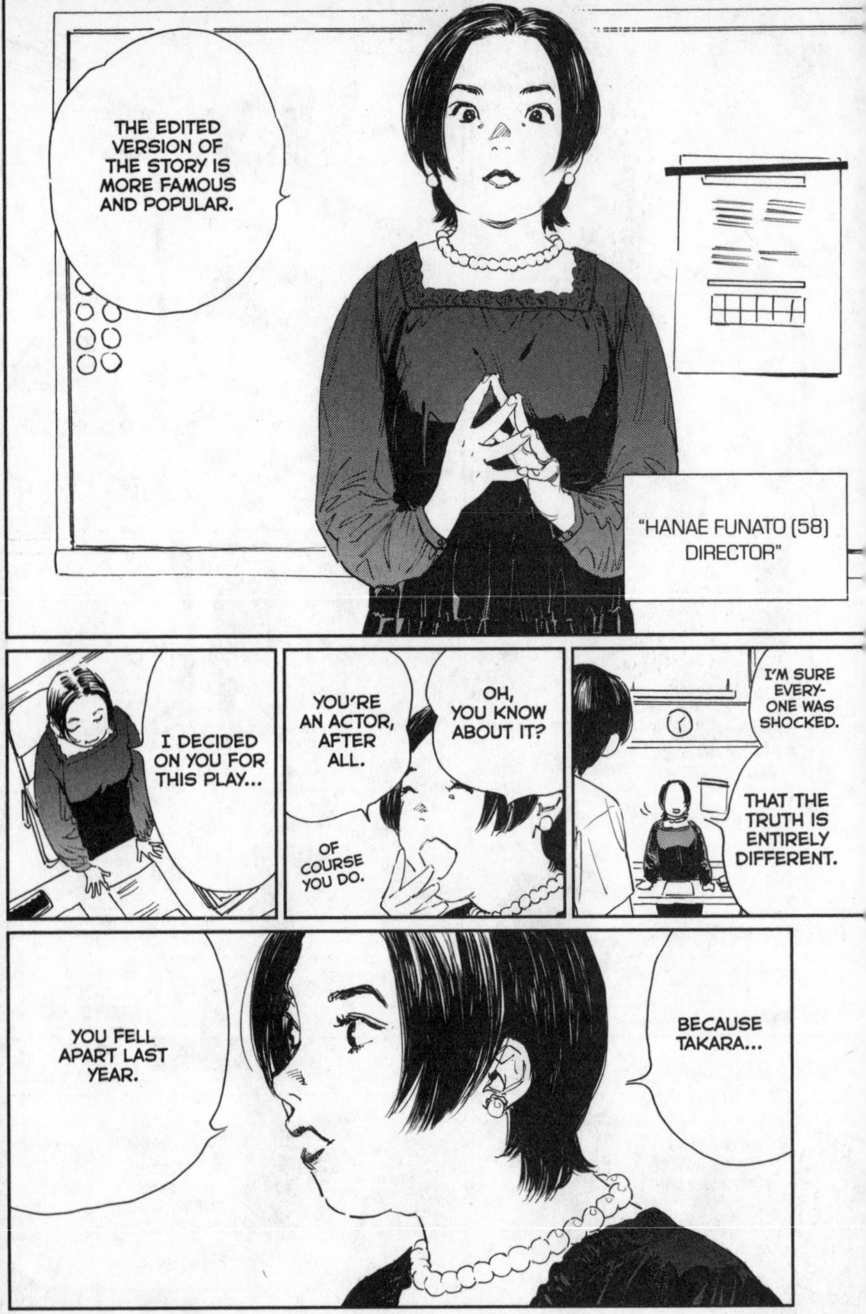
THE EDITED VERSION OF THE STORY IS MORE FAMOUS AND POPULAR.
"HANAE FUNATO (58) DIRECTOR"
I'M SURE EVERY-ONE WAS SHOCKED.
THAT THE TRUTH IS ENTIRELY DIFFERENT.
OH, YOU KNOW ABOUT IT?
YOU'RE AN ACTOR, AFTER ALL.
OF COURSE YOU DO.
I DECIDED ON YOU FOR THIS PLAY...
BECAUSE TAKARA...
YOU FELL APART LAST YEAR.

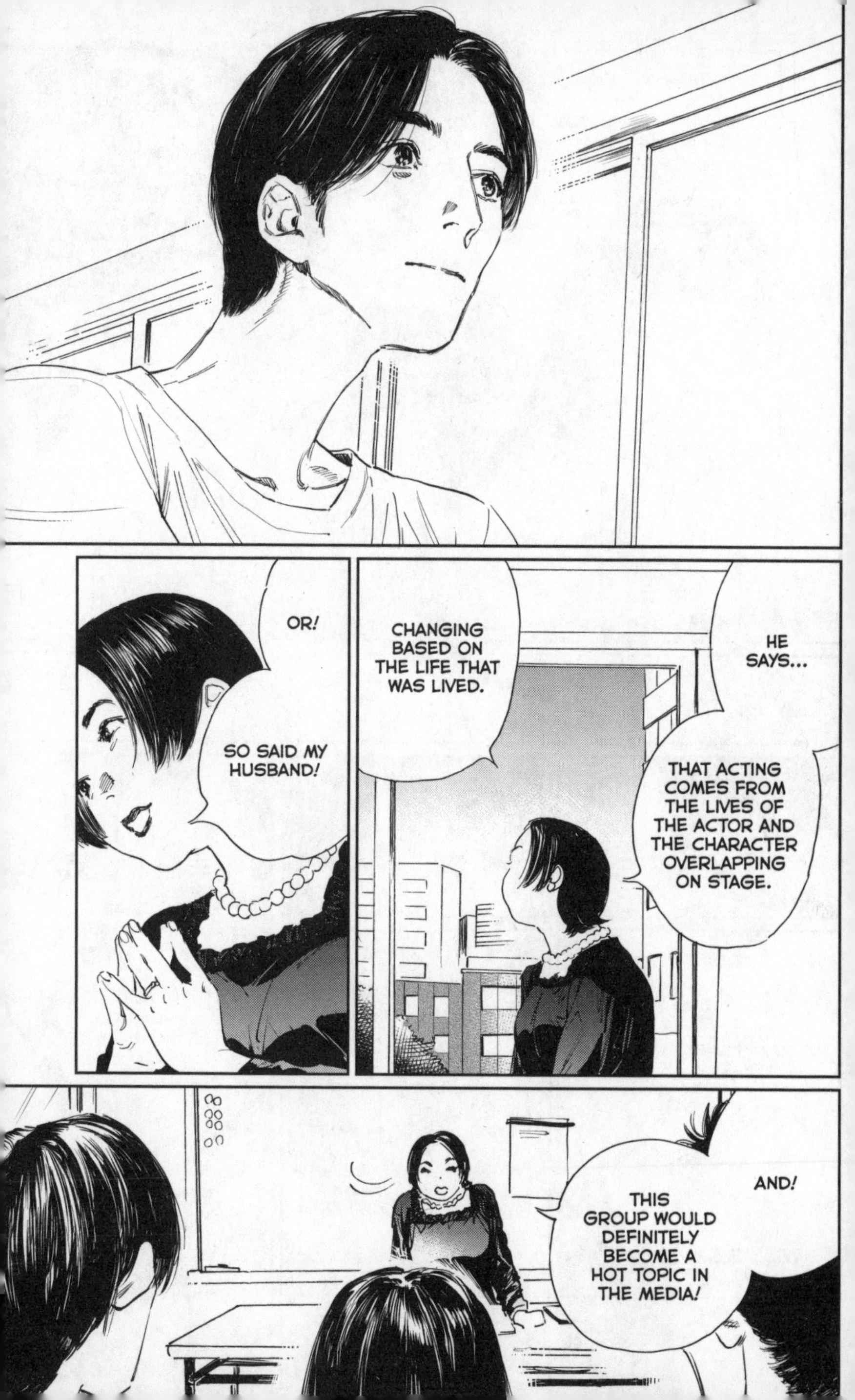
HE SAYS...
THAT ACTING COMES FROM THE LIVES OF THE ACTOR AND THE CHARACTER OVERLAPPING ON STAGE.
CHANGING BASED ON THE LIFE THAT WAS LIVED.
OR!
SO SAID MY HUSBAND!
AND!
THIS GROUP WOULD DEFINITELY BECOME A HOT TOPIC IN THE MEDIA!

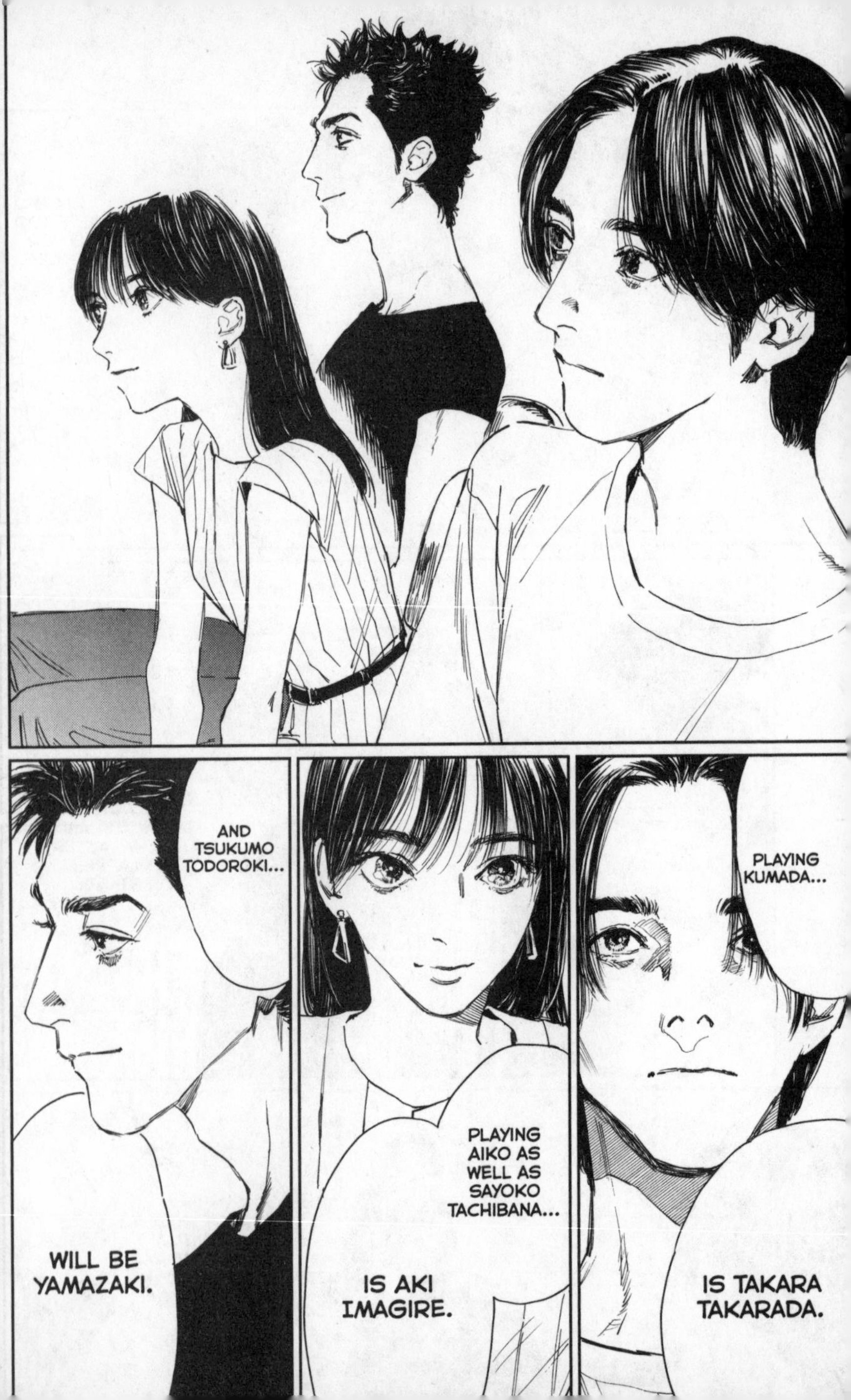
PLAYING KUMADA...
IS TAKARA TAKARADA.
PLAYING AIKO AS WELL AS SAYOKO TACHIBANA...
IS AKI IMAGIRE.
AND TSUKUMO TODOROKI...
WILL BE YAMAZAKI.

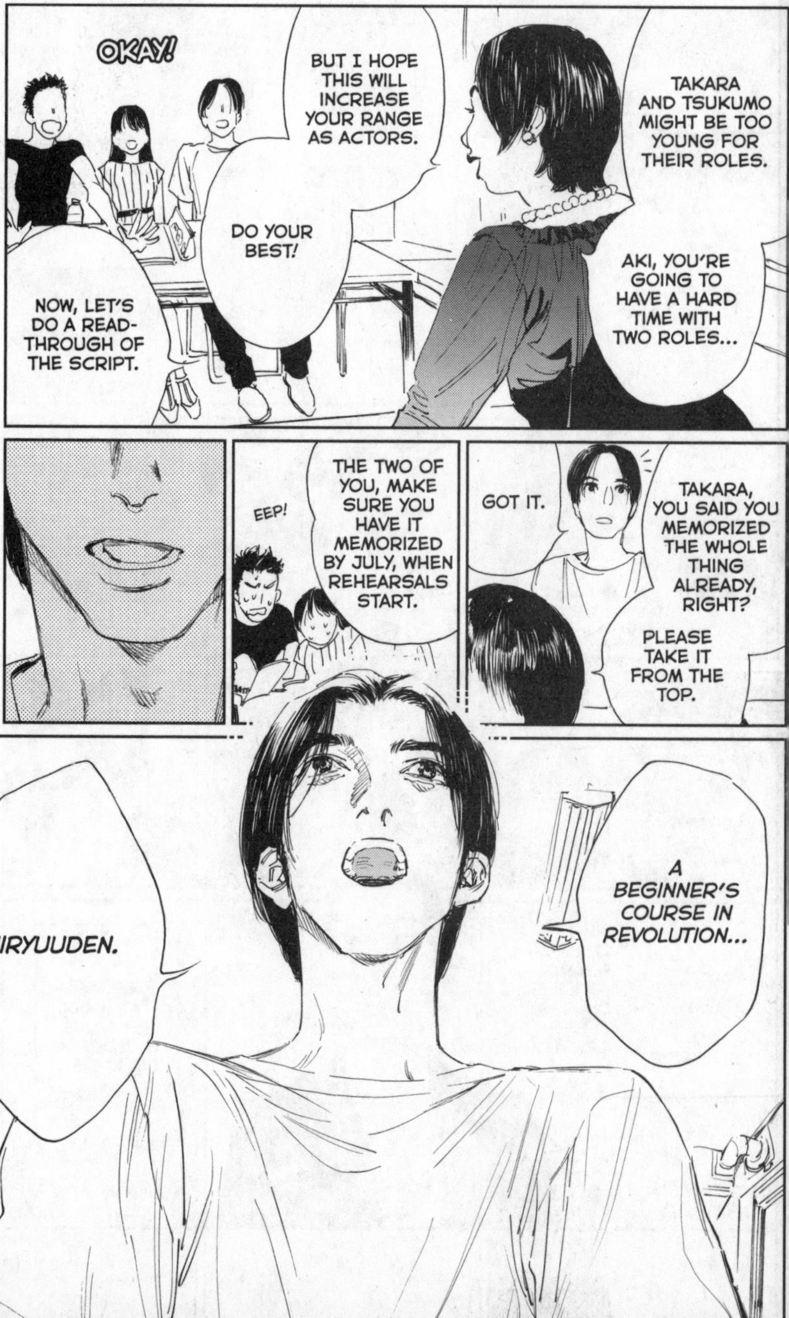
TAKARA AND TSUKUMO MIGHT BE TOO YOUNG FOR THEIR ROLES.
BUT I HOPE THIS WILL INCREASE YOUR RANGE AS ACTORS.
AKI, YOU'RE GOING TO HAVE A HARD TIME WITH TWO ROLES...
DO YOUR BEST!
OKAY!
NOW, LET'S DO A READ-THROUGH OF THE SCRIPT.
TAKARA, YOU SAID YOU MEMORIZED THE WHOLE THING ALREADY, RIGHT?
GOT IT.
PLEASE TAKE IT FROM THE TOP.
THE TWO OF YOU, MAKE SURE YOU HAVE IT MEMORIZED BY JULY, WHEN REHEARSALS START.
EEP!
A BEGINNER'S COURSE IN REVOLUTION...
HIRYUUDEN.

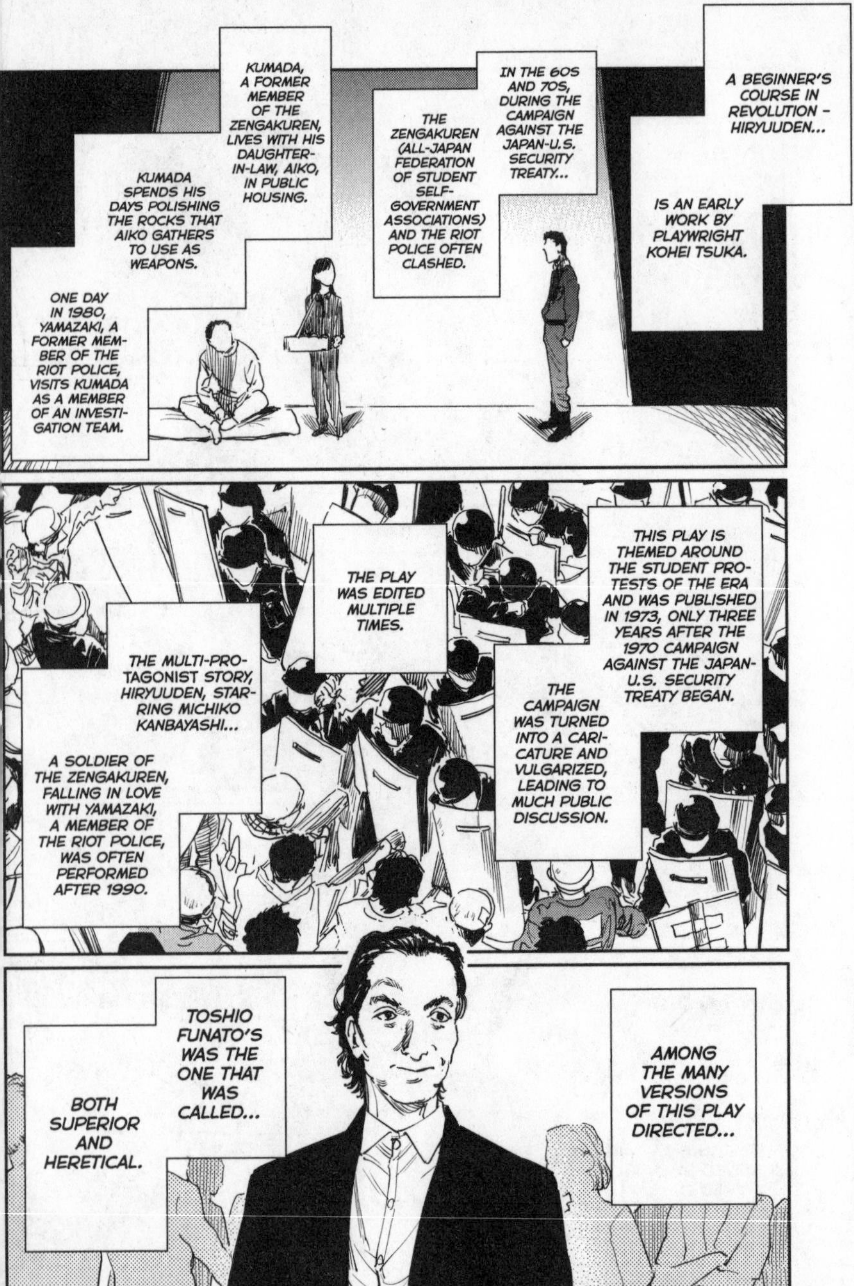

A BEGINNER'S COURSE IN REVOLUTION - HIRYUUDEN...
IS AN EARLY WORK BY PLAYWRIGHT KOHEI TSUKA.
IN THE 60S AND 70S, DURING THE CAMPAIGN AGAINST THE JAPAN-U.S. SECURITY TREATY...
THE ZENGAKUREN (ALL-JAPAN FEDERATION OF STUDENT SELF-GOVERNMENT ASSOCIATIONS) AND THE RIOT POLICE OFTEN CLASHED.
KUMADA, A FORMER MEMBER OF THE ZENGAKUREN, LIVES WITH HIS DAUGHTER-IN-LAW, AIKO, IN PUBLIC HOUSING.
KUMADA SPENDS HIS DAYS POLISHING THE ROCKS THAT AIKO GATHERS TO USE AS WEAPONS.
ONE DAY IN 1980, YAMAZAKI, A FORMER MEMBER OF THE RIOT POLICE, VISITS KUMADA AS A MEMBER OF AN INVESTIGATION TEAM.
THIS PLAY IS THEMED AROUND THE STUDENT PROTESTS OF THE ERA AND WAS PUBLISHED IN 1973, ONLY THREE YEARS AFTER THE 1970 CAMPAIGN AGAINST THE JAPAN-U.S. SECURITY TREATY BEGAN.
THE CAMPAIGN WAS TURNED INTO A CARICATURE AND VULGARIZED, LEADING TO MUCH PUBLIC DISCUSSION.
THE PLAY WAS EDITED MULTIPLE TIMES.
THE MULTI-PROTAGONIST STORY, HIRYUUDEN, STARRING MICHIKO KANBAYASHI...
A SOLDIER OF THE ZENGAKUREN, FALLING IN LOVE WITH YAMAZAKI, A MEMBER OF THE RIOT POLICE, WAS OFTEN PERFORMED AFTER 1990.
AMONG THE MANY VERSIONS OF THIS PLAY DIRECTED...
TOSHIO FUNATO'S WAS THE ONE THAT WAS CALLED...
BOTH SUPERIOR AND HERETICAL.

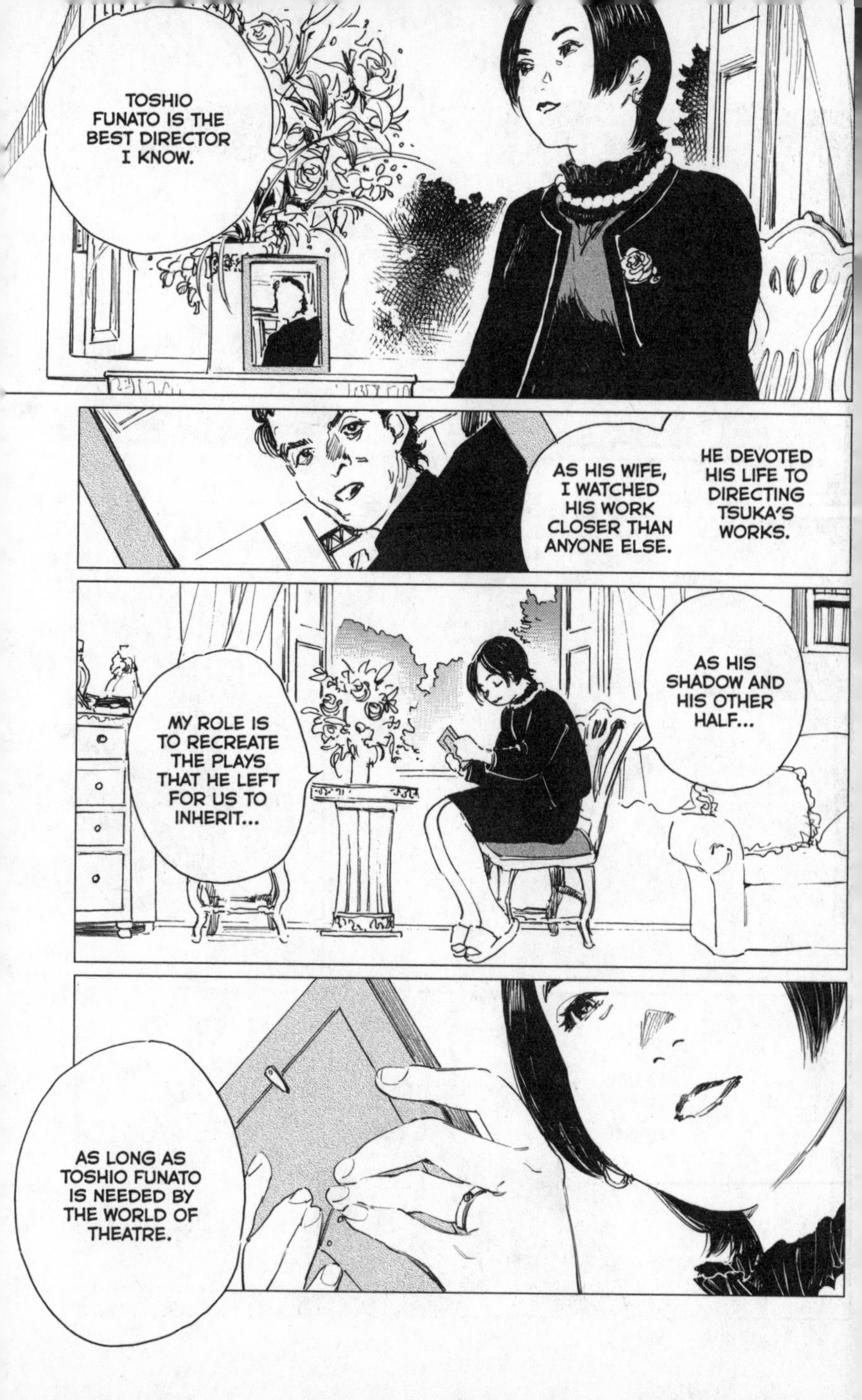
TOSHIO FUNATO IS THE BEST DIRECTOR I KNOW.
HE DEVOTED HIS LIFE TO DIRECTING TSUKA'S WORKS.
AS HIS WIFE, I WATCHED HIS WORK CLOSER THAN ANYONE ELSE.
AS HIS SHADOW AND HIS OTHER HALF...
MY ROLE IS TO RECREATE THE PLAYS THAT HE LEFT FOR US TO INHERIT...
AS LONG AS TOSHIO FUNATO IS NEEDED BY THE WORLD OF THEATRE.

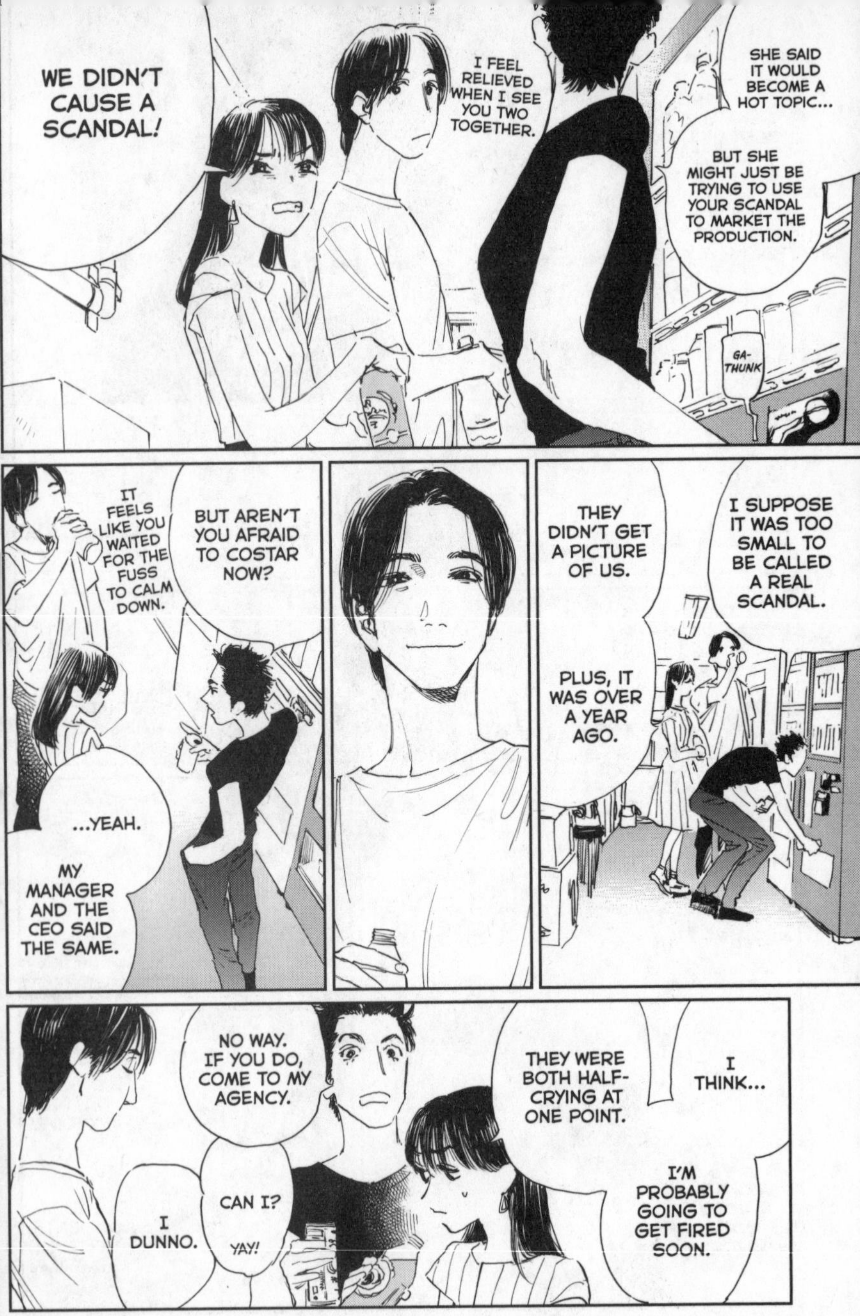
SHE SAID IT WOULD BECOME A HOT TOPIC...
BUT SHE MIGHT JUST BE TRYING TO USE YOUR SCANDAL TO MARKET THE PRODUCTION.
GA-THUNK
I FEEL RELIEVED WHEN I SEE YOU TWO TOGETHER.
WE DIDN'T CAUSE A SCANDAL!
I SUPPOSE IT WAS TOO SMALL TO BE CALLED A REAL SCANDAL.
THEY DIDN'T GET A PICTURE OF US.
PLUS, IT WAS OVER A YEAR AGO.
BUT AREN'T YOU AFRAID TO COSTAR NOW?
IT FEELS LIKE YOU WAITED FOR THE FUSS TO CALM DOWN.
...YEAH.
MY MANAGER AND THE CEO SAID THE SAME.
I THINK...
THEY WERE BOTH HALF-CRYING AT ONE POINT.
I'M PROBABLY GOING TO GET FIRED SOON.
NO WAY. IF YOU DO, COME TO MY AGENCY.
CAN I?
YAY!
I DUNNO.

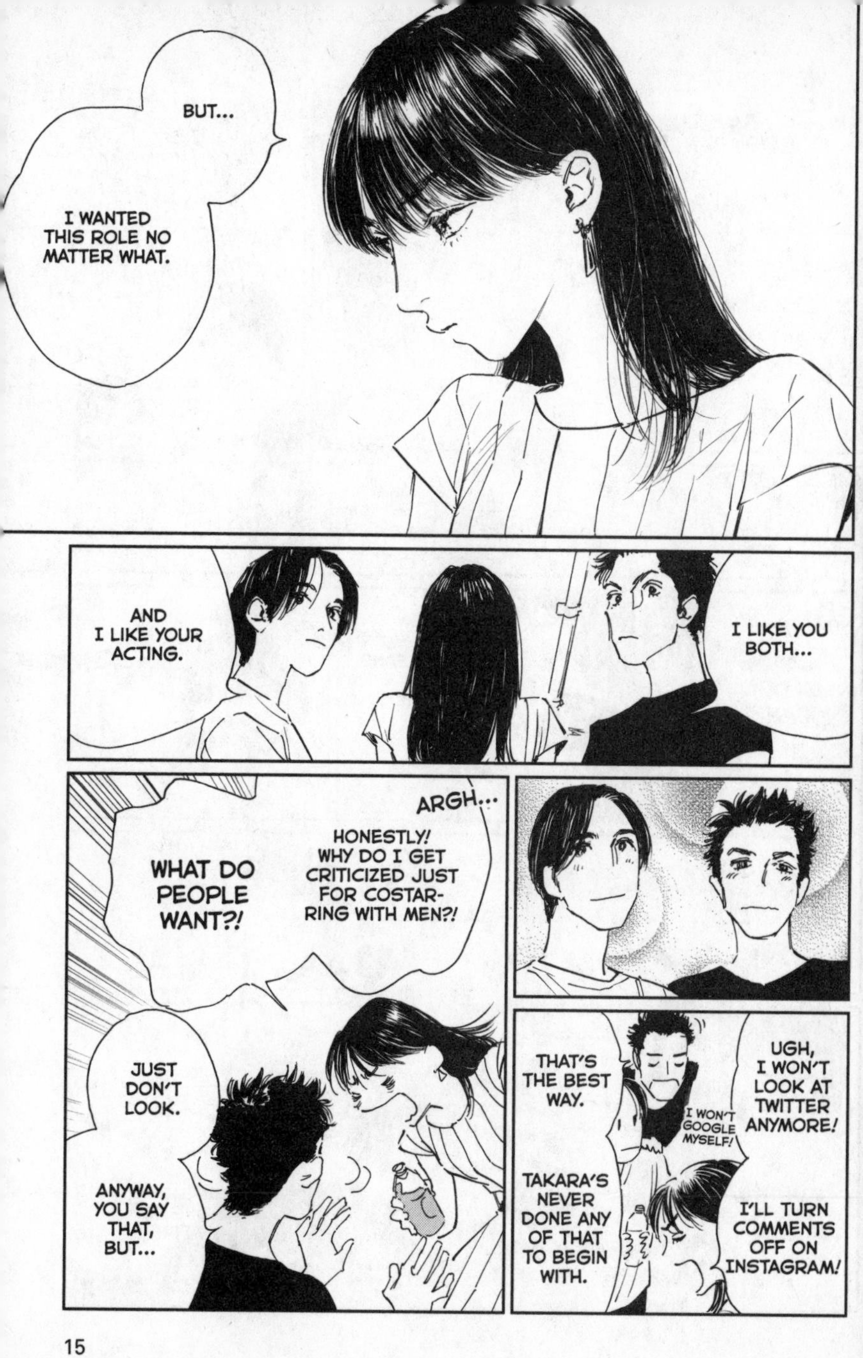
BUT...
I WANTED THIS ROLE NO MATTER WHAT.
I LIKE YOU BOTH...
AND I LIKE YOUR ACTING.
UGH, I WON'T LOOK AT TWITTER ANYMORE!
I WON'T GOOGLE MYSELF!
I'LL TURN COMMENTS OFF ON INSTAGRAM!
THAT'S THE BEST WAY.
TAKARA'S NEVER DONE ANY OF THAT TO BEGIN WITH.
ARGH...
HONESTLY! WHY DO I GET CRITICIZED JUST FOR COSTAR-RING WITH MEN?!
WHAT DO PEOPLE WANT?!
JUST DON'T LOOK.
ANYWAY, YOU SAY THAT, BUT...

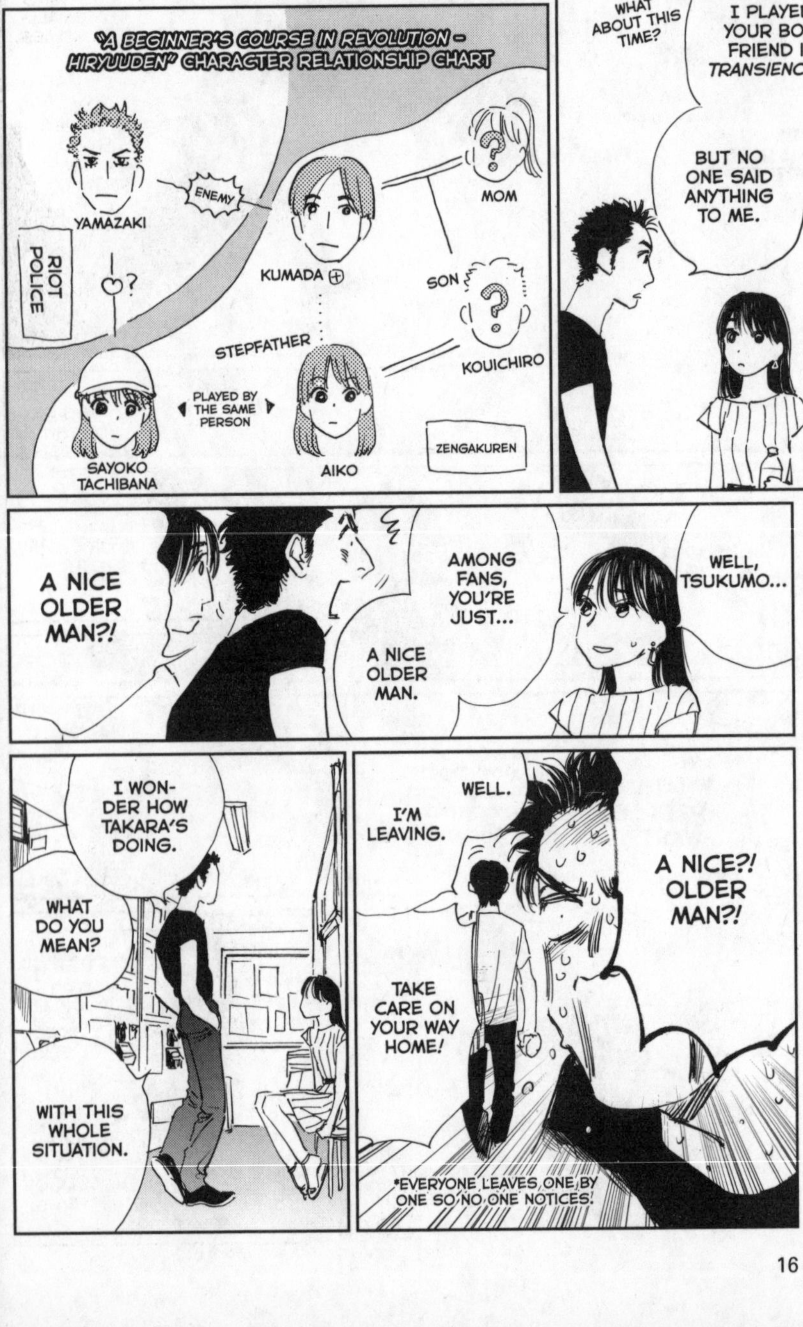
I PLAYED YOUR BOY-FRIEND IN *TRANSIENCE*...
BUT NO ONE SAID ANYTHING TO ME.
WHAT ABOUT THIS TIME?
"A BEGINNER'S COURSE IN REVOLUTION - HIRYUUDEN" CHARACTER RELATIONSHIP CHART
YAMAZAKI
ENEMY
KUMADA
MOM
SON
KOUICHIRO
RIOT POLICE
STEPFATHER
PLAYED BY THE SAME PERSON
SAYOKO TACHIBANA
AIKO
ZENGAKUREN
WELL, TSUKUMO...
AMONG FANS, YOU'RE JUST...
A NICE OLDER MAN.
A NICE OLDER MAN?!
WELL.
I'M LEAVING.
A NICE?! OLDER MAN?!
TAKE CARE ON YOUR WAY HOME!
*EVERYONE LEAVES ONE BY ONE SO NO ONE NOTICES.
I WON-DER HOW TAKARA'S DOING.
WHAT DO YOU MEAN?
WITH THIS WHOLE SITUATION.

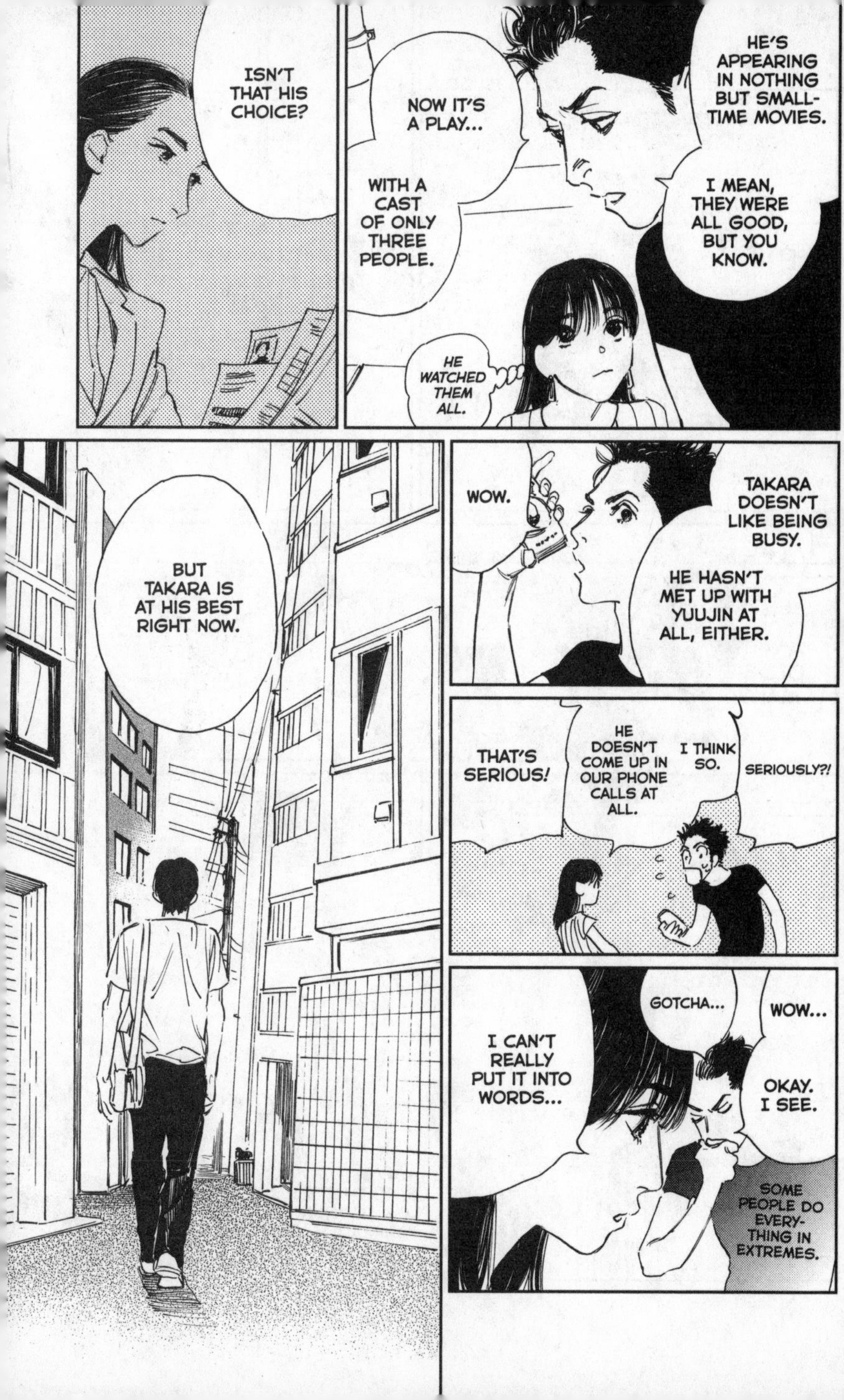
HE'S APPEARING IN NOTHING BUT SMALL-TIME MOVIES.
I MEAN, THEY WERE ALL GOOD, BUT YOU KNOW.
NOW IT'S A PLAY...
WITH A CAST OF ONLY THREE PEOPLE.
HE WATCHED THEM ALL.
ISN'T THAT HIS CHOICE?
TAKARA DOESN'T LIKE BEING BUSY.
HE HASN'T MET UP WITH YUUJIN AT ALL, EITHER.
WOW.
SERIOUSLY?!
I THINK SO.
HE DOESN'T COME UP IN OUR PHONE CALLS AT ALL.
THAT'S SERIOUS!
WOW...
OKAY. I SEE.
GOTCHA...
SOME PEOPLE DO EVERYTHING IN EXTREMES.
I CAN'T REALLY PUT IT INTO WORDS...
BUT TAKARA IS AT HIS BEST RIGHT NOW.

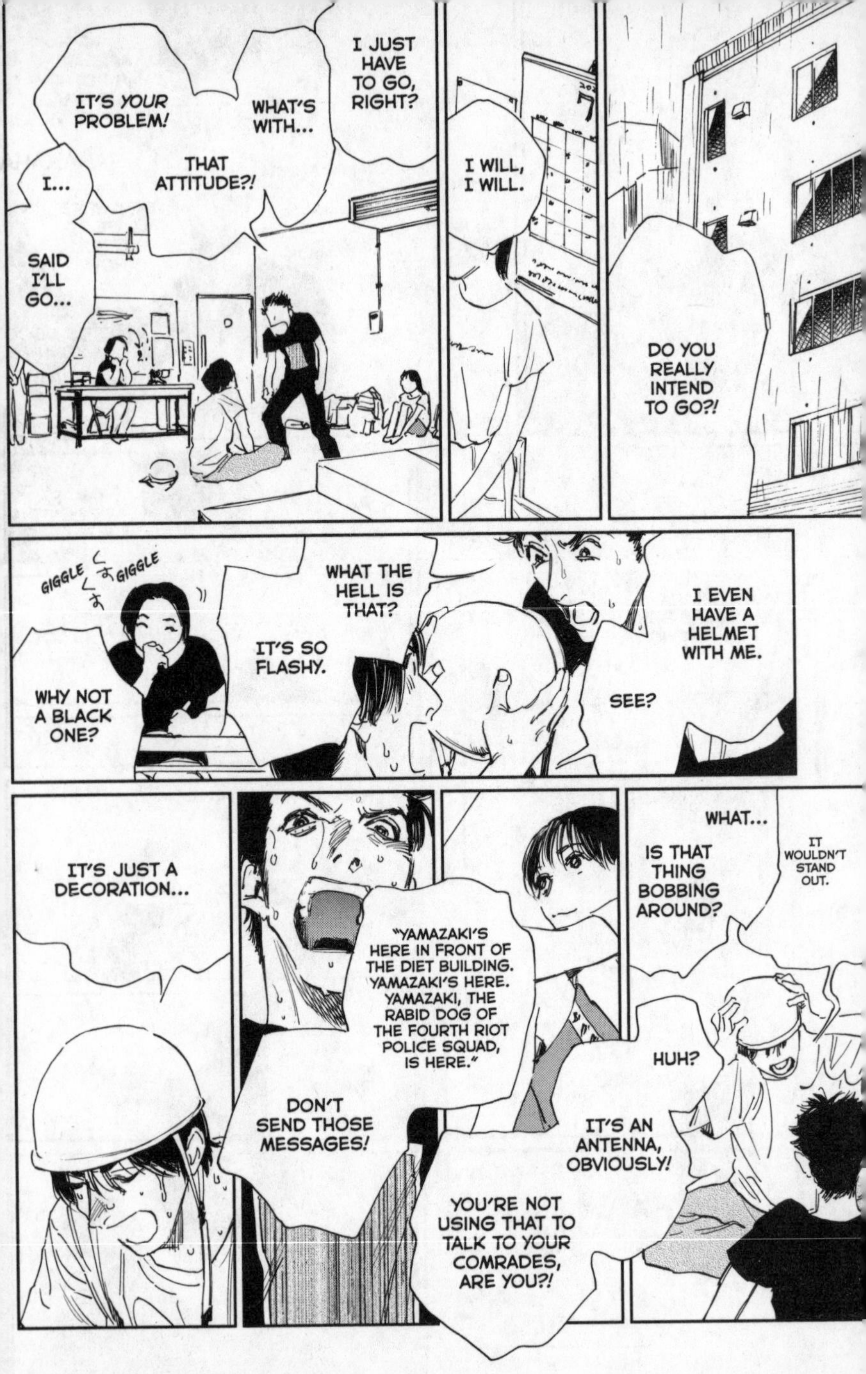
DO YOU REALLY INTEND TO GO?!
I WILL, I WILL.
I JUST HAVE TO GO, RIGHT?
WHAT'S WITH...
THAT ATTITUDE?!
IT'S *YOUR* PROBLEM!
I...
SAID I'LL GO...
I EVEN HAVE A HELMET WITH ME.
SEE?
WHAT THE HELL IS THAT?
IT'S SO FLASHY.
GIGGLE くすくす GIGGLE
WHY NOT A BLACK ONE?
IT WOULDN'T STAND OUT.
WHAT...
IS THAT THING BOBBING AROUND?
HUH?
IT'S AN ANTENNA, OBVIOUSLY!
YOU'RE NOT USING THAT TO TALK TO YOUR COMRADES, ARE YOU?!
"YAMAZAKI'S HERE IN FRONT OF THE DIET BUILDING. YAMAZAKI'S HERE. YAMAZAKI, THE RABID DOG OF THE FOURTH RIOT POLICE SQUAD, IS HERE."
DON'T SEND THOSE MESSAGES!
IT'S JUST A DECORATION...

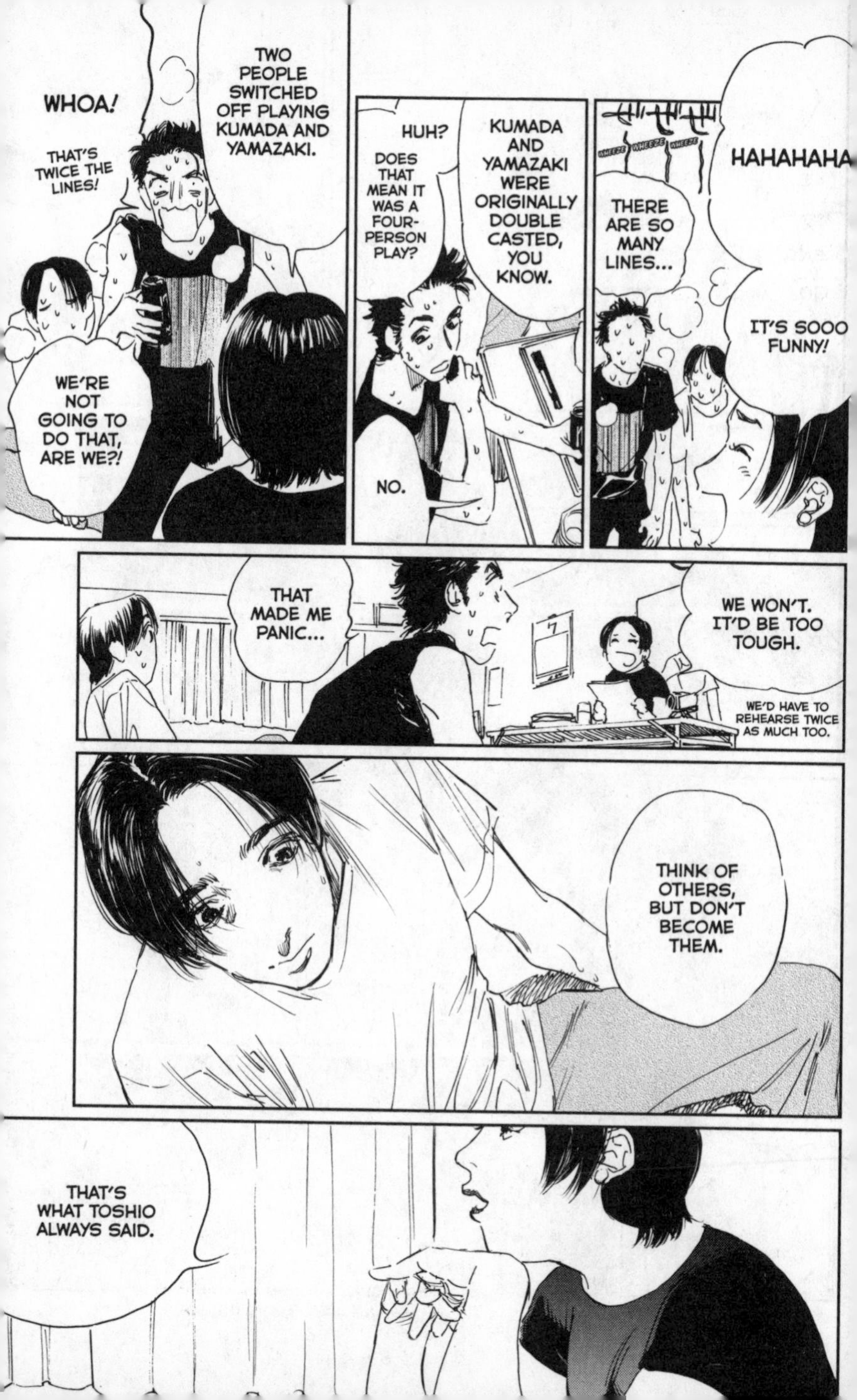
HAHAHAHA
WHEEZE WHEEZE WHEEZE
THERE ARE SO MANY LINES...
IT'S SOOO FUNNY!
KUMADA AND YAMAZAKI WERE ORIGINALLY DOUBLE CASTED, YOU KNOW.
HUH?
DOES THAT MEAN IT WAS A FOUR-PERSON PLAY?
NO.
TWO PEOPLE SWITCHED OFF PLAYING KUMADA AND YAMAZAKI.
WHOA!
THAT'S TWICE THE LINES!
WE'RE NOT GOING TO DO THAT, ARE WE?!
WE WON'T. IT'D BE TOO TOUGH.
WE'D HAVE TO REHEARSE TWICE AS MUCH TOO.
THAT MADE ME PANIC...
THINK OF OTHERS, BUT DON'T BECOME THEM.
THAT'S WHAT TOSHIO ALWAYS SAID.

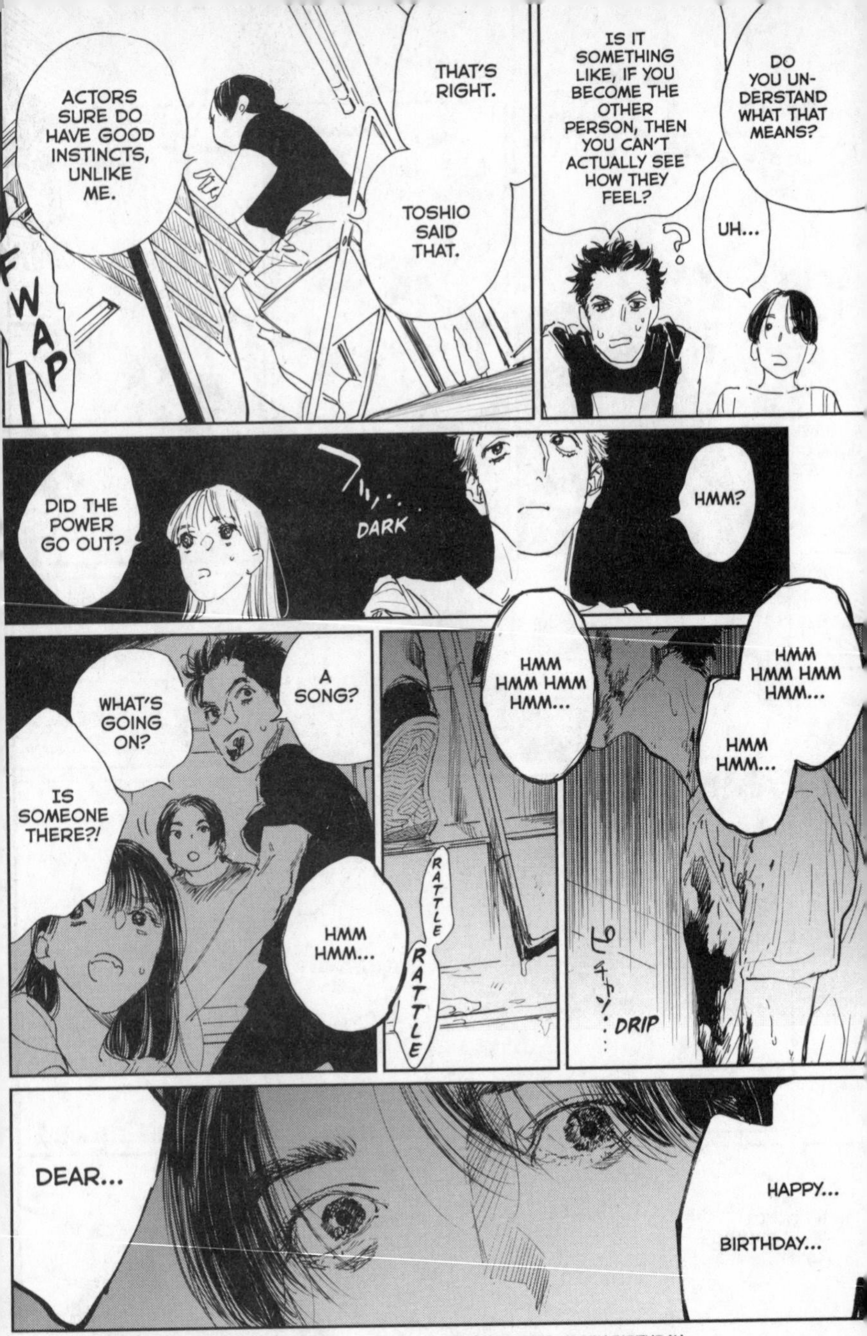
DO YOU UNDERSTAND WHAT THAT MEANS?
IS IT SOMETHING LIKE, IF YOU BECOME THE OTHER PERSON, THEN YOU CAN'T ACTUALLY SEE HOW THEY FEEL?
UH...
THAT'S RIGHT.
TOSHIO SAID THAT.
ACTORS SURE DO HAVE GOOD INSTINCTS, UNLIKE ME.
FWAP
HMM?
DARK
DID THE POWER GO OUT?
HMM HMM HMM HMM...
HMM HMM...
HMM HMM HMM HMM...
DRIP
RATTLE RATTLE
A SONG?
WHAT'S GOING ON?
IS SOMEONE THERE?!
HMM HMM...
HAPPY...
BIRTHDAY...
DEAR...
HE'S HUMMING HAPPY BIRTHDAY.

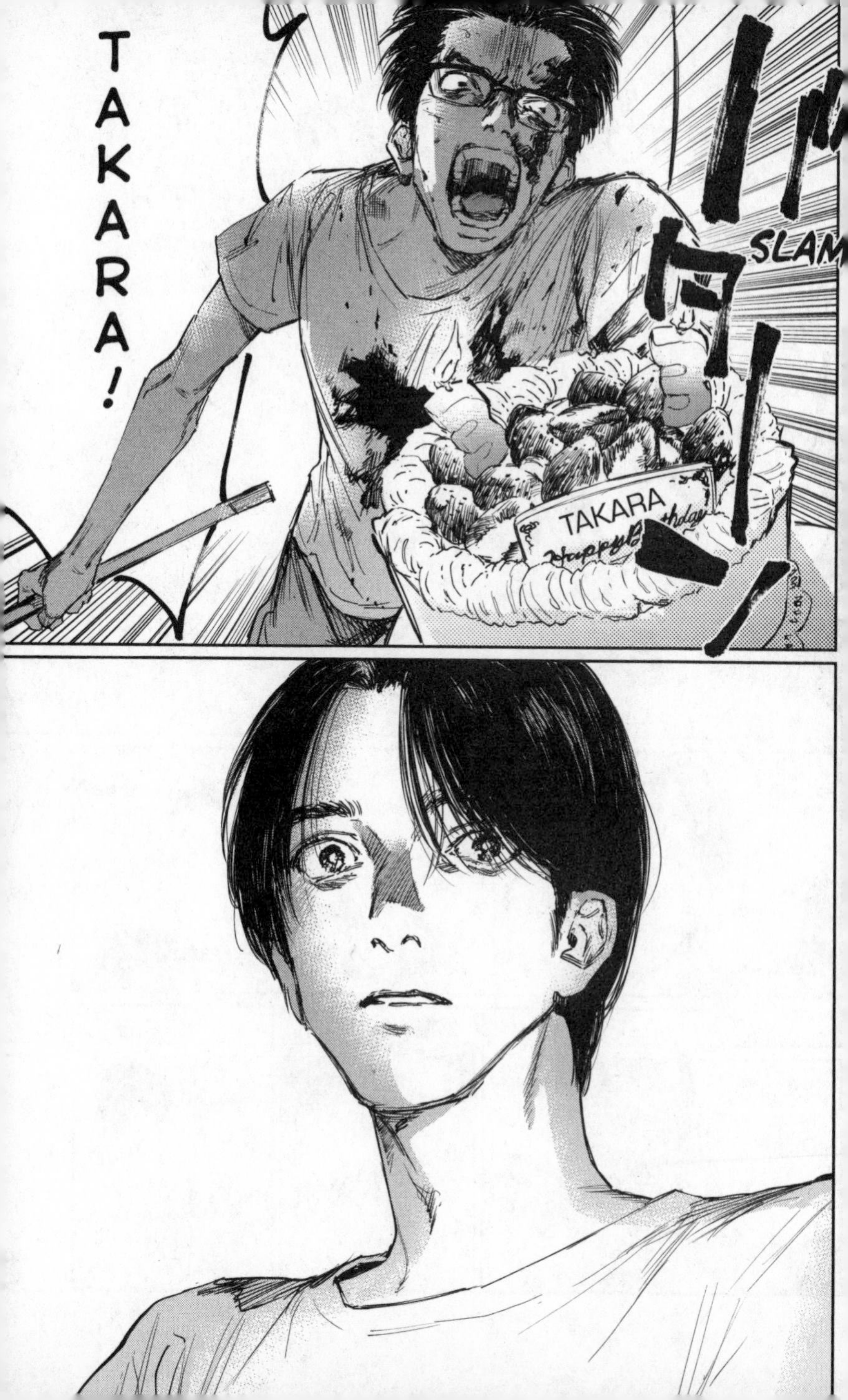
SLAM
TAKARA!
TAKARA
Happy Birthday

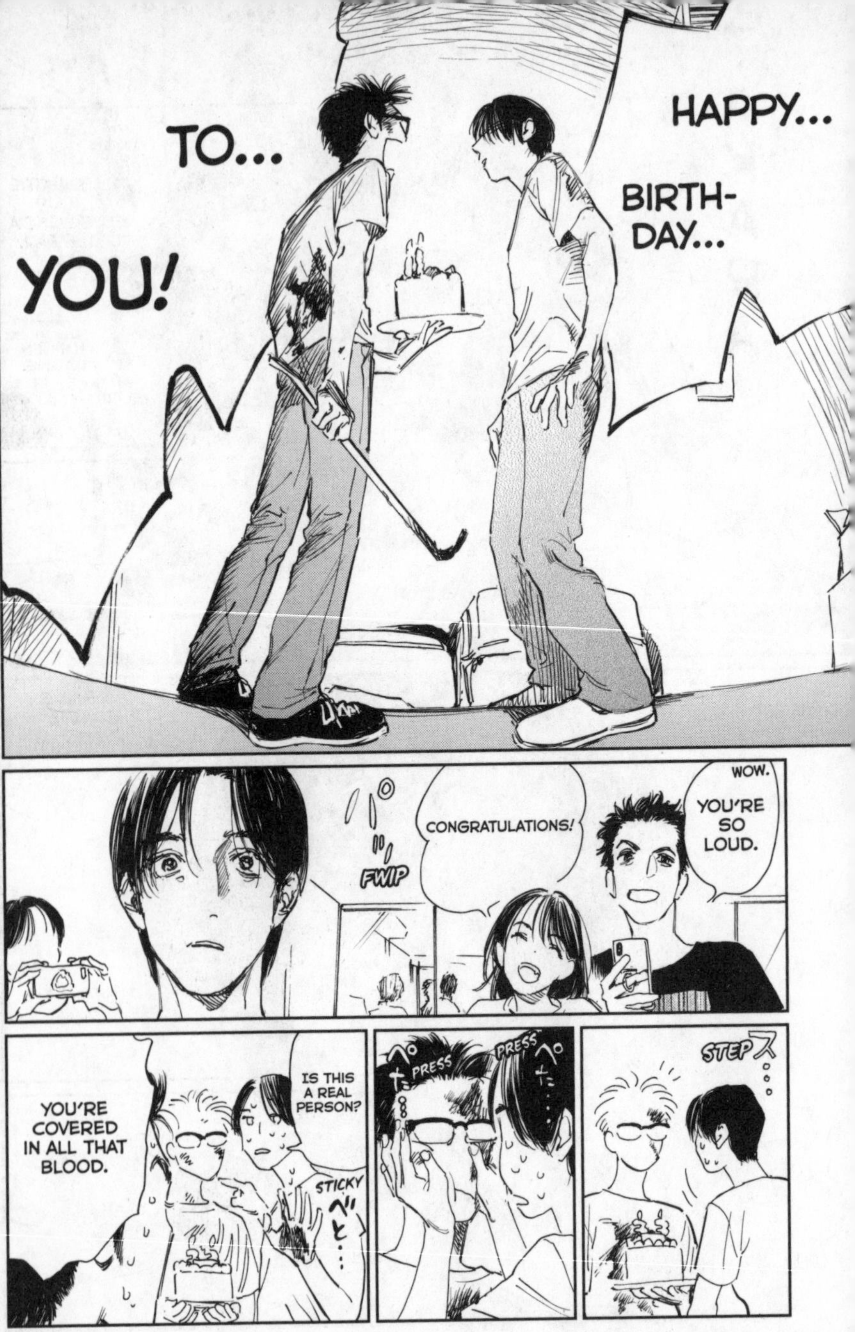
HAPPY...
BIRTH-DAY...
TO...
YOU!
WOW. YOU'RE SO LOUD.
CONGRATULATIONS!
FWIP
STEP ス
PRESS
PRESS
IS THIS A REAL PERSON?
STICKY べと…
YOU'RE COVERED IN ALL THAT BLOOD.

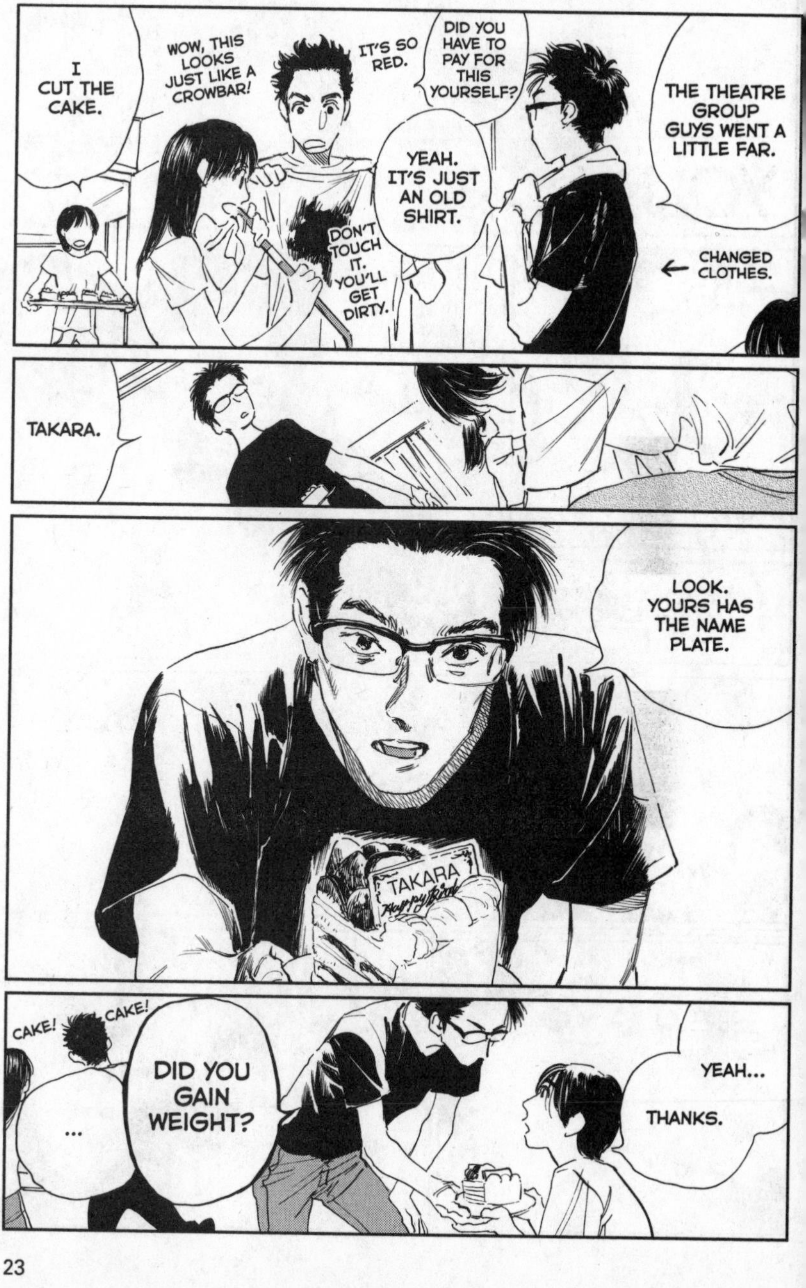
THE THEATRE GROUP GUYS WENT A LITTLE FAR.
CHANGED CLOTHES.
DID YOU HAVE TO PAY FOR THIS YOURSELF?
YEAH. IT'S JUST AN OLD SHIRT.
IT'S SO RED.
DON'T TOUCH IT. YOU'LL GET DIRTY.
WOW, THIS LOOKS JUST LIKE A CROWBAR!
I CUT THE CAKE.
TAKARA.
LOOK. YOURS HAS THE NAME PLATE.
TAKARA
YEAH...
THANKS.
DID YOU GAIN WEIGHT?
...
CAKE!
CAKE!

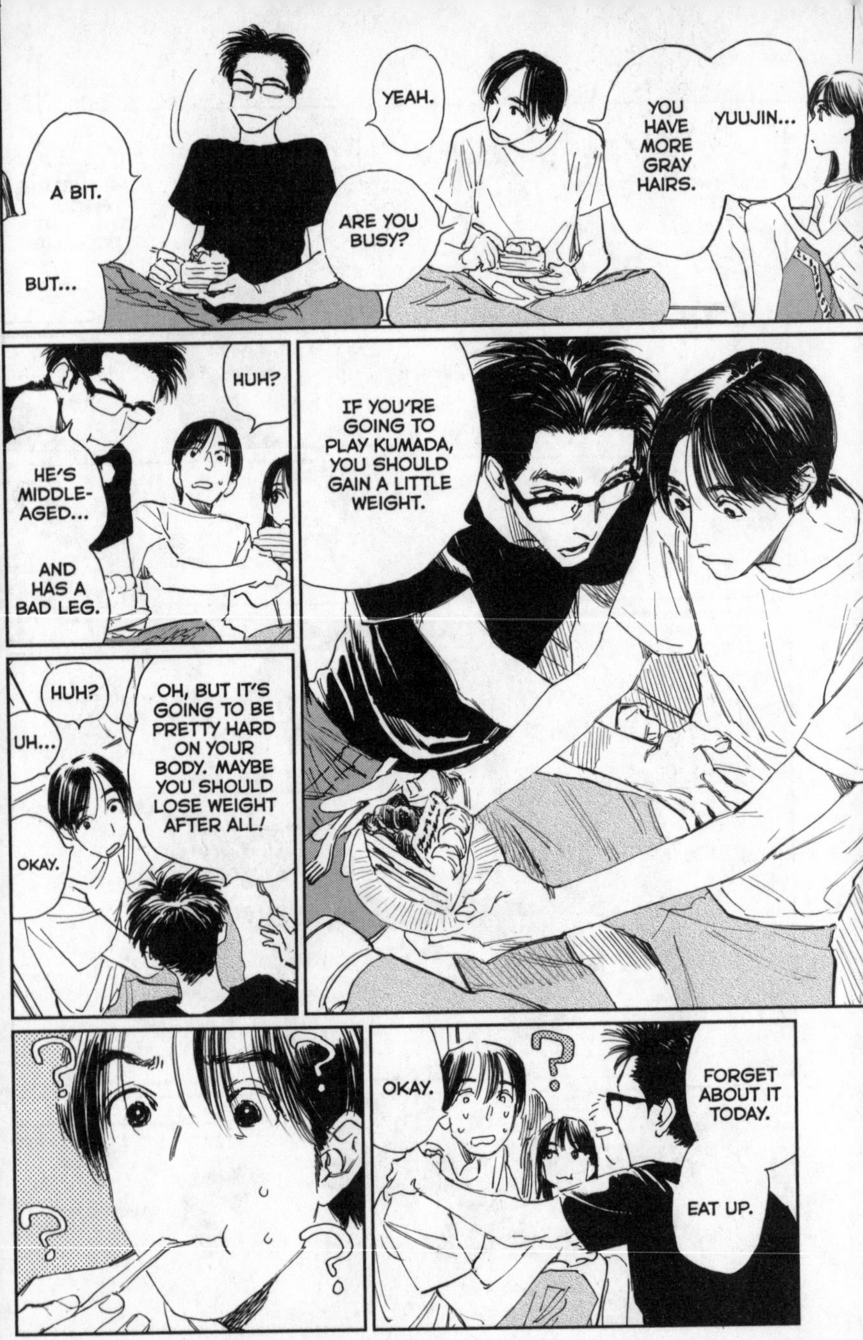
YUUJIN...
YOU HAVE MORE GRAY HAIRS.
YEAH.
ARE YOU BUSY?
A BIT.
BUT...
IF YOU'RE GOING TO PLAY KUMADA, YOU SHOULD GAIN A LITTLE WEIGHT.
HUH?
HE'S MIDDLE-AGED...
AND HAS A BAD LEG.
OH, BUT IT'S GOING TO BE PRETTY HARD ON YOUR BODY. MAYBE YOU SHOULD LOSE WEIGHT AFTER ALL!
HUH?
UH...
OKAY.
FORGET ABOUT IT TODAY.
OKAY.
EAT UP.

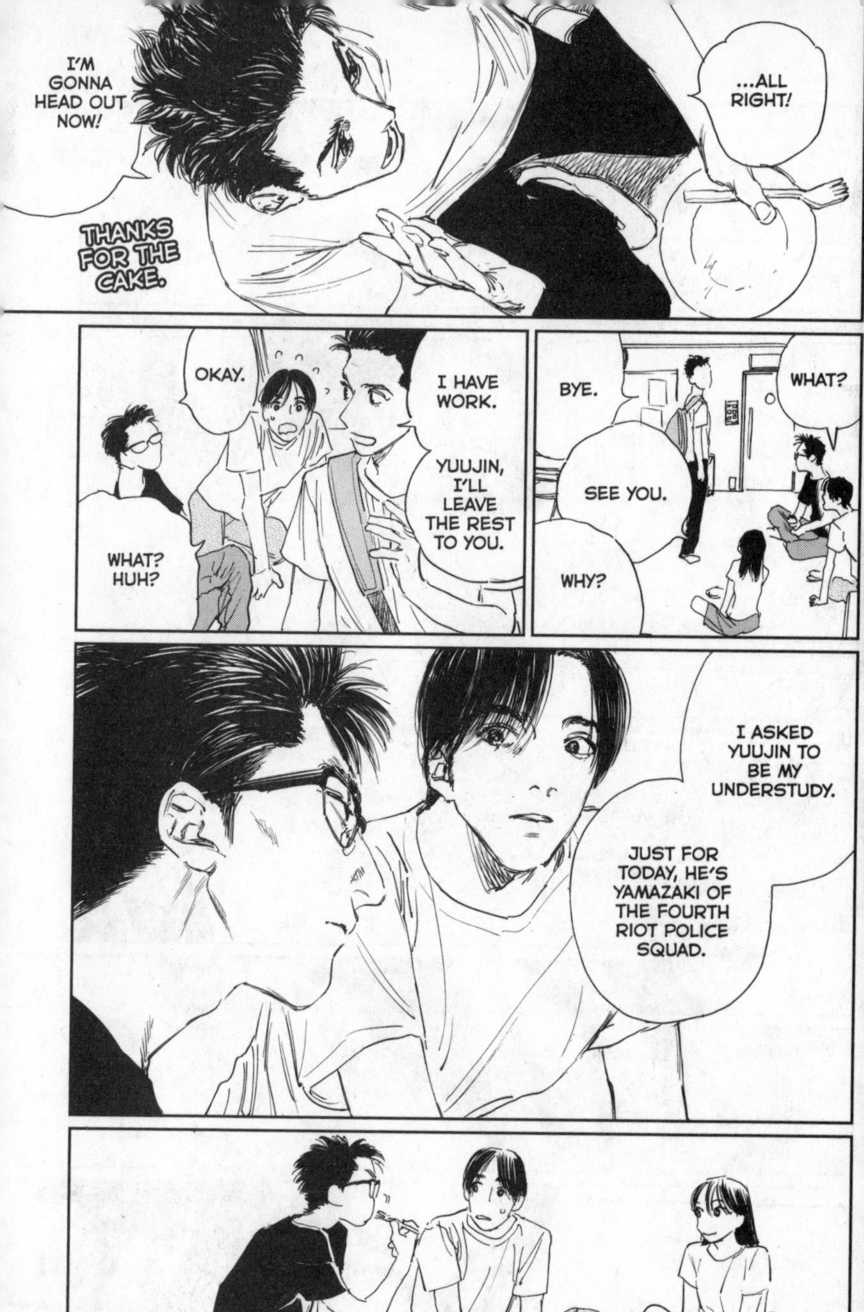
...ALL RIGHT!
I'M GONNA HEAD OUT NOW!
THANKS FOR THE CAKE.
WHAT?
BYE.
SEE YOU.
WHY?
I HAVE WORK.
YUUJIN, I'LL LEAVE THE REST TO YOU.
OKAY.
WHAT? HUH?
I ASKED YUUJIN TO BE MY UNDERSTUDY.
JUST FOR TODAY, HE'S YAMAZAKI OF THE FOURTH RIOT POLICE SQUAD.

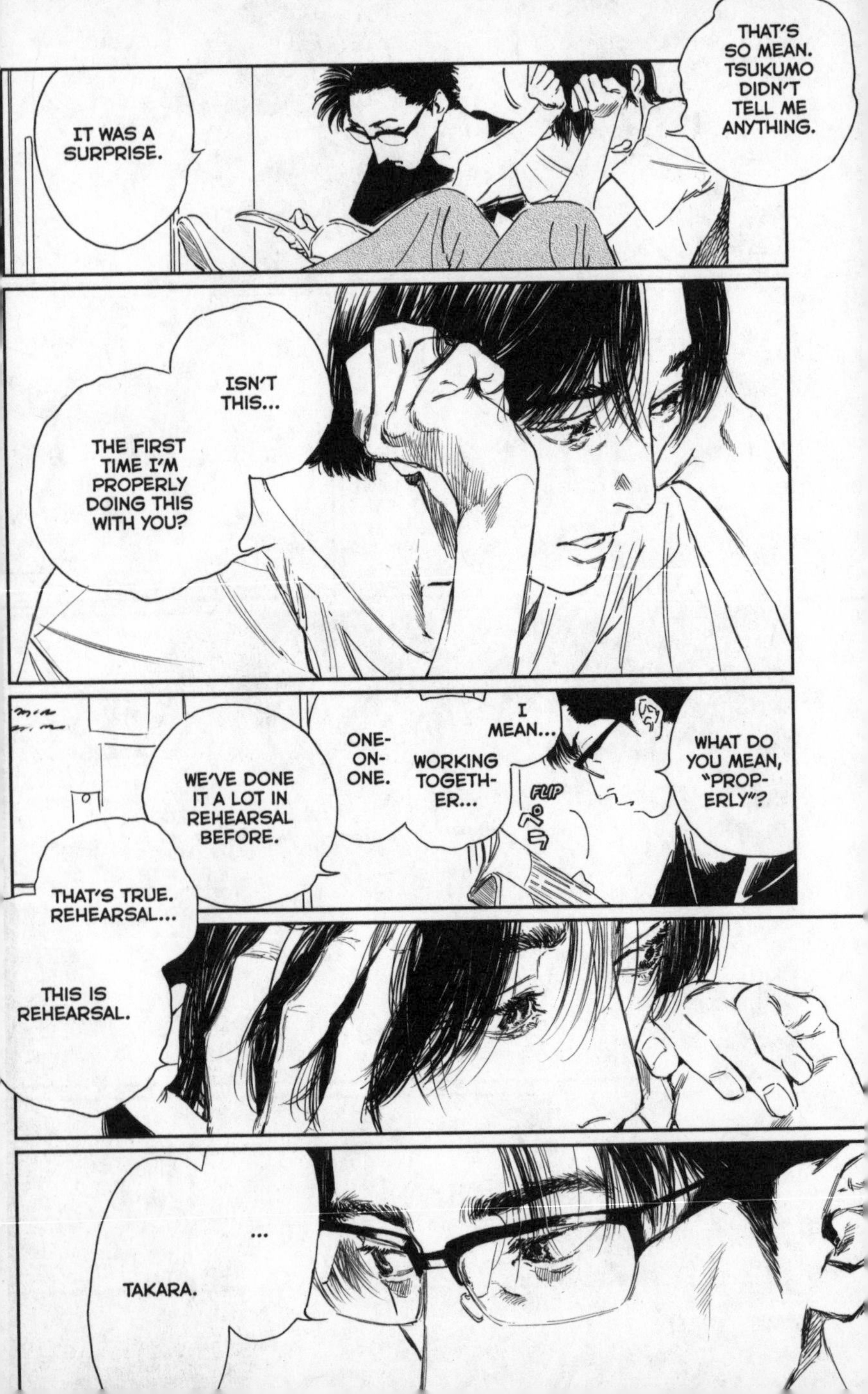
THAT'S SO MEAN. TSUKUMO DIDN'T TELL ME ANYTHING.
IT WAS A SURPRISE.
ISN'T THIS...
THE FIRST TIME I'M PROPERLY DOING THIS WITH YOU?
WHAT DO YOU MEAN, "PROPERLY"?
FLIP
I MEAN...
WORKING TOGETHER...
ONE-ON-ONE.
WE'VE DONE IT A LOT IN REHEARSAL BEFORE.
THAT'S TRUE. REHEARSAL...
THIS IS REHEARSAL.
...
TAKARA.

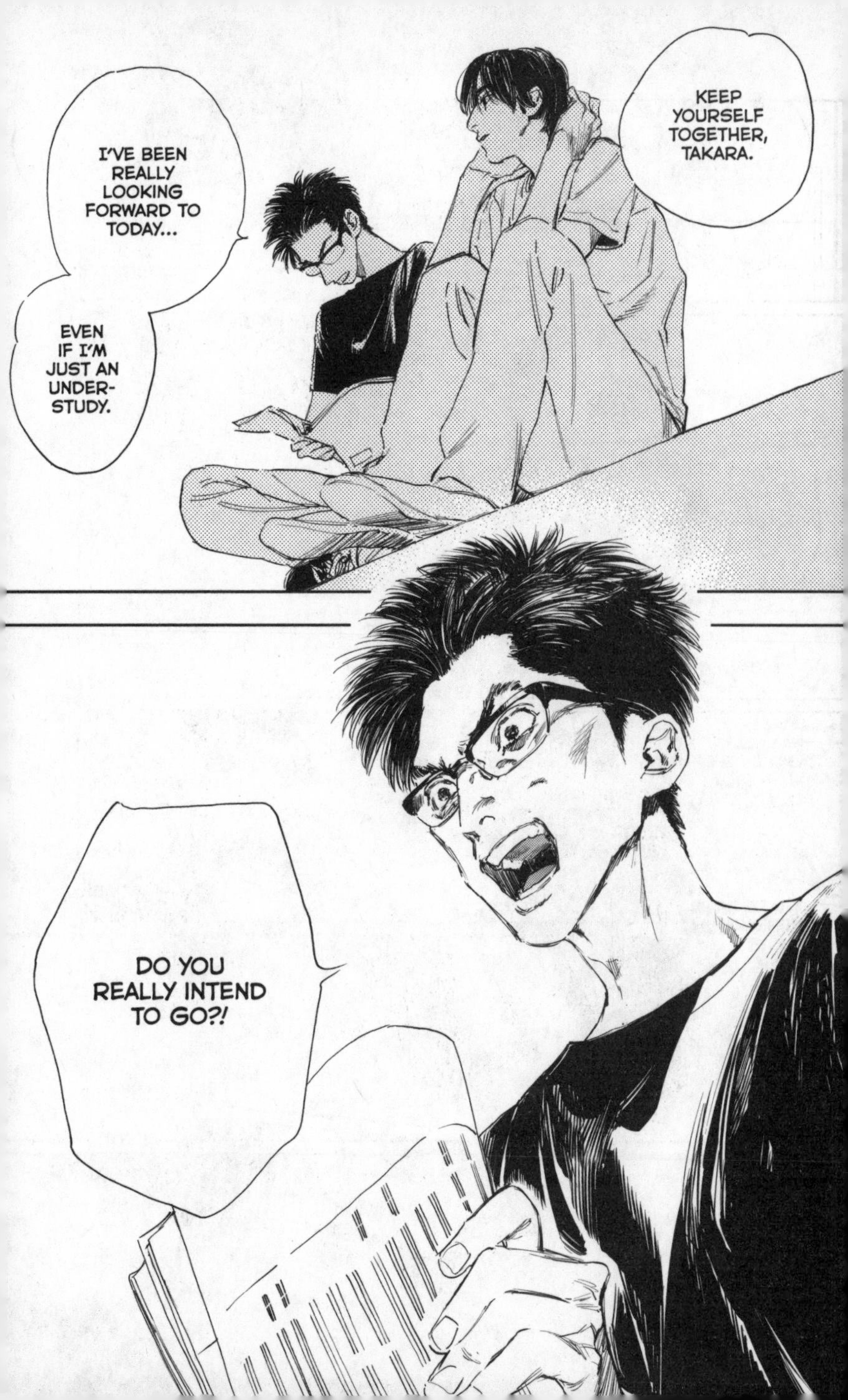
KEEP YOURSELF TOGETHER, TAKARA.
I'VE BEEN REALLY LOOKING FORWARD TO TODAY...
EVEN IF I'M JUST AN UNDER-STUDY.
DO YOU REALLY INTEND TO GO?!

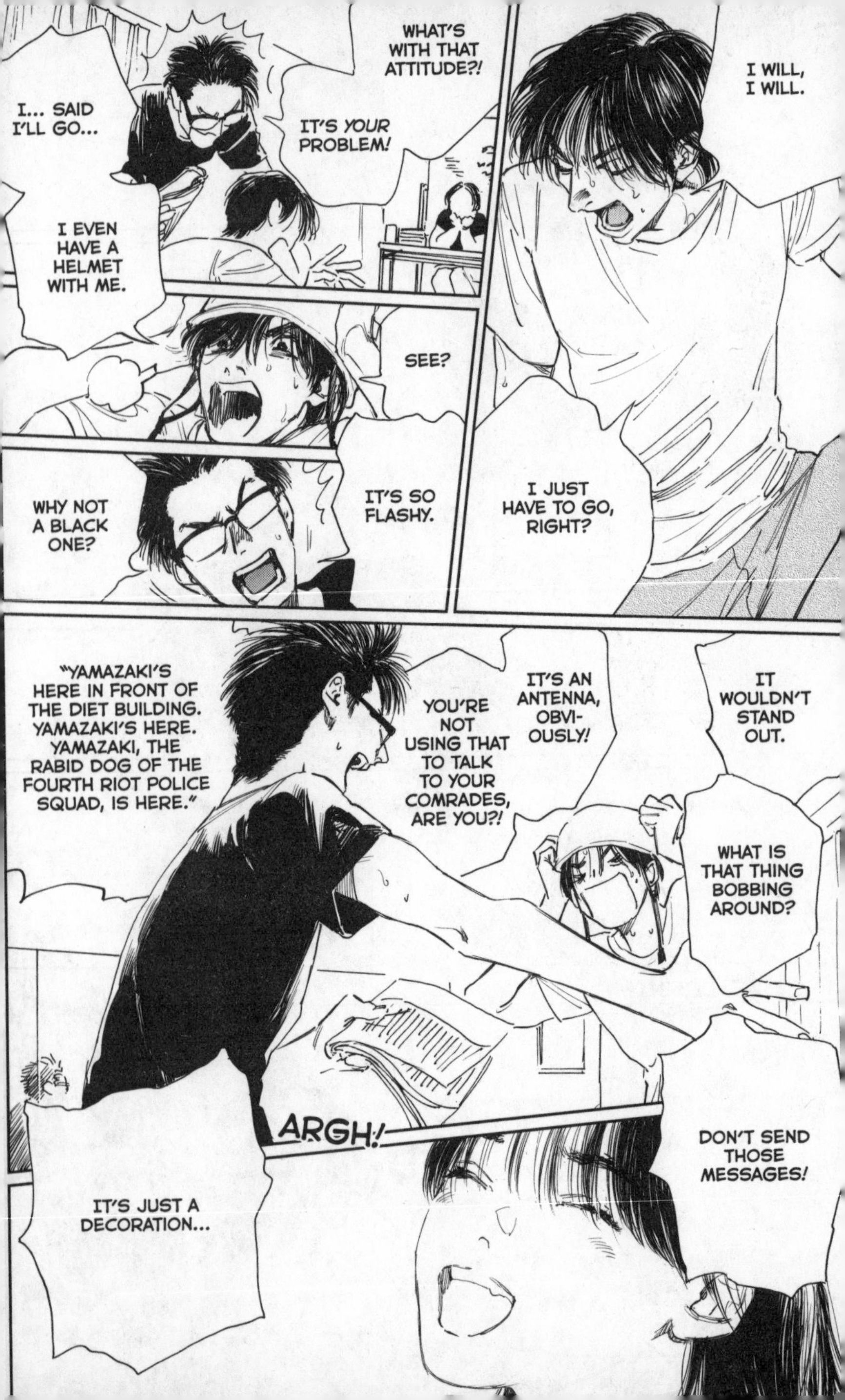
I WILL, I WILL.
I JUST HAVE TO GO, RIGHT?
WHAT'S WITH THAT ATTITUDE?!
IT'S *YOUR* PROBLEM!
I... SAID I'LL GO...
I EVEN HAVE A HELMET WITH ME.
SEE?
IT'S SO FLASHY.
WHY NOT A BLACK ONE?
IT WOULDN'T STAND OUT.
WHAT IS THAT THING BOBBING AROUND?
IT'S AN ANTENNA, OBVIOUSLY!
YOU'RE NOT USING THAT TO TALK TO YOUR COMRADES, ARE YOU?!
"YAMAZAKI'S HERE IN FRONT OF THE DIET BUILDING. YAMAZAKI'S HERE. YAMAZAKI, THE RABID DOG OF THE FOURTH RIOT POLICE SQUAD, IS HERE."
ARGH!
DON'T SEND THOSE MESSAGES!
IT'S JUST A DECORATION...

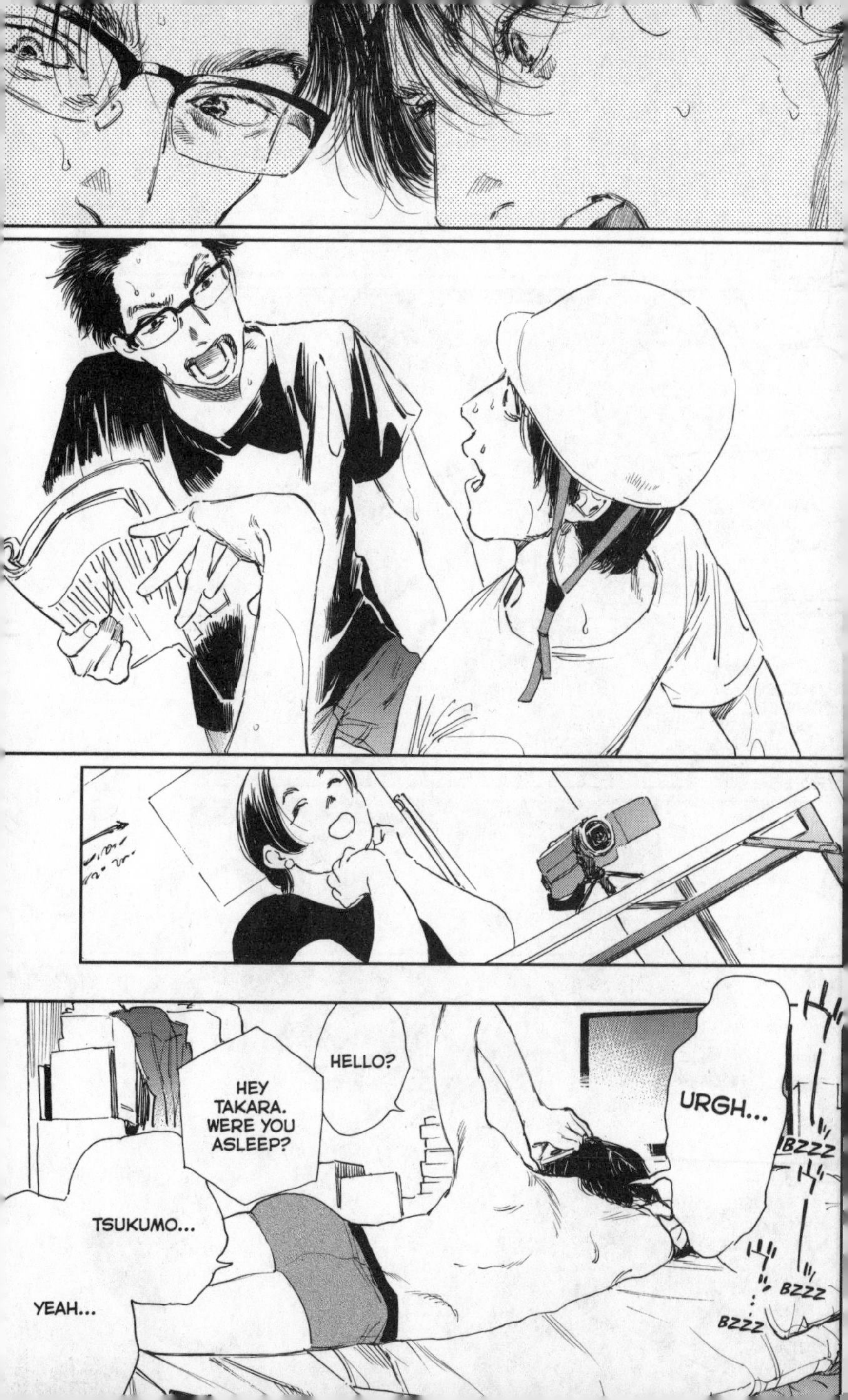
BZZZ
URGH...
BZZZ
BZZZ
HELLO?
HEY TAKARA. WERE YOU ASLEEP?
TSUKUMO...
YEAH...

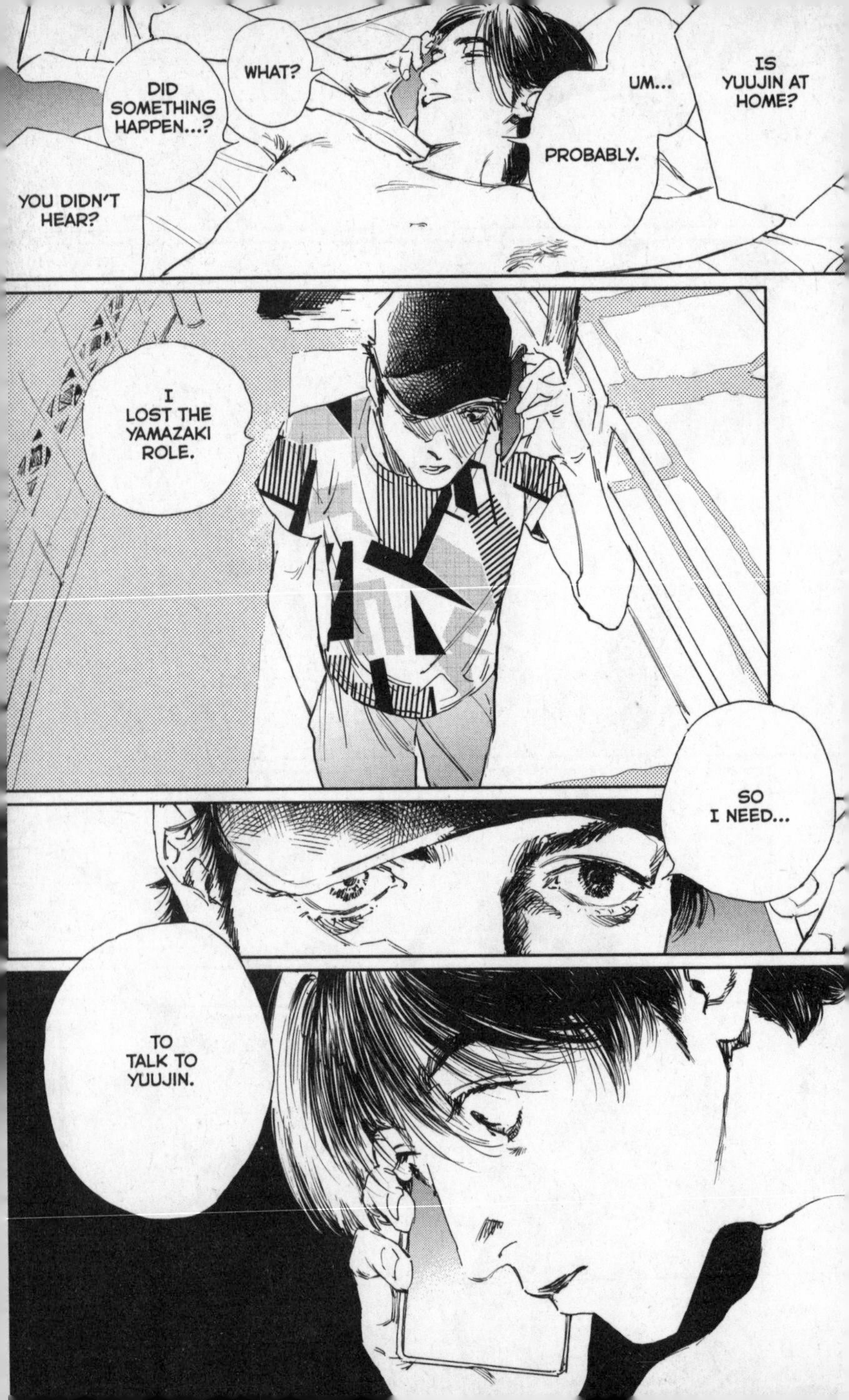
IS YUUJIN AT HOME?
UM...
PROBABLY.
WHAT?
DID SOMETHING HAPPEN...?
YOU DIDN'T HEAR?
I LOST THE YAMAZAKI ROLE.
SO I NEED...
TO TALK TO YUUJIN.

DOUBLE

CHAPTER 21 | MACBETH

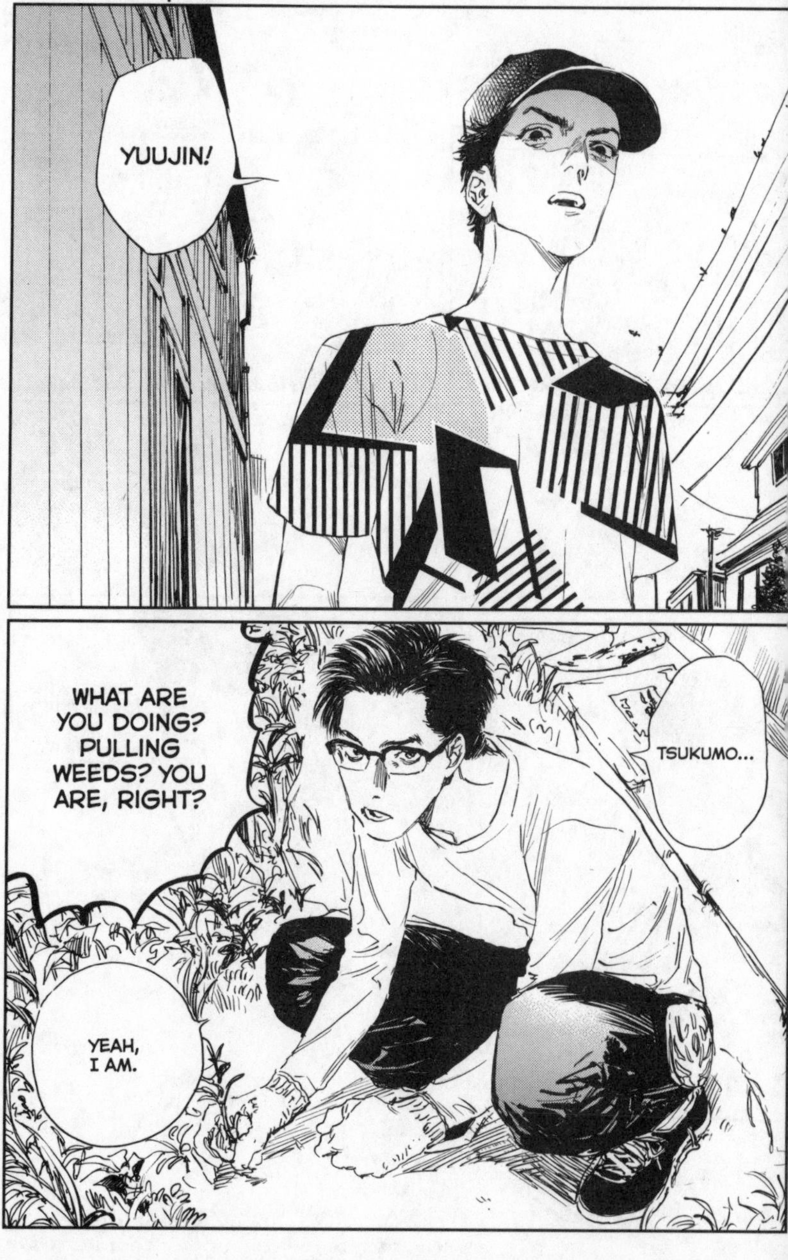
YUUJIN!
TSUKUMO...
WHAT ARE YOU DOING? PULLING WEEDS? YOU ARE, RIGHT?
YEAH, I AM.

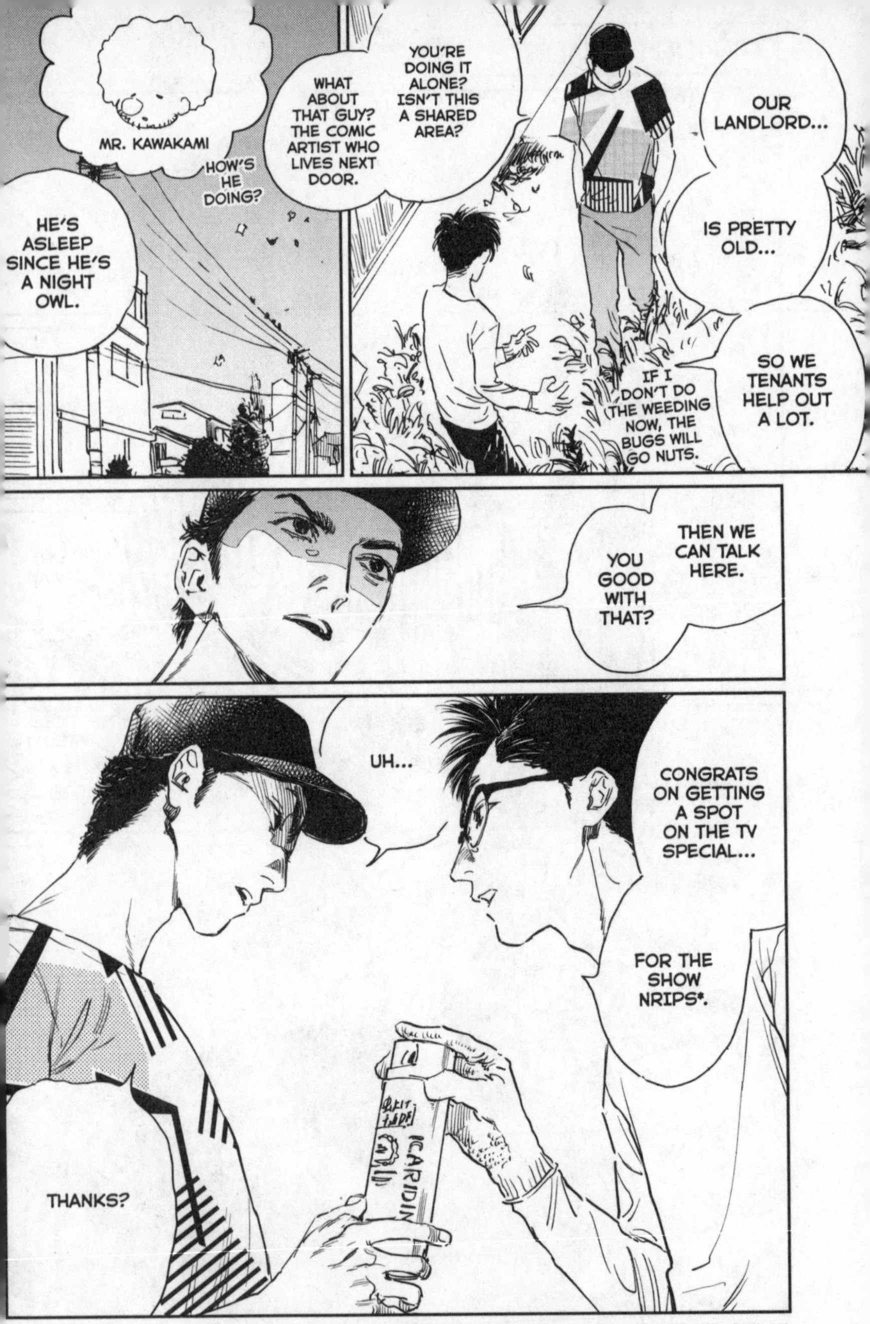
YOU'RE DOING IT ALONE? ISN'T THIS A SHARED AREA?
OUR LANDLORD...
IS PRETTY OLD...
SO WE TENANTS HELP OUT A LOT.
IF I DON'T DO THE WEEDING NOW, THE BUGS WILL GO NUTS.
WHAT ABOUT THAT GUY? THE COMIC ARTIST WHO LIVES NEXT DOOR.
MR. KAWAKAMI
HOW'S HE DOING?
HE'S ASLEEP SINCE HE'S A NIGHT OWL.
THEN WE CAN TALK HERE.
YOU GOOD WITH THAT?
CONGRATS ON GETTING A SPOT ON THE TV SPECIAL...
FOR THE SHOW NRIPS*.
UH...
THANKS?

* NATIONAL RESEARCH INSTITUTE OF POLICE SCIENCE, SIMILAR TO NCIS (NAVAL CRIMINAL INVESTIGATIVE SERVICE)

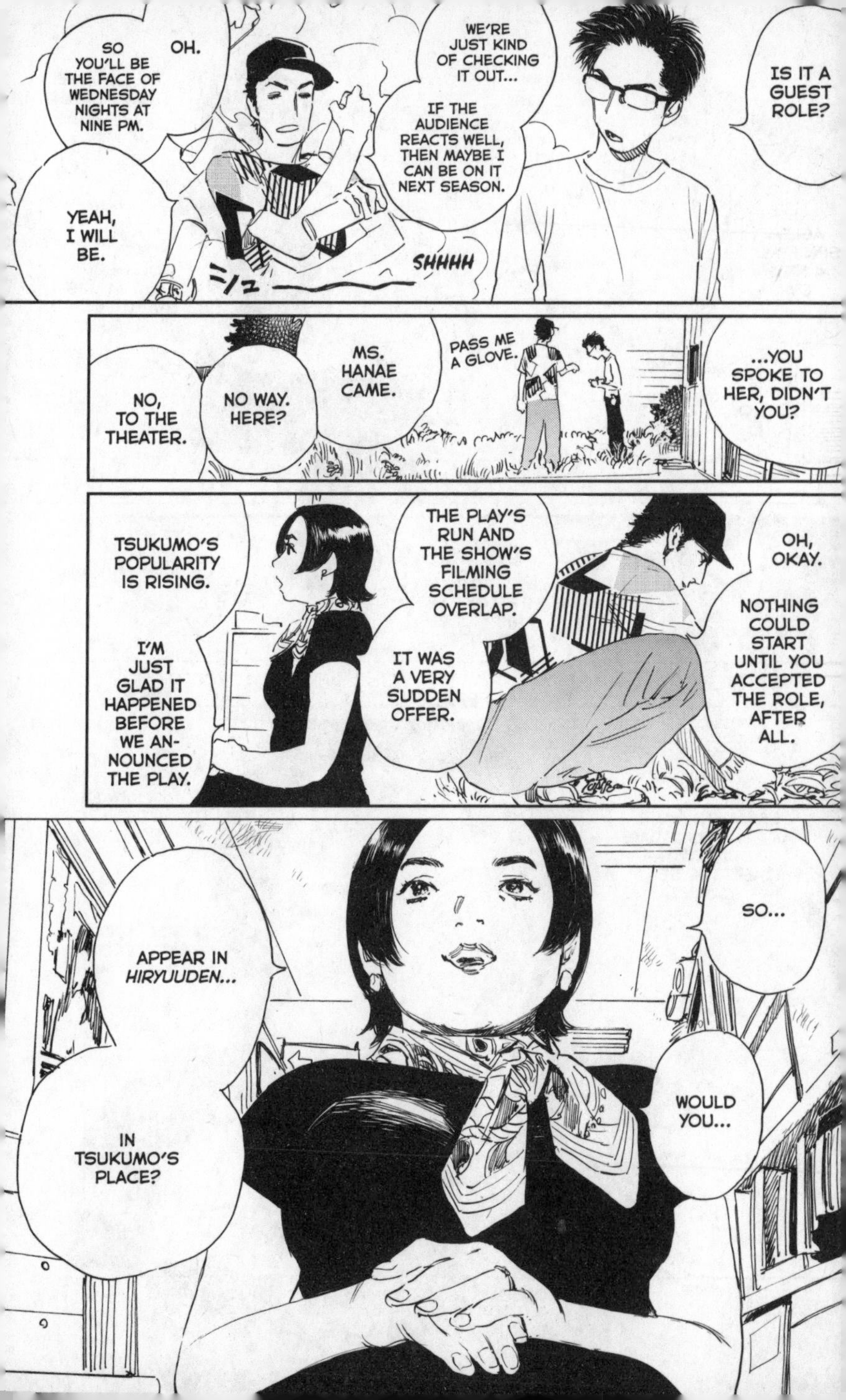

IS IT A GUEST ROLE?
WE'RE JUST KIND OF CHECKING IT OUT...
IF THE AUDIENCE REACTS WELL, THEN MAYBE I CAN BE ON IT NEXT SEASON.
SHHHH
OH.
SO YOU'LL BE THE FACE OF WEDNESDAY NIGHTS AT NINE PM.
YEAH, I WILL BE.
...YOU SPOKE TO HER, DIDN'T YOU?
PASS ME A GLOVE.
MS. HANAE CAME.
NO WAY. HERE?
NO, TO THE THEATER.
OH, OKAY.
NOTHING COULD START UNTIL YOU ACCEPTED THE ROLE, AFTER ALL.
THE PLAY'S RUN AND THE SHOW'S FILMING SCHEDULE OVERLAP.
IT WAS A VERY SUDDEN OFFER.
TSUKUMO'S POPULARITY IS RISING.
I'M JUST GLAD IT HAPPENED BEFORE WE AN-NOUNCED THE PLAY.
SO...
WOULD YOU...
APPEAR IN *HIRYUUDEN*...
IN TSUKUMO'S PLACE?

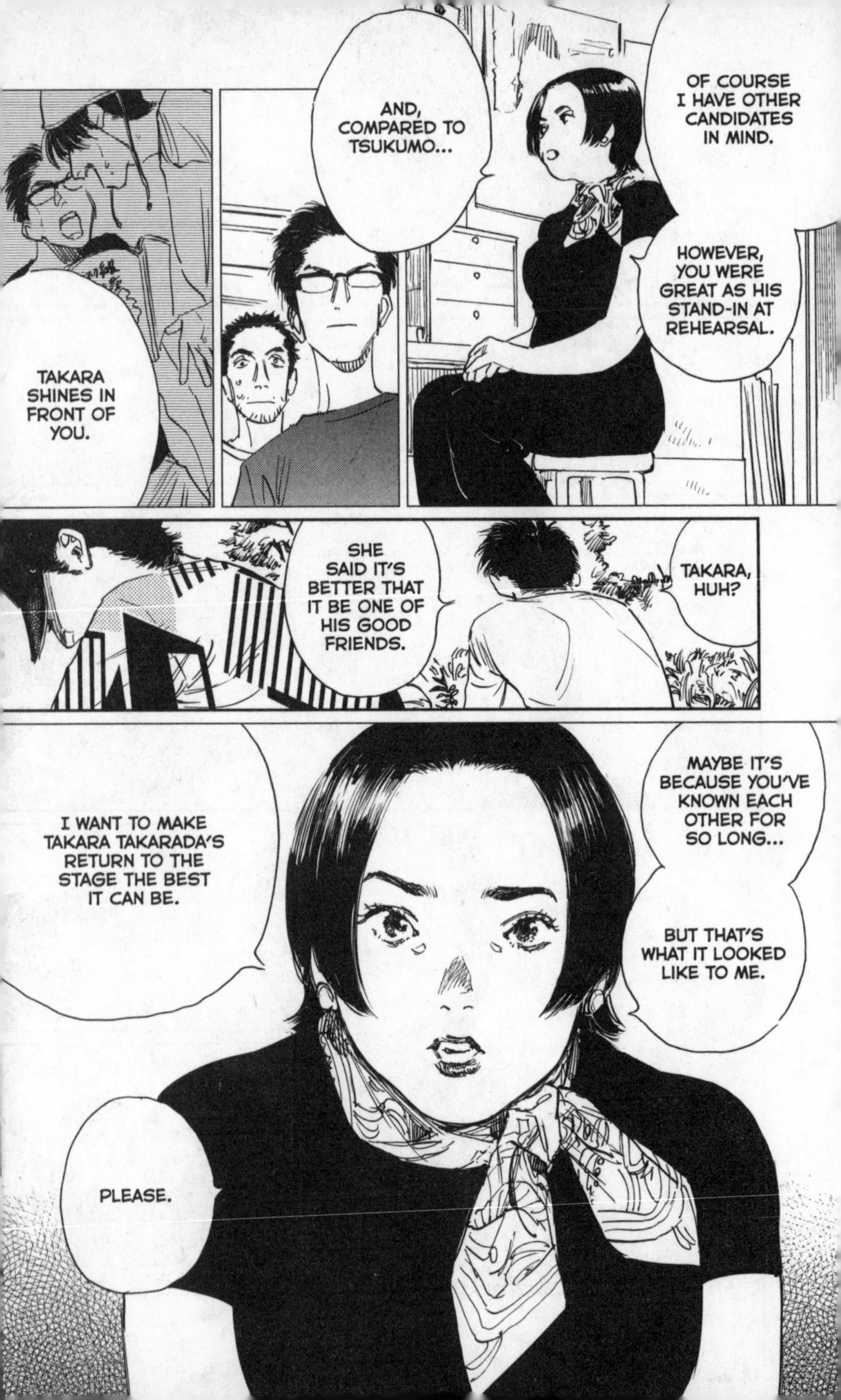
OF COURSE I HAVE OTHER CANDIDATES IN MIND.
HOWEVER, YOU WERE GREAT AS HIS STAND-IN AT REHEARSAL.
AND, COMPARED TO TSUKUMO...
TAKARA SHINES IN FRONT OF YOU.
TAKARA, HUH?
SHE SAID IT'S BETTER THAT IT BE ONE OF HIS GOOD FRIENDS.
MAYBE IT'S BECAUSE YOU'VE KNOWN EACH OTHER FOR SO LONG...
BUT THAT'S WHAT IT LOOKED LIKE TO ME.
I WANT TO MAKE TAKARA TAKARADA'S RETURN TO THE STAGE THE BEST IT CAN BE.
PLEASE.

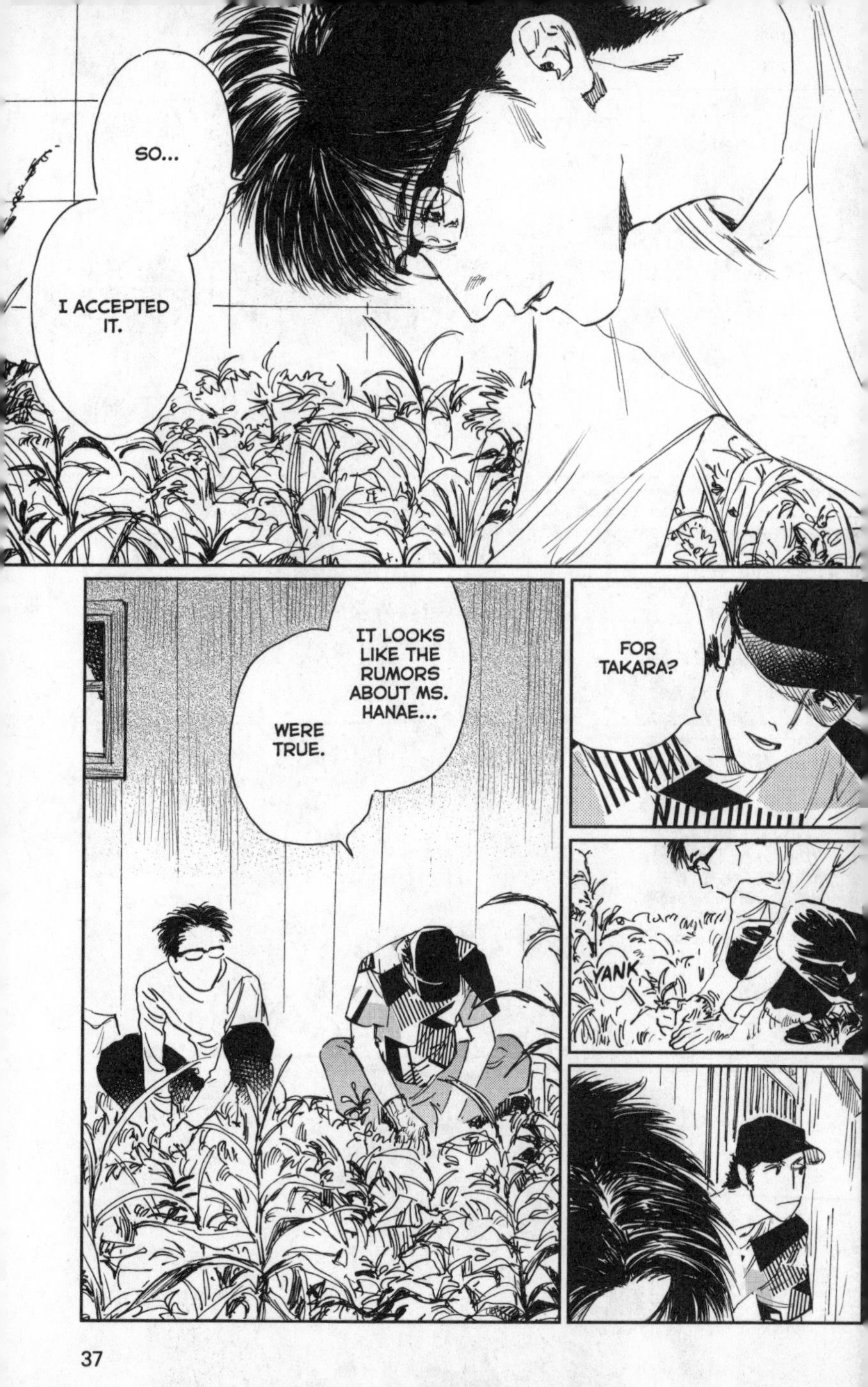
SO...
I ACCEPTED IT.
FOR TAKARA?
YANK
IT LOOKS LIKE THE RUMORS ABOUT MS. HANAE...
WERE TRUE.

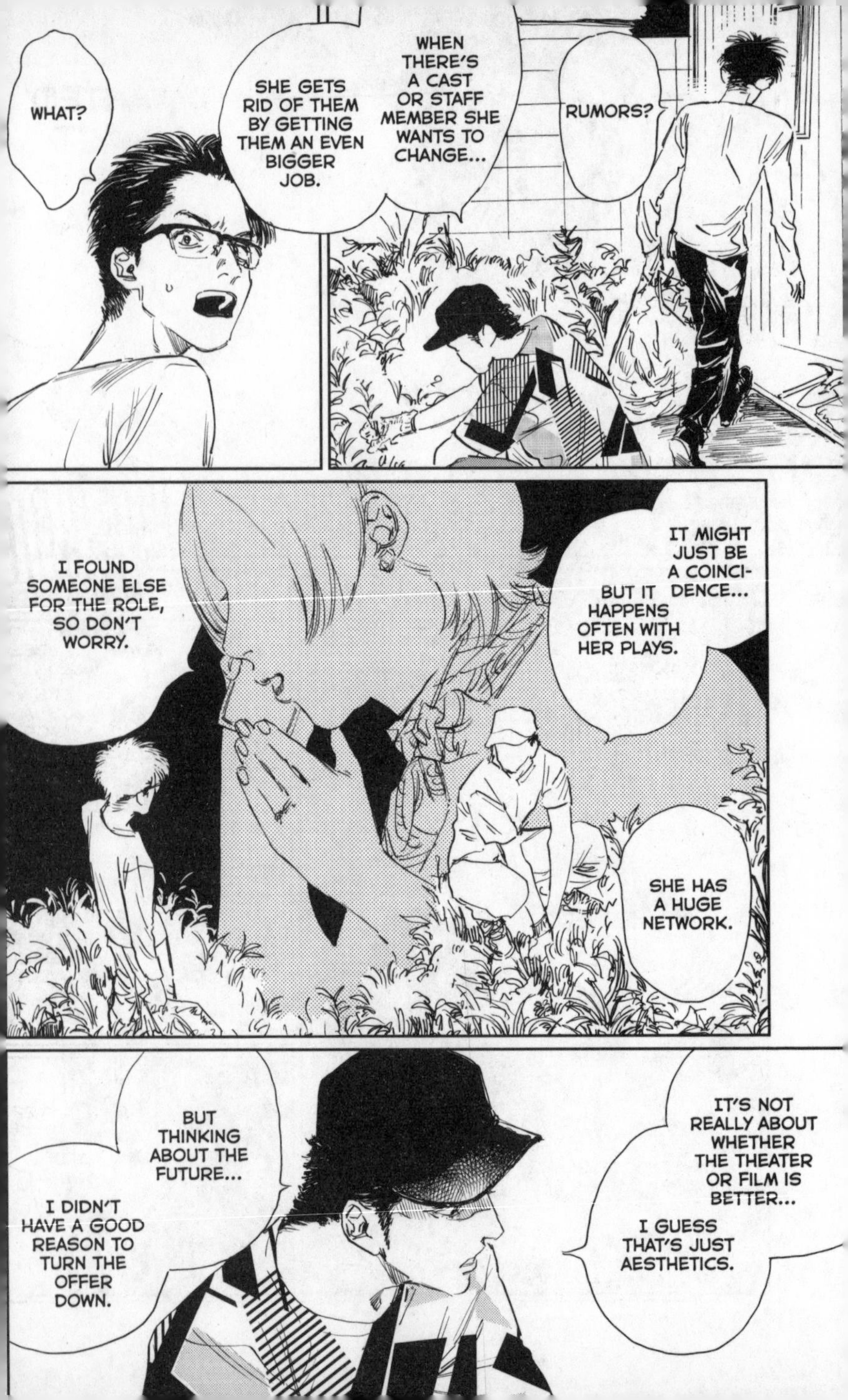
RUMORS?
WHEN THERE'S A CAST OR STAFF MEMBER SHE WANTS TO CHANGE...
SHE GETS RID OF THEM BY GETTING THEM AN EVEN BIGGER JOB.
WHAT?
IT MIGHT JUST BE A COINCIDENCE...
BUT IT HAPPENS OFTEN WITH HER PLAYS.
SHE HAS A HUGE NETWORK.
I FOUND SOMEONE ELSE FOR THE ROLE, SO DON'T WORRY.
IT'S NOT REALLY ABOUT WHETHER THE THEATER OR FILM IS BETTER...
I GUESS THAT'S JUST AESTHETICS.
BUT THINKING ABOUT THE FUTURE...
I DIDN'T HAVE A GOOD REASON TO TURN THE OFFER DOWN.

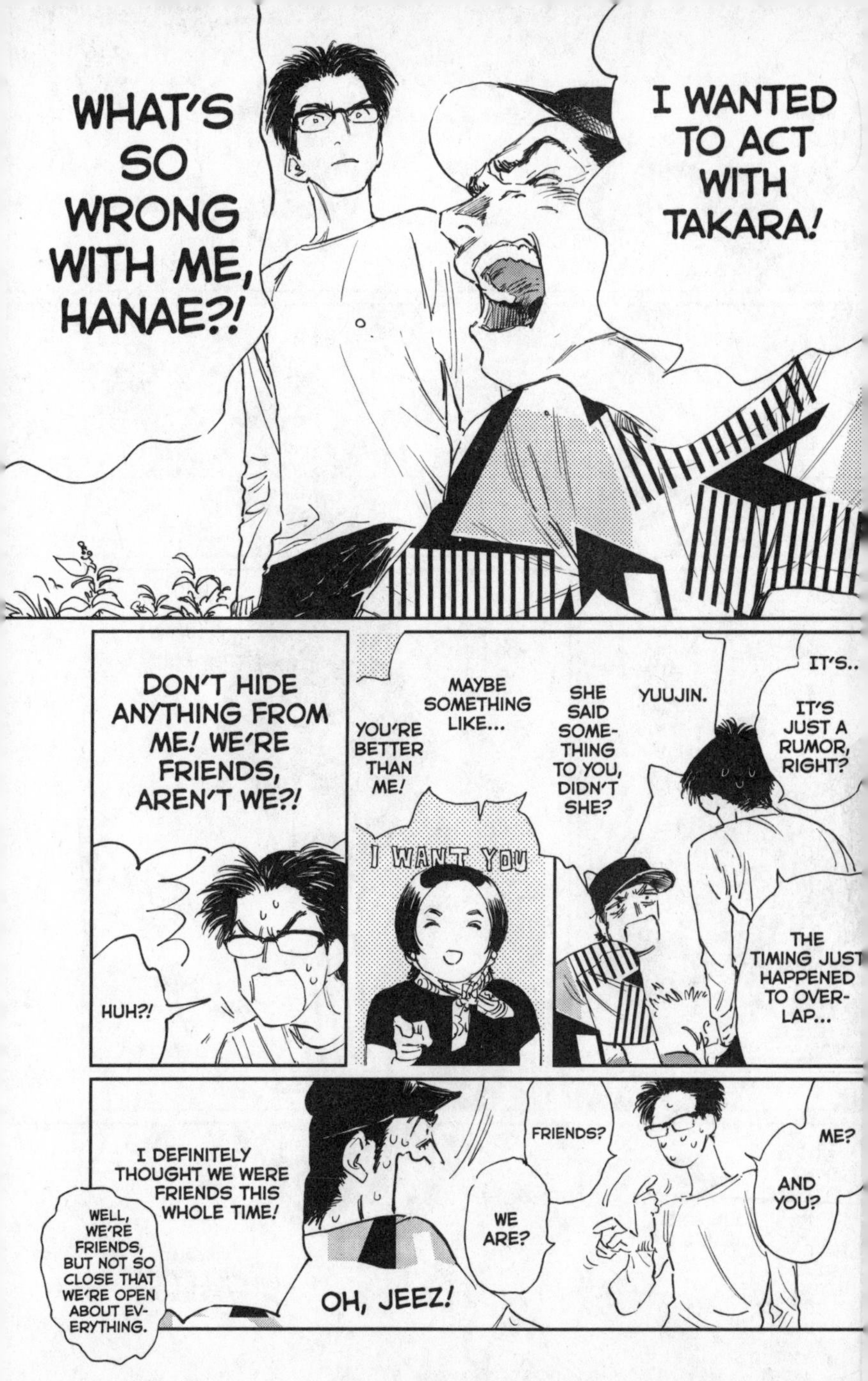
I WANTED TO ACT WITH TAKARA!
WHAT'S SO WRONG WITH ME, HANAE?!
IT'S..
IT'S JUST A RUMOR, RIGHT?
THE TIMING JUST HAPPENED TO OVER-LAP...
YUUJIN.
SHE SAID SOME-THING TO YOU, DIDN'T SHE?
MAYBE SOMETHING LIKE...
YOU'RE BETTER THAN ME!
I WANT YOU
DON'T HIDE ANYTHING FROM ME! WE'RE FRIENDS, AREN'T WE?!
HUH?!
ME?
AND YOU?
FRIENDS?
WE ARE?
I DEFINITELY THOUGHT WE WERE FRIENDS THIS WHOLE TIME!
OH, JEEZ!
WELL, WE'RE FRIENDS, BUT NOT SO CLOSE THAT WE'RE OPEN ABOUT EV-ERYTHING.

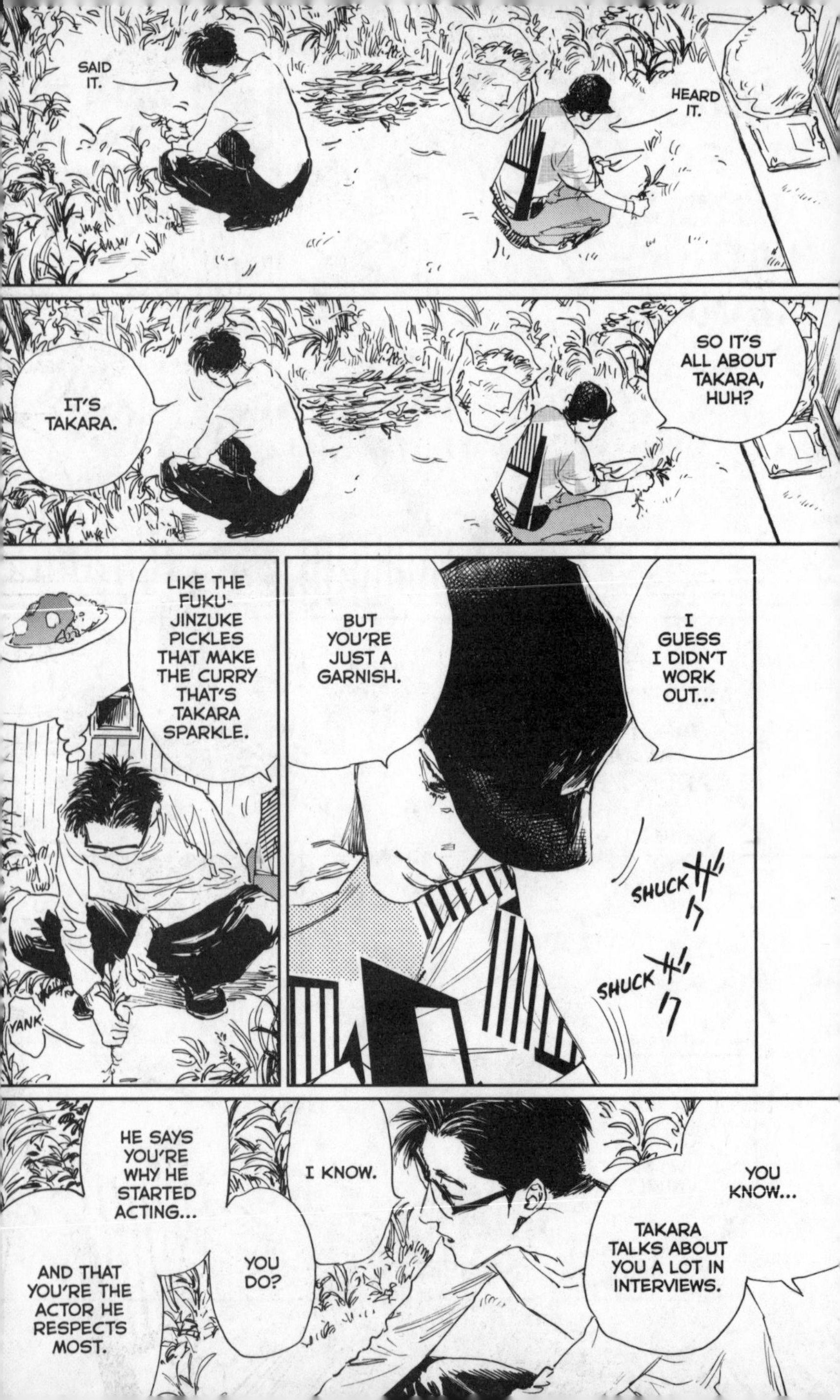
HEARD IT.
SAID IT.
SO IT'S ALL ABOUT TAKARA, HUH?
IT'S TAKARA.
I GUESS I DIDN'T WORK OUT...
BUT YOU'RE JUST A GARNISH.
SHUCK ザク
SHUCK ザク
LIKE THE FUKU-JINZUKE PICKLES THAT MAKE THE CURRY THAT'S TAKARA SPARKLE.
YANK
YOU KNOW...
TAKARA TALKS ABOUT YOU A LOT IN INTERVIEWS.
I KNOW.
YOU DO?
HE SAYS YOU'RE WHY HE STARTED ACTING...
AND THAT YOU'RE THE ACTOR HE RESPECTS MOST.

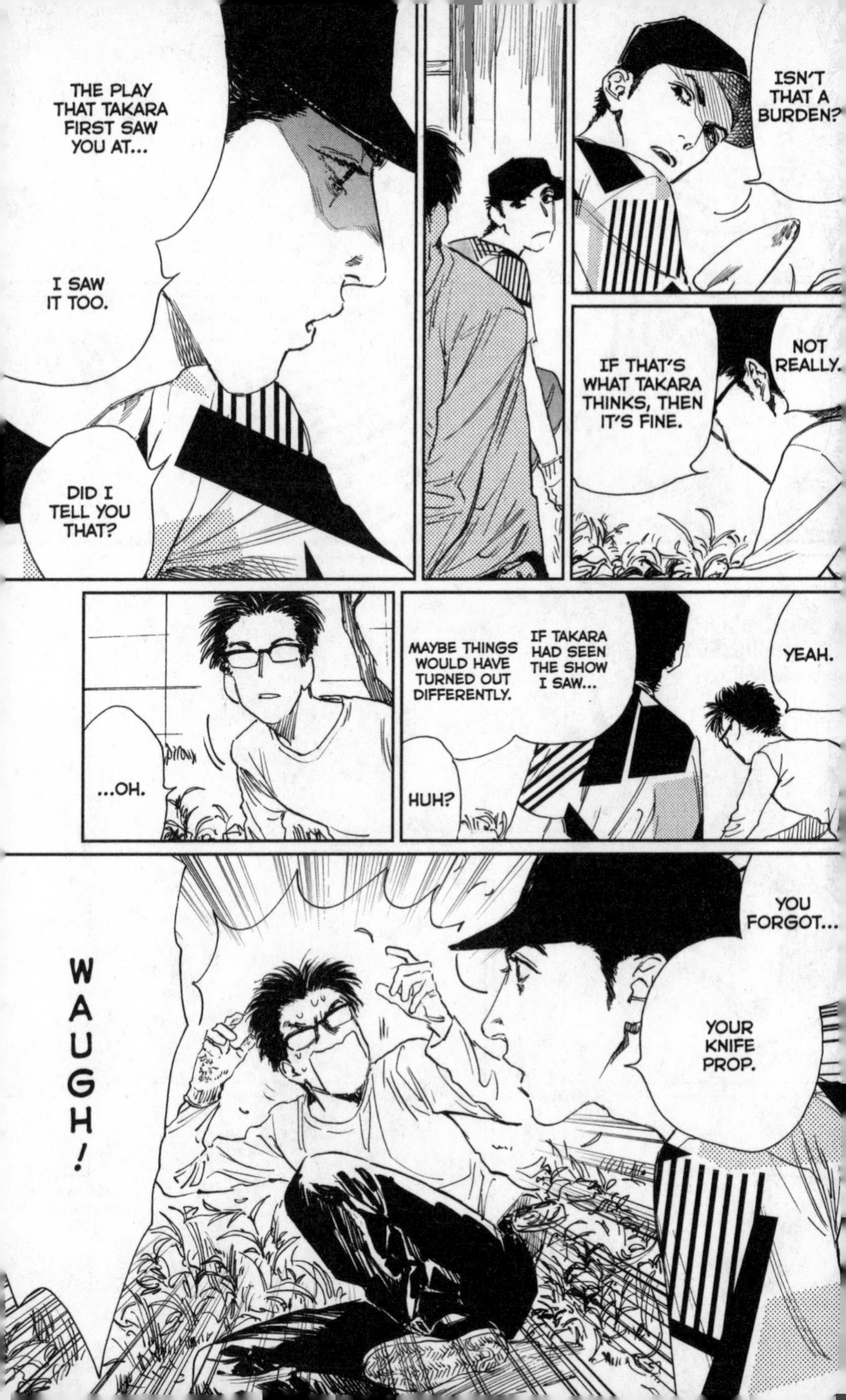
ISN'T THAT A BURDEN?
NOT REALLY.
IF THAT'S WHAT TAKARA THINKS, THEN IT'S FINE.
THE PLAY THAT TAKARA FIRST SAW YOU AT...
I SAW IT TOO.
DID I TELL YOU THAT?
YEAH.
IF TAKARA HAD SEEN THE SHOW I SAW...
MAYBE THINGS WOULD HAVE TURNED OUT DIFFERENTLY.
HUH?
...OH.
YOU FORGOT...
YOUR KNIFE PROP.
WAUGH!

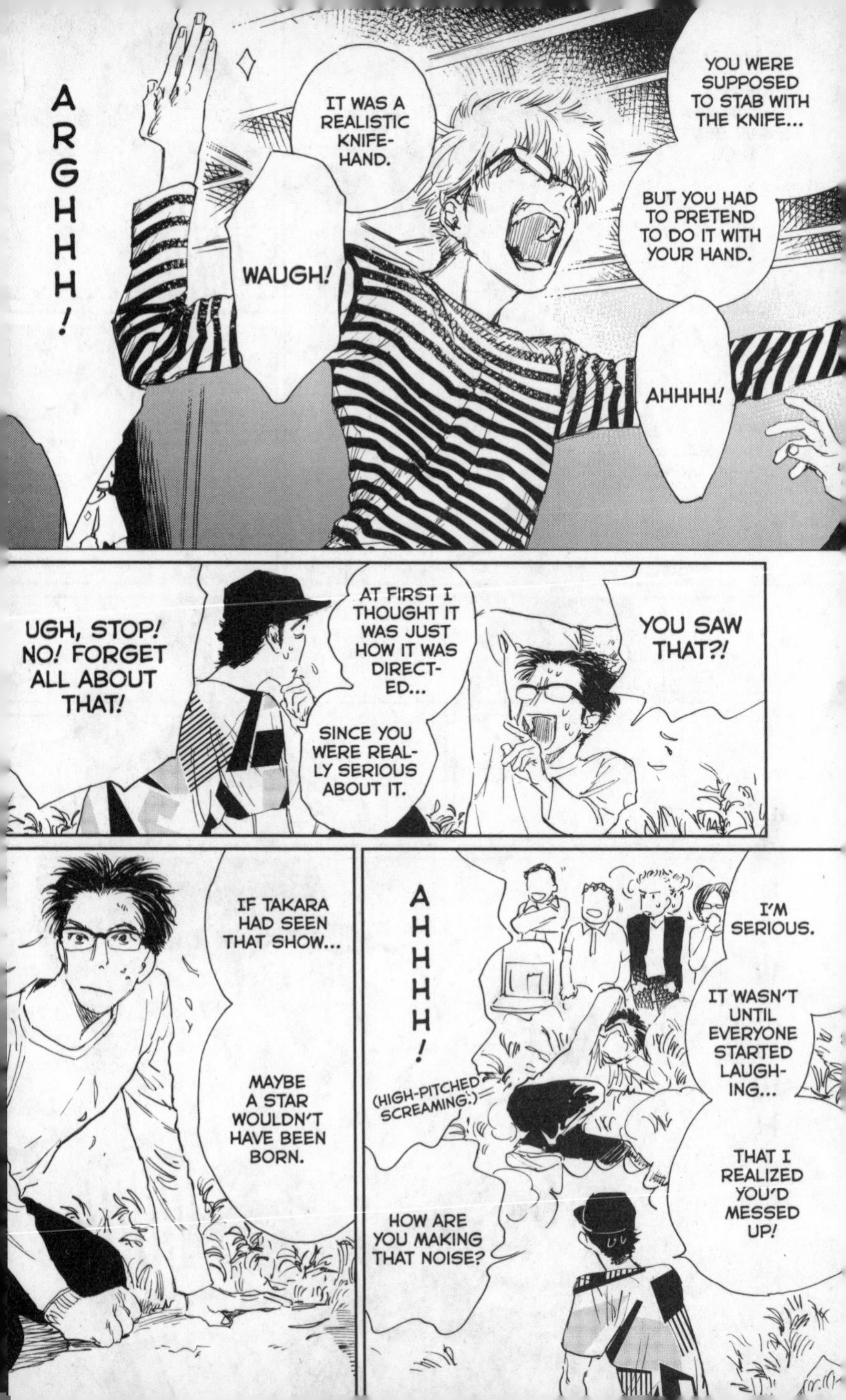

YOU WERE SUPPOSED TO STAB WITH THE KNIFE...
BUT YOU HAD TO PRETEND TO DO IT WITH YOUR HAND.
AHHHH!
IT WAS A REALISTIC KNIFE-HAND.
WAUGH!
ARGHHH!
YOU SAW THAT?!
AT FIRST I THOUGHT IT WAS JUST HOW IT WAS DIRECTED...
SINCE YOU WERE REALLY SERIOUS ABOUT IT.
UGH, STOP! NO! FORGET ALL ABOUT THAT!
I'M SERIOUS.
IT WASN'T UNTIL EVERYONE STARTED LAUGHING...
THAT I REALIZED YOU'D MESSED UP!
AHHHH!
(HIGH-PITCHED SCREAMING.)
HOW ARE YOU MAKING THAT NOISE?
IF TAKARA HAD SEEN THAT SHOW...
MAYBE A STAR WOULDN'T HAVE BEEN BORN.

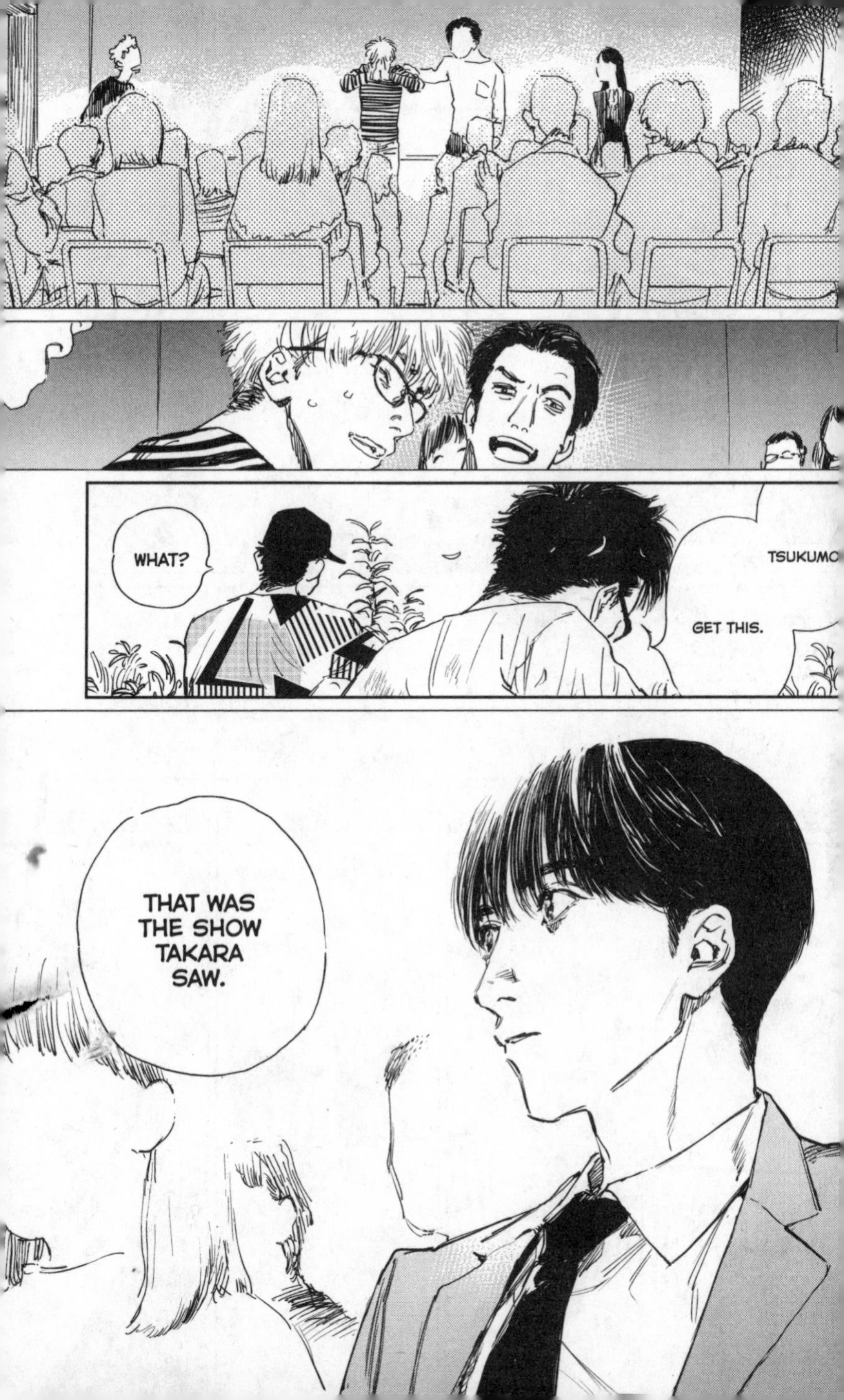
TSUKUMO
GET THIS.
WHAT?
THAT WAS THE SHOW TAKARA SAW.

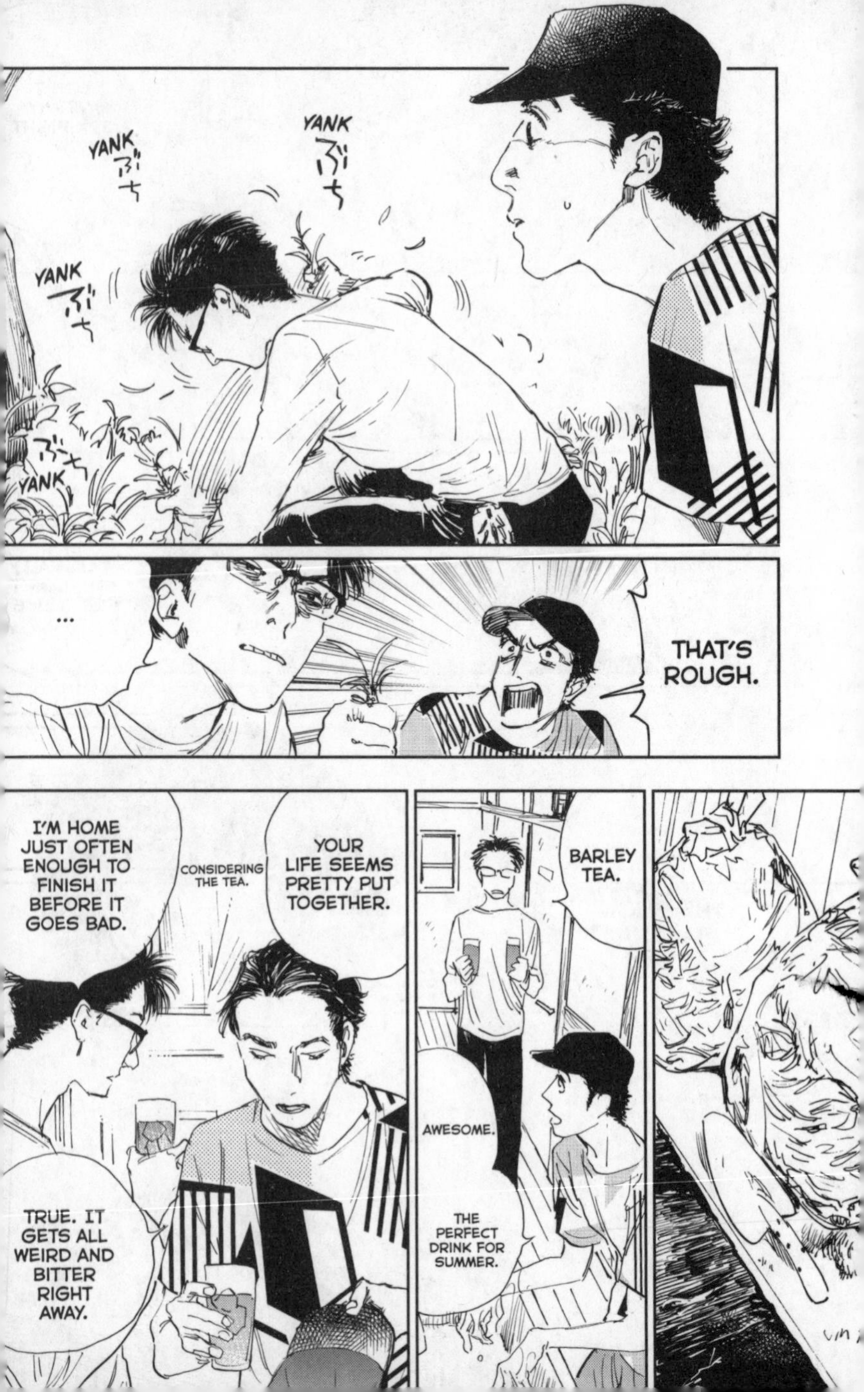
YANK
ぶち
YANK
ぶち
YANK
ぶち
ぶち
YANK
THAT'S ROUGH.
...
BARLEY TEA.
AWESOME.
THE PERFECT DRINK FOR SUMMER.
YOUR LIFE SEEMS PRETTY PUT TOGETHER.
CONSIDERING THE TEA.
I'M HOME JUST OFTEN ENOUGH TO FINISH IT BEFORE IT GOES BAD.
TRUE. IT GETS ALL WEIRD AND BITTER RIGHT AWAY.

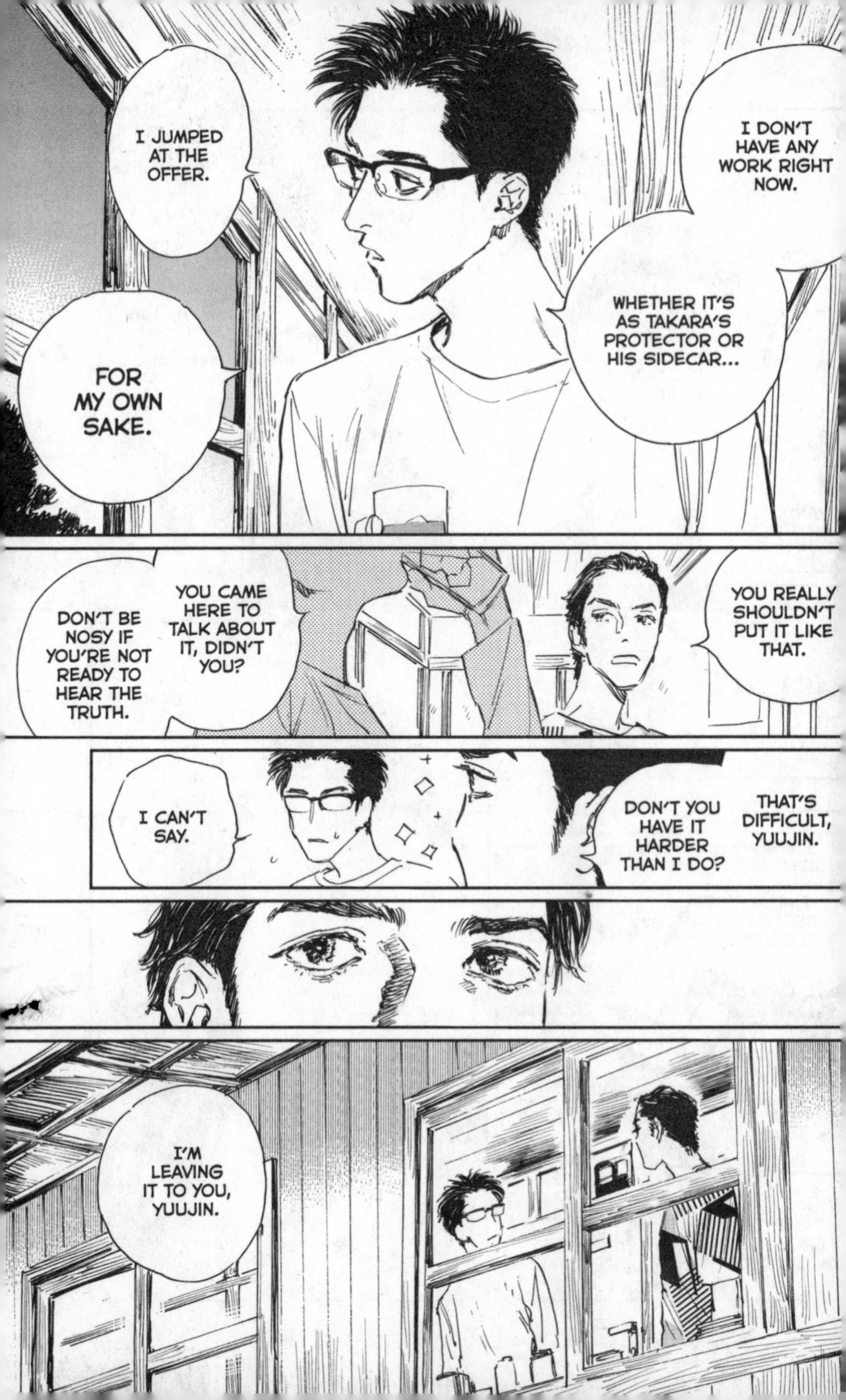
I DON'T HAVE ANY WORK RIGHT NOW.
WHETHER IT'S AS TAKARA'S PROTECTOR OR HIS SIDECAR...
I JUMPED AT THE OFFER.
FOR MY OWN SAKE.
YOU REALLY SHOULDN'T PUT IT LIKE THAT.
YOU CAME HERE TO TALK ABOUT IT, DIDN'T YOU?
DON'T BE NOSY IF YOU'RE NOT READY TO HEAR THE TRUTH.
THAT'S DIFFICULT, YUUJIN.
DON'T YOU HAVE IT HARDER THAN I DO?
I CAN'T SAY.
I'M LEAVING IT TO YOU, YUUJIN.

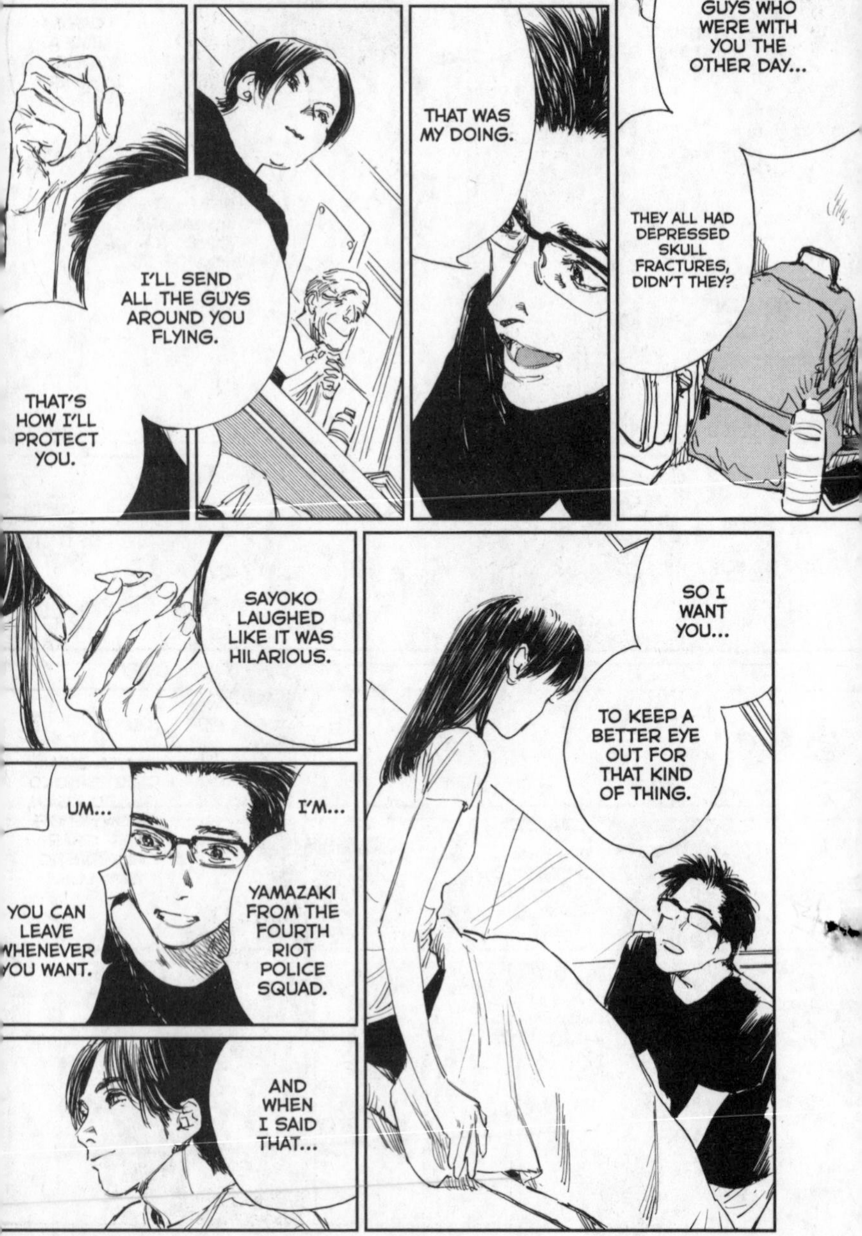
THE THREE GUYS WHO WERE WITH YOU THE OTHER DAY...
THEY ALL HAD DEPRESSED SKULL FRACTURES, DIDN'T THEY?
THAT WAS MY DOING.
I'LL SEND ALL THE GUYS AROUND YOU FLYING.
THAT'S HOW I'LL PROTECT YOU.
SO I WANT YOU...
TO KEEP A BETTER EYE OUT FOR THAT KIND OF THING.
SAYOKO LAUGHED LIKE IT WAS HILARIOUS.
I'M...
YAMAZAKI FROM THE FOURTH RIOT POLICE SQUAD.
UM...
YOU CAN LEAVE WHENEVER YOU WANT.
AND WHEN I SAID THAT...

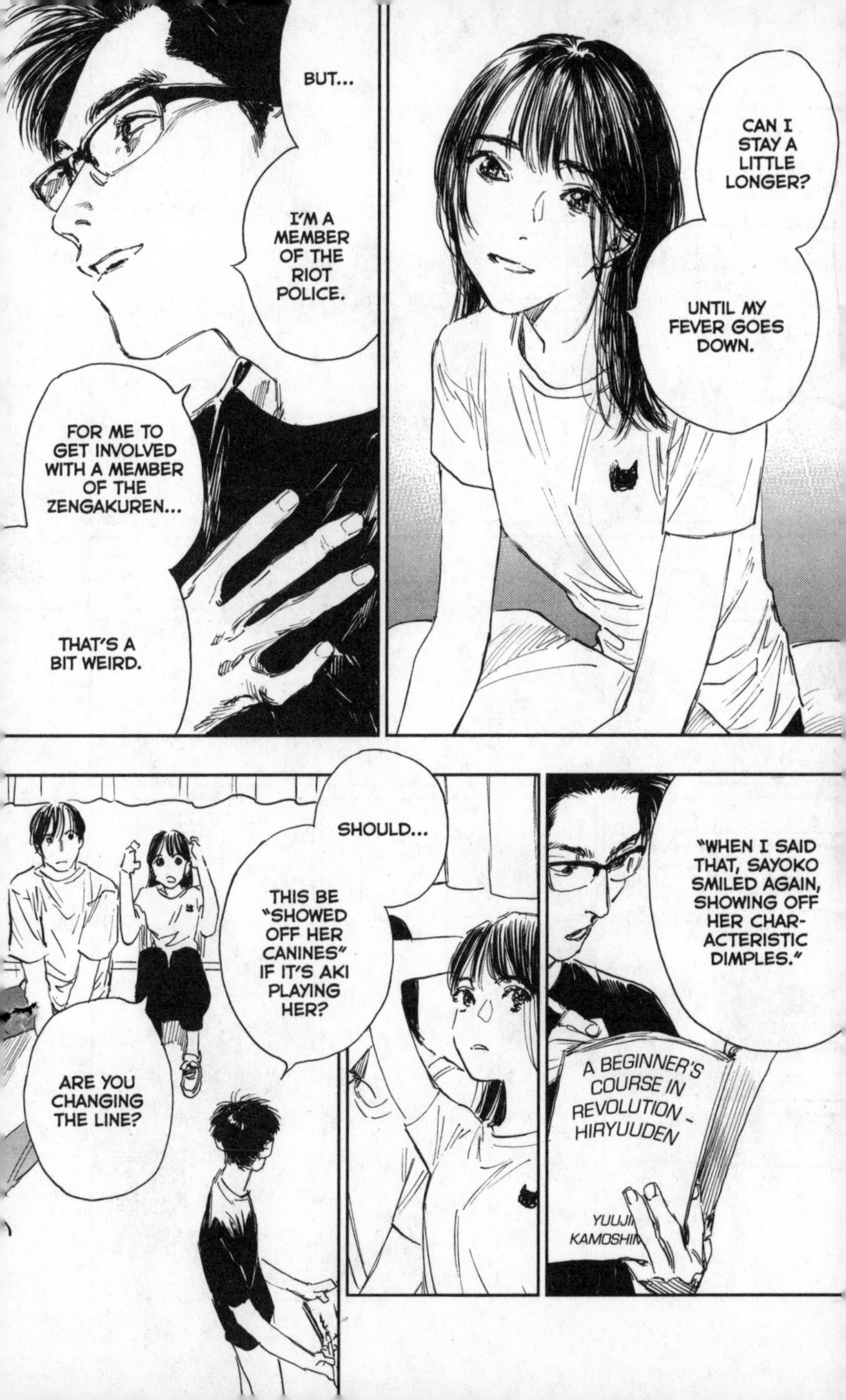
CAN I STAY A LITTLE LONGER?
UNTIL MY FEVER GOES DOWN.
BUT...
I'M A MEMBER OF THE RIOT POLICE.
FOR ME TO GET INVOLVED WITH A MEMBER OF THE ZENGAKUREN...
THAT'S A BIT WEIRD.
"WHEN I SAID THAT, SAYOKO SMILED AGAIN, SHOWING OFF HER CHAR-ACTERISTIC DIMPLES."
A BEGINNER'S COURSE IN REVOLUTION - HIRYUUDEN
SHOULD...
THIS BE "SHOWED OFF HER CANINES" IF IT'S AKI PLAYING HER?
ARE YOU CHANGING THE LINE?

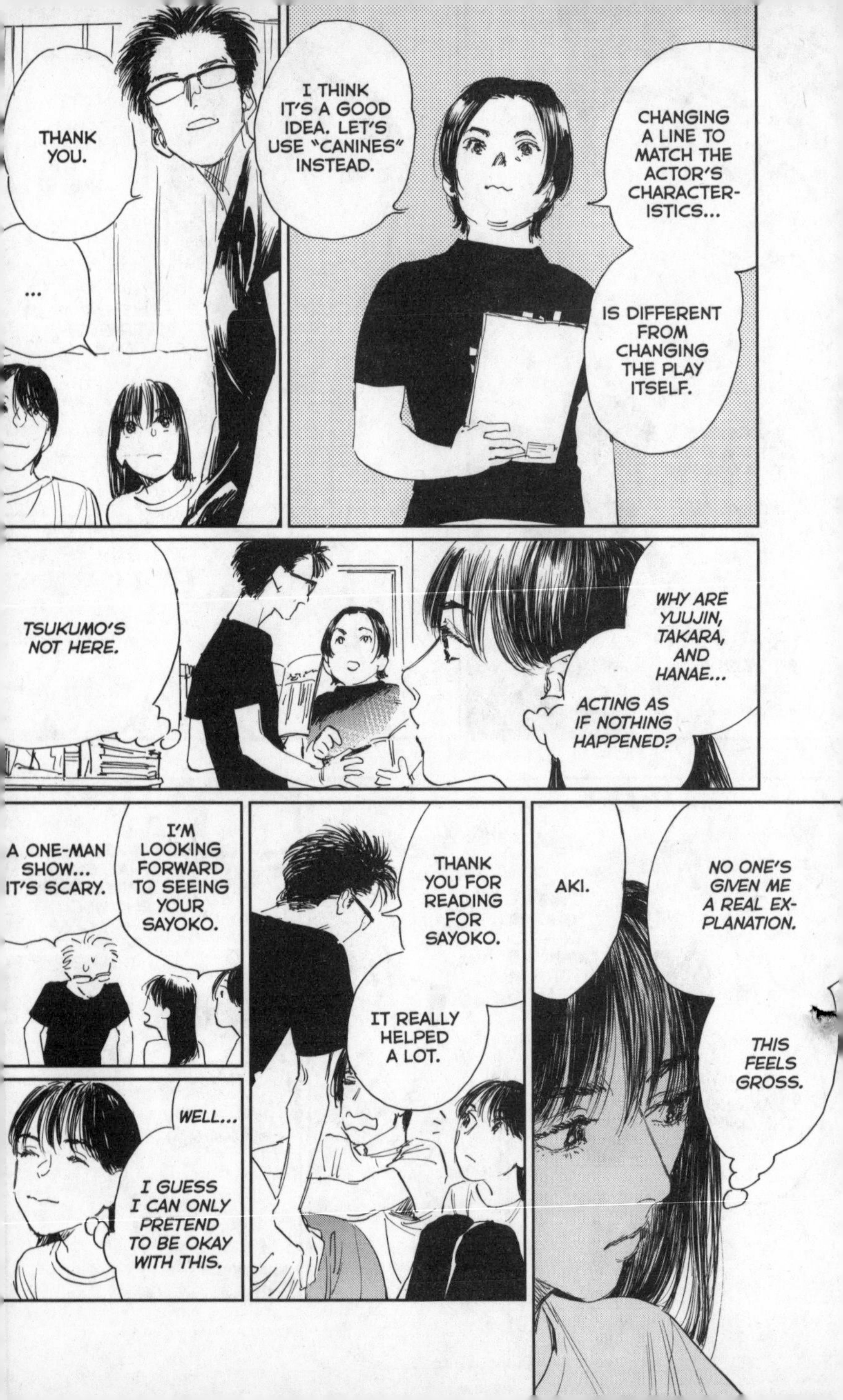
CHANGING A LINE TO MATCH THE ACTOR'S CHARACTER-ISTICS...
IS DIFFERENT FROM CHANGING THE PLAY ITSELF.
I THINK IT'S A GOOD IDEA. LET'S USE "CANINES" INSTEAD.
THANK YOU.
...
WHY ARE YUUJIN, TAKARA, AND HANAE...
ACTING AS IF NOTHING HAPPENED?
TSUKUMO'S NOT HERE.
NO ONE'S GIVEN ME A REAL EX-PLANATION.
AKI.
THIS FEELS GROSS.
THANK YOU FOR READING FOR SAYOKO.
IT REALLY HELPED A LOT.
I'M LOOKING FORWARD TO SEEING YOUR SAYOKO.
A ONE-MAN SHOW... IT'S SCARY.
WELL...
I GUESS I CAN ONLY PRETEND TO BE OKAY WITH THIS.

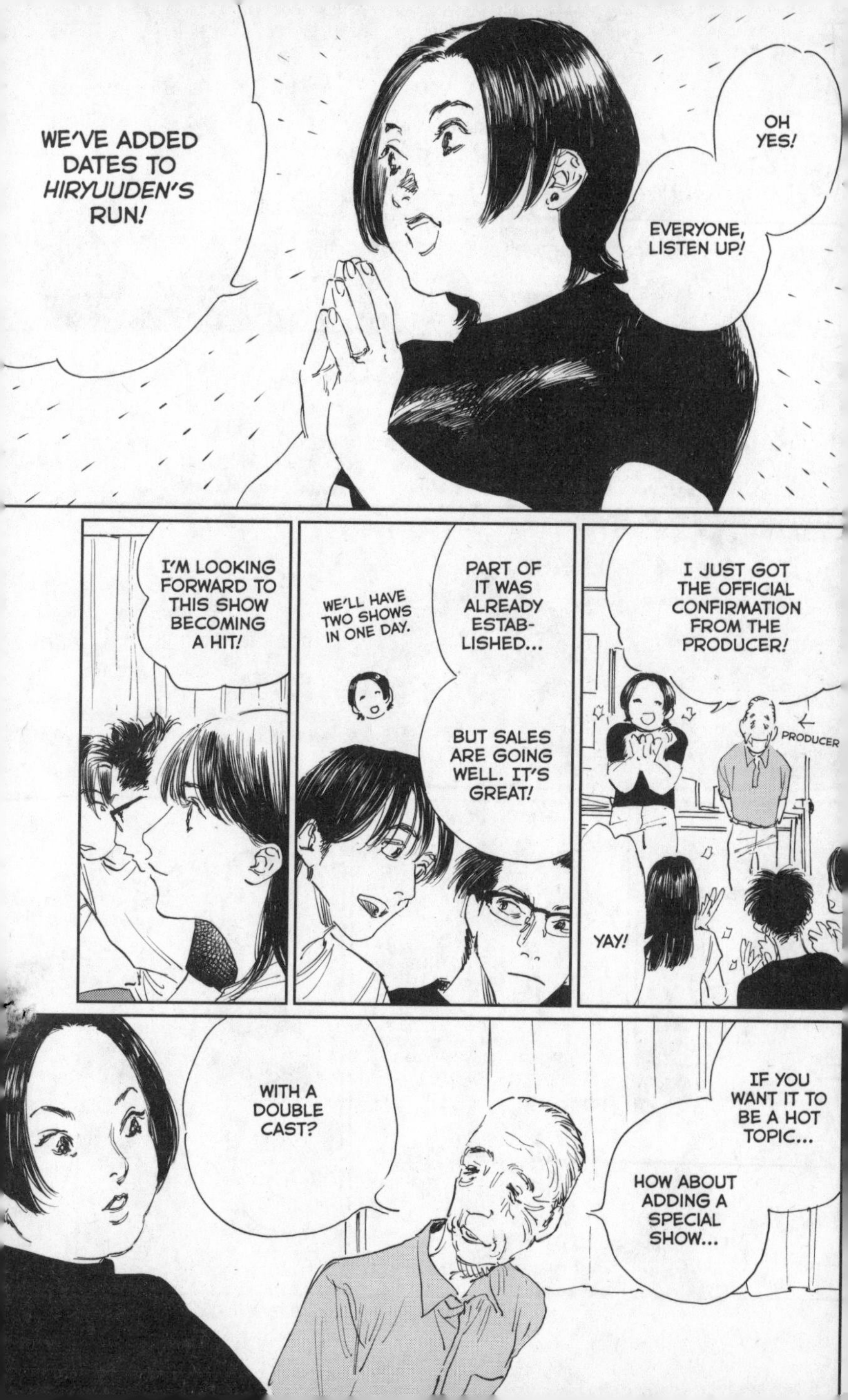
OH YES!
EVERYONE, LISTEN UP!
WE'VE ADDED DATES TO *HIRYUUDEN'S* RUN!
I JUST GOT THE OFFICIAL CONFIRMATION FROM THE PRODUCER!
PRODUCER
YAY!
PART OF IT WAS ALREADY ESTAB-LISHED...
WE'LL HAVE TWO SHOWS IN ONE DAY.
BUT SALES ARE GOING WELL. IT'S GREAT!
I'M LOOKING FORWARD TO THIS SHOW BECOMING A HIT!
IF YOU WANT IT TO BE A HOT TOPIC...
HOW ABOUT ADDING A SPECIAL SHOW...
WITH A DOUBLE CAST?

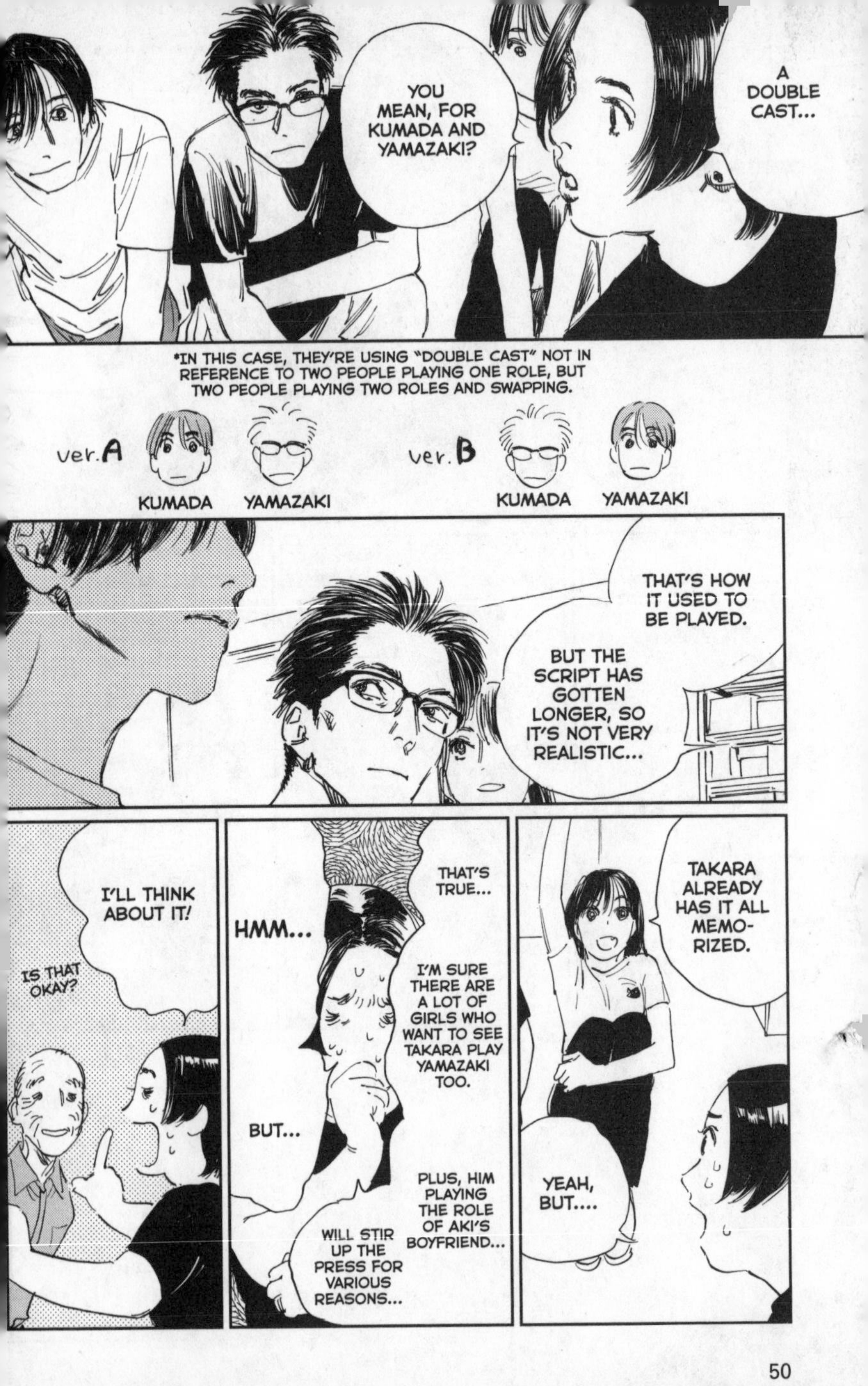
A DOUBLE CAST...
YOU MEAN, FOR KUMADA AND YAMAZAKI?
*IN THIS CASE, THEY'RE USING "DOUBLE CAST" NOT IN REFERENCE TO TWO PEOPLE PLAYING ONE ROLE, BUT TWO PEOPLE PLAYING TWO ROLES AND SWAPPING.
ver.A
KUMADA
YAMAZAKI
ver.B
KUMADA
YAMAZAKI
THAT'S HOW IT USED TO BE PLAYED.
BUT THE SCRIPT HAS GOTTEN LONGER, SO IT'S NOT VERY REALISTIC...
TAKARA ALREADY HAS IT ALL MEMO-RIZED.
YEAH, BUT....
THAT'S TRUE...
HMM...
I'M SURE THERE ARE A LOT OF GIRLS WHO WANT TO SEE TAKARA PLAY YAMAZAKI TOO.
BUT...
PLUS, HIM PLAYING THE ROLE OF AKI'S BOYFRIEND...
WILL STIR UP THE PRESS FOR VARIOUS REASONS...
I'LL THINK ABOUT IT!
IS THAT OKAY?

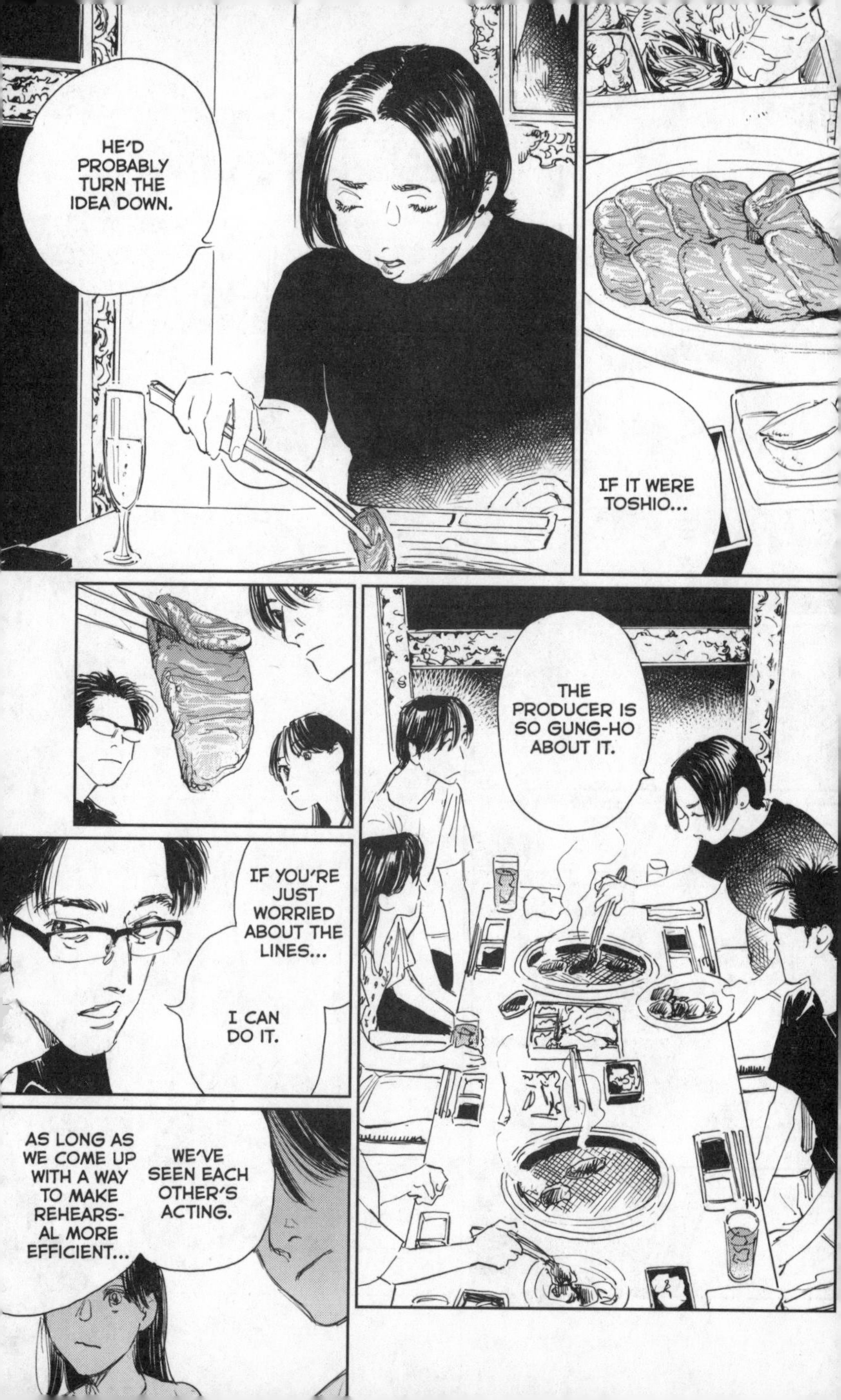
IF IT WERE TOSHIO...
HE'D PROBABLY TURN THE IDEA DOWN.
THE PRODUCER IS SO GUNG-HO ABOUT IT.
IF YOU'RE JUST WORRIED ABOUT THE LINES...
I CAN DO IT.
WE'VE SEEN EACH OTHER'S ACTING.
AS LONG AS WE COME UP WITH A WAY TO MAKE REHEARS-AL MORE EFFICIENT...

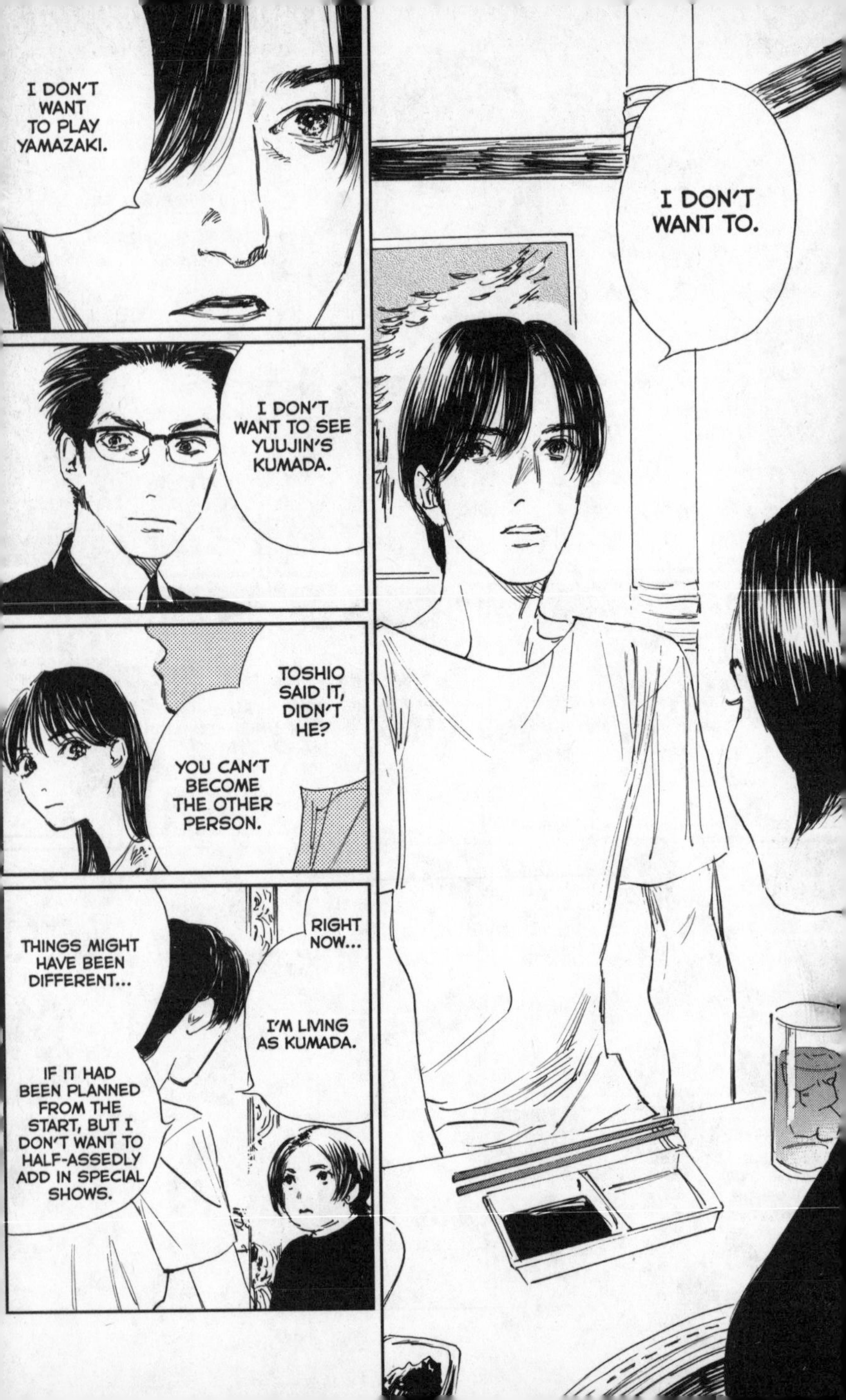
I DON'T WANT TO.
I DON'T WANT TO PLAY YAMAZAKI.
I DON'T WANT TO SEE YUUJIN'S KUMADA.
TOSHIO SAID IT, DIDN'T HE?
YOU CAN'T BECOME THE OTHER PERSON.
RIGHT NOW...
I'M LIVING AS KUMADA.
THINGS MIGHT HAVE BEEN DIFFERENT...
IF IT HAD BEEN PLANNED FROM THE START, BUT I DON'T WANT TO HALF-ASSEDLY ADD IN SPECIAL SHOWS.

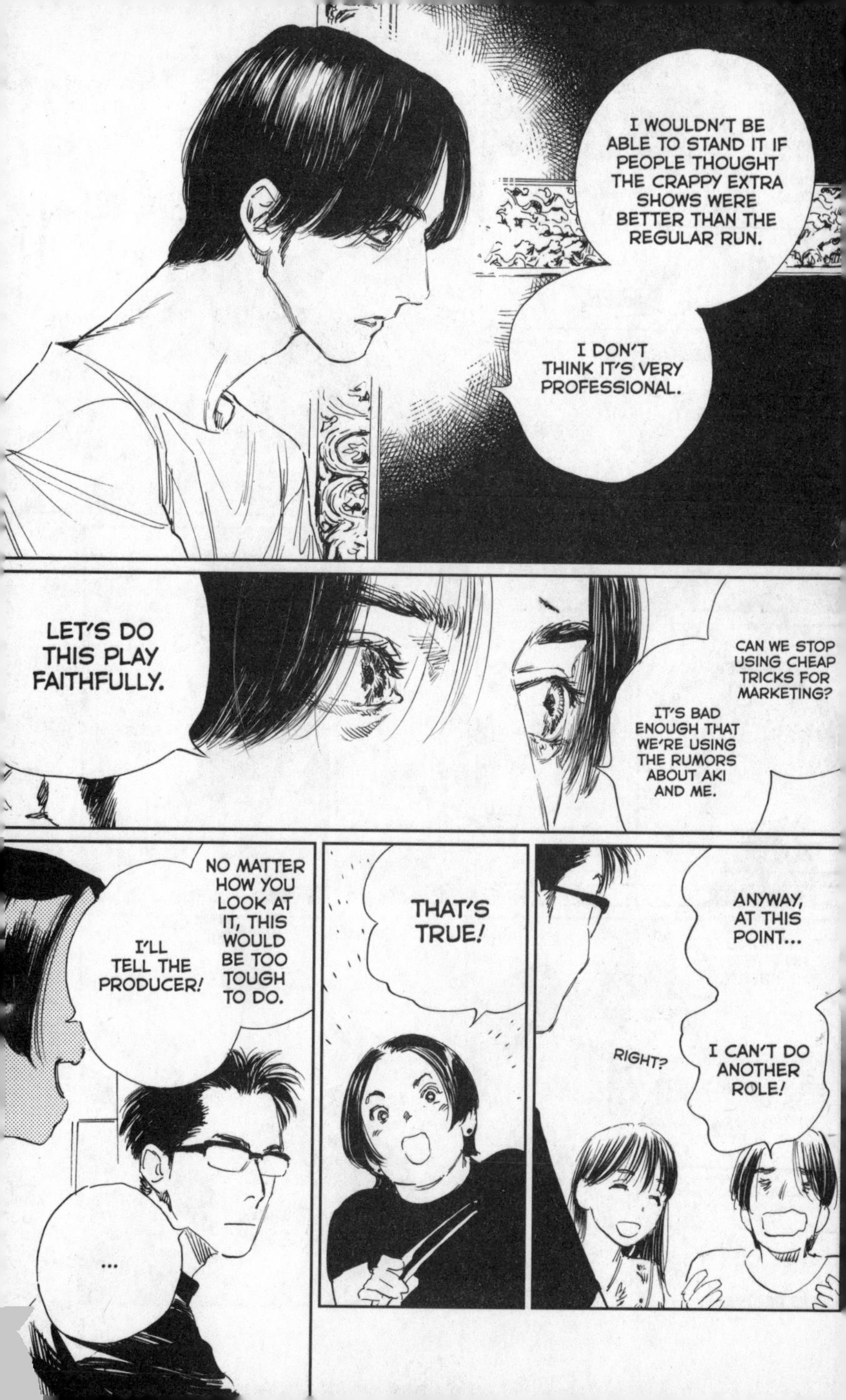
I WOULDN'T BE ABLE TO STAND IT IF PEOPLE THOUGHT THE CRAPPY EXTRA SHOWS WERE BETTER THAN THE REGULAR RUN.
I DON'T THINK IT'S VERY PROFESSIONAL.
CAN WE STOP USING CHEAP TRICKS FOR MARKETING?
IT'S BAD ENOUGH THAT WE'RE USING THE RUMORS ABOUT AKI AND ME.
LET'S DO THIS PLAY FAITHFULLY.
ANYWAY, AT THIS POINT...
I CAN'T DO ANOTHER ROLE!
RIGHT?
THAT'S TRUE!
NO MATTER HOW YOU LOOK AT IT, THIS WOULD BE TOO TOUGH TO DO.
I'LL TELL THE PRODUCER!
...

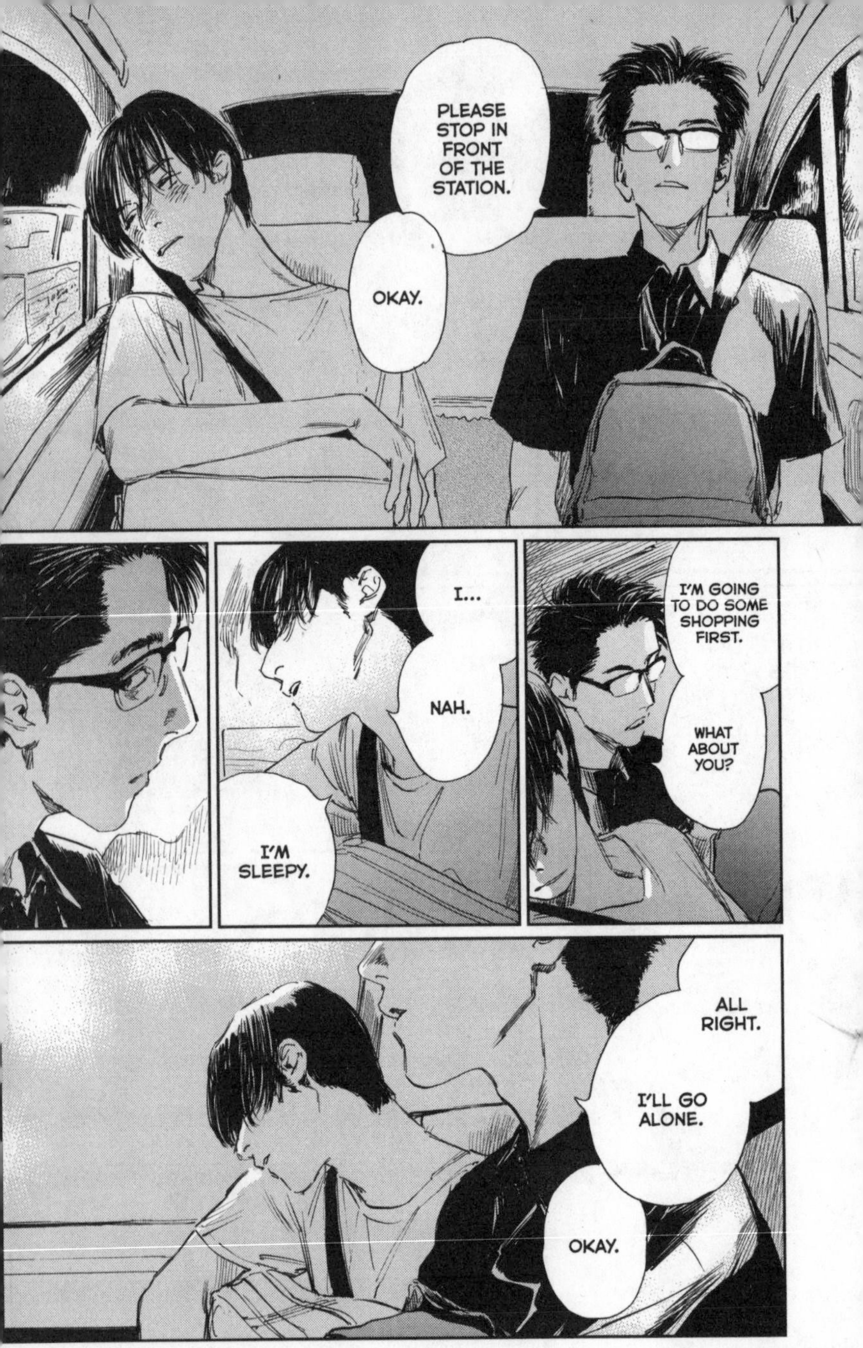
PLEASE STOP IN FRONT OF THE STATION.
OKAY.
I'M GOING TO DO SOME SHOPPING FIRST.
WHAT ABOUT YOU?
I...
NAH.
I'M SLEEPY.
ALL RIGHT.
I'LL GO ALONE.
OKAY.

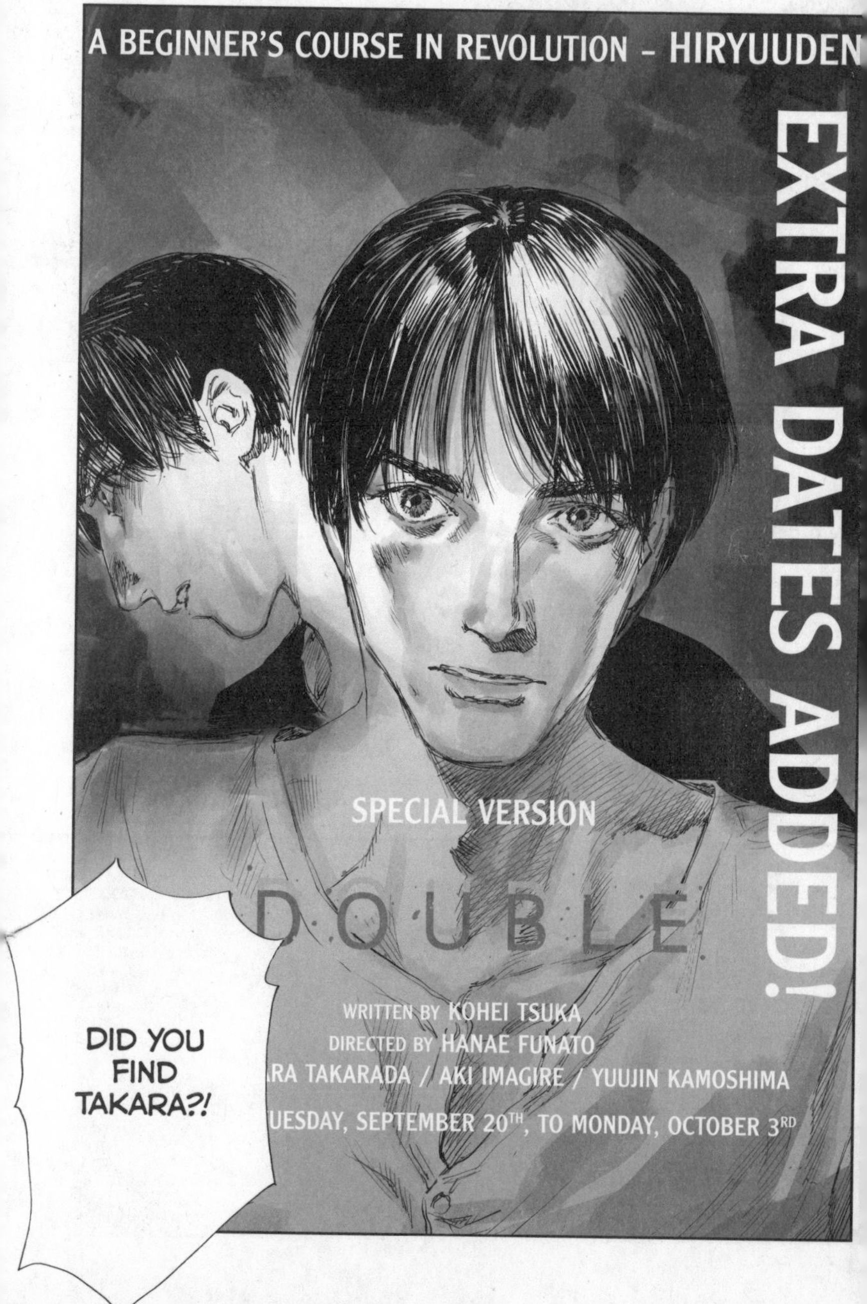
A BEGINNER'S COURSE IN REVOLUTION – HIRYUUDEN
EXTRA DATES ADDED!
SPECIAL VERSION
DOUBLE
WRITTEN BY KOHEI TSUKA
DIRECTED BY HANAE FUNATO
RA TAKARADA / AKI IMAGIRE / YUUJIN KAMOSHIMA
UESDAY, SEPTEMBER 20TH, TO MONDAY, OCTOBER 3RD
DID YOU FIND TAKARA?!

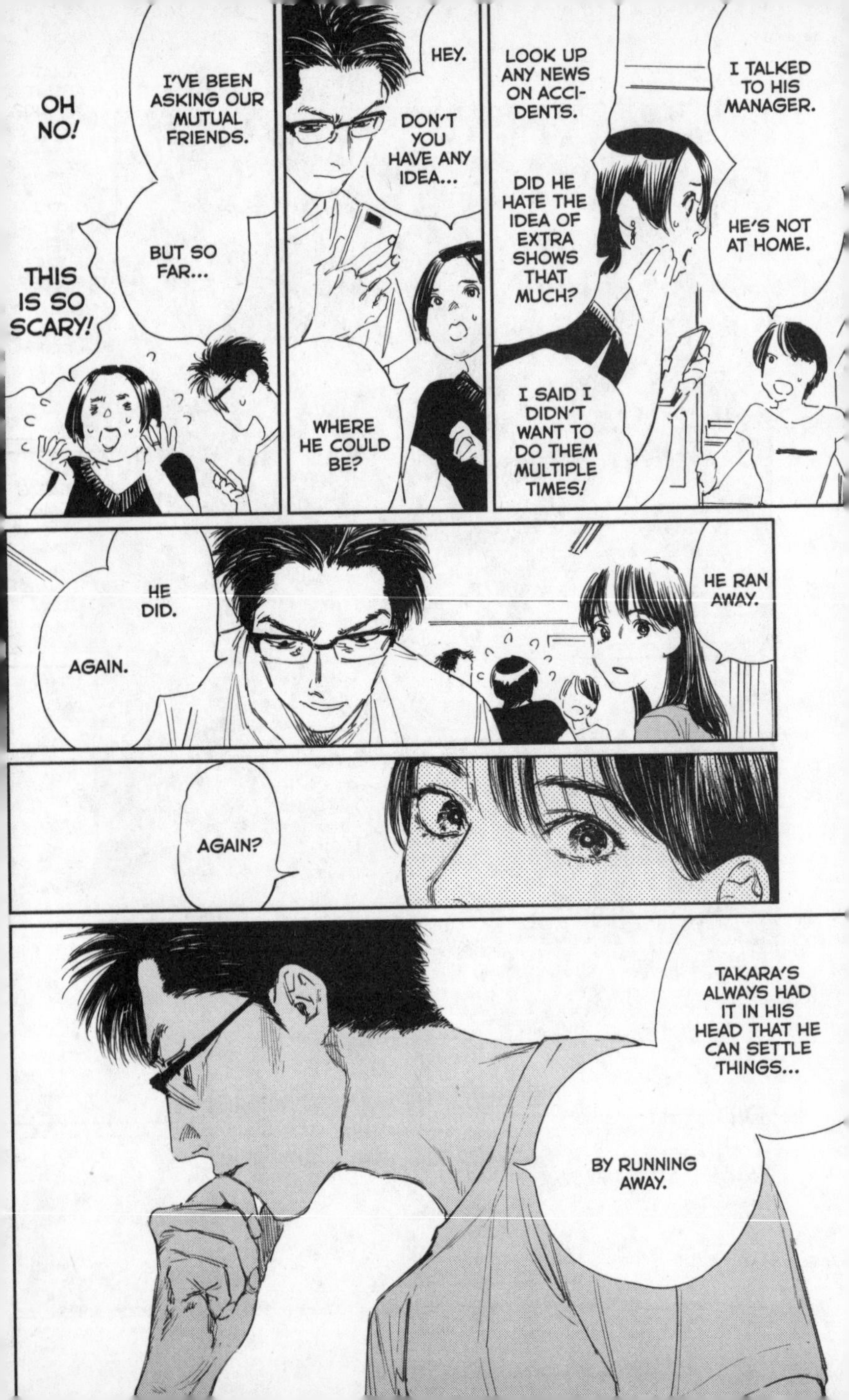
I TALKED TO HIS MANAGER.
HE'S NOT AT HOME.
LOOK UP ANY NEWS ON ACCI-DENTS.
DID HE HATE THE IDEA OF EXTRA SHOWS THAT MUCH?
I SAID I DIDN'T WANT TO DO THEM MULTIPLE TIMES!
HEY.
DON'T YOU HAVE ANY IDEA...
WHERE HE COULD BE?
I'VE BEEN ASKING OUR MUTUAL FRIENDS.
BUT SO FAR...
OH NO!
THIS IS SO SCARY!
HE RAN AWAY.
HE DID.
AGAIN.
AGAIN?
TAKARA'S ALWAYS HAD IT IN HIS HEAD THAT HE CAN SETTLE THINGS...
BY RUNNING AWAY.

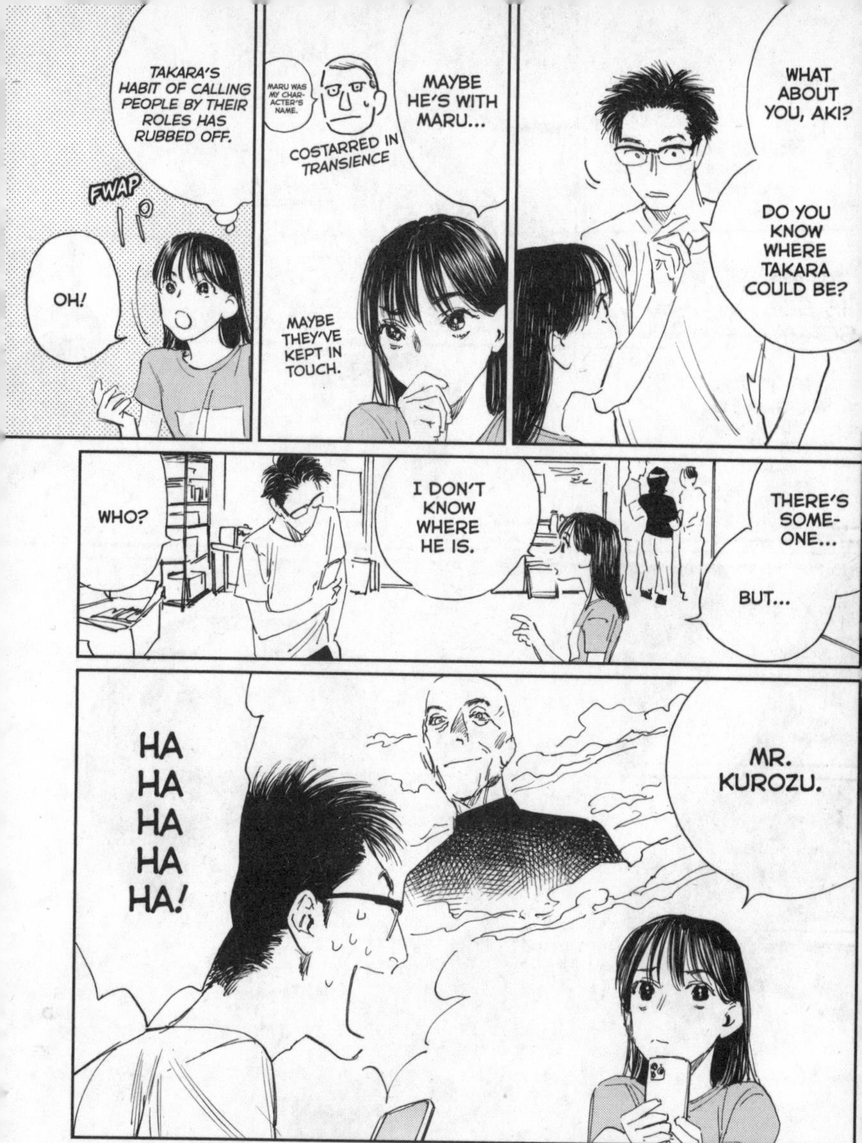
WHAT ABOUT YOU, AKI?
DO YOU KNOW WHERE TAKARA COULD BE?
MAYBE HE'S WITH MARU...
MARU WAS MY CHARACTER'S NAME.
COSTARRED IN TRANSIENCE
MAYBE THEY'VE KEPT IN TOUCH.
TAKARA'S HABIT OF CALLING PEOPLE BY THEIR ROLES HAS RUBBED OFF.
FWAP
OH!
THERE'S SOMEONE...
BUT...
I DON'T KNOW WHERE HE IS.
WHO?
MR. KUROZU.
HA HA HA HA HA!
SORRY.
I DIDN'T MEAN TO BE THAT LOUD.
I DIDN'T EXPECT TO HEAR THAT NAME.
MR. KUROZU, THE DIRECTOR...

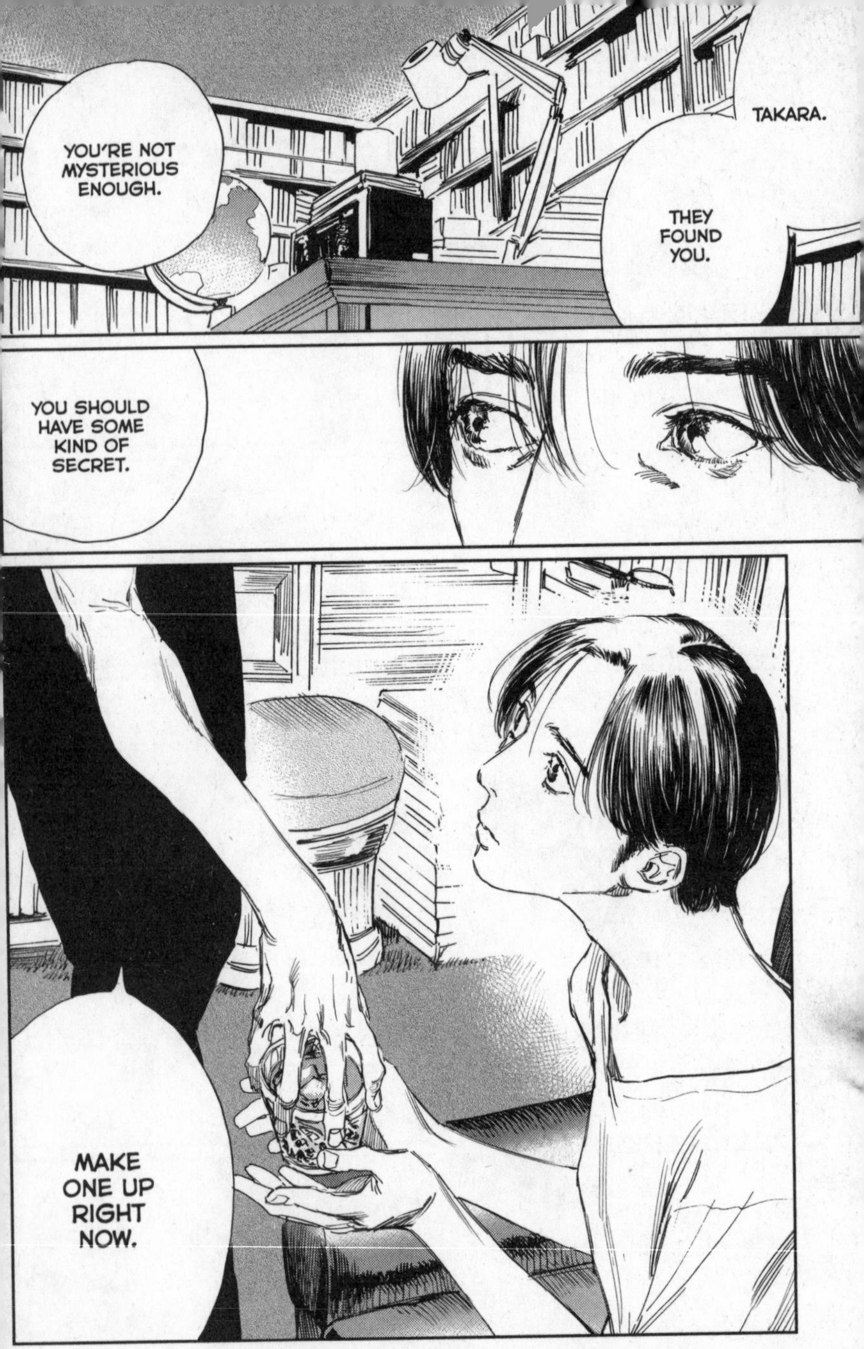
TAKARA.
THEY FOUND YOU.
YOU'RE NOT MYSTERIOUS ENOUGH.
YOU SHOULD HAVE SOME KIND OF SECRET.
MAKE ONE UP RIGHT NOW.

DOUBLE

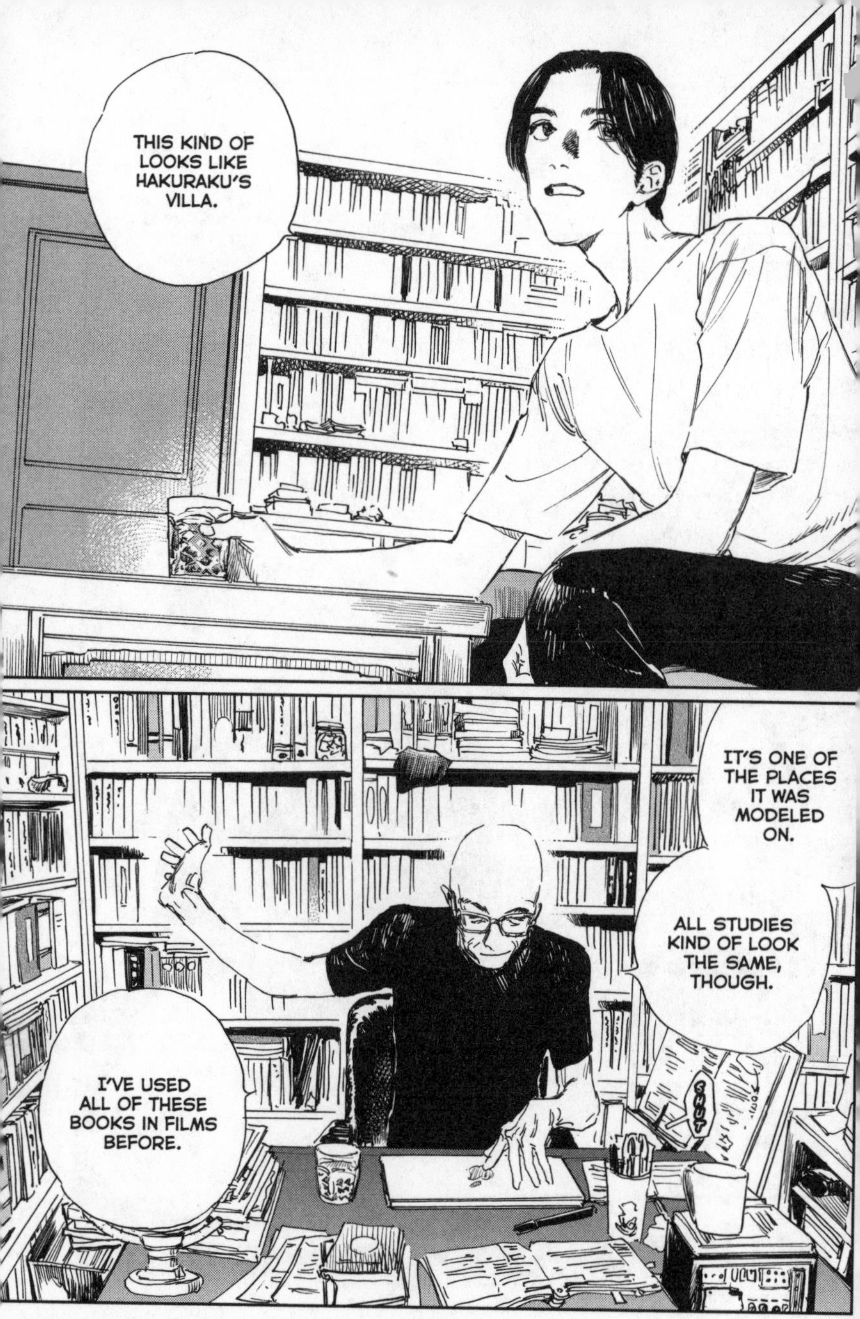
THIS KIND OF LOOKS LIKE HAKURAKU'S VILLA.
IT'S ONE OF THE PLACES IT WAS MODELED ON.
ALL STUDIES KIND OF LOOK THE SAME, THOUGH.
SHUT
I'VE USED ALL OF THESE BOOKS IN FILMS BEFORE.

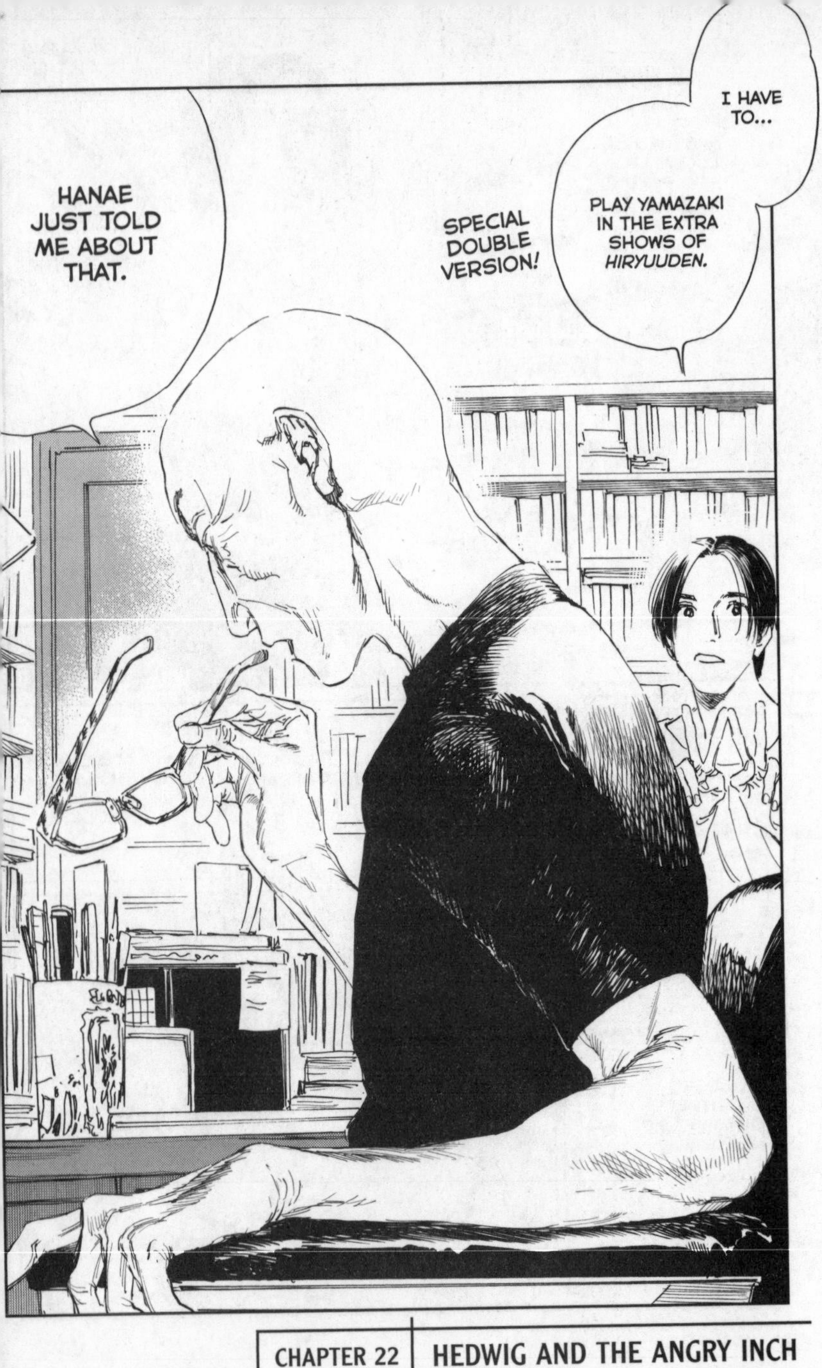
I HAVE TO...
PLAY YAMAZAKI IN THE EXTRA SHOWS OF *HIRYUUDEN.*
SPECIAL DOUBLE VERSION!
HANAE JUST TOLD ME ABOUT THAT.

CHAPTER 22 | HEDWIG AND THE ANGRY INCH

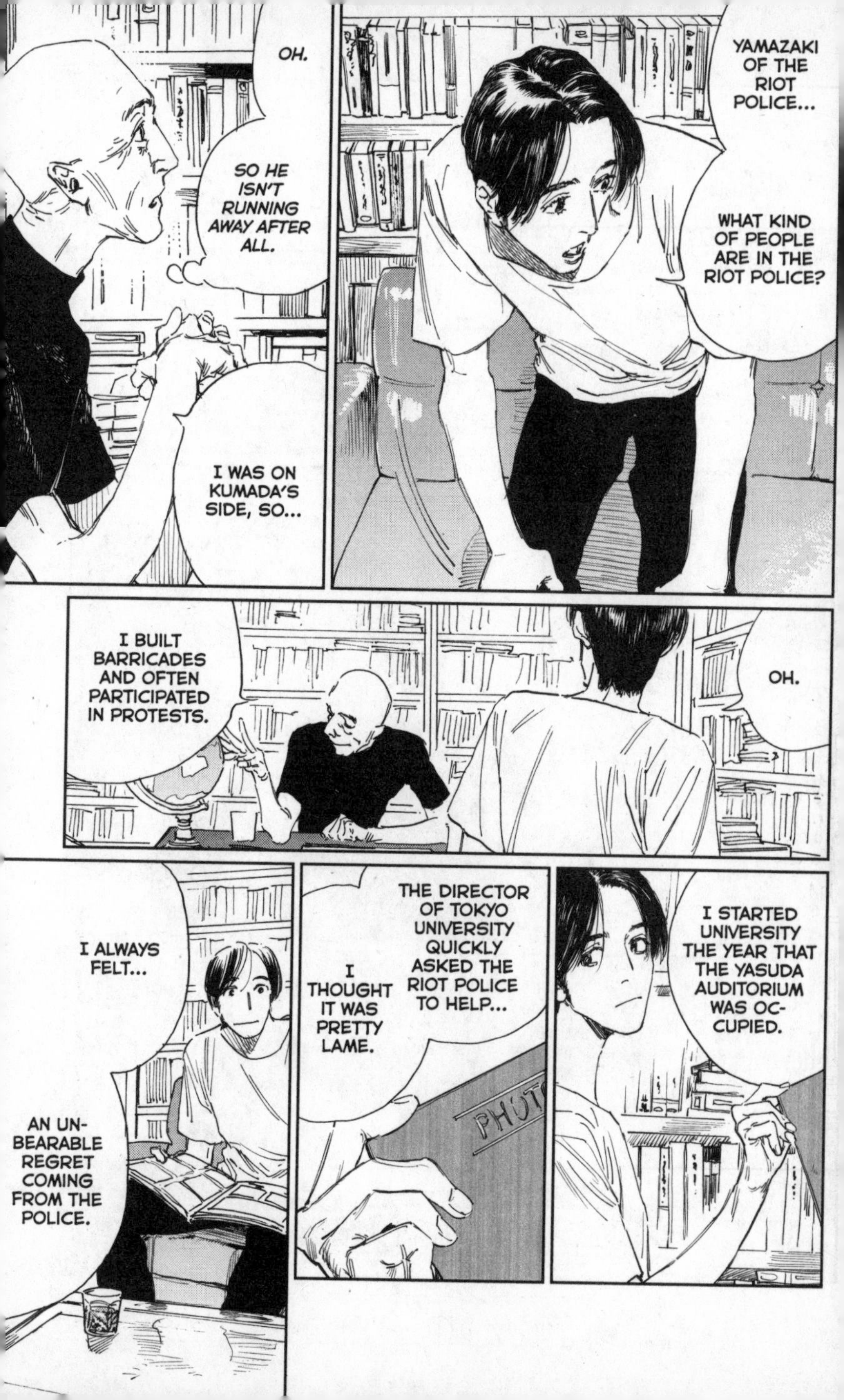
YAMAZAKI OF THE RIOT POLICE...
WHAT KIND OF PEOPLE ARE IN THE RIOT POLICE?
OH.
SO HE ISN'T RUNNING AWAY AFTER ALL.
I WAS ON KUMADA'S SIDE, SO...
OH.
I BUILT BARRICADES AND OFTEN PARTICIPATED IN PROTESTS.
I STARTED UNIVERSITY THE YEAR THAT THE YASUDA AUDITORIUM WAS OC-CUPIED.
THE DIRECTOR OF TOKYO UNIVERSITY QUICKLY ASKED THE RIOT POLICE TO HELP...
I THOUGHT IT WAS PRETTY LAME.
I ALWAYS FELT...
AN UN-BEARABLE REGRET COMING FROM THE POLICE.

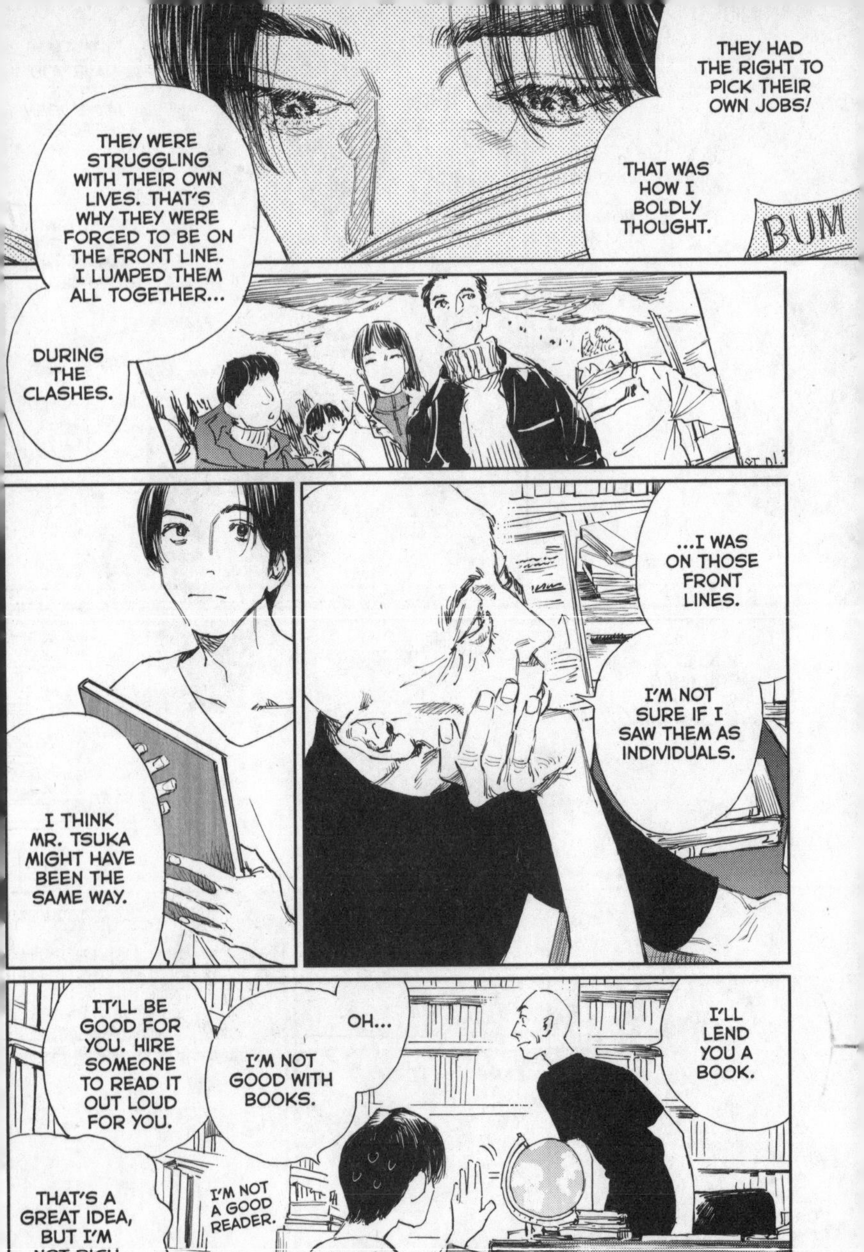
THEY HAD THE RIGHT TO PICK THEIR OWN JOBS!
THAT WAS HOW I BOLDLY THOUGHT.
BUM
THEY WERE STRUGGLING WITH THEIR OWN LIVES. THAT'S WHY THEY WERE FORCED TO BE ON THE FRONT LINE. I LUMPED THEM ALL TOGETHER...
DURING THE CLASHES.
...I WAS ON THOSE FRONT LINES.
I'M NOT SURE IF I SAW THEM AS INDIVIDUALS.
I THINK MR. TSUKA MIGHT HAVE BEEN THE SAME WAY.
I'LL LEND YOU A BOOK.
OH...
I'M NOT GOOD WITH BOOKS.
IT'LL BE GOOD FOR YOU. HIRE SOMEONE TO READ IT OUT LOUD FOR YOU.
I'M NOT A GOOD READER.
THAT'S A GREAT IDEA, BUT I'M NOT RICH LIKE YOU!

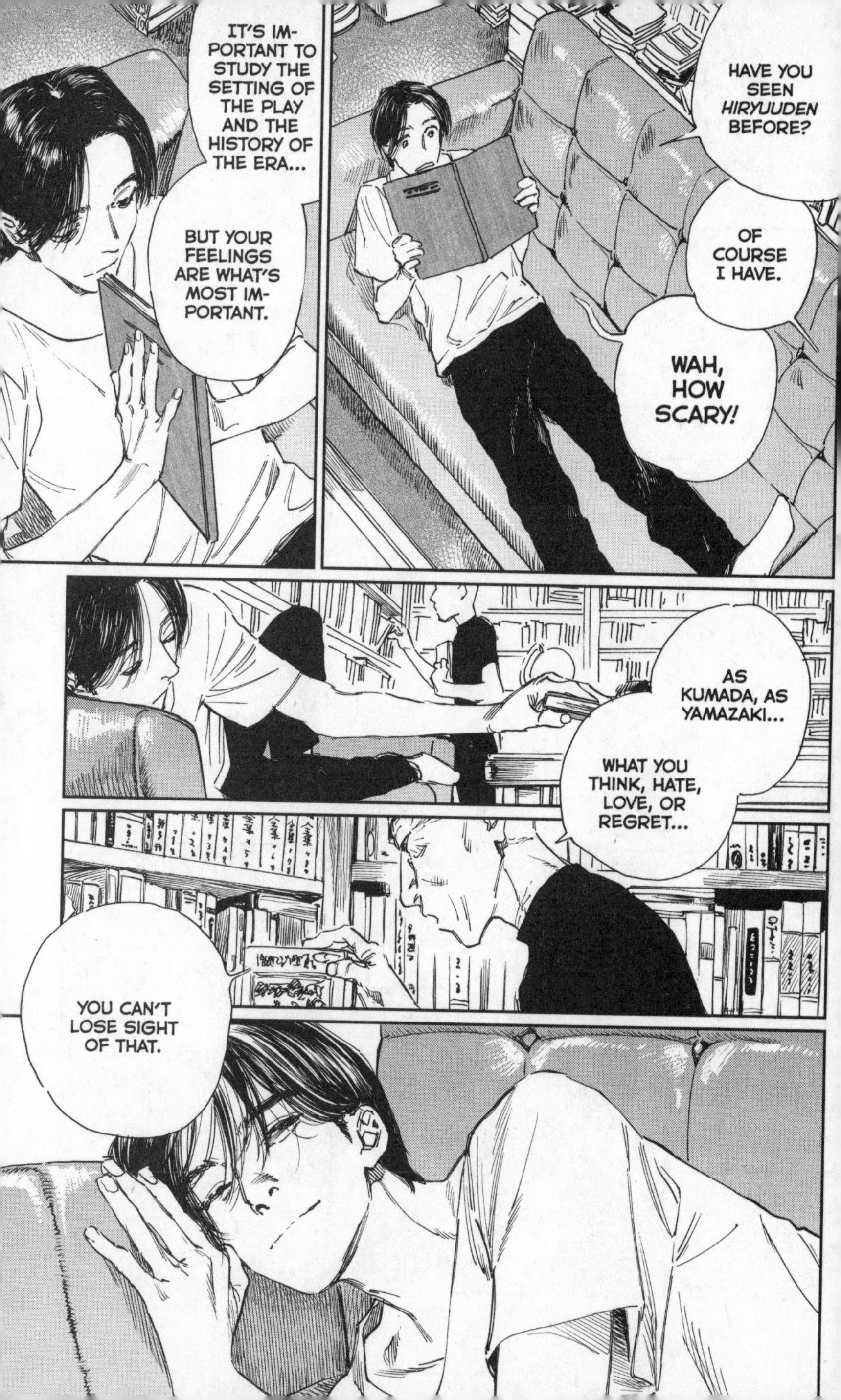
HAVE YOU SEEN *HIRYUUDEN* BEFORE?
OF COURSE I HAVE.
WAH, HOW SCARY!
IT'S IMPORTANT TO STUDY THE SETTING OF THE PLAY AND THE HISTORY OF THE ERA...
BUT YOUR FEELINGS ARE WHAT'S MOST IMPORTANT.
AS KUMADA, AS YAMAZAKI...
WHAT YOU THINK, HATE, LOVE, OR REGRET...
YOU CAN'T LOSE SIGHT OF THAT.

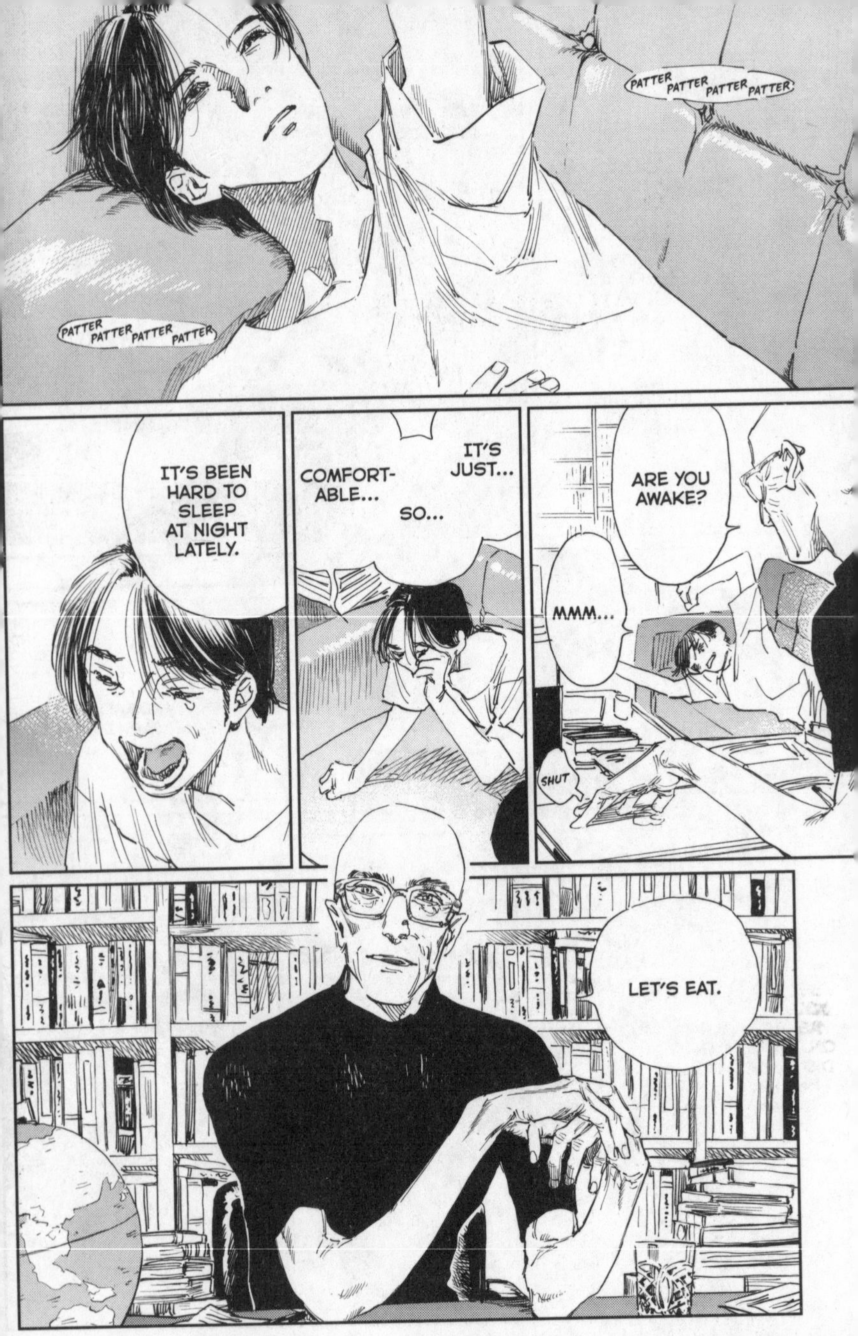
PATTER PATTER PATTER PATTER
PATTER PATTER PATTER PATTER
ARE YOU AWAKE?
MMM...
SHUT
IT'S JUST...
COMFORT-ABLE...
SO...
IT'S BEEN HARD TO SLEEP AT NIGHT LATELY.
LET'S EAT.

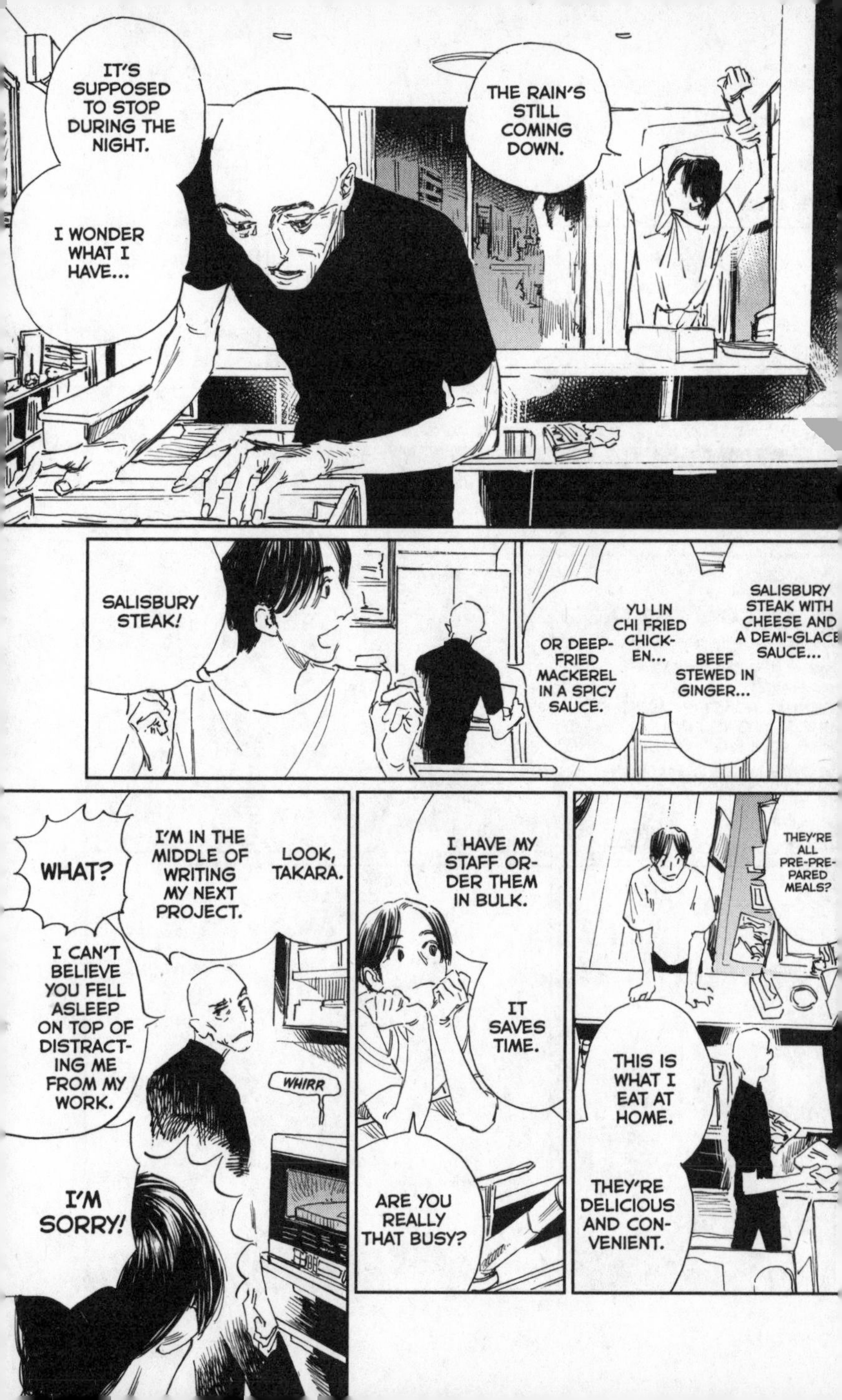
THE RAIN'S STILL COMING DOWN.
IT'S SUPPOSED TO STOP DURING THE NIGHT.
I WONDER WHAT I HAVE...
SALISBURY STEAK WITH CHEESE AND A DEMI-GLACE SAUCE...
BEEF STEWED IN GINGER...
YU LIN CHI FRIED CHICK-EN...
OR DEEP-FRIED MACKEREL IN A SPICY SAUCE.
SALISBURY STEAK!
THEY'RE ALL PRE-PRE-PARED MEALS?
THIS IS WHAT I EAT AT HOME.
THEY'RE DELICIOUS AND CON-VENIENT.
I HAVE MY STAFF OR-DER THEM IN BULK.
IT SAVES TIME.
ARE YOU REALLY THAT BUSY?
LOOK, TAKARA.
I'M IN THE MIDDLE OF WRITING MY NEXT PROJECT.
WHAT?
I CAN'T BELIEVE YOU FELL ASLEEP ON TOP OF DISTRACT-ING ME FROM MY WORK.
WHIRR
I'M SORRY!

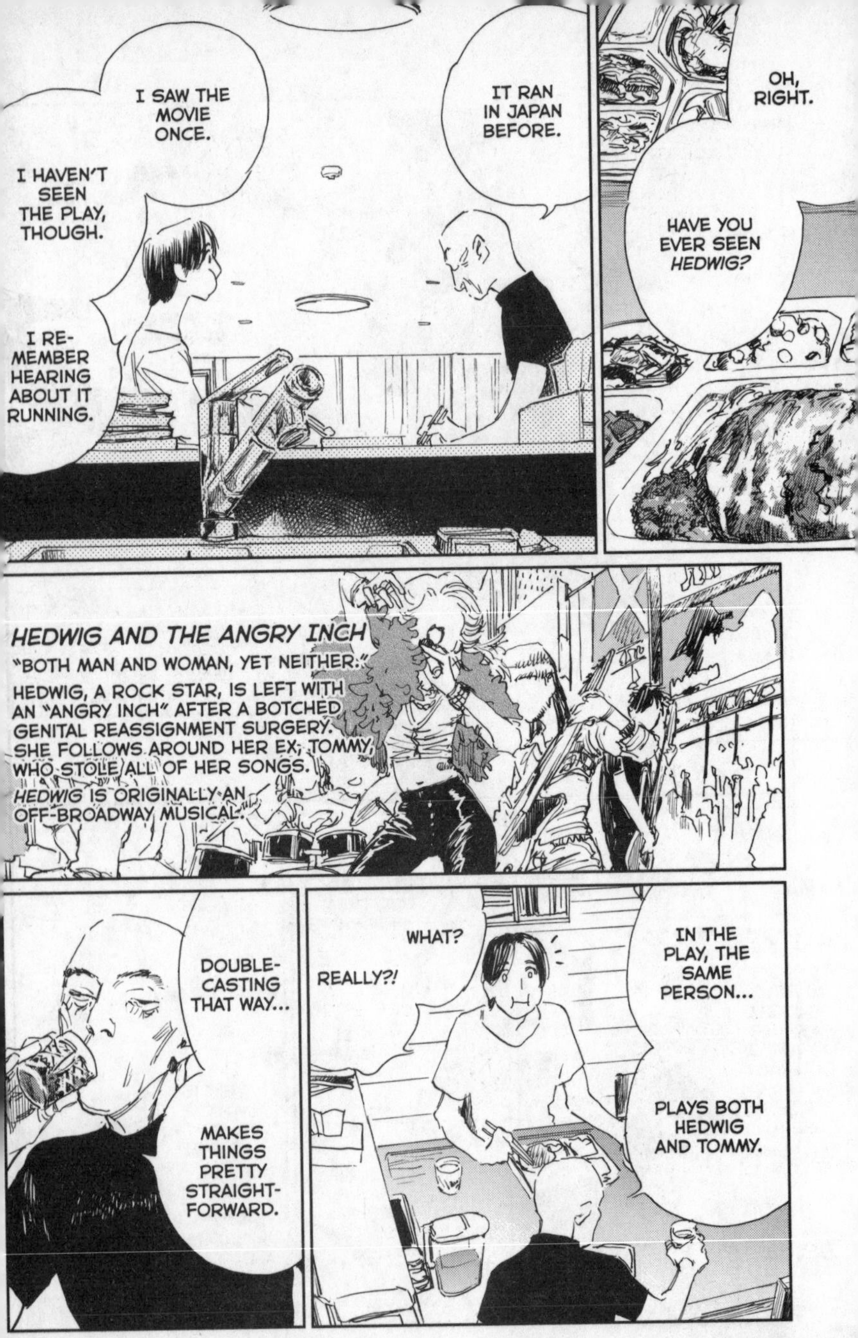
OH, RIGHT.
HAVE YOU EVER SEEN *HEDWIG?*
IT RAN IN JAPAN BEFORE.
I SAW THE MOVIE ONCE.
I HAVEN'T SEEN THE PLAY, THOUGH.
I RE-MEMBER HEARING ABOUT IT RUNNING.
HEDWIG AND THE ANGRY INCH
"BOTH MAN AND WOMAN, YET NEITHER."
HEDWIG, A ROCK STAR, IS LEFT WITH AN "ANGRY INCH" AFTER A BOTCHED GENITAL REASSIGNMENT SURGERY. SHE FOLLOWS AROUND HER EX, TOMMY, WHO STOLE ALL OF HER SONGS.
HEDWIG IS ORIGINALLY AN OFF-BROADWAY MUSICAL.
IN THE PLAY, THE SAME PERSON...
PLAYS BOTH HEDWIG AND TOMMY.
WHAT?
REALLY?!
DOUBLE-CASTING THAT WAY...
MAKES THINGS PRETTY STRAIGHT-FORWARD.

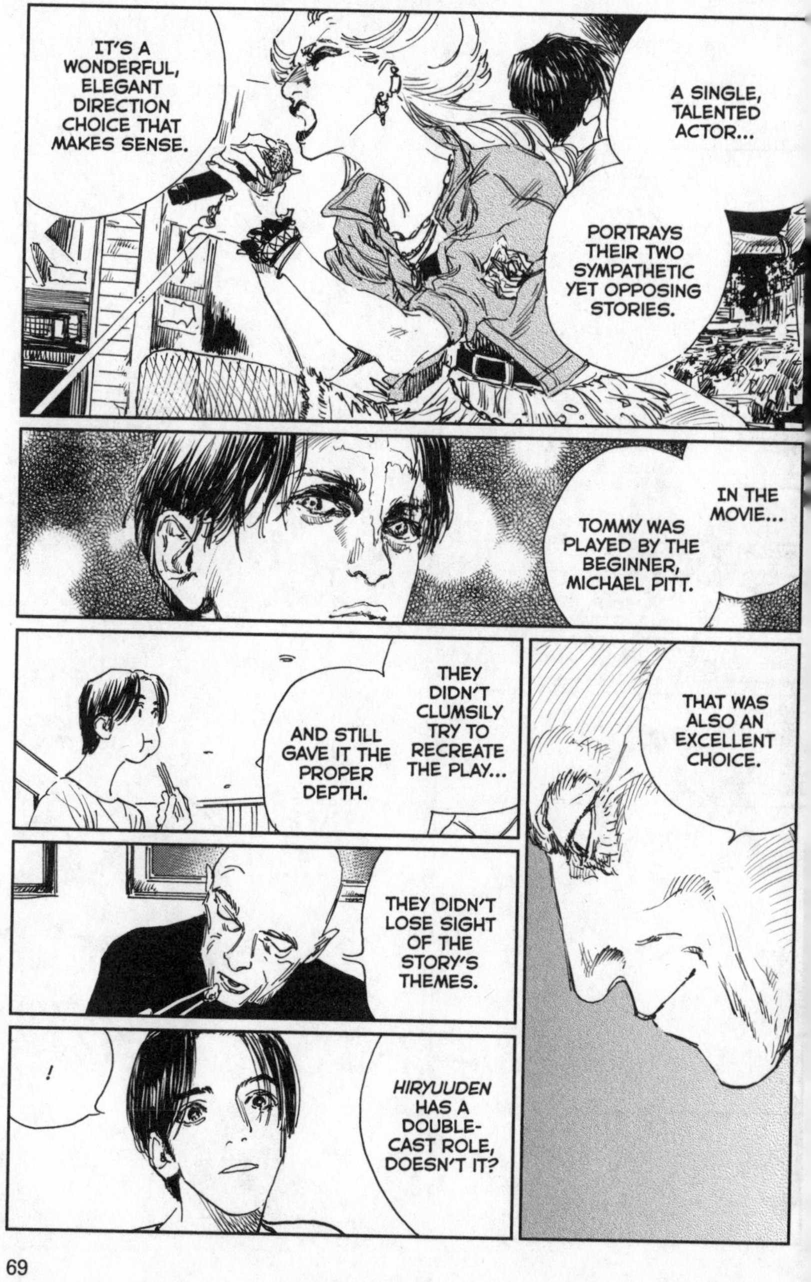
A SINGLE, TALENTED ACTOR...
PORTRAYS THEIR TWO SYMPATHETIC YET OPPOSING STORIES.
IT'S A WONDERFUL, ELEGANT DIRECTION CHOICE THAT MAKES SENSE.
IN THE MOVIE...
TOMMY WAS PLAYED BY THE BEGINNER, MICHAEL PITT.
THAT WAS ALSO AN EXCELLENT CHOICE.
THEY DIDN'T CLUMSILY TRY TO RECREATE THE PLAY...
AND STILL GAVE IT THE PROPER DEPTH.
THEY DIDN'T LOSE SIGHT OF THE STORY'S THEMES.
HIRYUUDEN HAS A DOUBLE-CAST ROLE, DOESN'T IT?
!

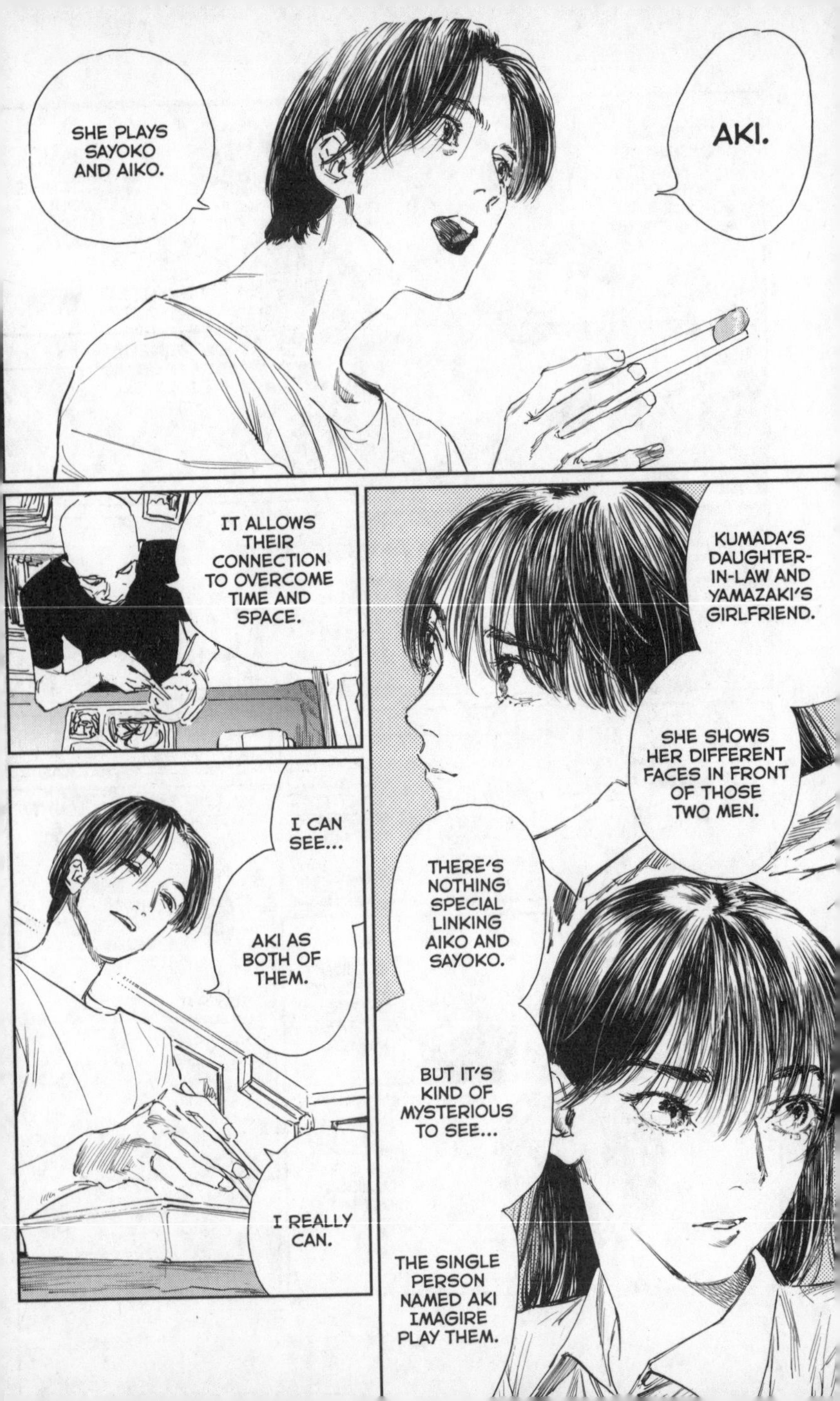
AKI.
SHE PLAYS SAYOKO AND AIKO.
KUMADA'S DAUGHTER-IN-LAW AND YAMAZAKI'S GIRLFRIEND.
SHE SHOWS HER DIFFERENT FACES IN FRONT OF THOSE TWO MEN.
THERE'S NOTHING SPECIAL LINKING AIKO AND SAYOKO.
BUT IT'S KIND OF MYSTERIOUS TO SEE...
THE SINGLE PERSON NAMED AKI IMAGIRE PLAY THEM.
IT ALLOWS THEIR CONNECTION TO OVERCOME TIME AND SPACE.
I CAN SEE...
AKI AS BOTH OF THEM.
I REALLY CAN.

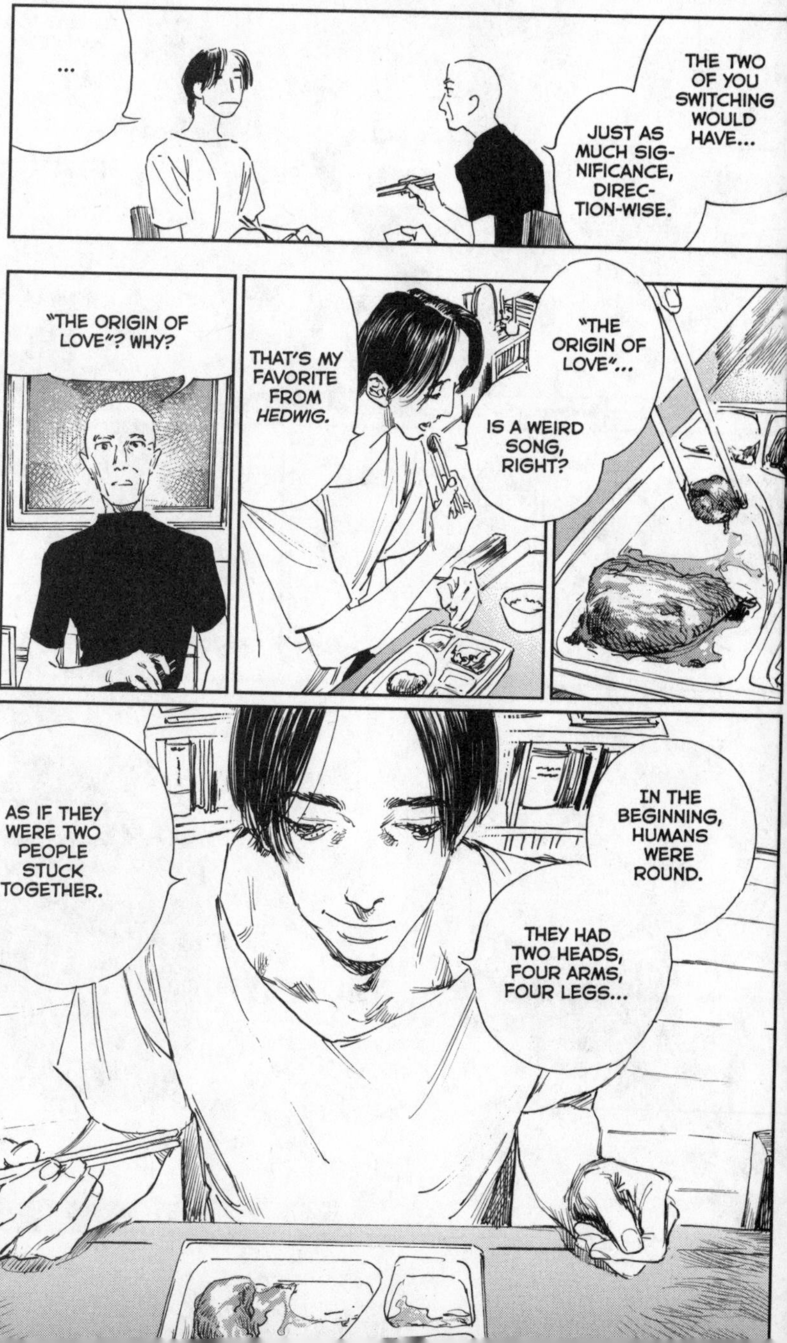
THE TWO OF YOU SWITCHING WOULD HAVE...
JUST AS MUCH SIGNIFICANCE, DIRECTION-WISE.
...
"THE ORIGIN OF LOVE"...
IS A WEIRD SONG, RIGHT?
THAT'S MY FAVORITE FROM *HEDWIG.*
"THE ORIGIN OF LOVE"? WHY?
IN THE BEGINNING, HUMANS WERE ROUND.
THEY HAD TWO HEADS, FOUR ARMS, FOUR LEGS...
AS IF THEY WERE TWO PEOPLE STUCK TOGETHER.

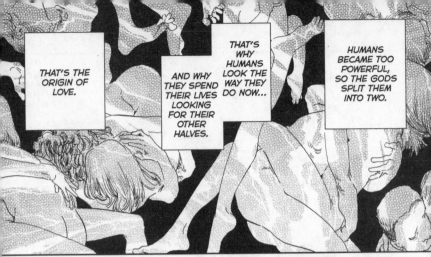

HUMANS BECAME TOO POWERFUL, SO THE GODS SPLIT THEM INTO TWO.
THAT'S WHY HUMANS LOOK THE WAY THEY DO NOW...
AND WHY THEY SPEND THEIR LIVES LOOKING FOR THEIR OTHER HALVES.
THAT'S THE ORIGIN OF LOVE.
ARISTOP-HANES.
?
THAT COMES FROM PLATO'S *SYMPOSIUM*, YOU KNOW.
OH...
SO...
YOU SHOULD READ MORE.
NNGH...
WANT SOME KIWI?
YEAH.
"YOU'RE THE OTHER HALF TO MY ORANGE."
THUNK

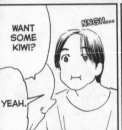

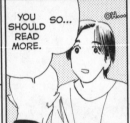

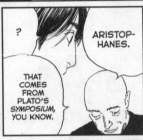

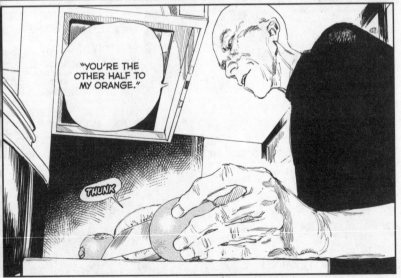

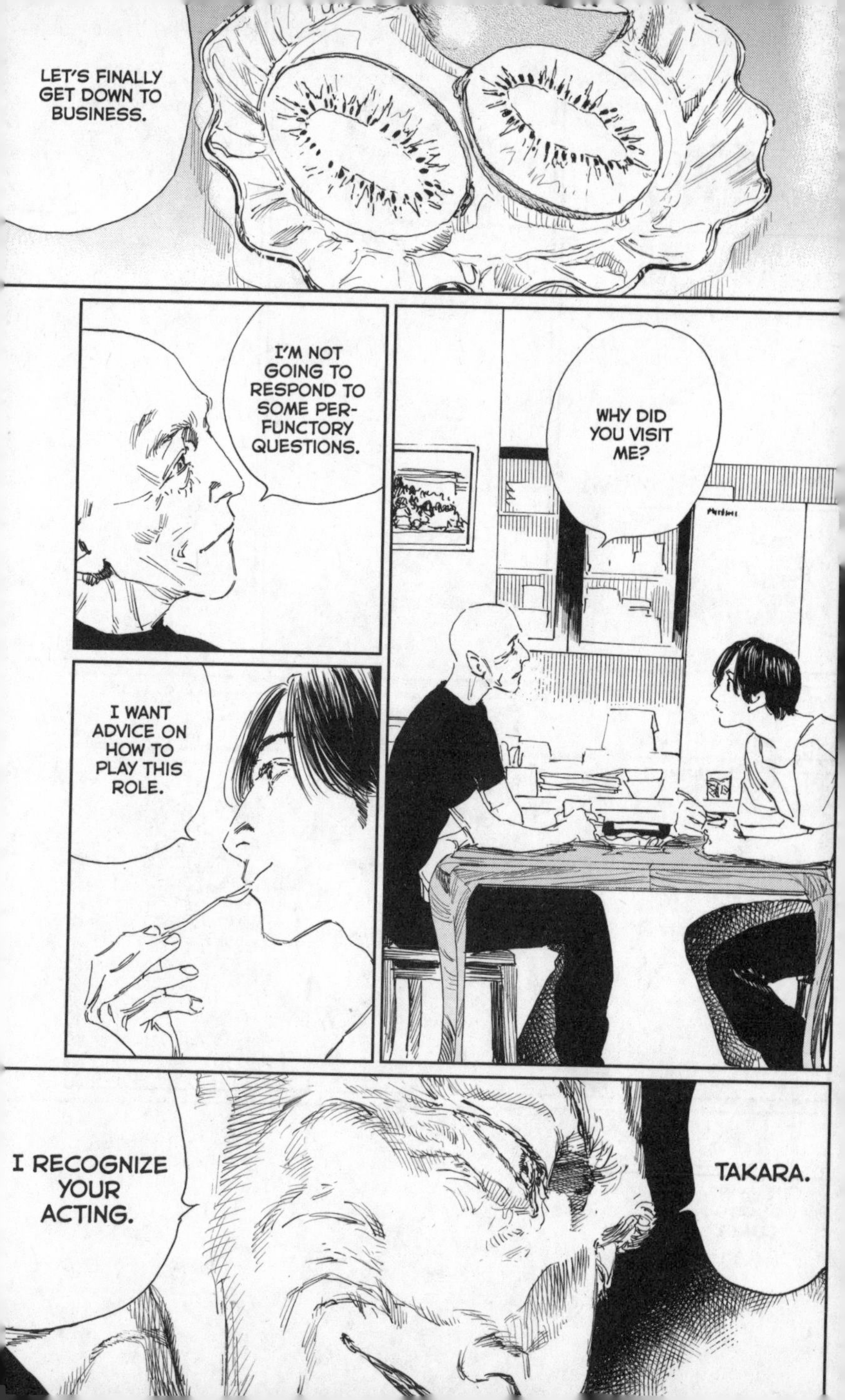
LET'S FINALLY GET DOWN TO BUSINESS.
WHY DID YOU VISIT ME?
I'M NOT GOING TO RESPOND TO SOME PER-FUNCTORY QUESTIONS.
I WANT ADVICE ON HOW TO PLAY THIS ROLE.
TAKARA.
I RECOGNIZE YOUR ACTING.

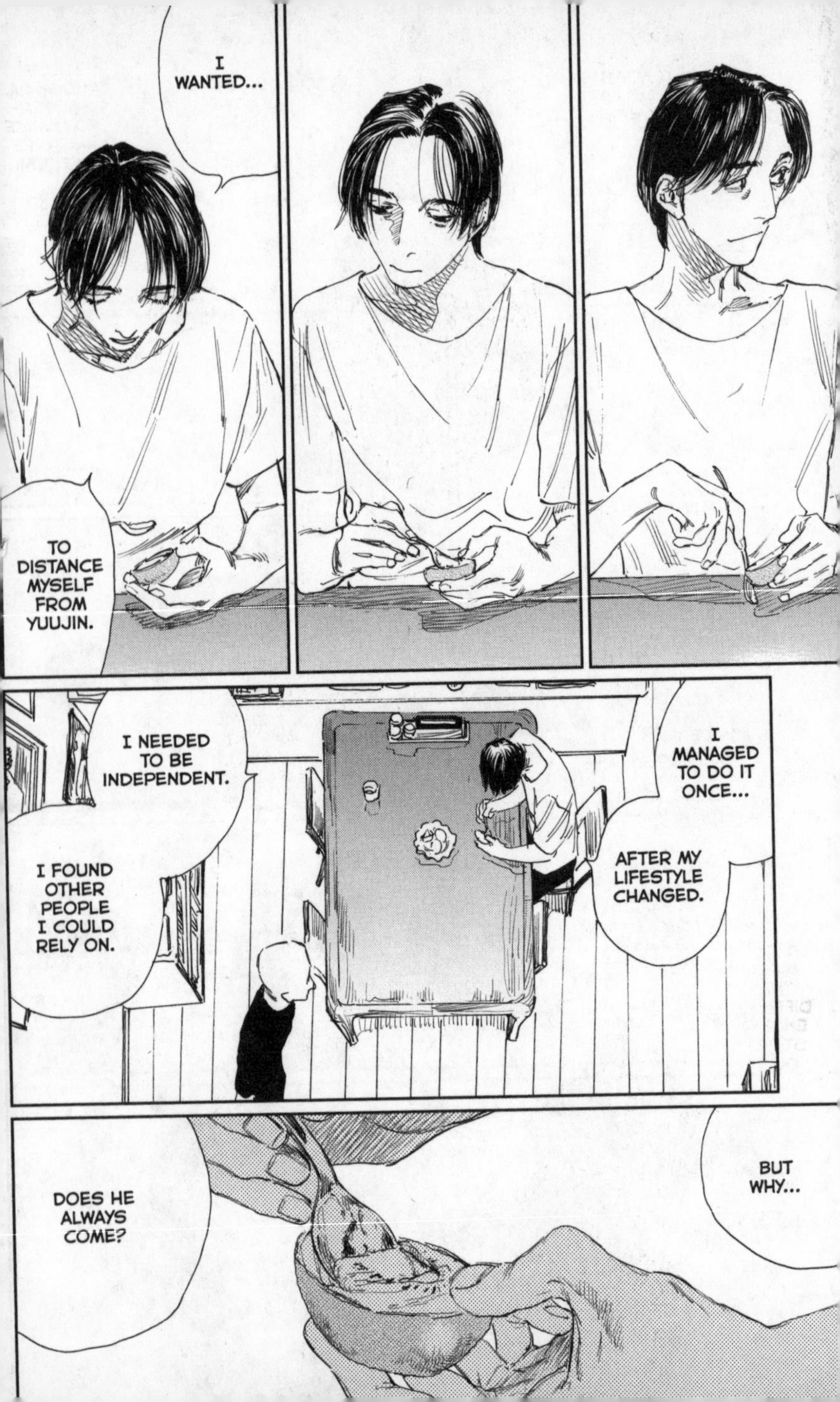
I WANTED...
TO DISTANCE MYSELF FROM YUUJIN.
I MANAGED TO DO IT ONCE...
AFTER MY LIFESTYLE CHANGED.
I NEEDED TO BE INDEPENDENT.
I FOUND OTHER PEOPLE I COULD RELY ON.
BUT WHY...
DOES HE ALWAYS COME?

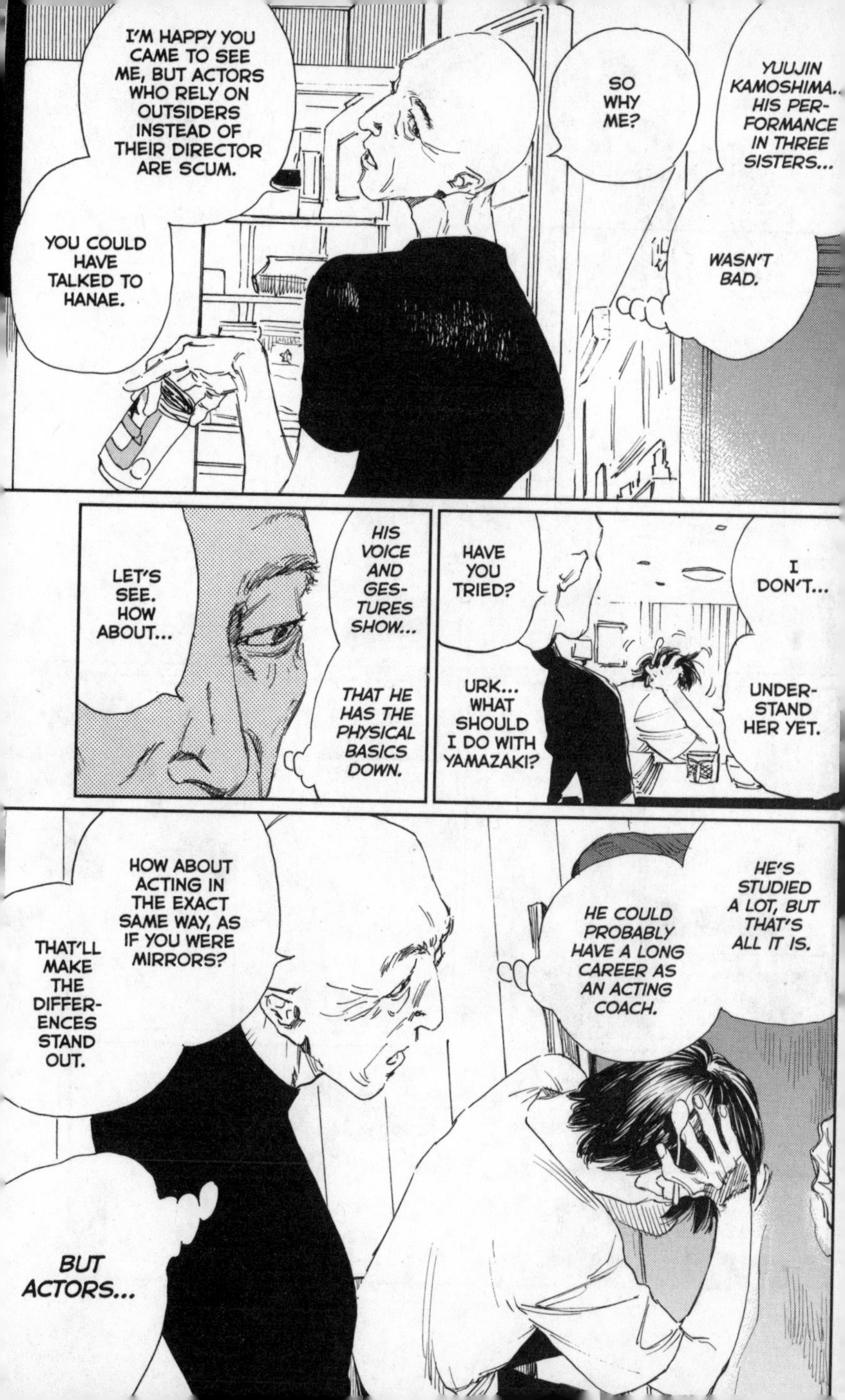
YUUJIN KAMOSHIMA.. HIS PERFORMANCE IN THREE SISTERS...
WASN'T BAD.
SO WHY ME?
I'M HAPPY YOU CAME TO SEE ME, BUT ACTORS WHO RELY ON OUTSIDERS INSTEAD OF THEIR DIRECTOR ARE SCUM.
YOU COULD HAVE TALKED TO HANAE.
I DON'T...
UNDERSTAND HER YET.
HAVE YOU TRIED?
URK... WHAT SHOULD I DO WITH YAMAZAKI?
HIS VOICE AND GESTURES SHOW...
THAT HE HAS THE PHYSICAL BASICS DOWN.
LET'S SEE. HOW ABOUT...
HE'S STUDIED A LOT, BUT THAT'S ALL IT IS.
HE COULD PROBABLY HAVE A LONG CAREER AS AN ACTING COACH.
HOW ABOUT ACTING IN THE EXACT SAME WAY, AS IF YOU WERE MIRRORS?
THAT'LL MAKE THE DIFFERENCES STAND OUT.
BUT ACTORS...

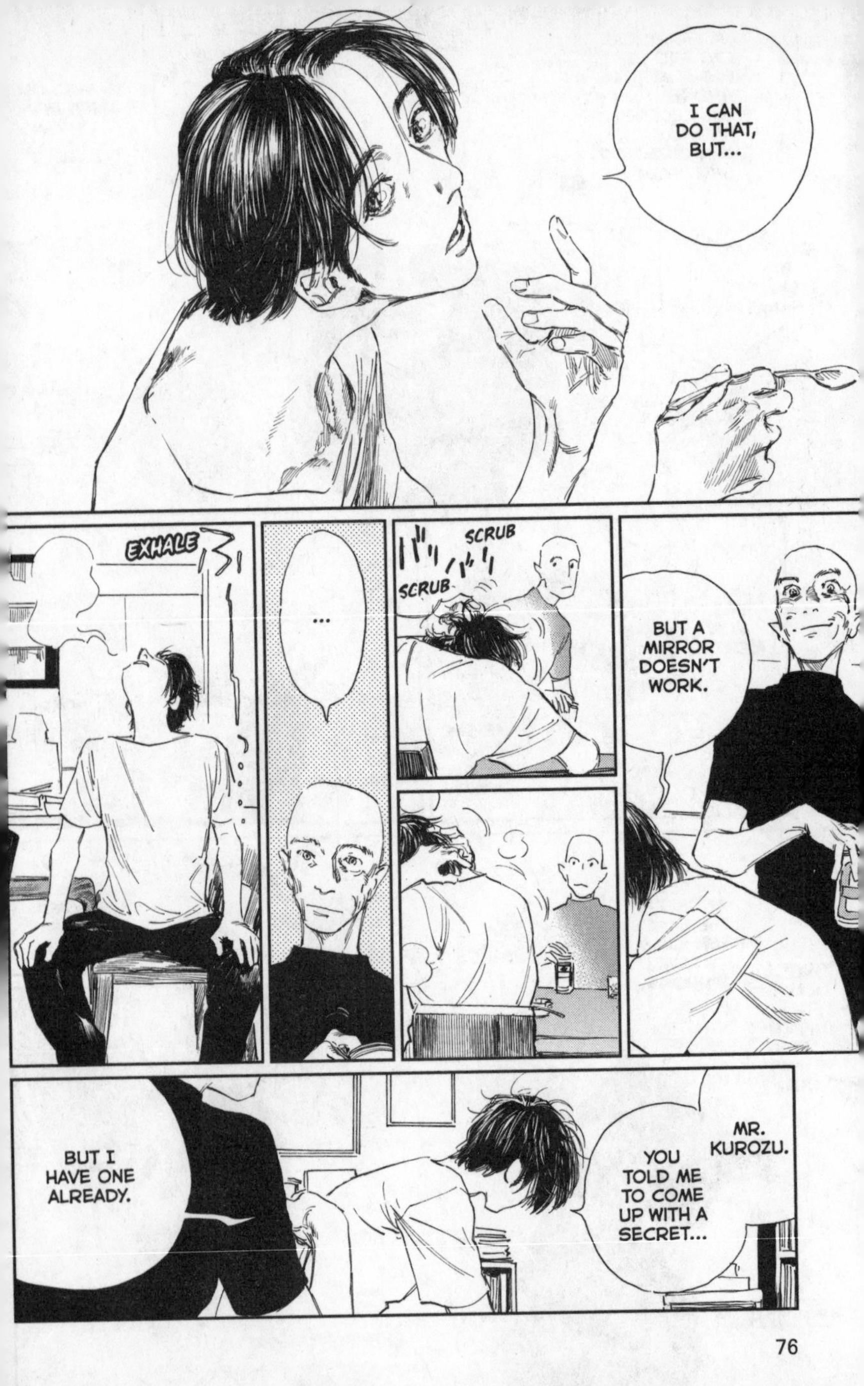
I CAN DO THAT, BUT...
BUT A MIRROR DOESN'T WORK.
SCRUB
SCRUB
...
EXHALE
MR. KUROZU.
YOU TOLD ME TO COME UP WITH A SECRET...
BUT I HAVE ONE ALREADY.

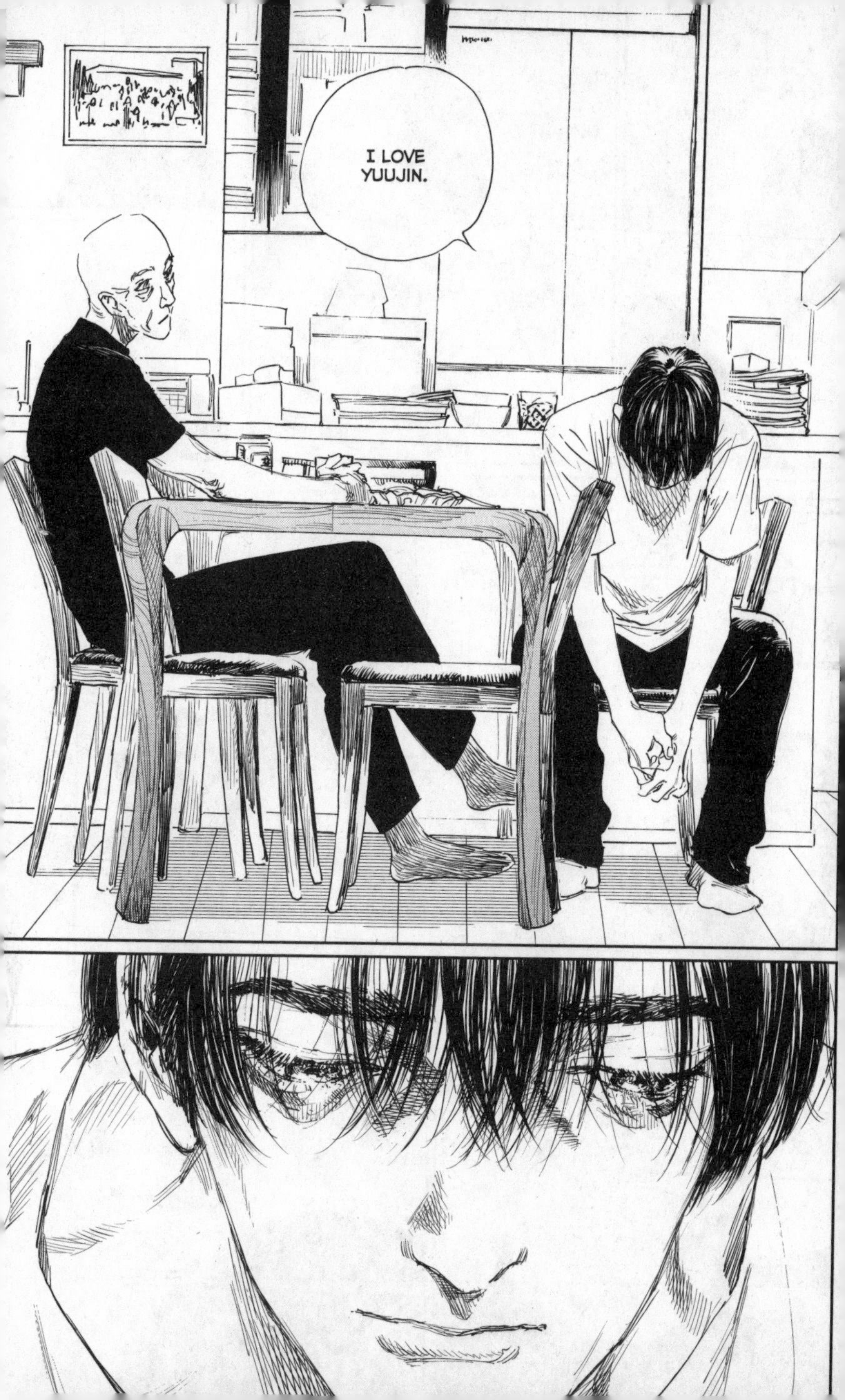
I LOVE YUUJIN.

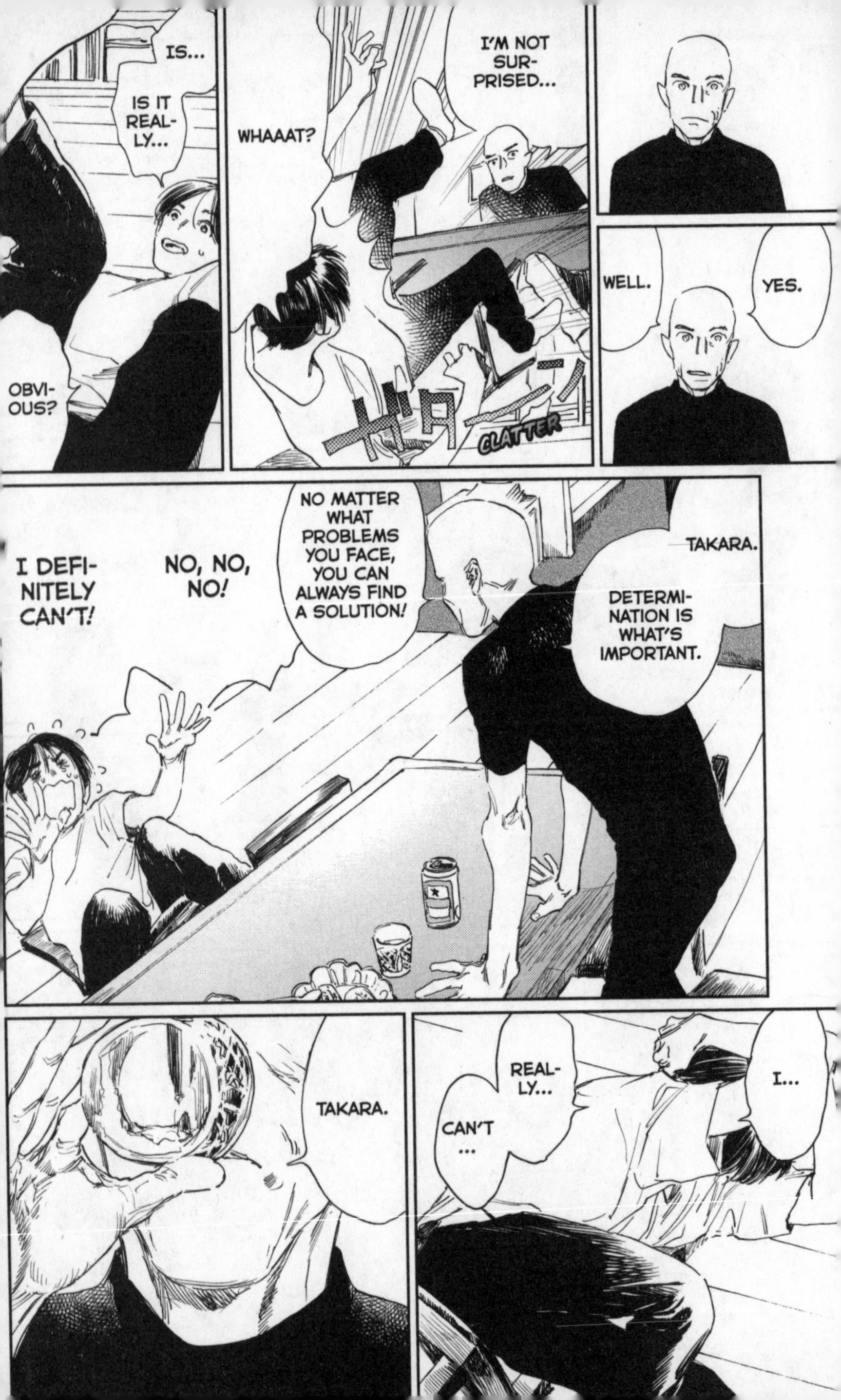
YES.
WELL.
I'M NOT SURPRISED...
WHAAAT?
CLATTER
IS...
IS IT REALLY...
OBVIOUS?
TAKARA.
DETERMINATION IS WHAT'S IMPORTANT.
NO MATTER WHAT PROBLEMS YOU FACE, YOU CAN ALWAYS FIND A SOLUTION!
NO, NO, NO!
I DEFINITELY CAN'T!
I...
REALLY...
CAN'T...
TAKARA.

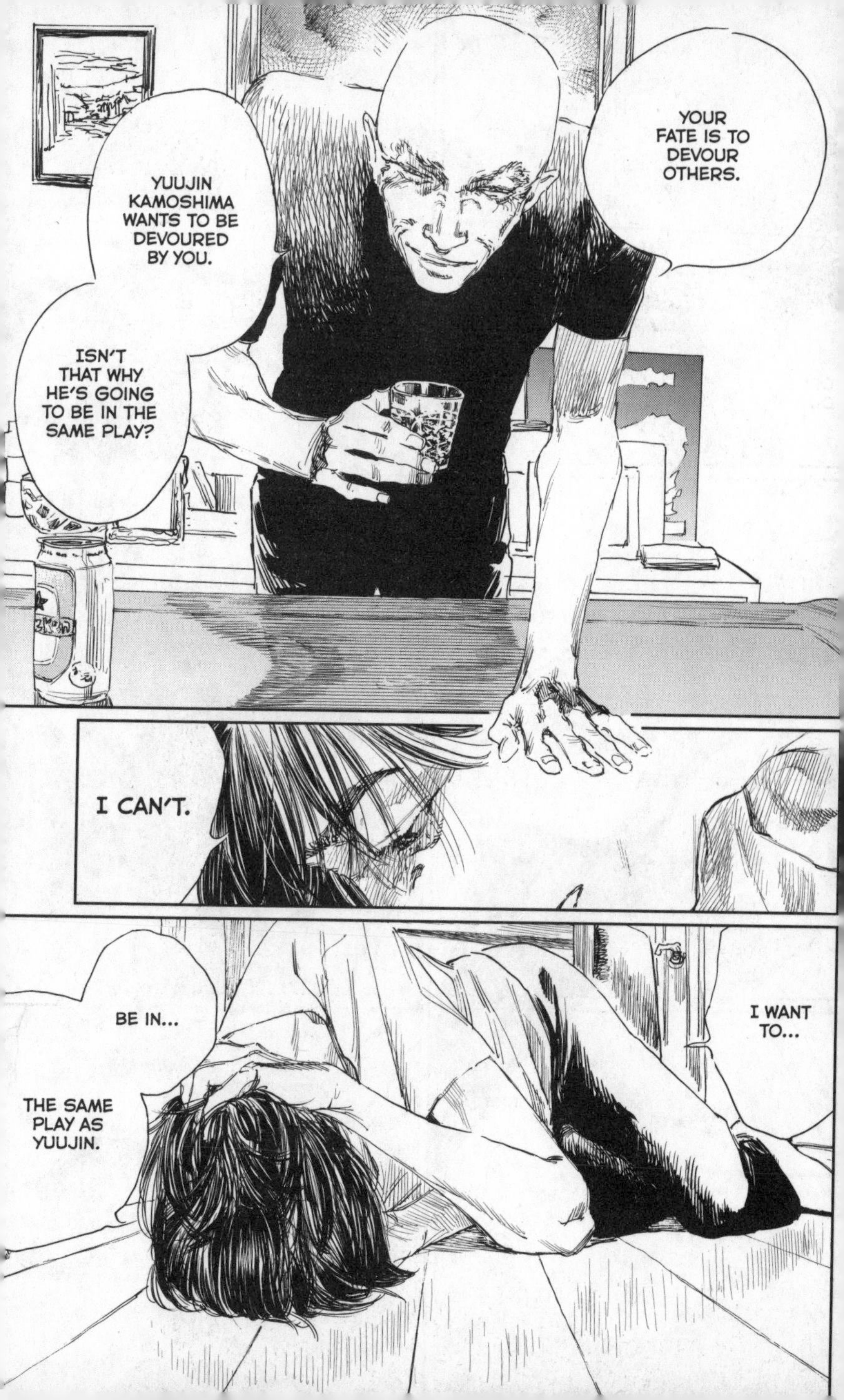
YOUR FATE IS TO DEVOUR OTHERS.
YUUJIN KAMOSHIMA WANTS TO BE DEVOURED BY YOU.
ISN'T THAT WHY HE'S GOING TO BE IN THE SAME PLAY?
I CAN'T.
I WANT TO...
BE IN...
THE SAME PLAY AS YUUJIN.

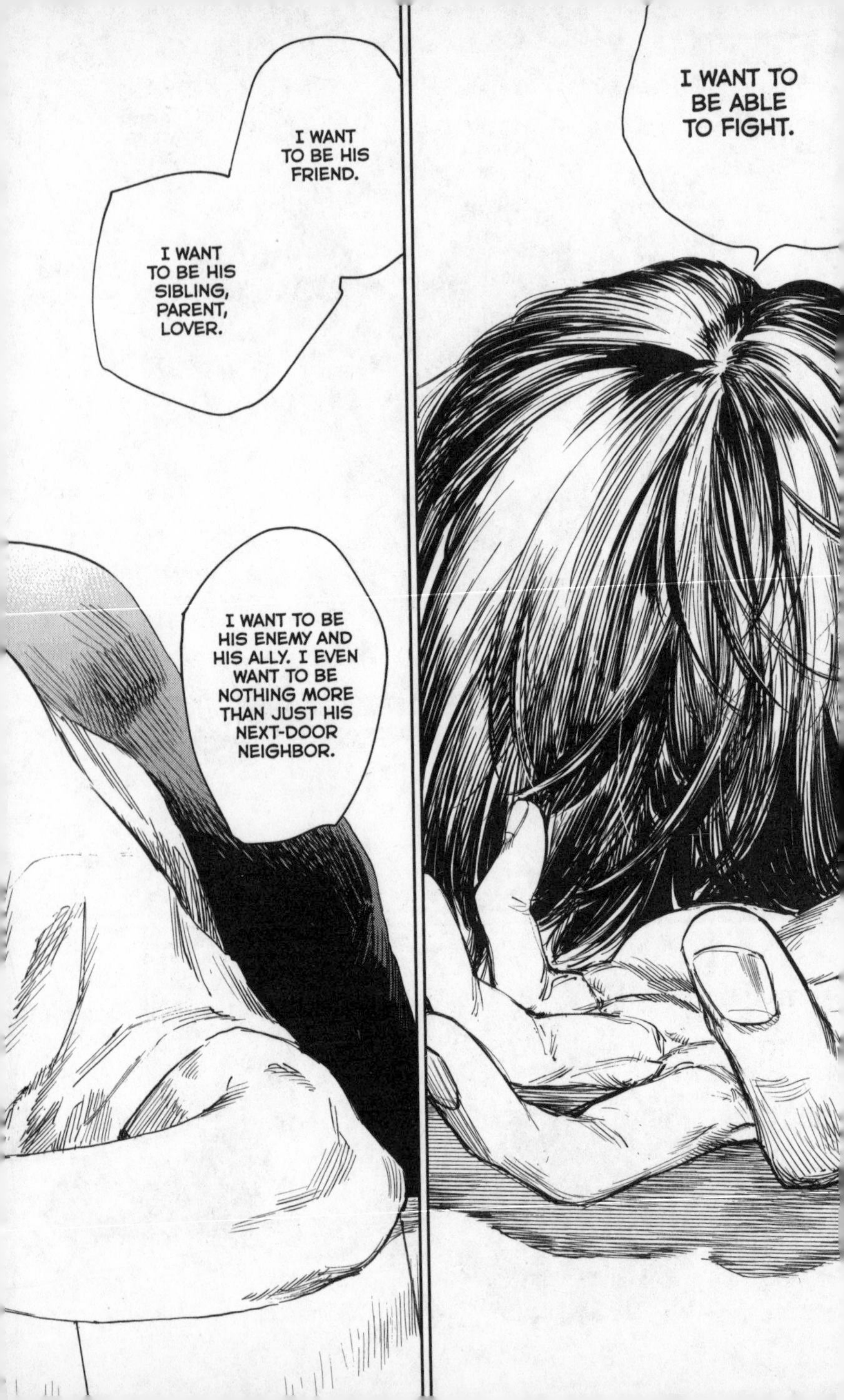
I WANT TO BE ABLE TO FIGHT.
I WANT TO BE HIS FRIEND.
I WANT TO BE HIS SIBLING, PARENT, LOVER.
I WANT TO BE HIS ENEMY AND HIS ALLY. I EVEN WANT TO BE NOTHING MORE THAN JUST HIS NEXT-DOOR NEIGHBOR.

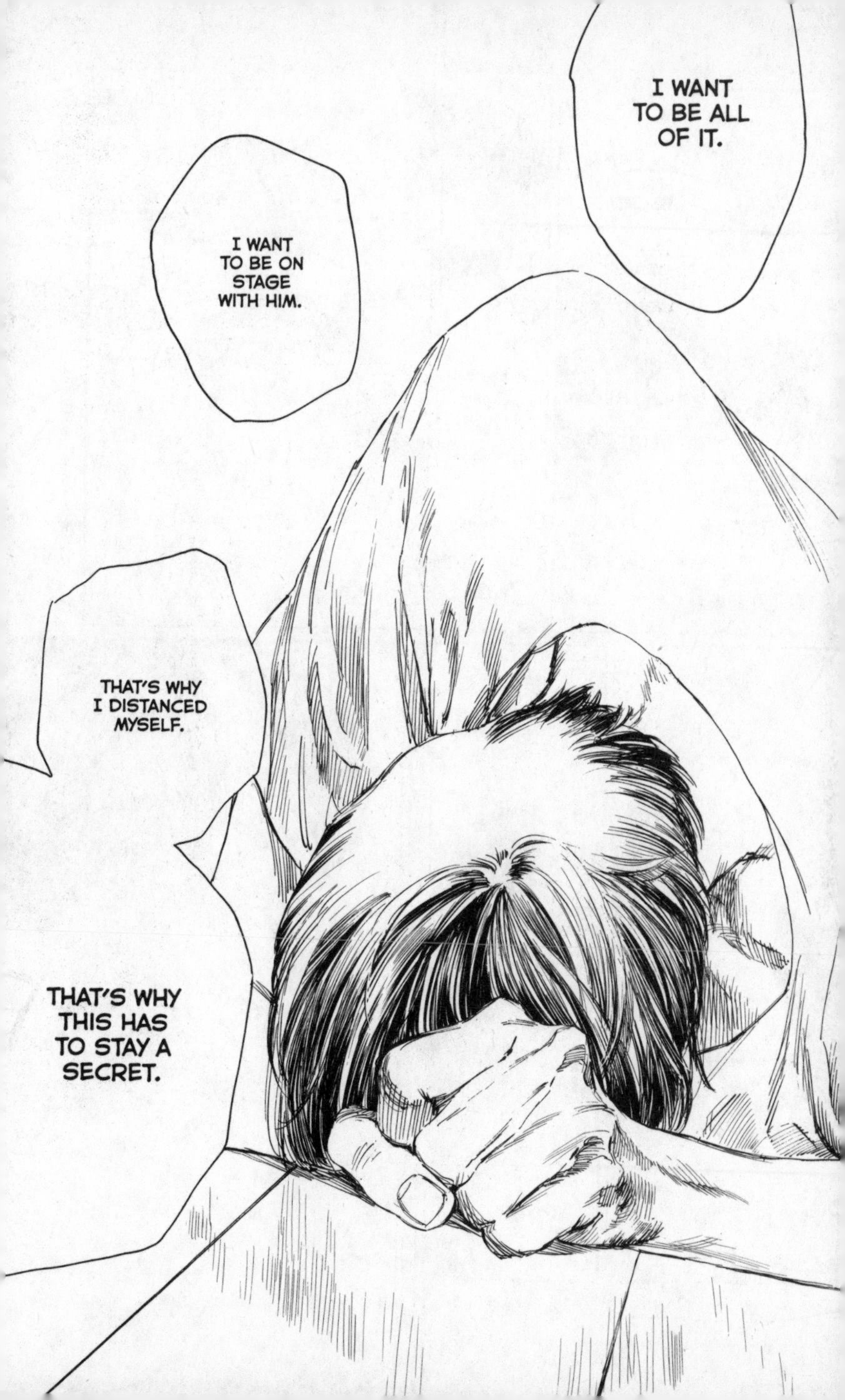
I WANT TO BE ALL OF IT.
I WANT TO BE ON STAGE WITH HIM.
THAT'S WHY I DISTANCED MYSELF.
THAT'S WHY THIS HAS TO STAY A SECRET.

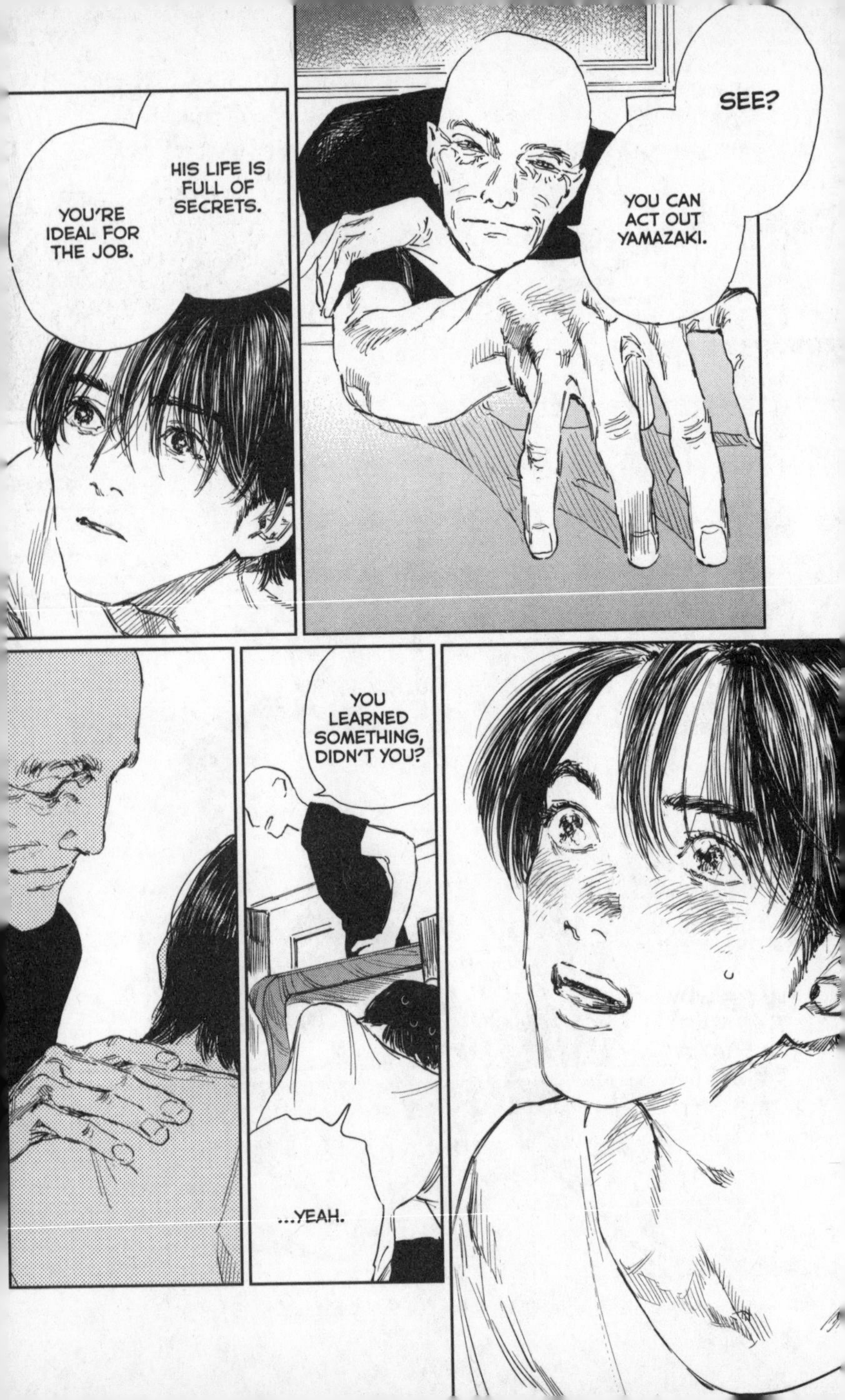
SEE?
YOU CAN ACT OUT YAMAZAKI.
HIS LIFE IS FULL OF SECRETS.
YOU'RE IDEAL FOR THE JOB.
YOU LEARNED SOMETHING, DIDN'T YOU?
...YEAH.

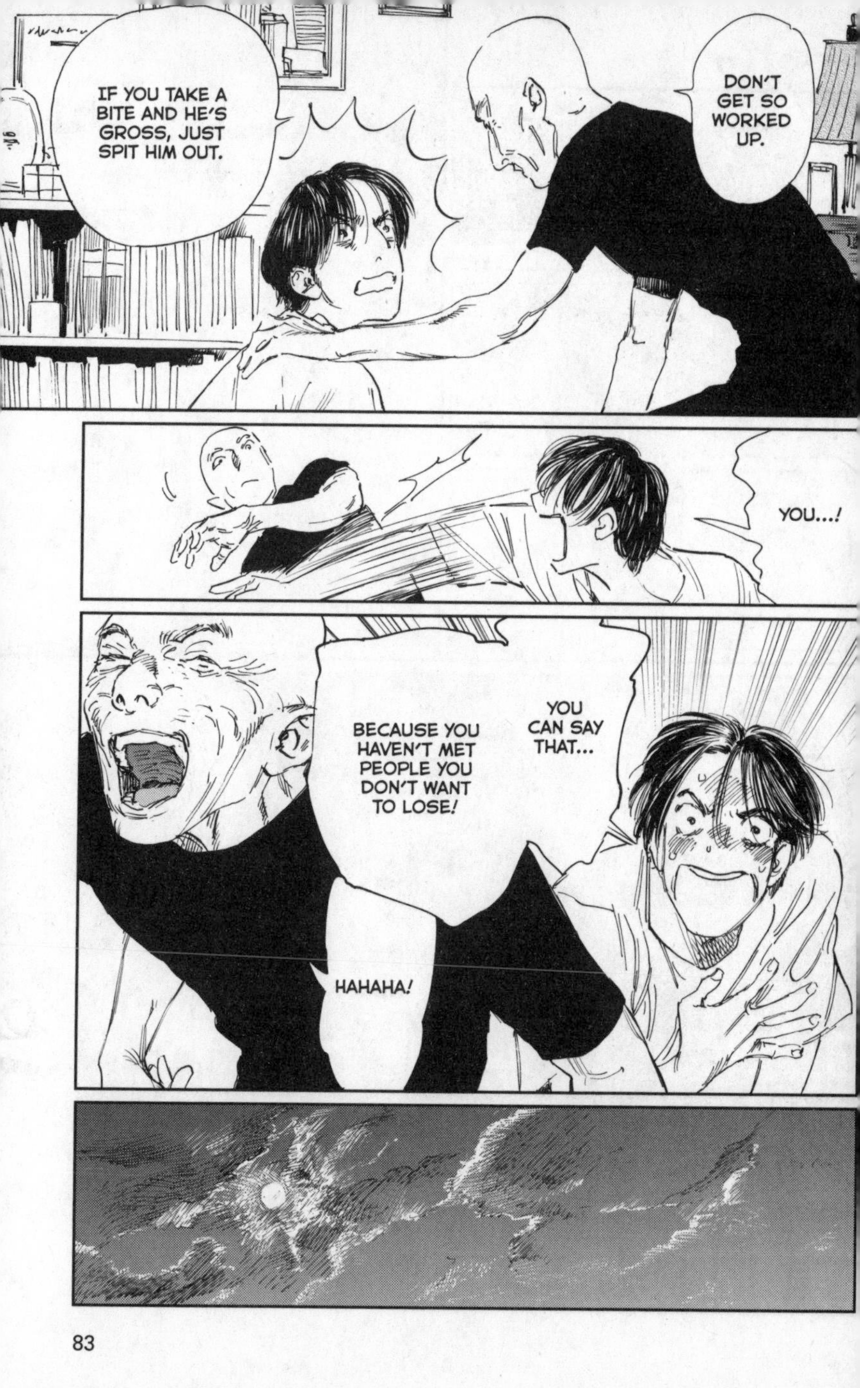
DON'T GET SO WORKED UP.
IF YOU TAKE A BITE AND HE'S GROSS, JUST SPIT HIM OUT.
YOU...!
YOU CAN SAY THAT...
BECAUSE YOU HAVEN'T MET PEOPLE YOU DON'T WANT TO LOSE!
HAHAHA!

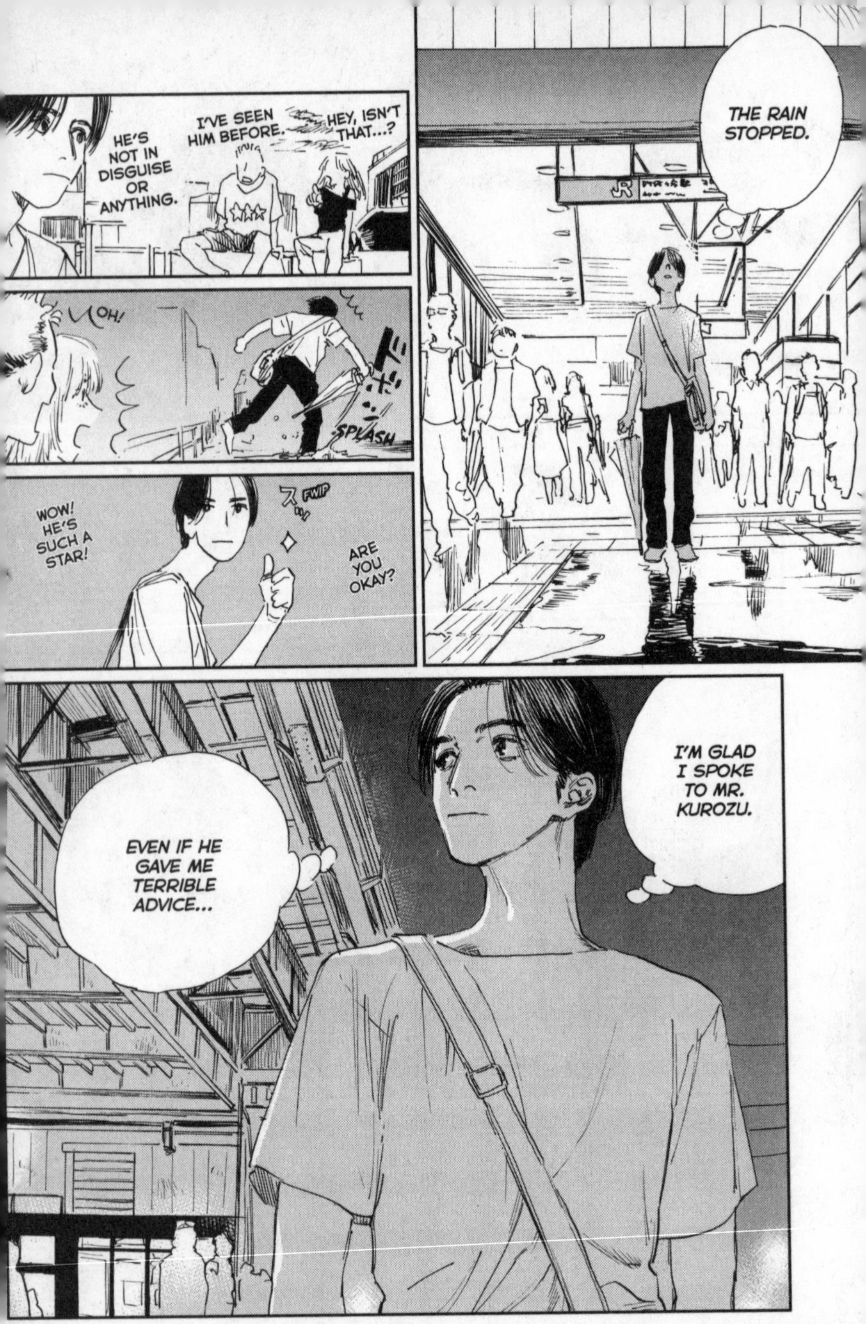
THE RAIN STOPPED.
HEY, ISN'T THAT...?
I'VE SEEN HIM BEFORE.
HE'S NOT IN DISGUISE OR ANYTHING.
OH!
SPLASH
FWIP
ARE YOU OKAY?
WOW! HE'S SUCH A STAR!
I'M GLAD I SPOKE TO MR. KUROZU.
EVEN IF HE GAVE ME TERRIBLE ADVICE...

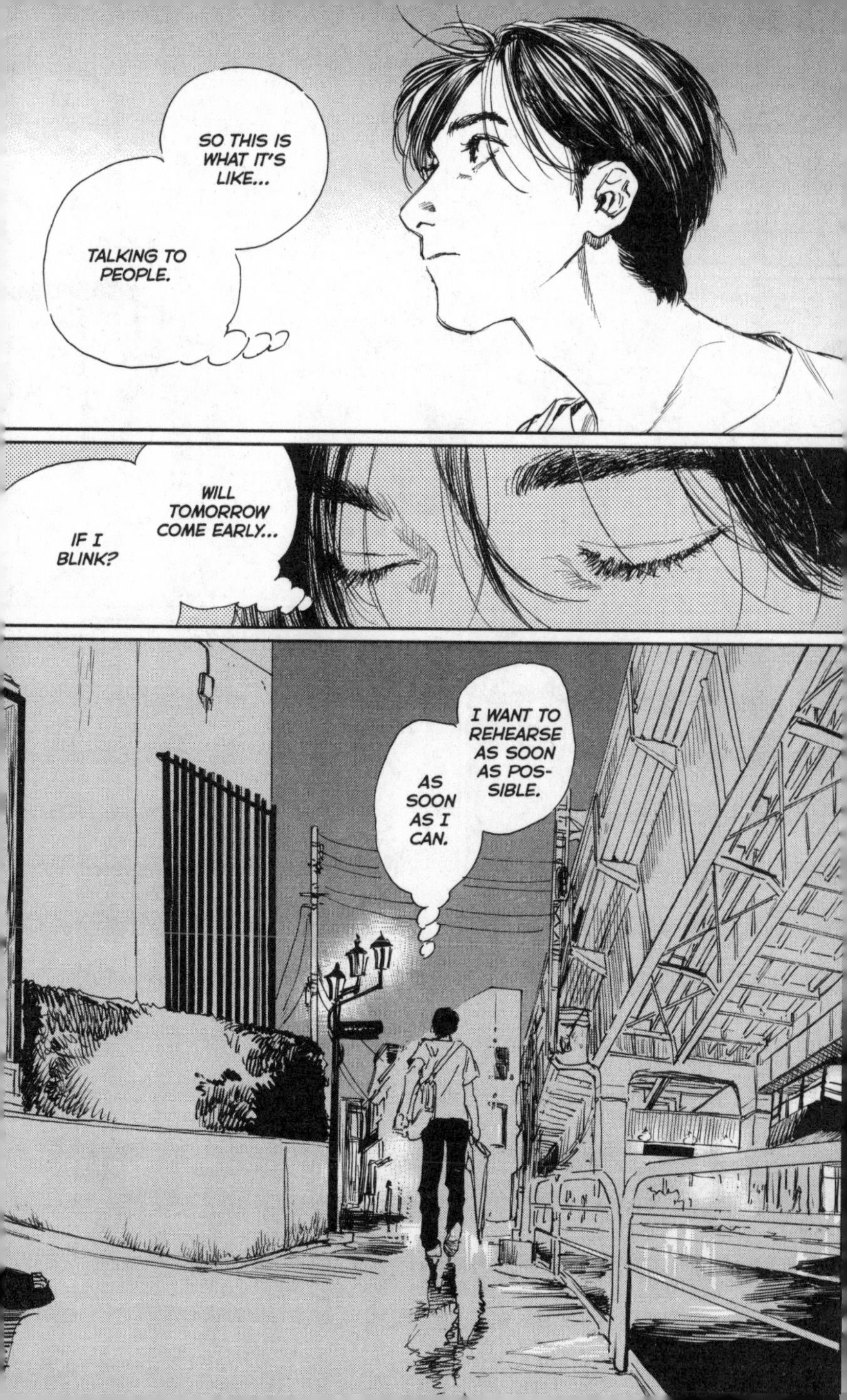
SO THIS IS WHAT IT'S LIKE...
TALKING TO PEOPLE.
WILL TOMORROW COME EARLY...
IF I BLINK?
I WANT TO REHEARSE AS SOON AS POS-SIBLE.
AS SOON AS I CAN.

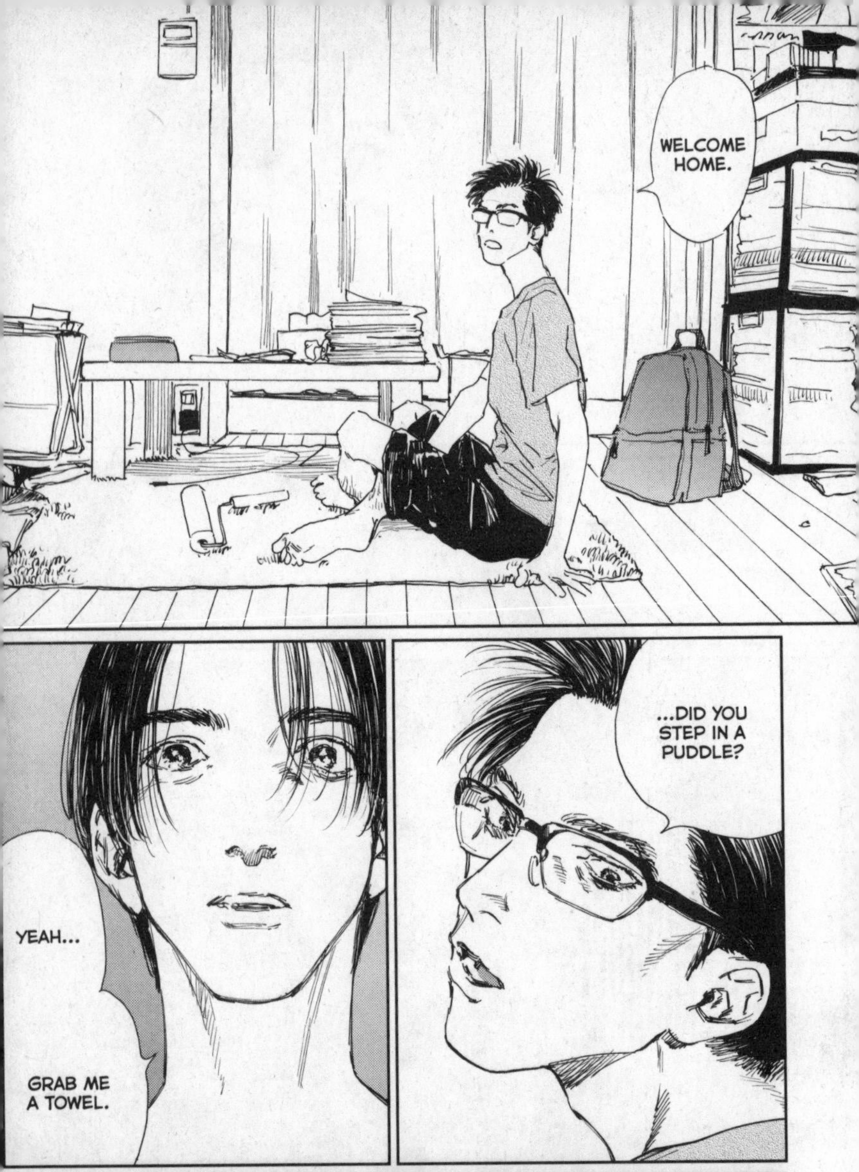
WELCOME HOME.
...DID YOU STEP IN A PUDDLE?
YEAH...
GRAB ME A TOWEL.
WHAT IS IT YOU PEOPLE WISH IN BEING AT EACH OTHER'S SIDE?

SYMPOSIUM, PLATO
TRANSLATED BY R.E. ALLEN
YALE UNIVERSITY PRESS

DOUBLE

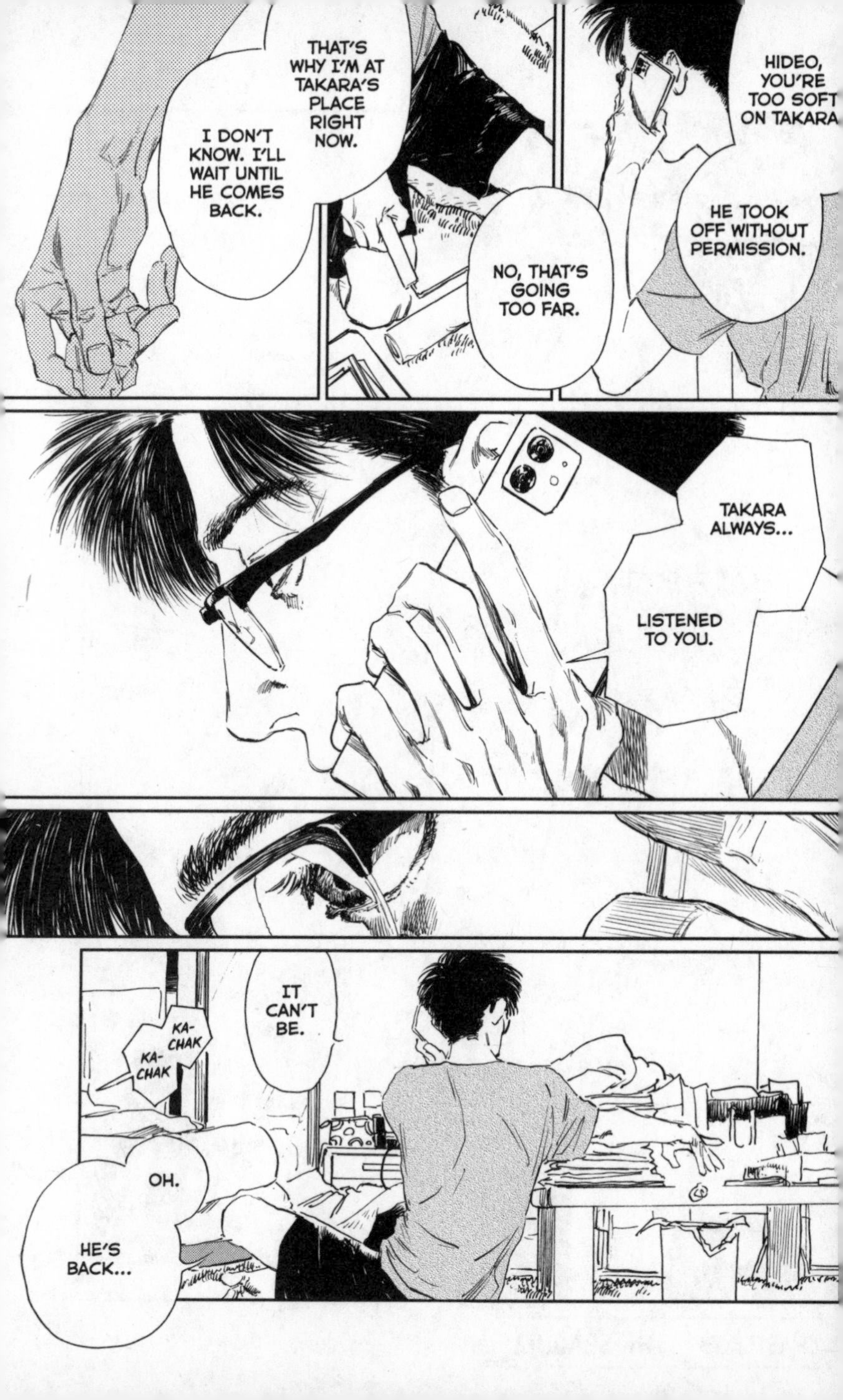
HIDEO, YOU'RE TOO SOFT ON TAKARA.
HE TOOK OFF WITHOUT PERMISSION.
NO, THAT'S GOING TOO FAR.
THAT'S WHY I'M AT TAKARA'S PLACE RIGHT NOW.
I DON'T KNOW. I'LL WAIT UNTIL HE COMES BACK.
TAKARA ALWAYS...
LISTENED TO YOU.
IT CAN'T BE.
KA-CHAK
KA-CHAK
OH.
HE'S BACK...

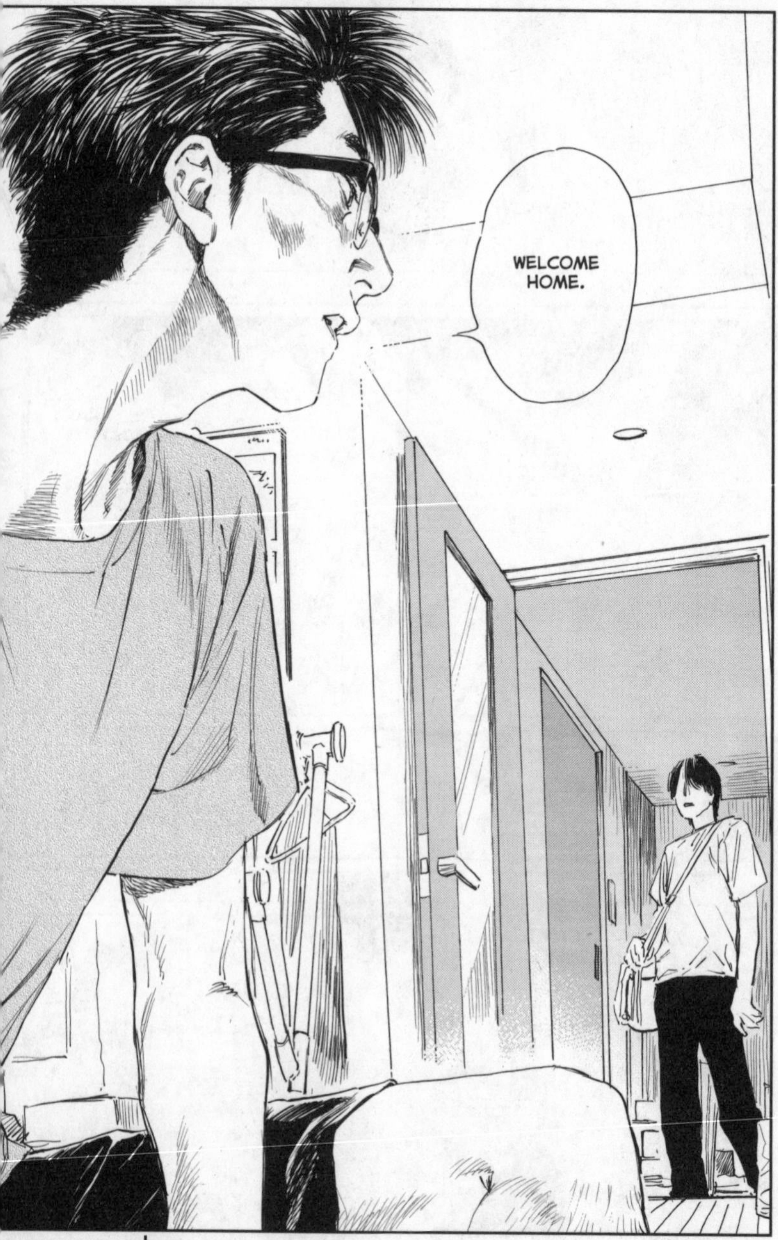
WELCOME HOME.

CHAPTER 23 | THE SEAGULL

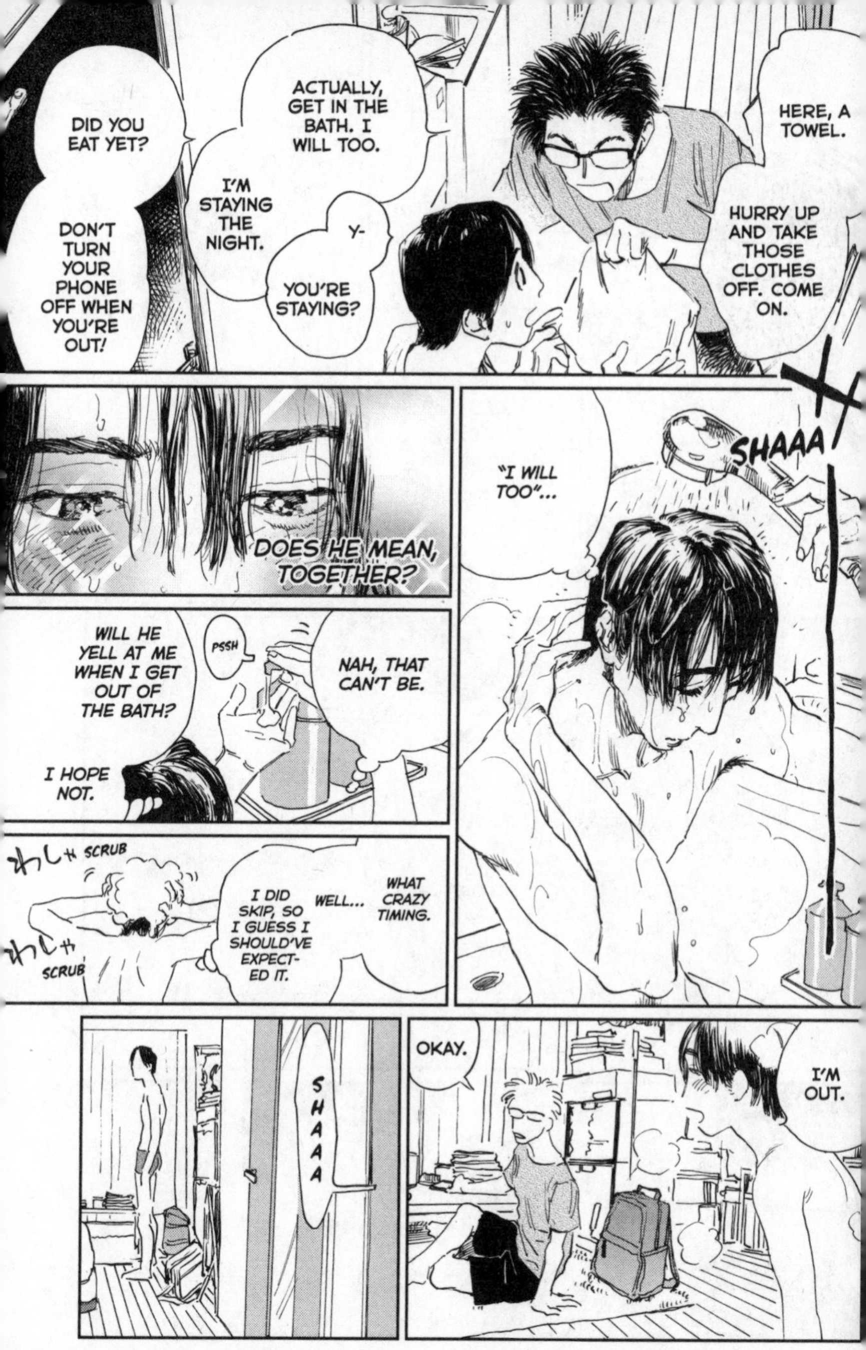
HERE, A TOWEL.
HURRY UP AND TAKE THOSE CLOTHES OFF. COME ON.
ACTUALLY, GET IN THE BATH. I WILL TOO.
I'M STAYING THE NIGHT.
Y-
YOU'RE STAYING?
DID YOU EAT YET?
DON'T TURN YOUR PHONE OFF WHEN YOU'RE OUT!
SHAAA
"I WILL TOO"...
DOES HE MEAN, TOGETHER?
NAH, THAT CAN'T BE.
PSSH
WILL HE YELL AT ME WHEN I GET OUT OF THE BATH?
I HOPE NOT.
WHAT CRAZY TIMING.
WELL...
I DID SKIP, SO I GUESS I SHOULD'VE EXPECTED IT.
SCRUB
SCRUB
I'M OUT.
OKAY.
SHAAAA

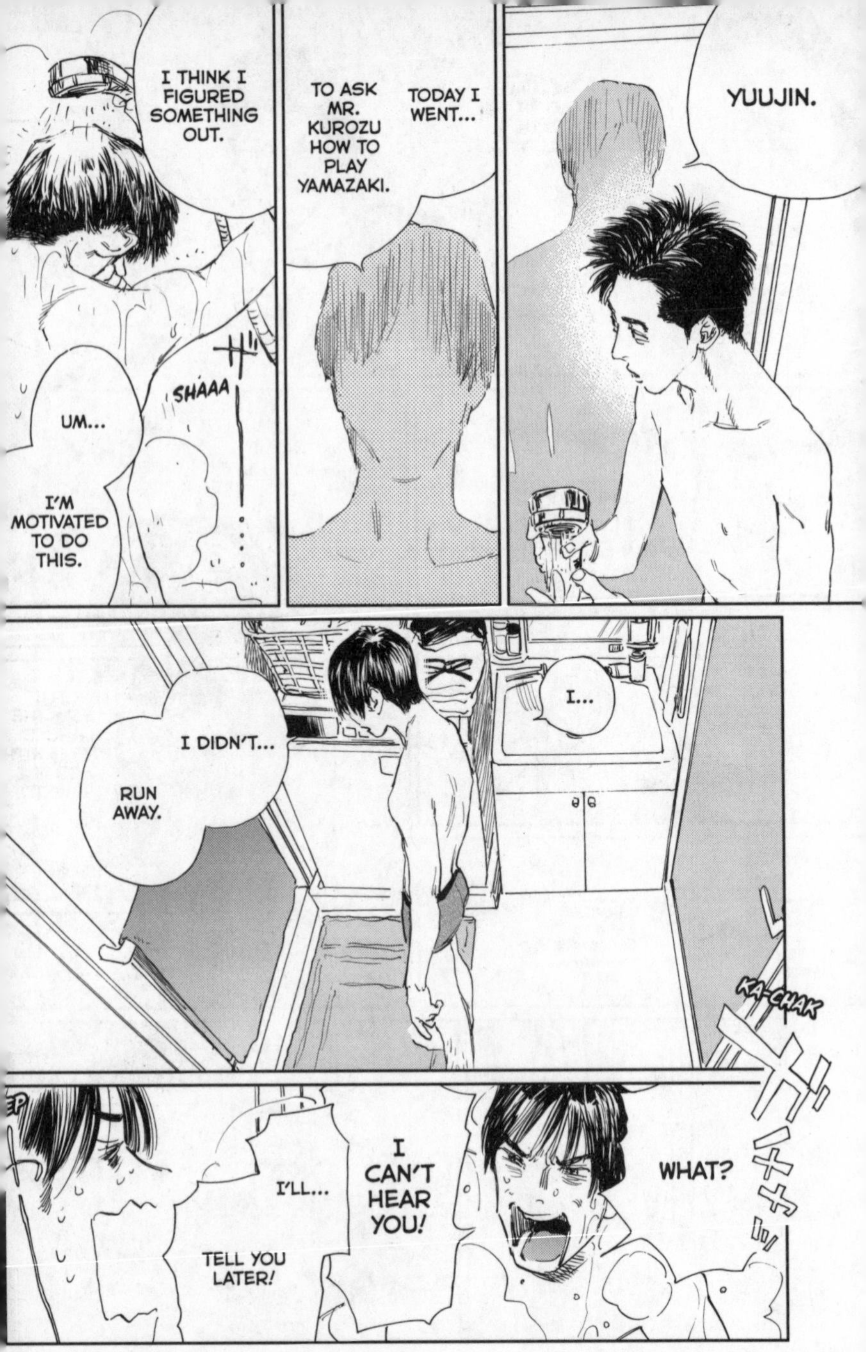
YUUJIN.
TODAY I WENT...
TO ASK MR. KUROZU HOW TO PLAY YAMAZAKI.
I THINK I FIGURED SOMETHING OUT.
SHAAA
UM...
I'M MOTIVATED TO DO THIS.
KA-CHAK
I...
I DIDN'T...
RUN AWAY.
WHAT?
I CAN'T HEAR YOU!
I'LL...
TELL YOU LATER!

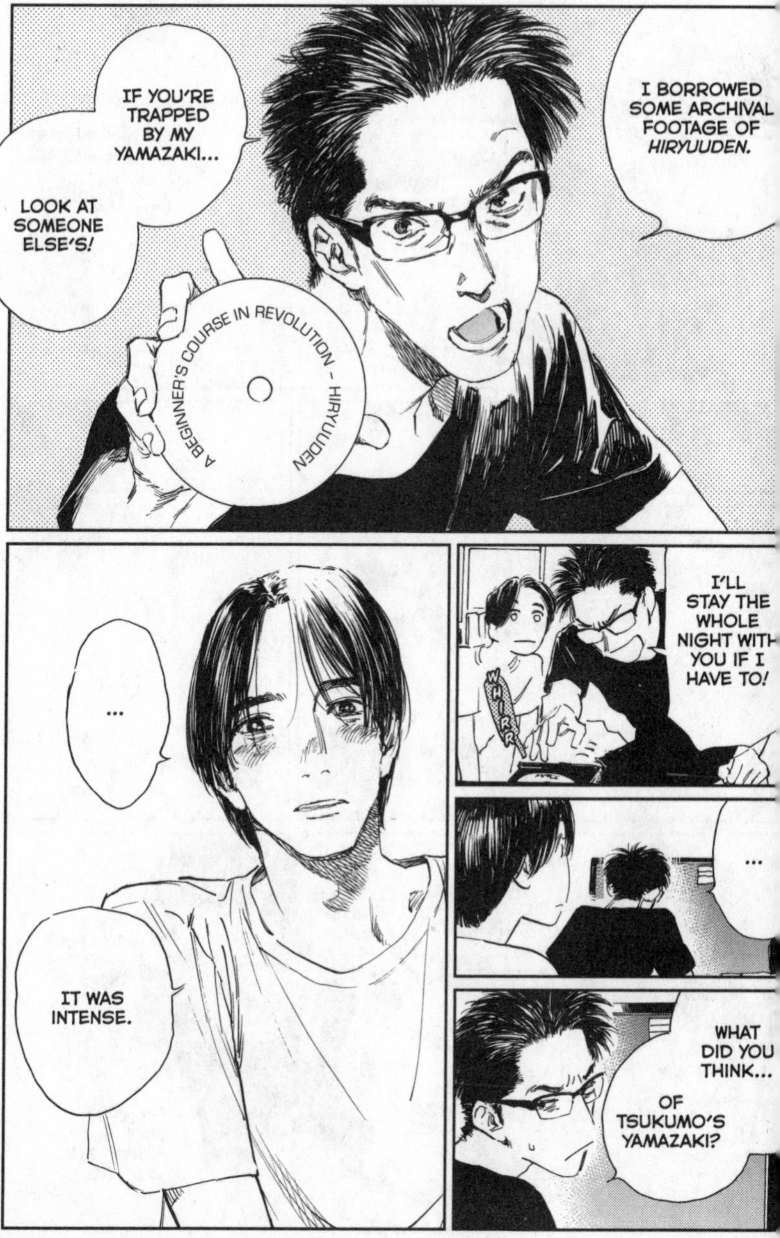
I BORROWED SOME ARCHIVAL FOOTAGE OF *HIRYUUDEN.*
IF YOU'RE TRAPPED BY MY YAMAZAKI...
LOOK AT SOMEONE ELSE'S!
A BEGINNER'S COURSE IN REVOLUTION – HIRYUUDEN
I'LL STAY THE WHOLE NIGHT WITH YOU IF I HAVE TO!
WHIRR
...
WHAT DID YOU THINK...
OF TSUKUMO'S YAMAZAKI?
...
IT WAS INTENSE.

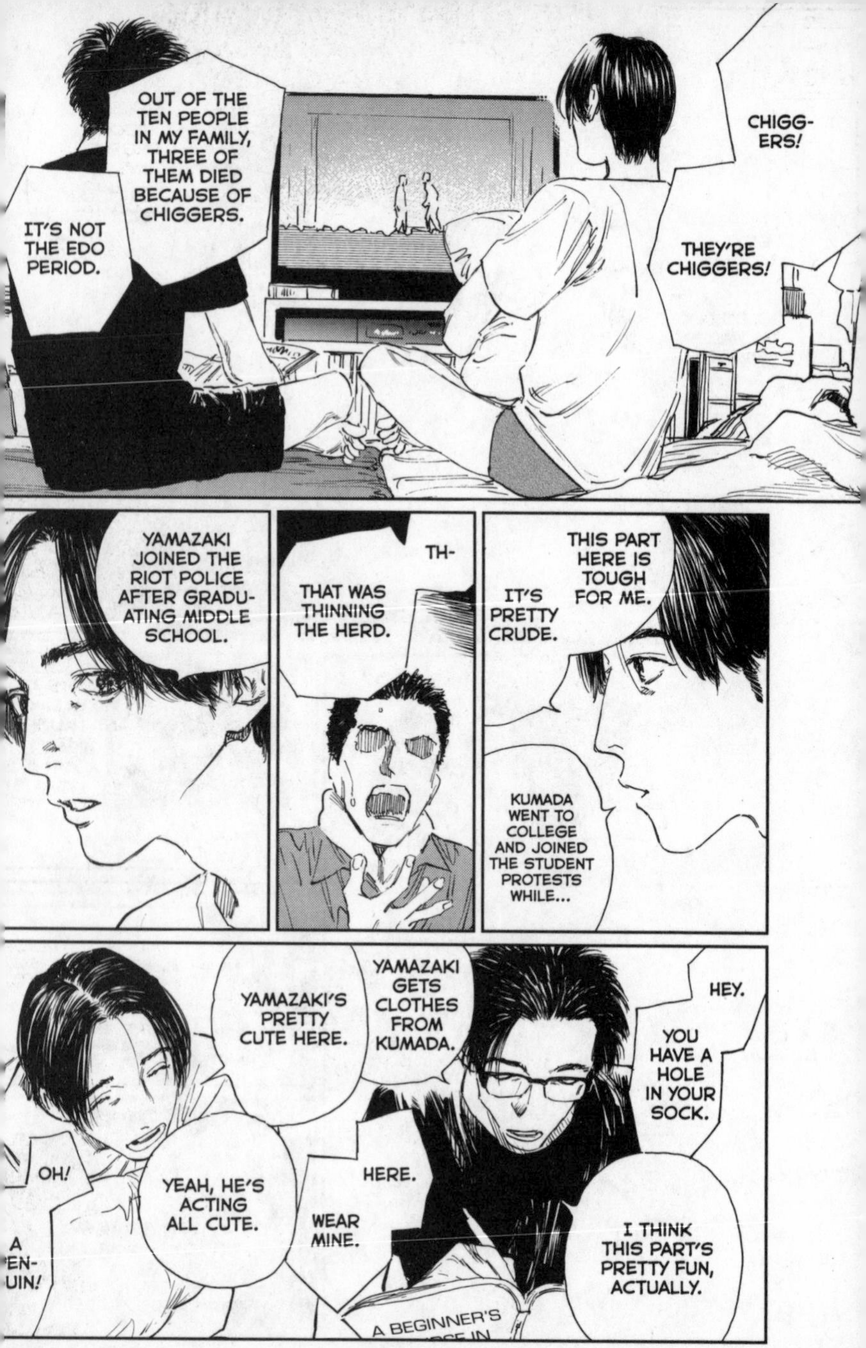
CHIGG-ERS!
THEY'RE CHIGGERS!
OUT OF THE TEN PEOPLE IN MY FAMILY, THREE OF THEM DIED BECAUSE OF CHIGGERS.
IT'S NOT THE EDO PERIOD.
THIS PART HERE IS TOUGH FOR ME.
IT'S PRETTY CRUDE.
KUMADA WENT TO COLLEGE AND JOINED THE STUDENT PROTESTS WHILE...
TH-
THAT WAS THINNING THE HERD.
YAMAZAKI JOINED THE RIOT POLICE AFTER GRADU-ATING MIDDLE SCHOOL.
HEY.
YOU HAVE A HOLE IN YOUR SOCK.
YAMAZAKI GETS CLOTHES FROM KUMADA.
I THINK THIS PART'S PRETTY FUN, ACTUALLY.
HERE.
WEAR MINE.
A BEGINNER'S
YAMAZAKI'S PRETTY CUTE HERE.
YEAH, HE'S ACTING ALL CUTE.
OH!
A
EN-
UIN!

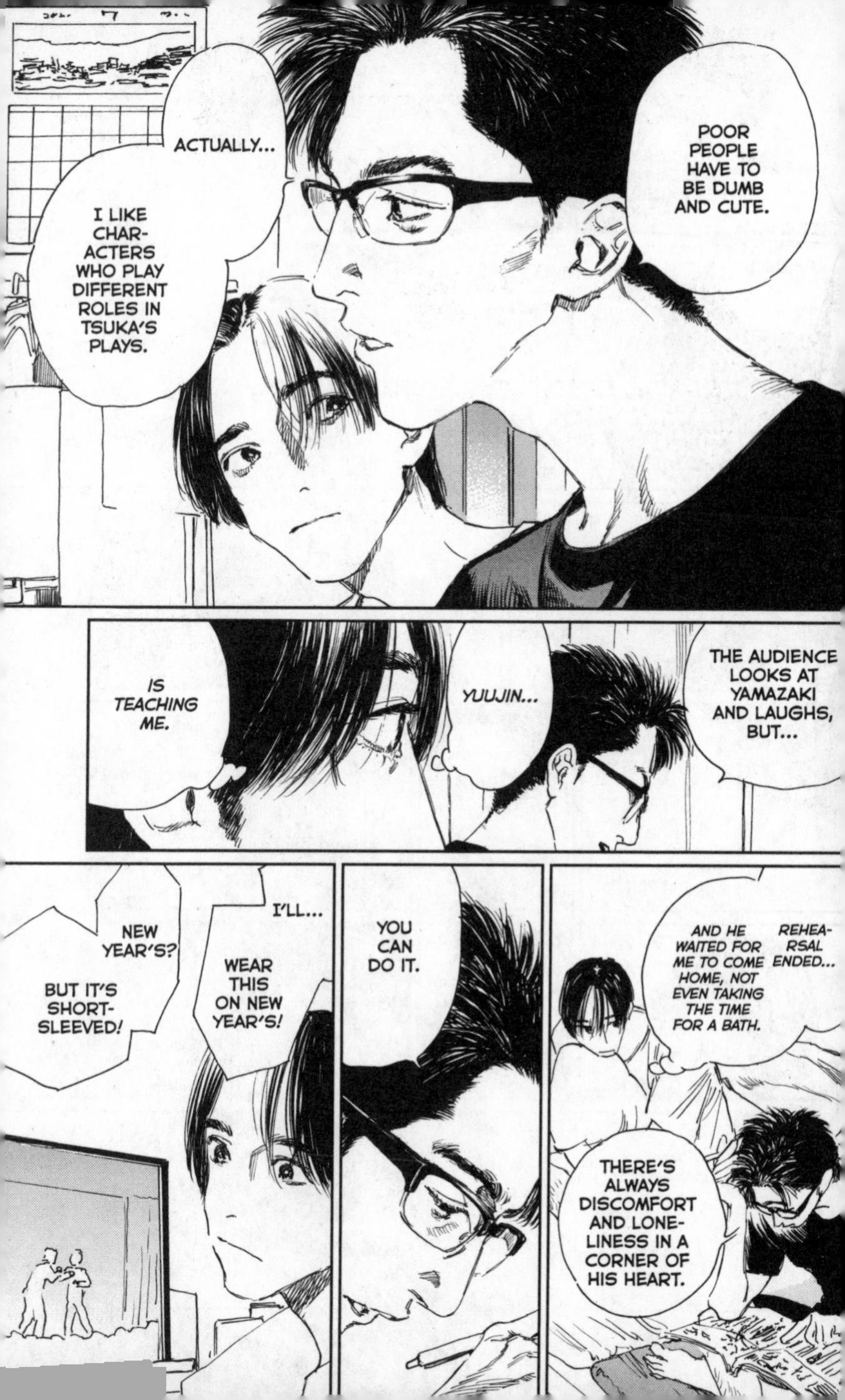

POOR PEOPLE HAVE TO BE DUMB AND CUTE.
ACTUALLY...
I LIKE CHARACTERS WHO PLAY DIFFERENT ROLES IN TSUKA'S PLAYS.
THE AUDIENCE LOOKS AT YAMAZAKI AND LAUGHS, BUT...
YUUJIN...
IS TEACHING ME.
REHEARSAL ENDED...
AND HE WAITED FOR ME TO COME HOME, NOT EVEN TAKING THE TIME FOR A BATH.
THERE'S ALWAYS DISCOMFORT AND LONELINESS IN A CORNER OF HIS HEART.
YOU CAN DO IT.
I'LL...
WEAR THIS ON NEW YEAR'S!
NEW YEAR'S?
BUT IT'S SHORT-SLEEVED!

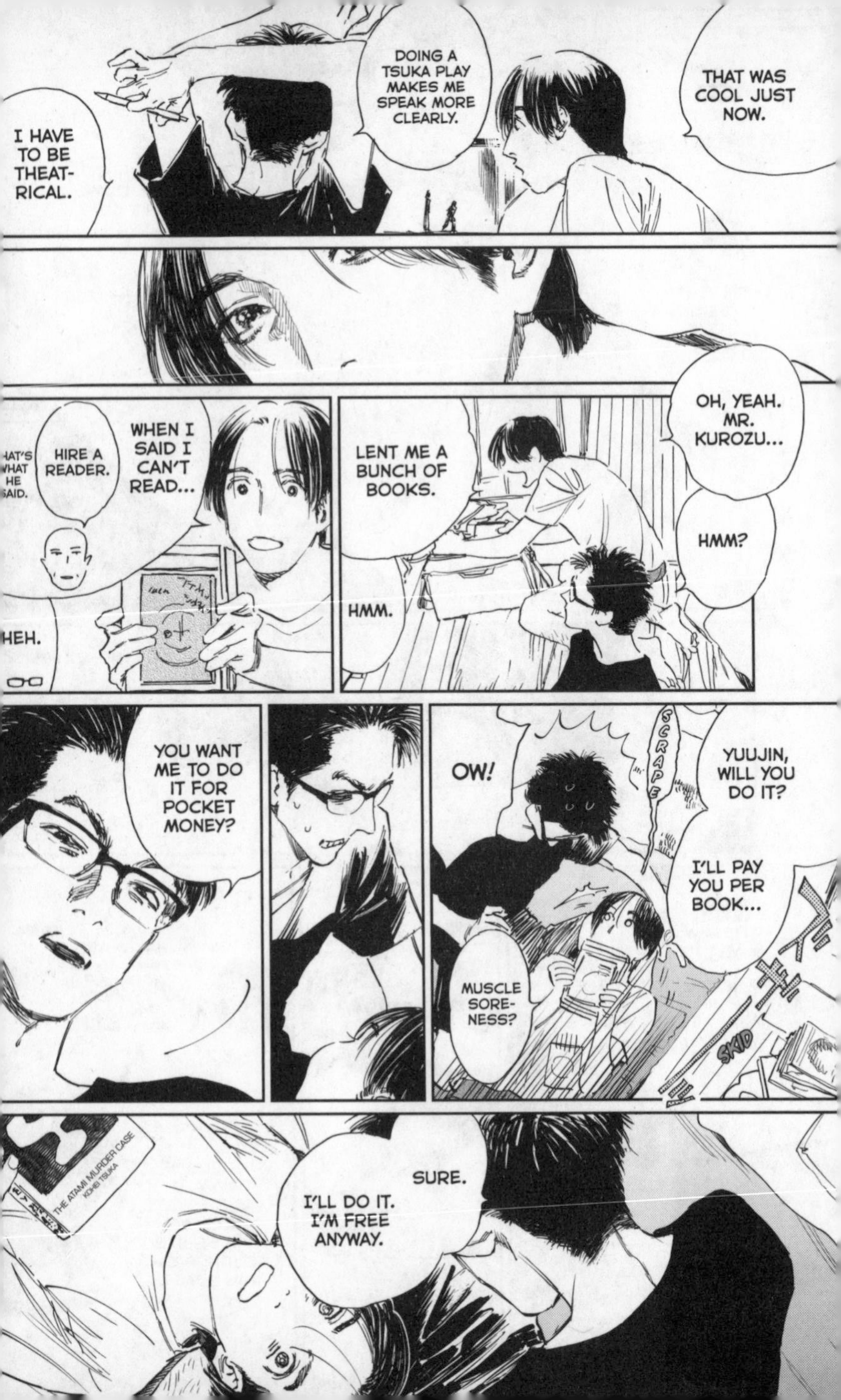
THAT WAS COOL JUST NOW.
DOING A TSUKA PLAY MAKES ME SPEAK MORE CLEARLY.
I HAVE TO BE THEAT-RICAL.
OH, YEAH. MR. KUROZU...
HMM?
LENT ME A BUNCH OF BOOKS.
HMM.
WHEN I SAID I CAN'T READ...
HIRE A READER.
HAT'S WHAT HE SAID.
HEH.
YUUJIN, WILL YOU DO IT?
I'LL PAY YOU PER BOOK...
SCRAPE
OW!
MUSCLE SORE-NESS?
SKID
YOU WANT ME TO DO IT FOR POCKET MONEY?
SURE.
I'LL DO IT. I'M FREE ANYWAY.
THE ATAMI MURDER CASE
KOHEI TSUKA

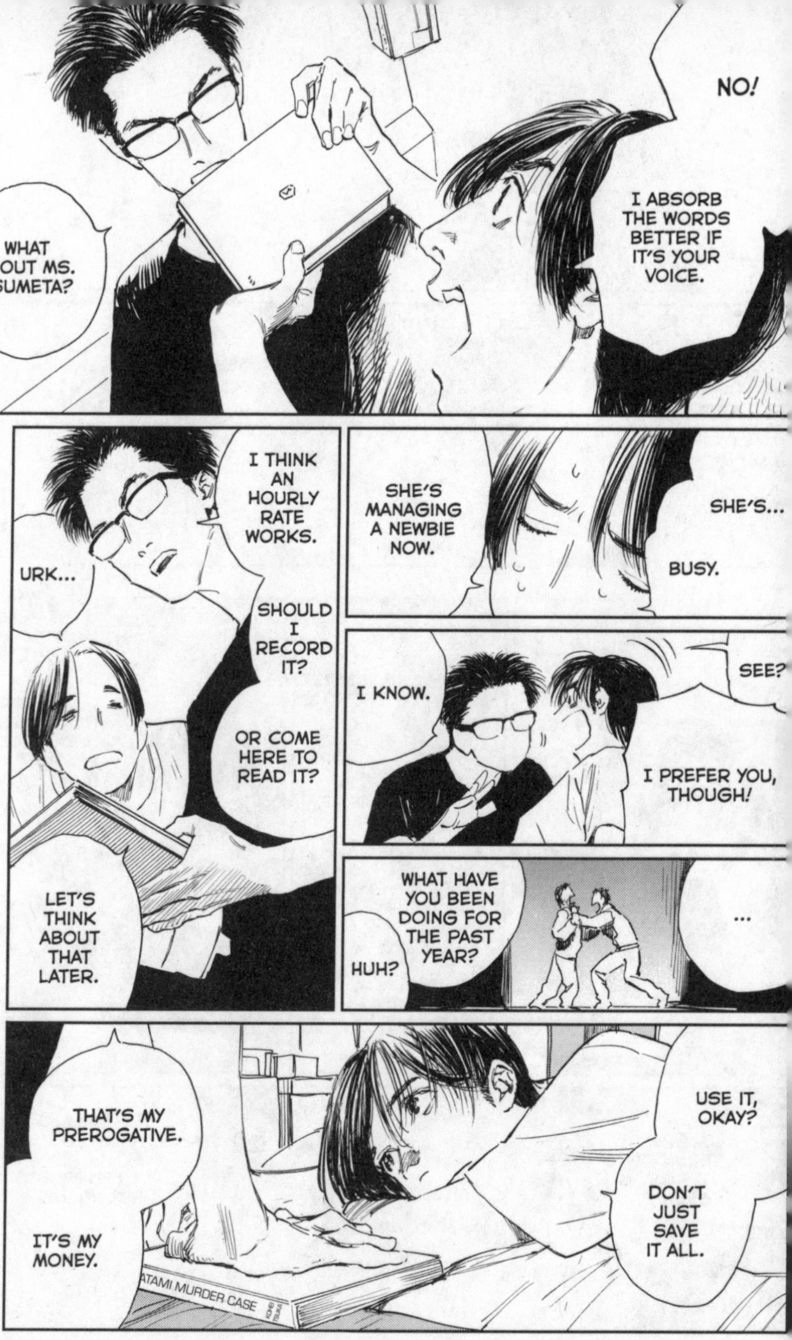
NO!
I ABSORB THE WORDS BETTER IF IT'S YOUR VOICE.
WHAT ABOUT MS. TSUMETA?
SHE'S...
BUSY.
SHE'S MANAGING A NEWBIE NOW.
SEE?
I PREFER YOU, THOUGH!
I KNOW.
...
WHAT HAVE YOU BEEN DOING FOR THE PAST YEAR?
HUH?
I THINK AN HOURLY RATE WORKS.
URK...
SHOULD I RECORD IT?
OR COME HERE TO READ IT?
LET'S THINK ABOUT THAT LATER.
USE IT, OKAY?
DON'T JUST SAVE IT ALL.
THAT'S MY PREROGATIVE.
IT'S MY MONEY.
ATAMI MURDER CASE

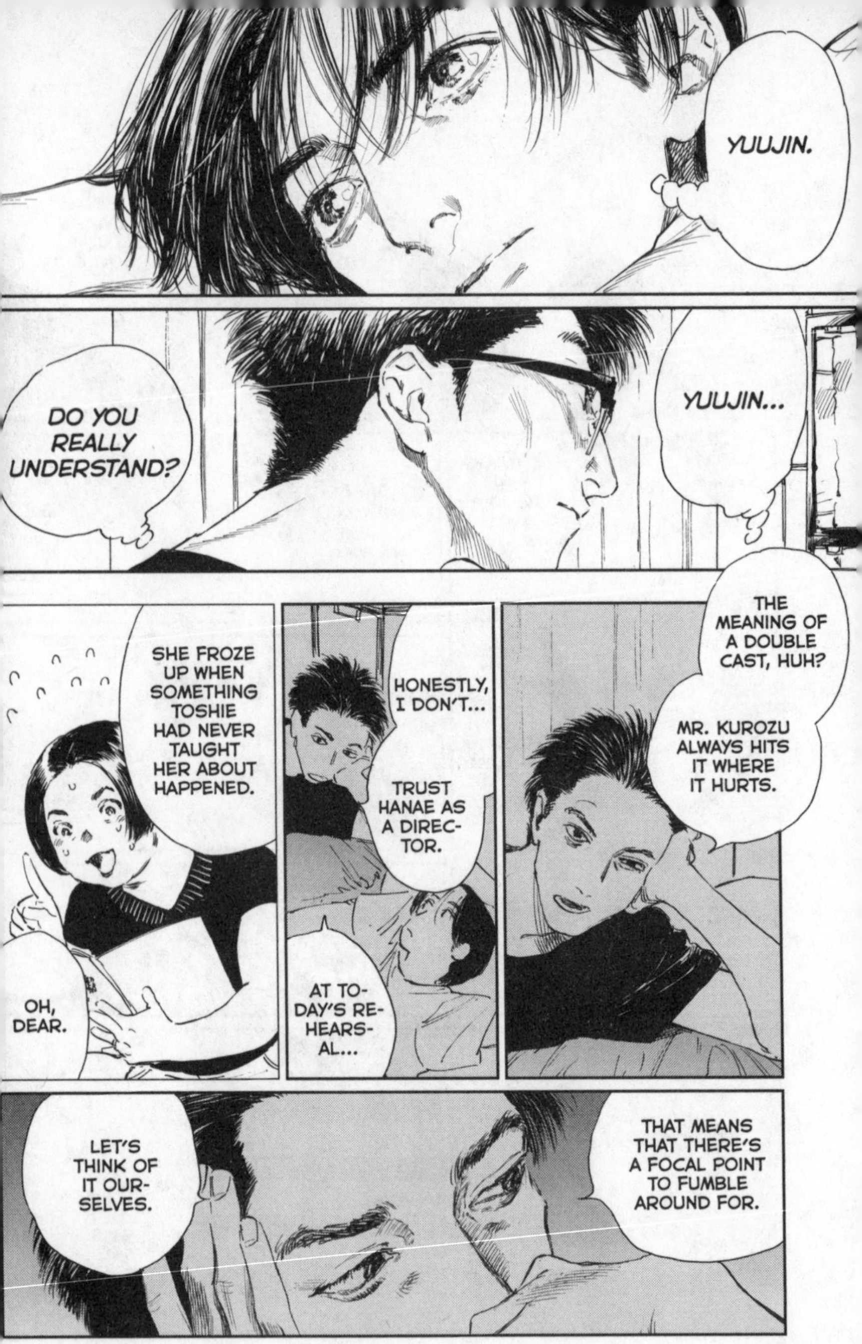
YUUJIN.
YUUJIN...
DO YOU REALLY UNDERSTAND?
THE MEANING OF A DOUBLE CAST, HUH?
MR. KUROZU ALWAYS HITS IT WHERE IT HURTS.
HONESTLY, I DON'T...
TRUST HANAE AS A DIRECTOR.
AT TO-DAY'S RE-HEARS-AL...
SHE FROZE UP WHEN SOMETHING TOSHIE HAD NEVER TAUGHT HER ABOUT HAPPENED.
OH, DEAR.
THAT MEANS THAT THERE'S A FOCAL POINT TO FUMBLE AROUND FOR.
LET'S THINK OF IT OUR-SELVES.

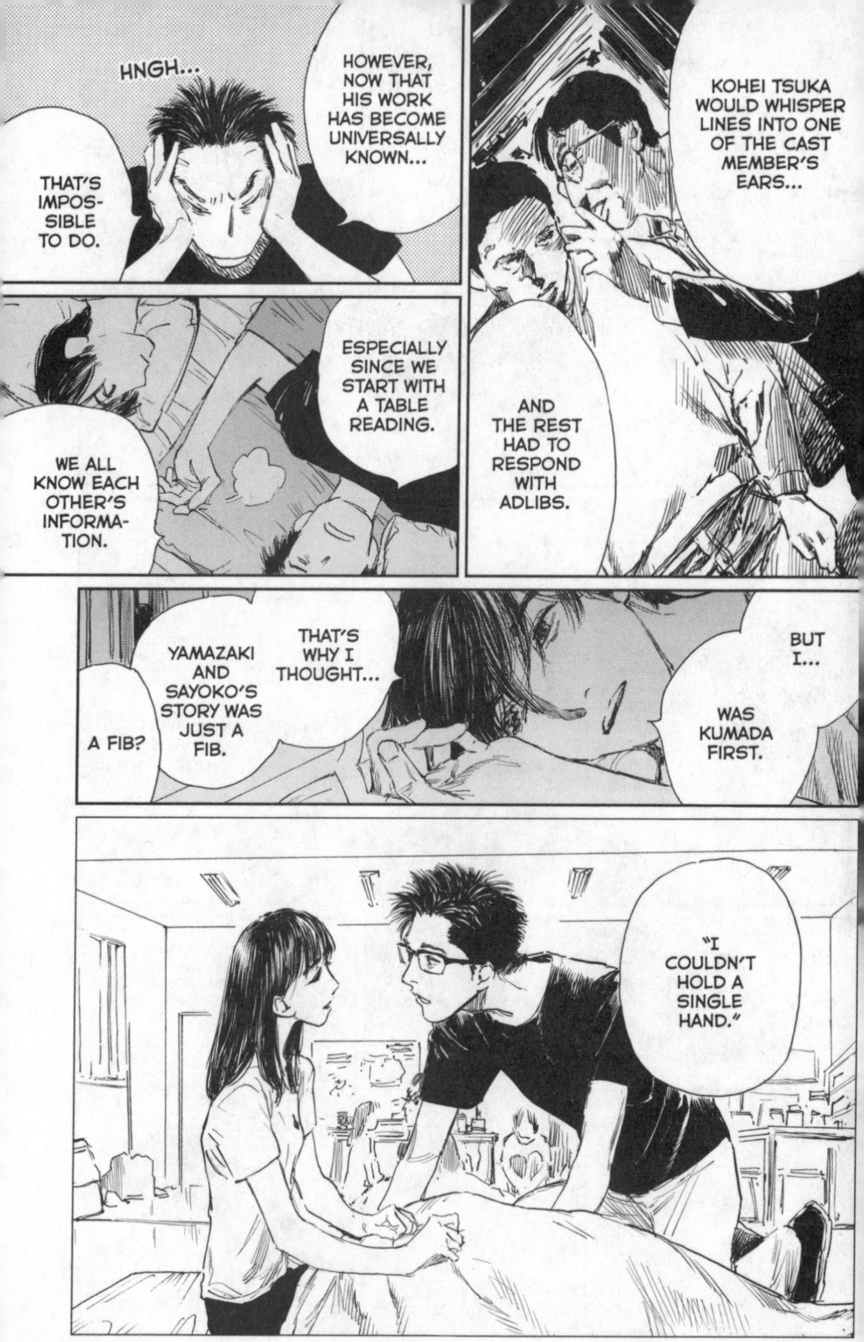
KOHEI TSUKA WOULD WHISPER LINES INTO ONE OF THE CAST MEMBER'S EARS...
AND THE REST HAD TO RESPOND WITH ADLIBS.
HOWEVER, NOW THAT HIS WORK HAS BECOME UNIVERSALLY KNOWN...
HNGH...
THAT'S IMPOSSIBLE TO DO.
ESPECIALLY SINCE WE START WITH A TABLE READING.
WE ALL KNOW EACH OTHER'S INFORMATION.
BUT I...
WAS KUMADA FIRST.
THAT'S WHY I THOUGHT...
YAMAZAKI AND SAYOKO'S STORY WAS JUST A FIB.
A FIB?
"I COULDN'T HOLD A SINGLE HAND."

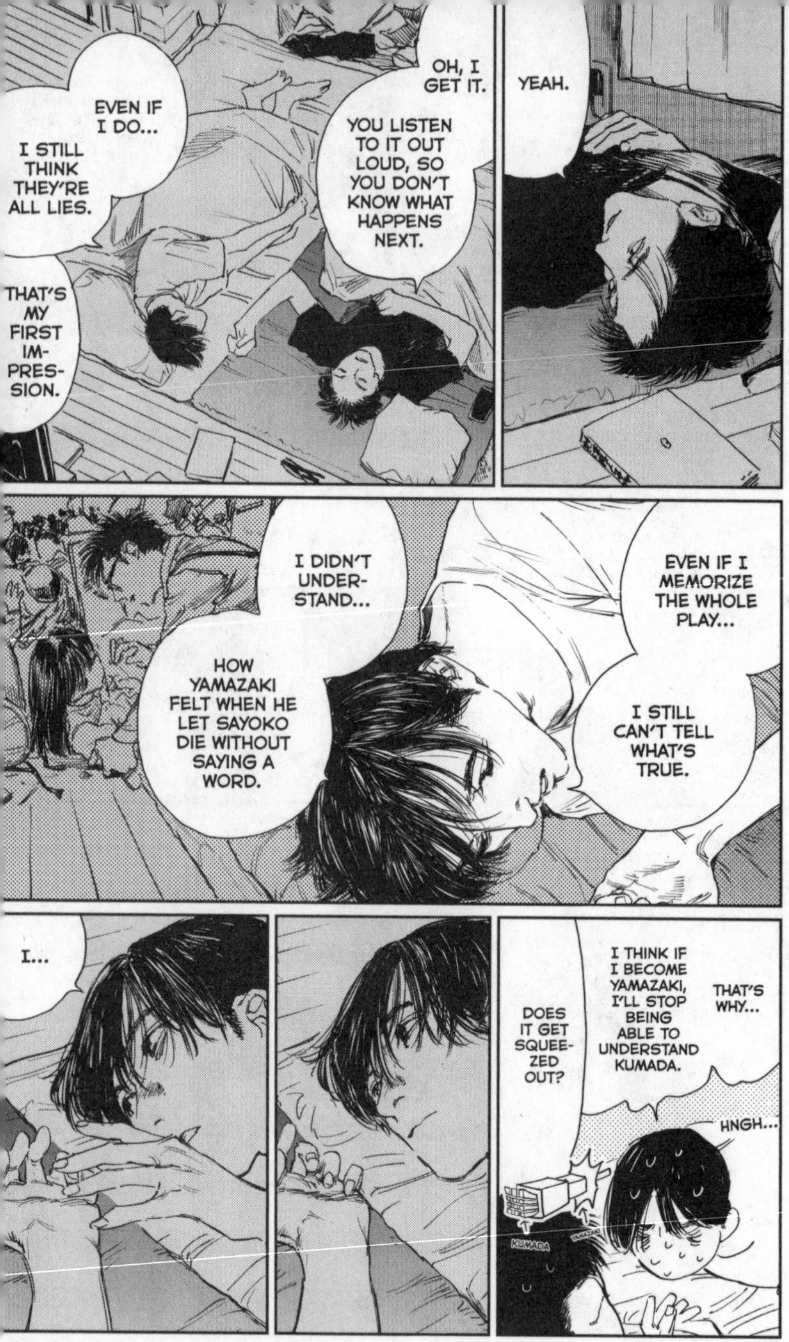
YEAH.
OH, I GET IT.
YOU LISTEN TO IT OUT LOUD, SO YOU DON'T KNOW WHAT HAPPENS NEXT.
EVEN IF I DO...
I STILL THINK THEY'RE ALL LIES.
THAT'S MY FIRST IMPRESSION.
EVEN IF I MEMORIZE THE WHOLE PLAY...
I STILL CAN'T TELL WHAT'S TRUE.
I DIDN'T UNDERSTAND...
HOW YAMAZAKI FELT WHEN HE LET SAYOKO DIE WITHOUT SAYING A WORD.
THAT'S WHY...
I THINK IF I BECOME YAMAZAKI, I'LL STOP BEING ABLE TO UNDERSTAND KUMADA.
DOES IT GET SQUEEZED OUT?
HNGH...
YAMAZAKI
KUMADA
I...

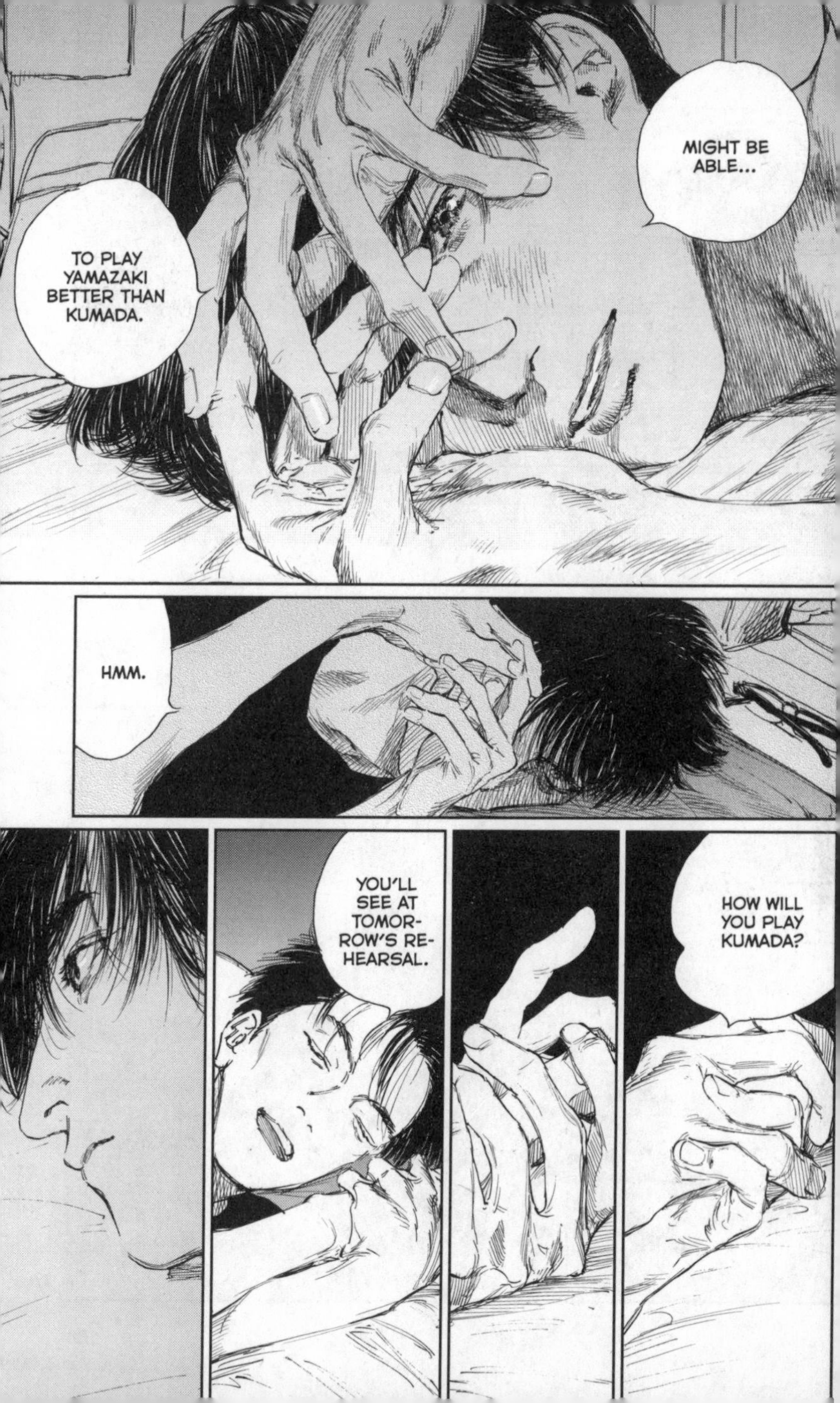
MIGHT BE ABLE...
TO PLAY YAMAZAKI BETTER THAN KUMADA.
HMM.
HOW WILL YOU PLAY KUMADA?
YOU'LL SEE AT TOMOR-ROW'S RE-HEARSAL.

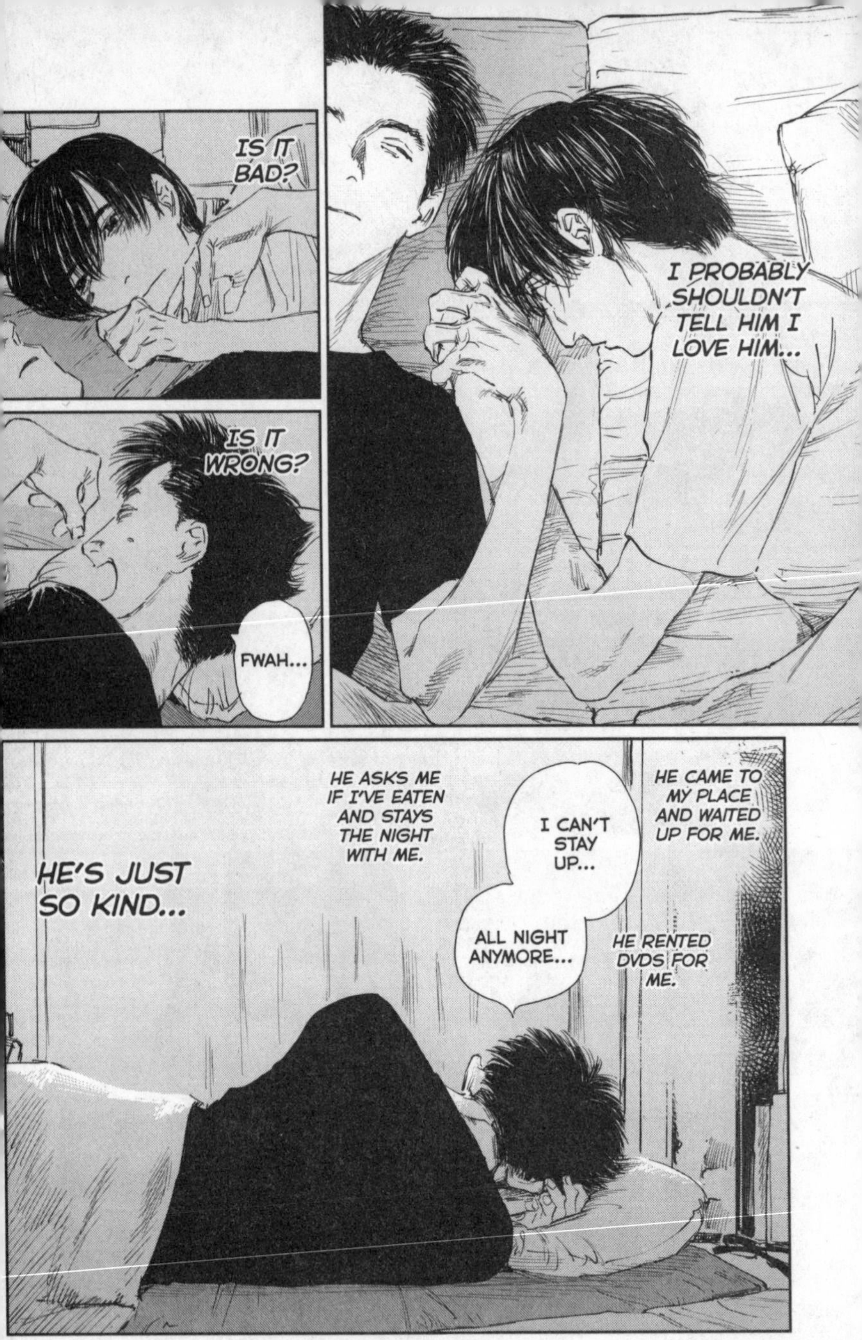
I PROBABLY SHOULDN'T TELL HIM I LOVE HIM...
IS IT BAD?
IS IT WRONG?
FWAH...
HE CAME TO MY PLACE AND WAITED UP FOR ME.
HE RENTED DVDS FOR ME.
I CAN'T STAY UP...
ALL NIGHT ANYMORE...
HE ASKS ME IF I'VE EATEN AND STAYS THE NIGHT WITH ME.
HE'S JUST SO KIND...

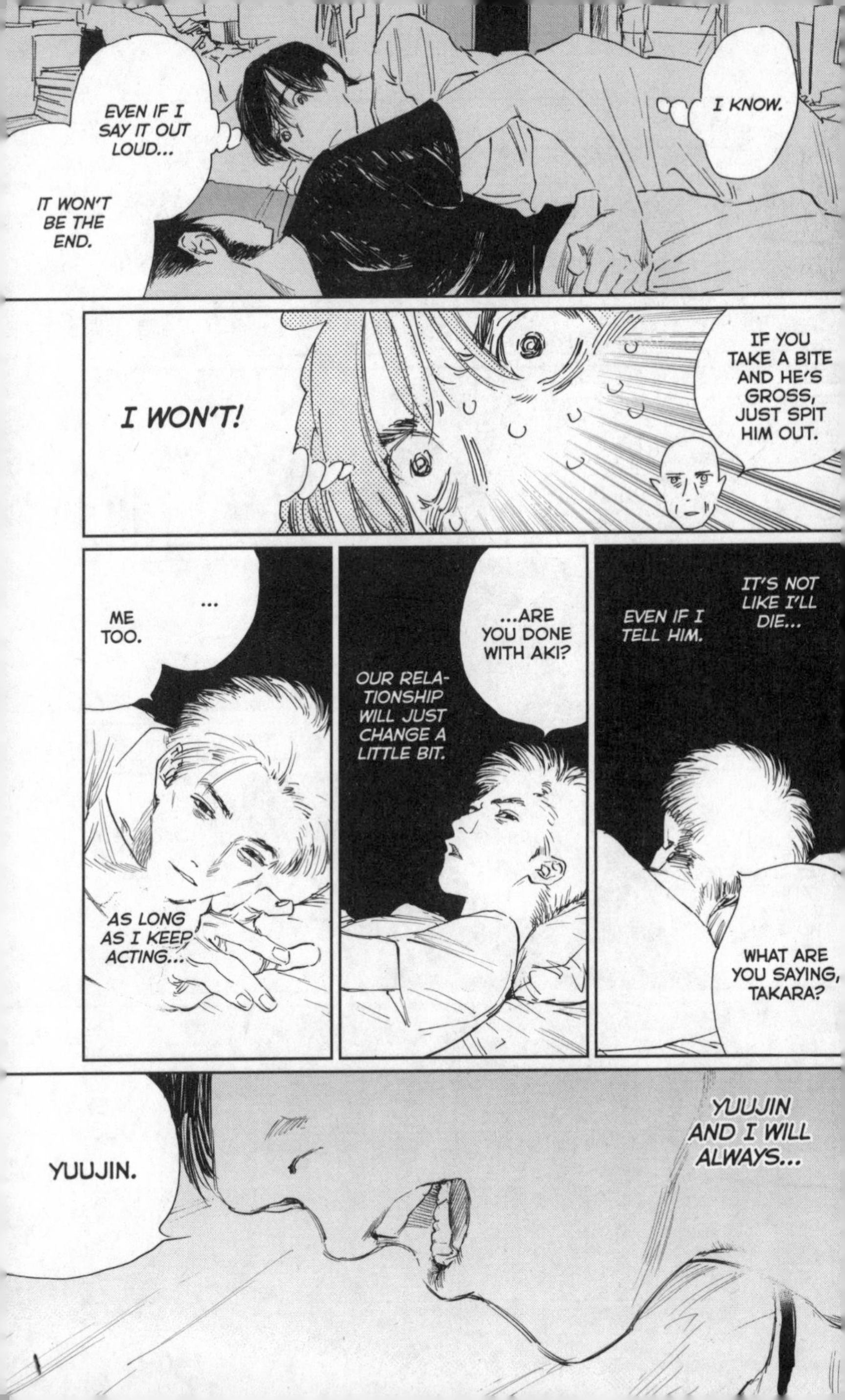

I KNOW.
EVEN IF I SAY IT OUT LOUD...
IT WON'T BE THE END.
IF YOU TAKE A BITE AND HE'S GROSS, JUST SPIT HIM OUT.
I WON'T!
IT'S NOT LIKE I'LL DIE...
EVEN IF I TELL HIM.
WHAT ARE YOU SAYING, TAKARA?
...ARE YOU DONE WITH AKI?
OUR RELA-TIONSHIP WILL JUST CHANGE A LITTLE BIT.
...
ME TOO.
AS LONG AS I KEEP ACTING...
YUUJIN AND I WILL ALWAYS...
YUUJIN.

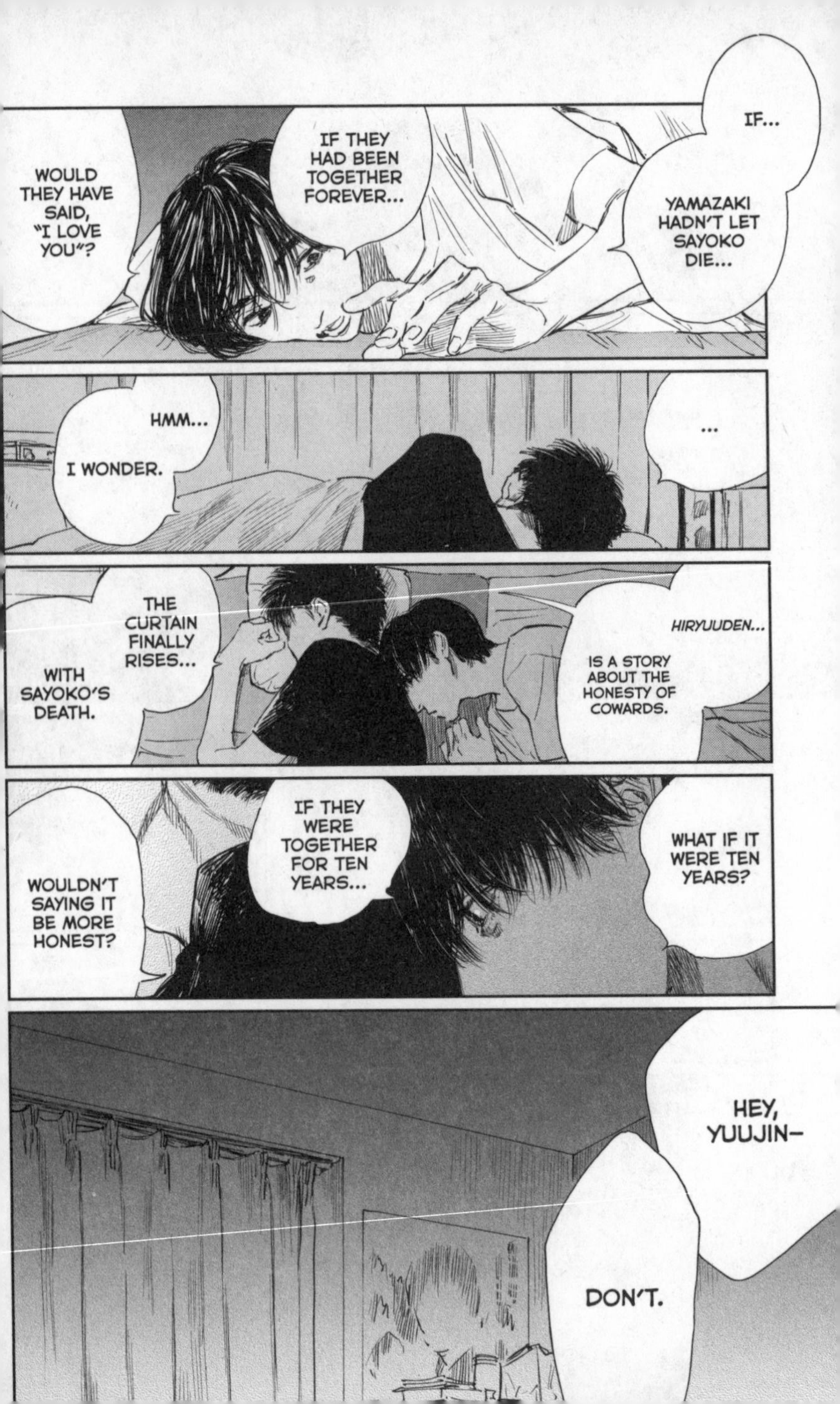
IF...
YAMAZAKI HADN'T LET SAYOKO DIE...
IF THEY HAD BEEN TOGETHER FOREVER...
WOULD THEY HAVE SAID, "I LOVE YOU"?
...
HMM...
I WONDER.
HIRYUUDEN...
IS A STORY ABOUT THE HONESTY OF COWARDS.
THE CURTAIN FINALLY RISES...
WITH SAYOKO'S DEATH.
WHAT IF IT WERE TEN YEARS?
IF THEY WERE TOGETHER FOR TEN YEARS...
WOULDN'T SAYING IT BE MORE HONEST?
HEY, YUUJIN–
DON'T.

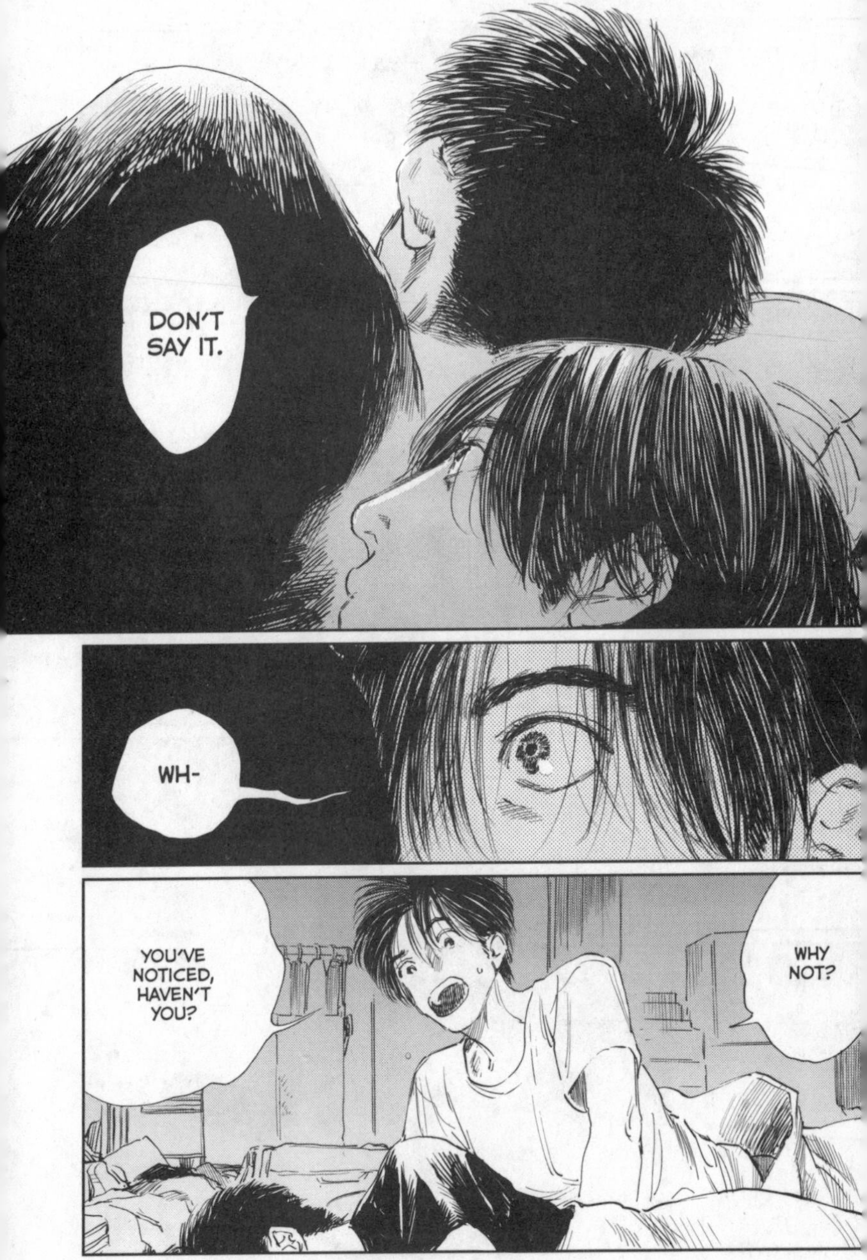
DON'T SAY IT.
WH-
WHY NOT?
YOU'VE NOTICED, HAVEN'T YOU?

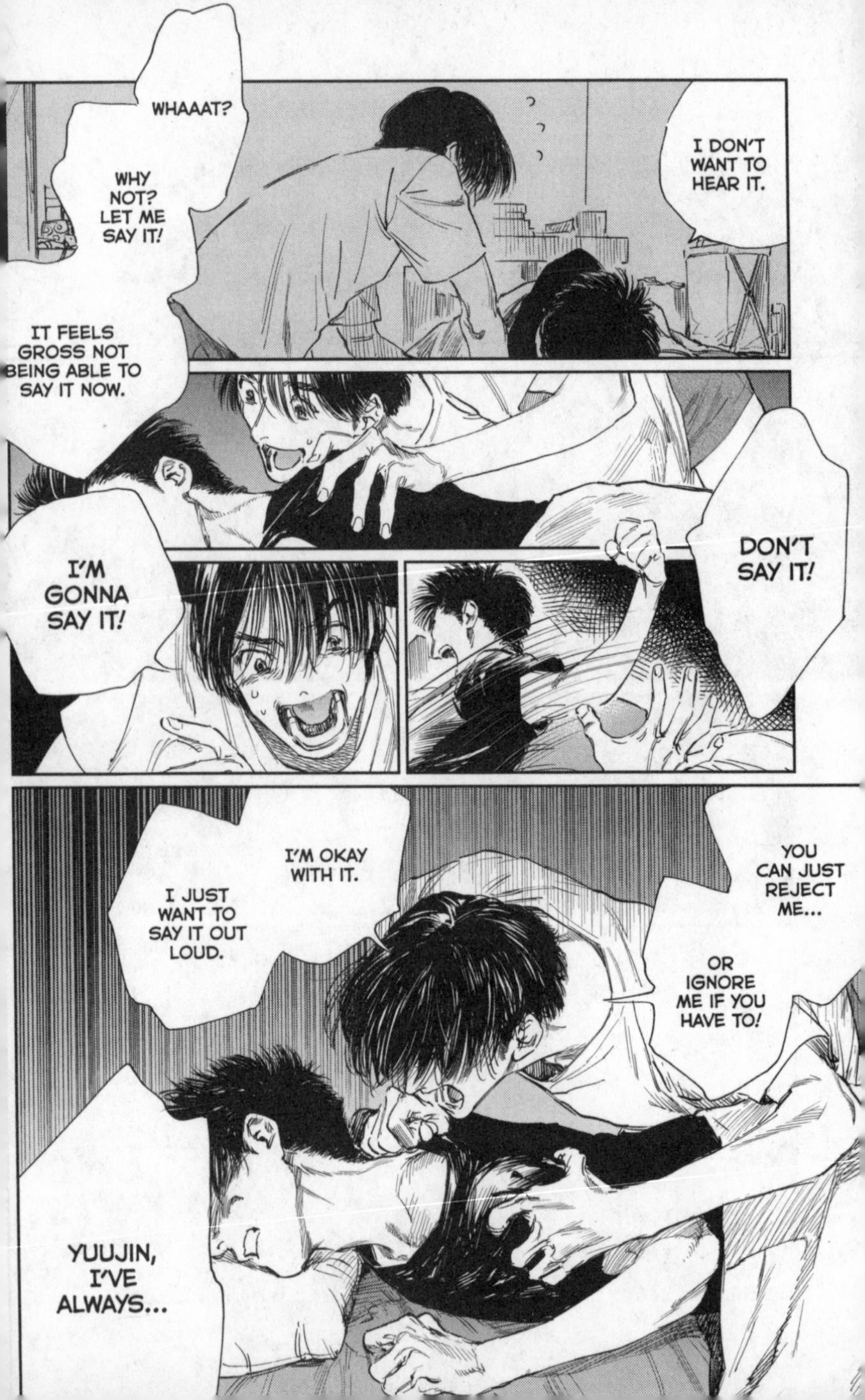
I DON'T WANT TO HEAR IT.
WHAAAT?
WHY NOT? LET ME SAY IT!
IT FEELS GROSS NOT BEING ABLE TO SAY IT NOW.
DON'T SAY IT!
I'M GONNA SAY IT!
YOU CAN JUST REJECT ME...
OR IGNORE ME IF YOU HAVE TO!
I'M OKAY WITH IT.
I JUST WANT TO SAY IT OUT LOUD.
YUUJIN, I'VE ALWAYS...

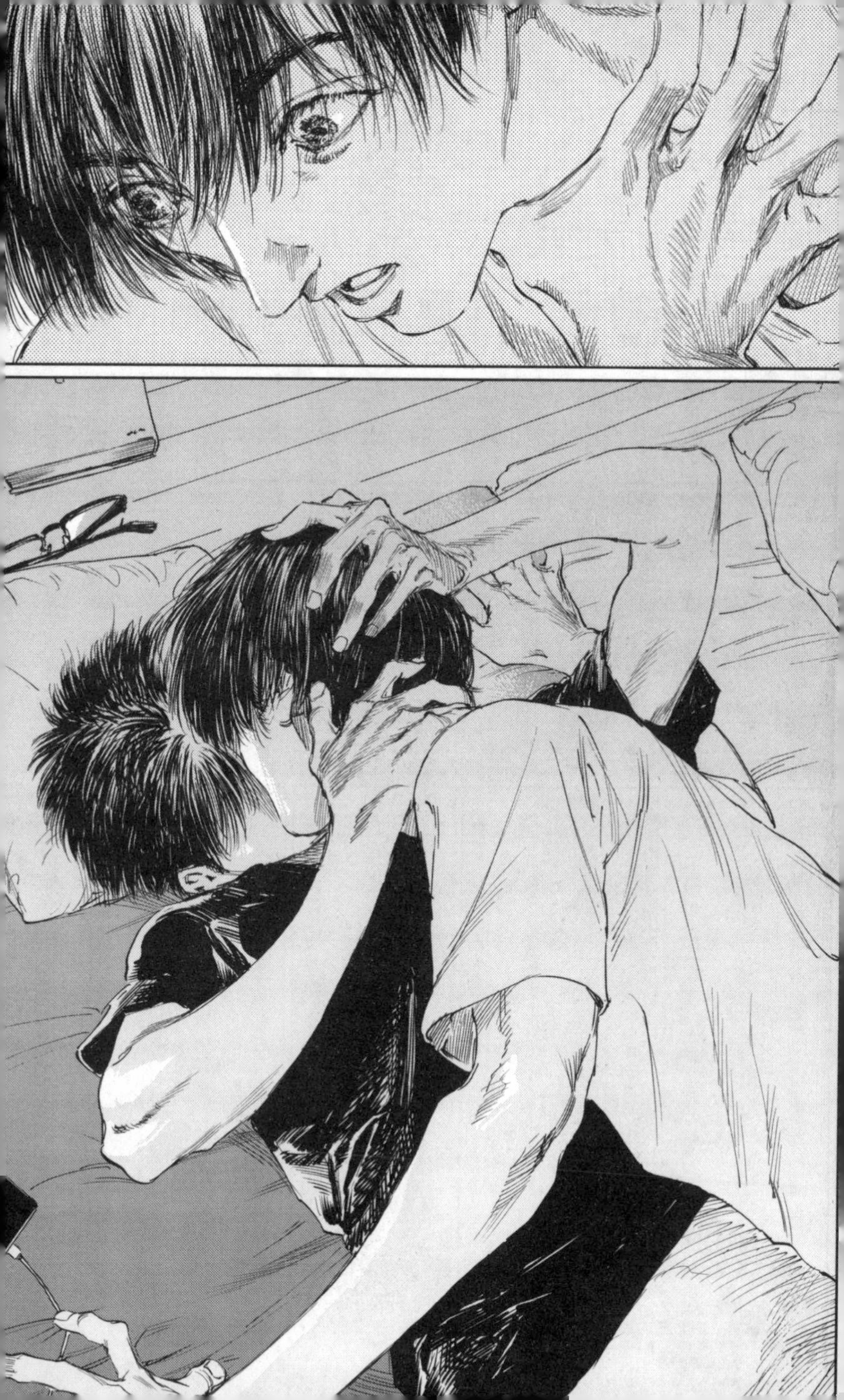

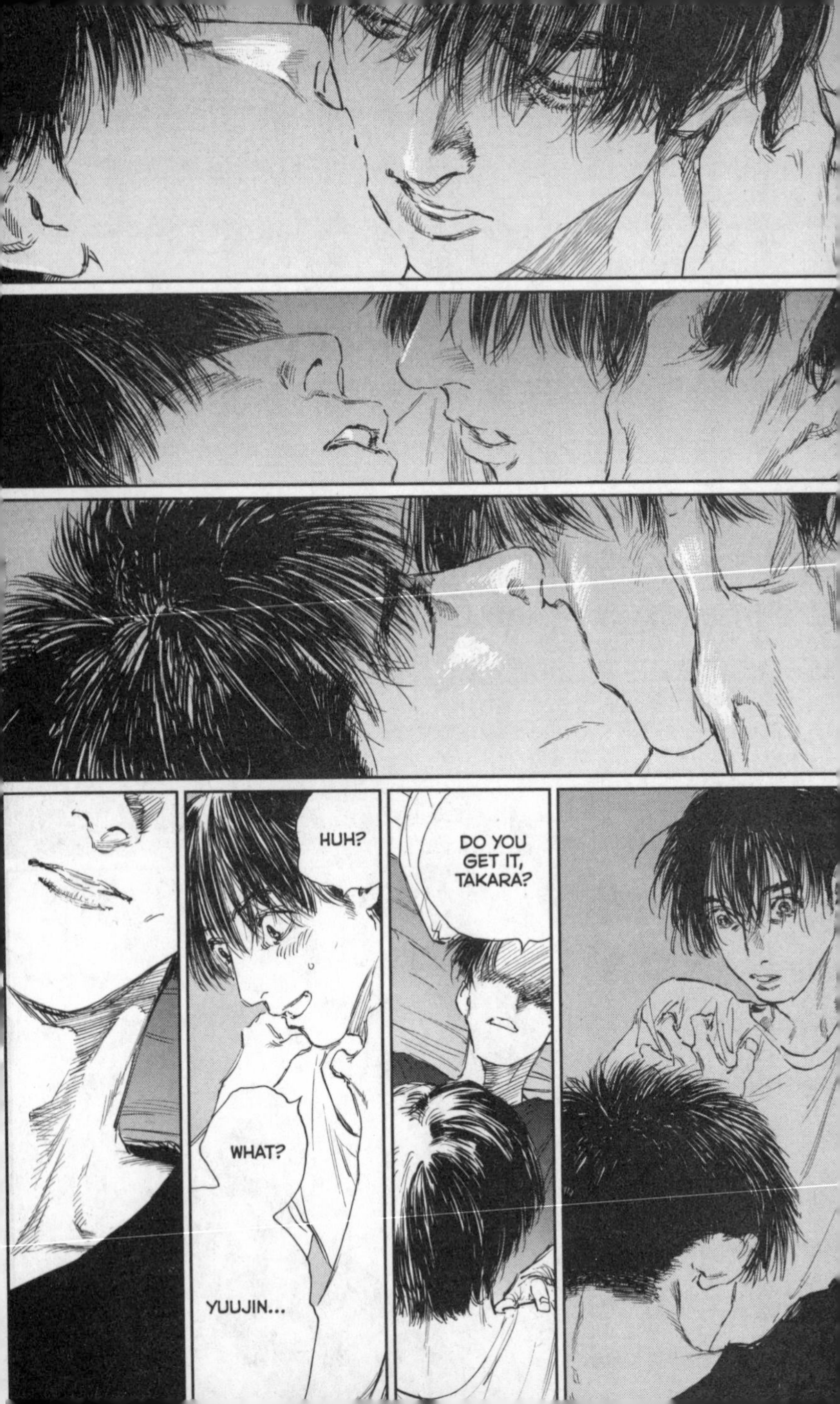
DO YOU GET IT, TAKARA?
HUH?
WHAT?
YUUJIN...

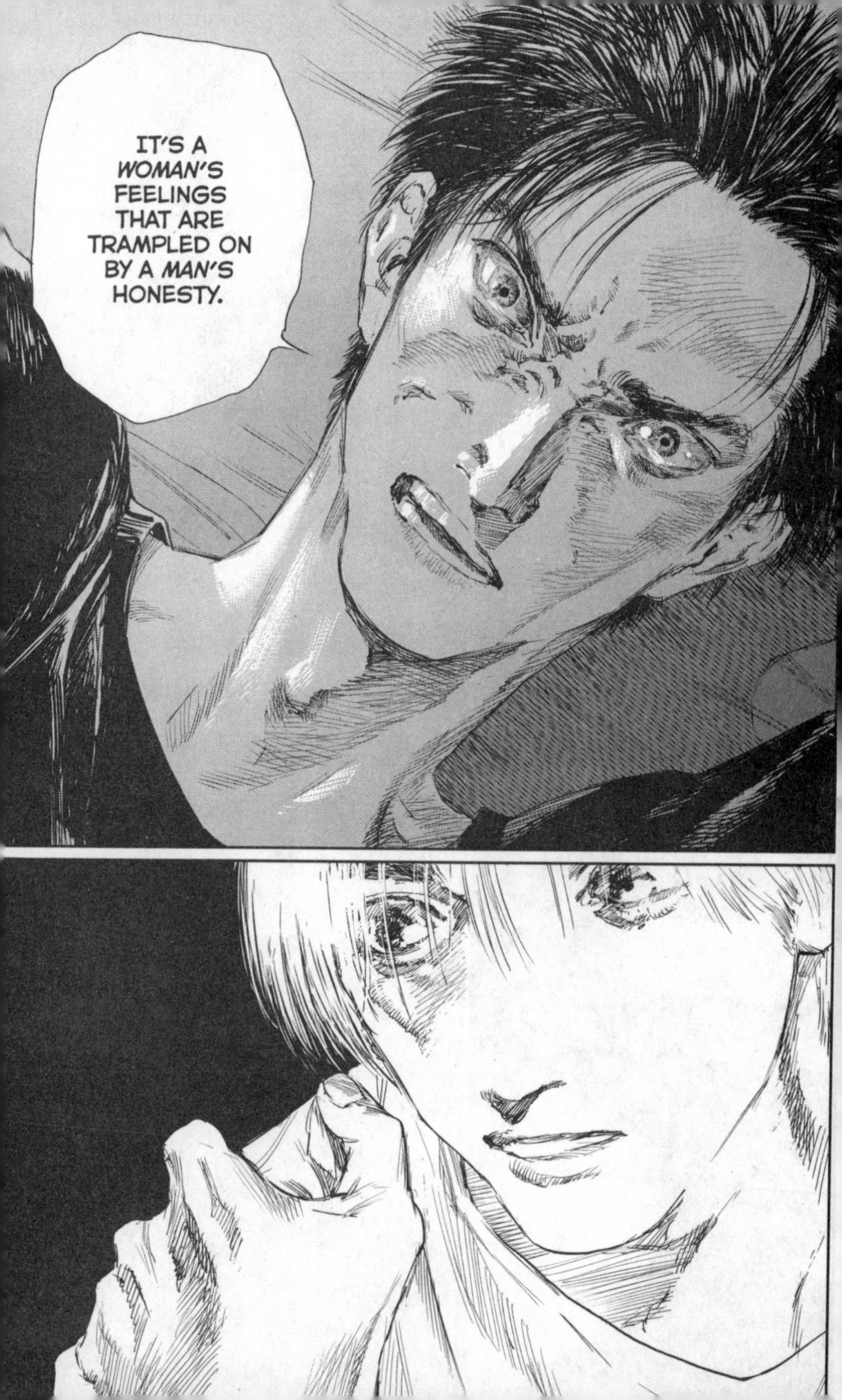
IT'S A *WOMAN'S* FEELINGS THAT ARE TRAMPLED ON BY A *MAN'S* HONESTY.

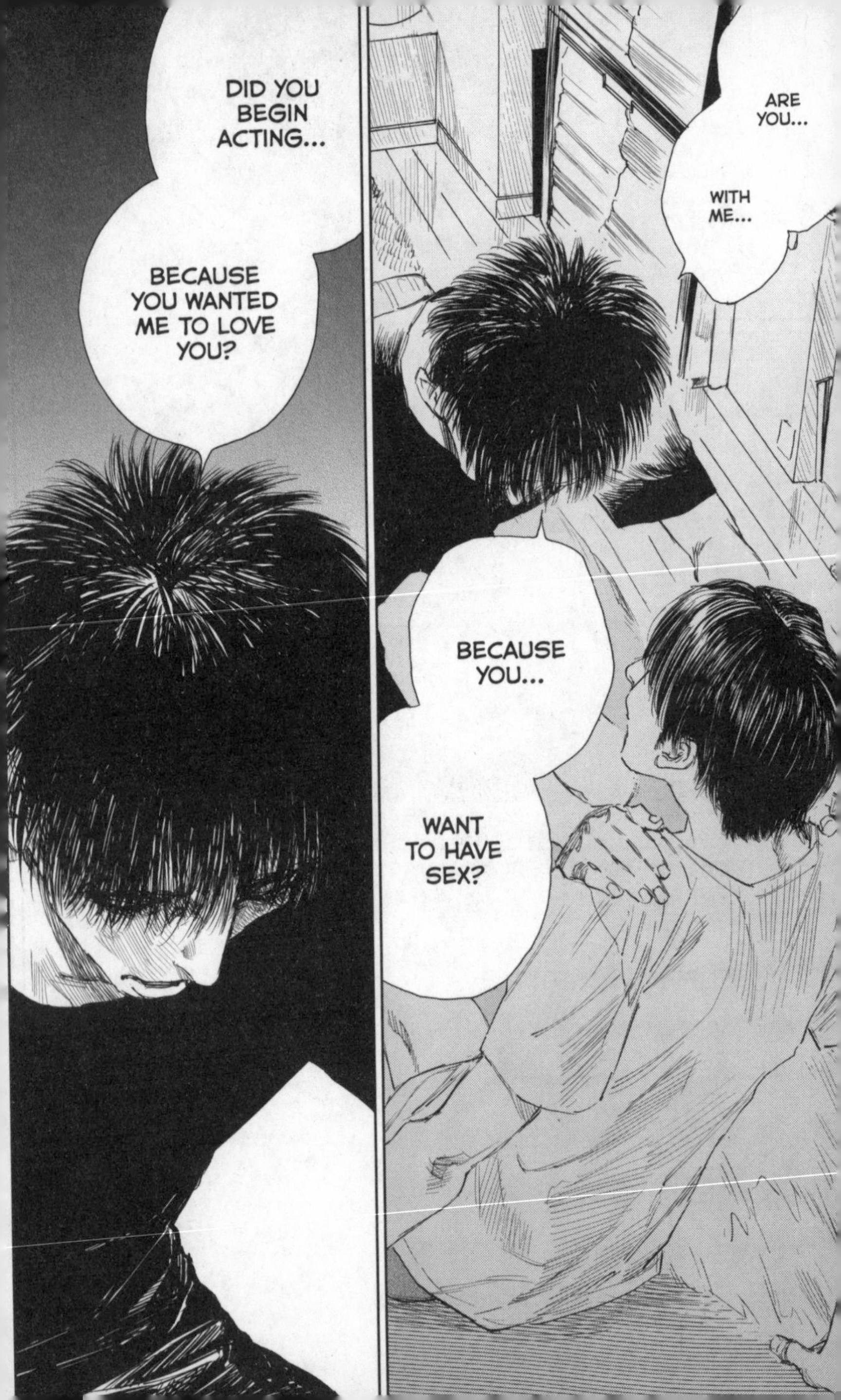
ARE YOU...
WITH ME...
BECAUSE YOU...
WANT TO HAVE SEX?
DID YOU BEGIN ACTING...
BECAUSE YOU WANTED ME TO LOVE YOU?

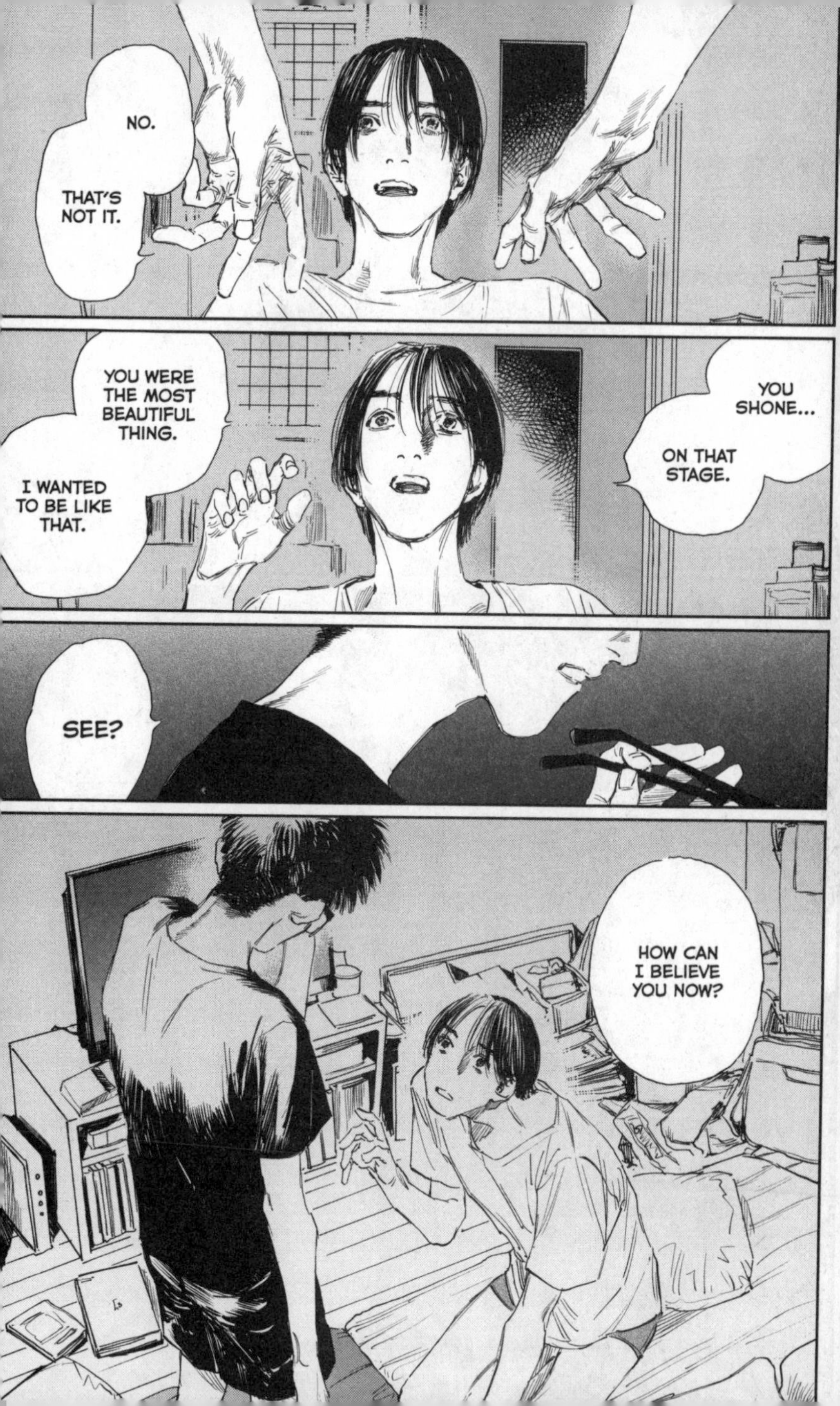
NO.
THAT'S NOT IT.
YOU SHONE...
ON THAT STAGE.
YOU WERE THE MOST BEAUTIFUL THING.
I WANTED TO BE LIKE THAT.
SEE?
HOW CAN I BELIEVE YOU NOW?

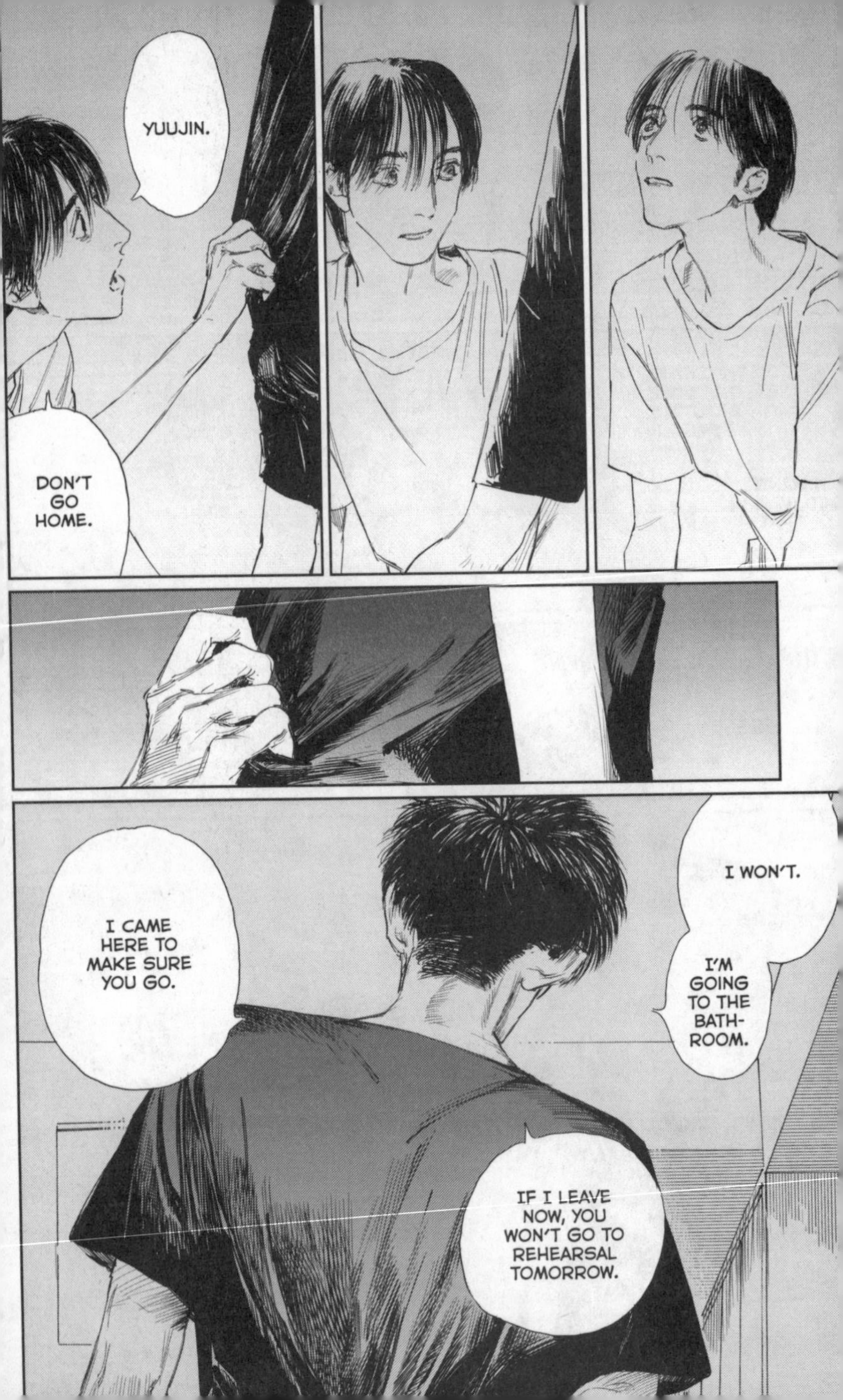
YUUJIN.
DON'T GO HOME.
I WON'T.
I'M GOING TO THE BATH-ROOM.
I CAME HERE TO MAKE SURE YOU GO.
IF I LEAVE NOW, YOU WON'T GO TO REHEARSAL TOMORROW.

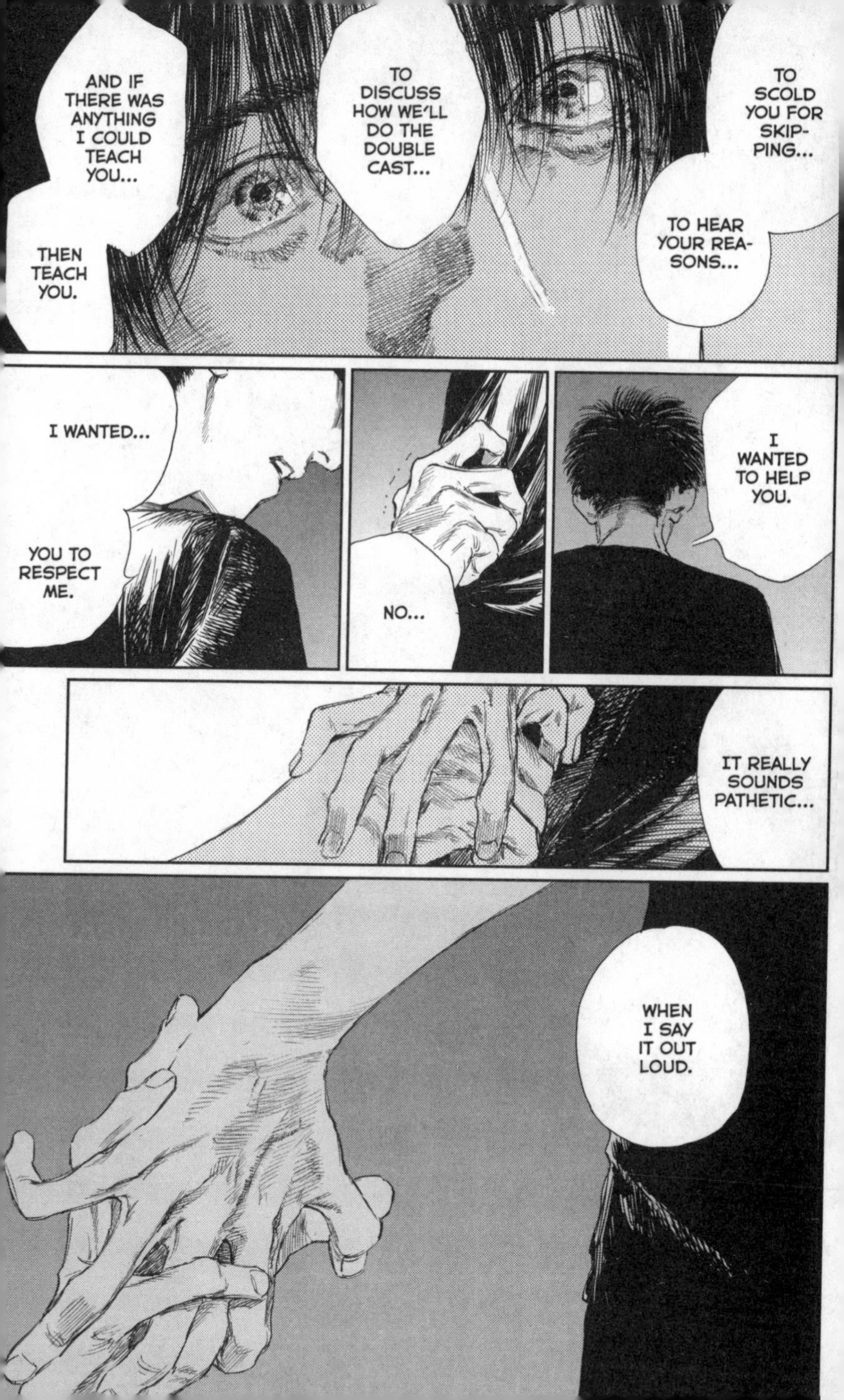
TO SCOLD YOU FOR SKIP-PING...
TO HEAR YOUR REA-SONS...
TO DISCUSS HOW WE'LL DO THE DOUBLE CAST...
AND IF THERE WAS ANYTHING I COULD TEACH YOU...
THEN TEACH YOU.
I WANTED TO HELP YOU.
NO...
I WANTED...
YOU TO RESPECT ME.
IT REALLY SOUNDS PATHETIC...
WHEN I SAY IT OUT LOUD.

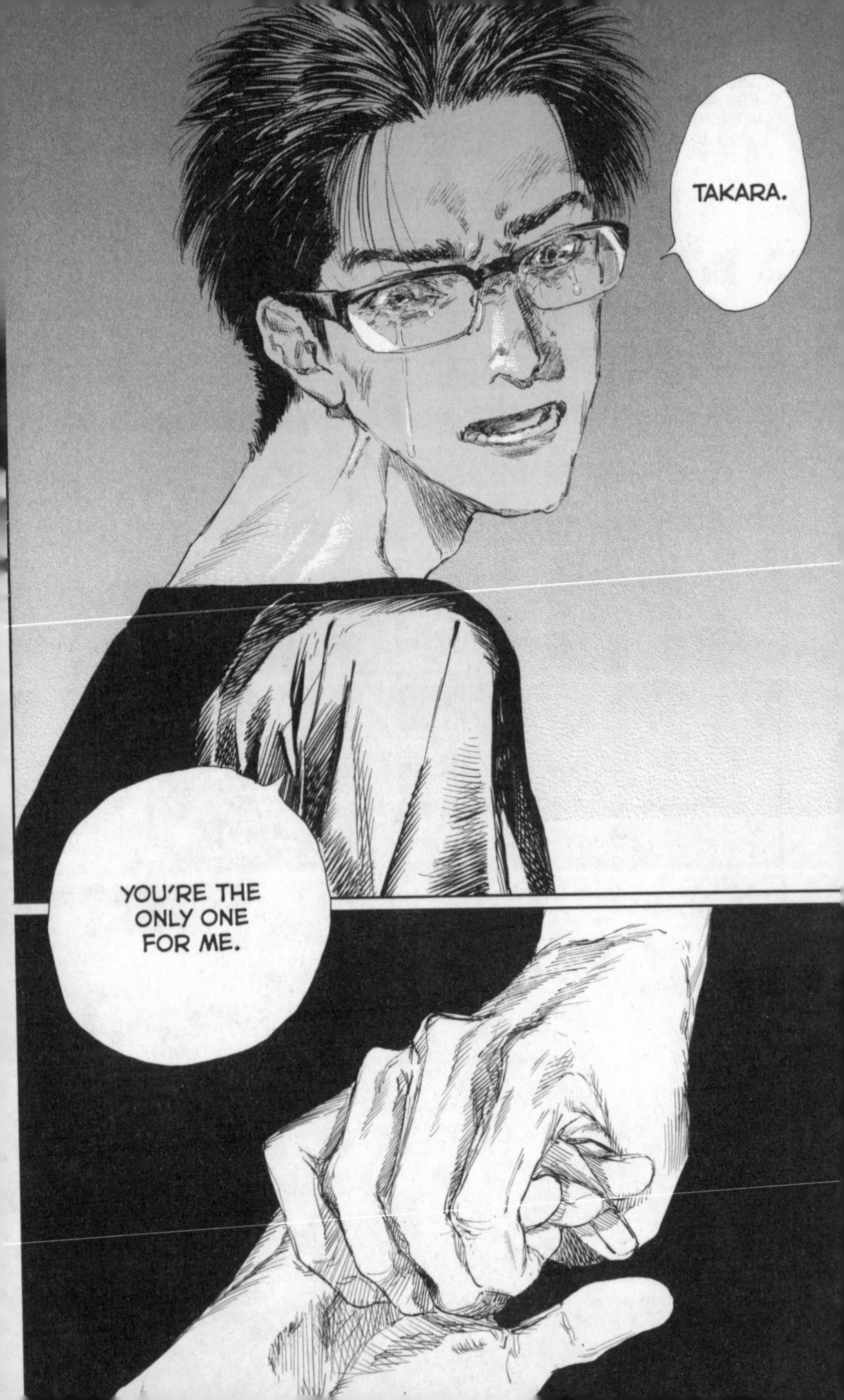
TAKARA.
YOU'RE THE ONLY ONE FOR ME.

DOUBLE

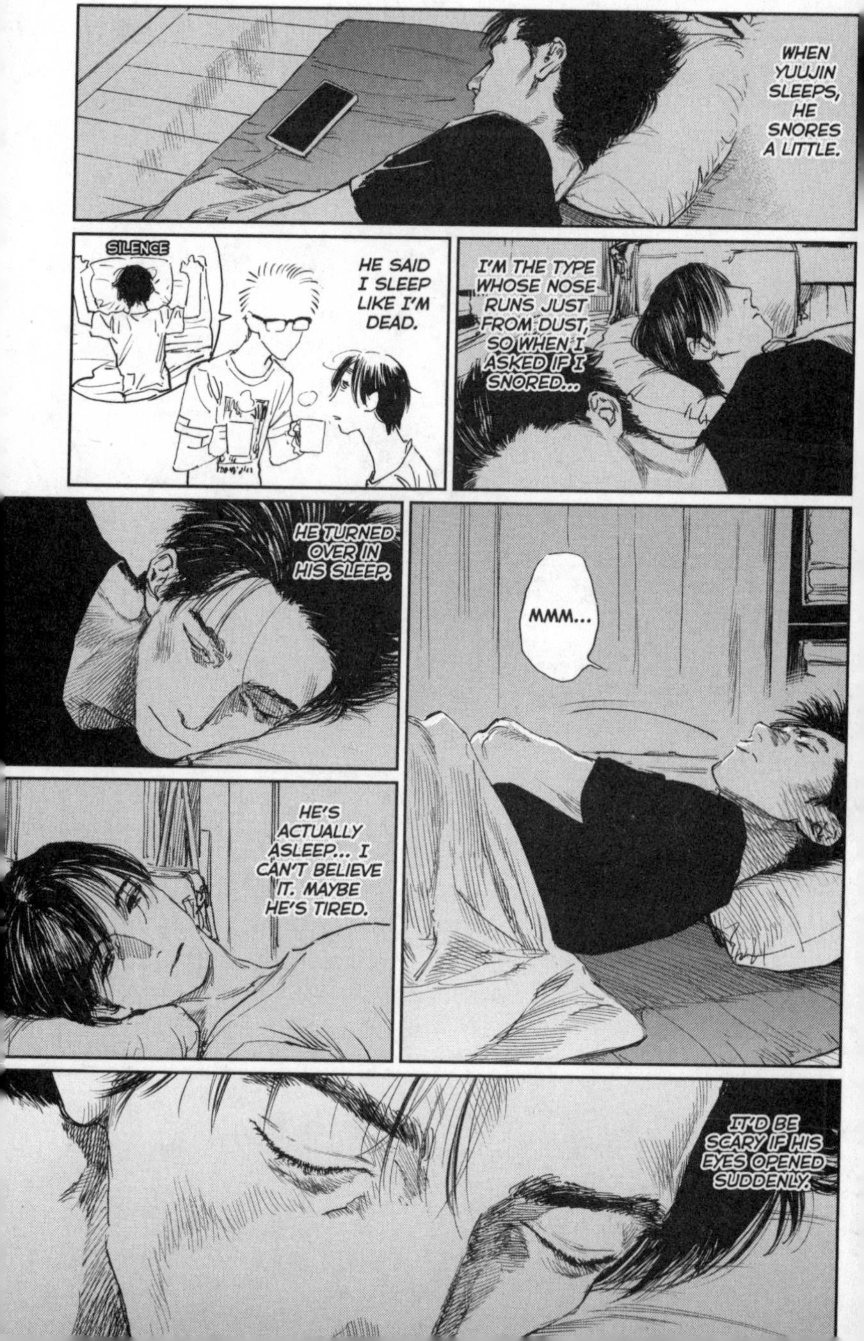

WHEN YUUJIN SLEEPS, HE SNORES A LITTLE.
I'M THE TYPE WHOSE NOSE RUNS JUST FROM DUST, SO WHEN I ASKED IF I SNORED...
HE SAID I SLEEP LIKE I'M DEAD.
SILENCE
MMM...
HE TURNED OVER IN HIS SLEEP.
HE'S ACTUALLY ASLEEP... I CAN'T BELIEVE IT. MAYBE HE'S TIRED.
IT'D BE SCARY IF HIS EYES OPENED SUDDENLY.

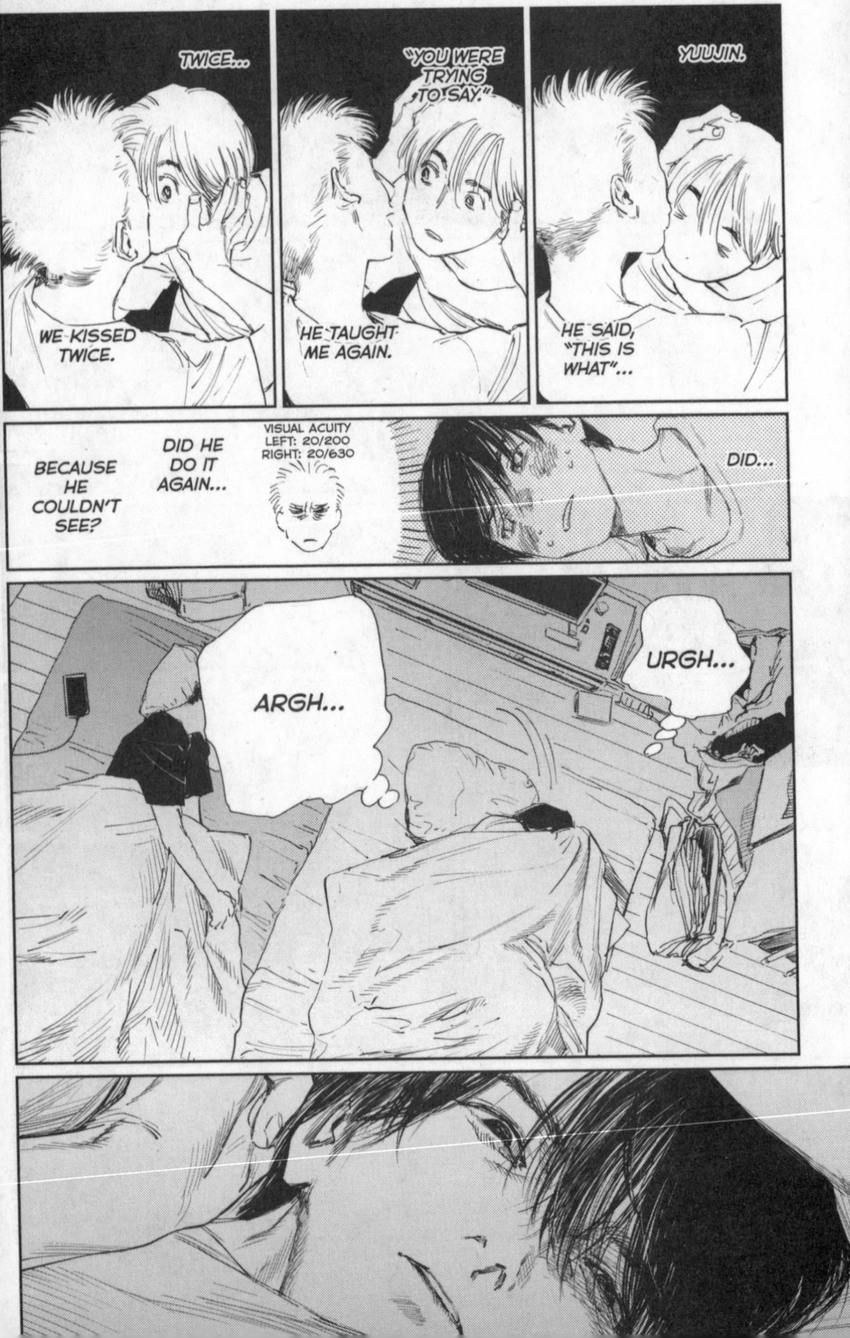
YUUJIN.
HE SAID, "THIS IS WHAT"...
"YOU WERE TRYING TO SAY."
HE TAUGHT ME AGAIN.
TWICE...
WE KISSED TWICE.
DID...
VISUAL ACUITY LEFT: 20/200 RIGHT: 20/630
DID HE DO IT AGAIN...
BECAUSE HE COULDN'T SEE?
URGH...
ARGH...

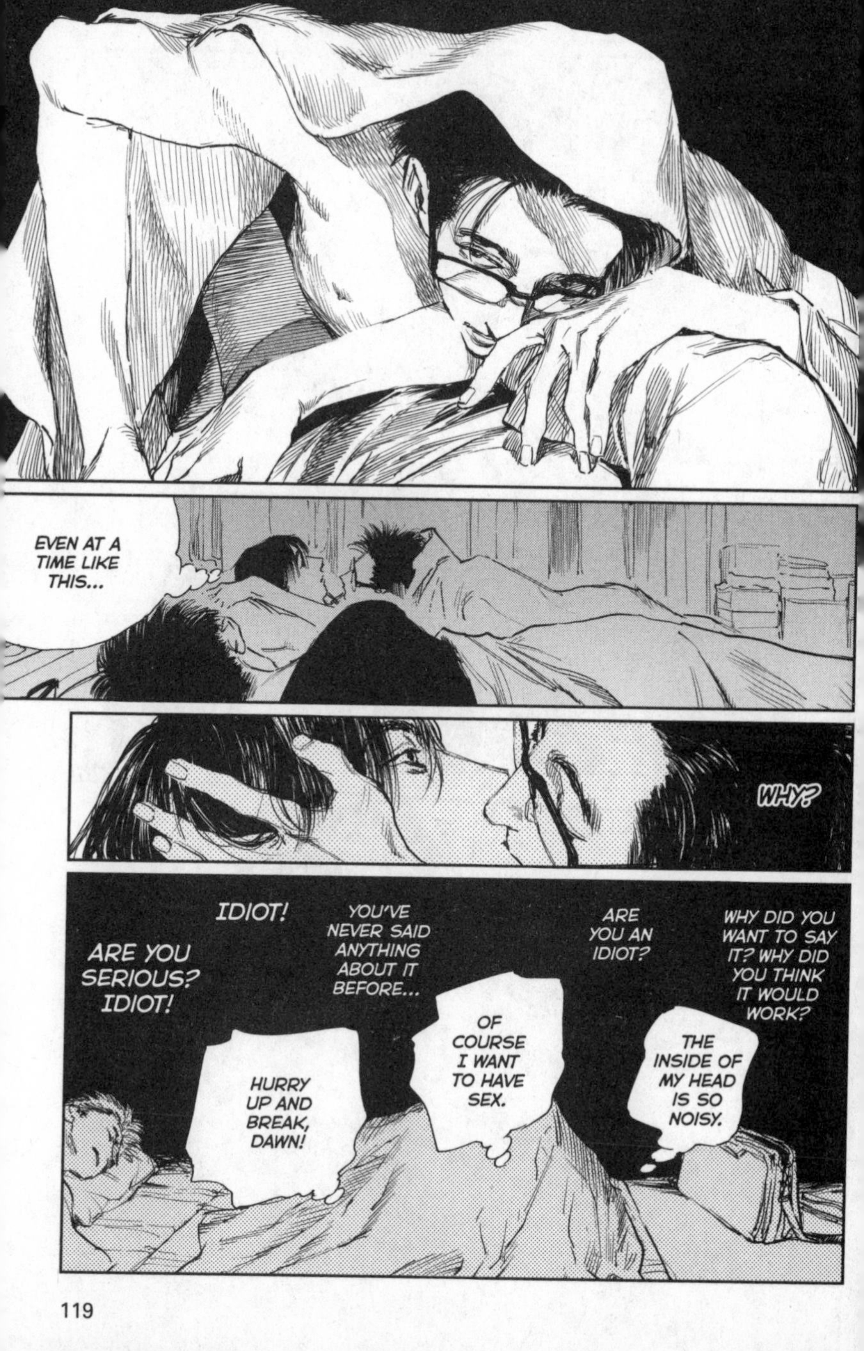
EVEN AT A TIME LIKE THIS...
WHY?
WHY DID YOU WANT TO SAY IT? WHY DID YOU THINK IT WOULD WORK?
ARE YOU AN IDIOT?
THE INSIDE OF MY HEAD IS SO NOISY.
YOU'VE NEVER SAID ANYTHING ABOUT IT BEFORE...
OF COURSE I WANT TO HAVE SEX.
IDIOT!
ARE YOU SERIOUS? IDIOT!
HURRY UP AND BREAK, DAWN!

CHAPTER 24 | CALIGULA

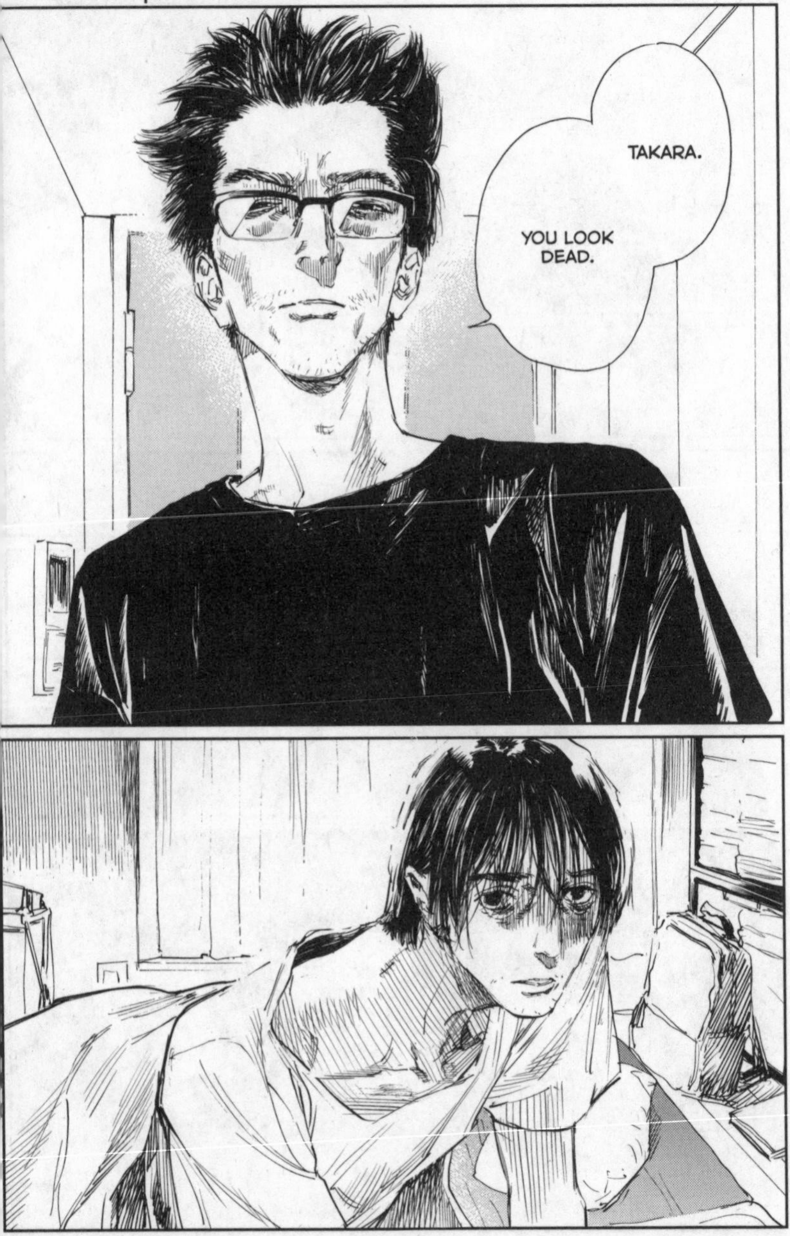
TAKARA.
YOU LOOK DEAD.

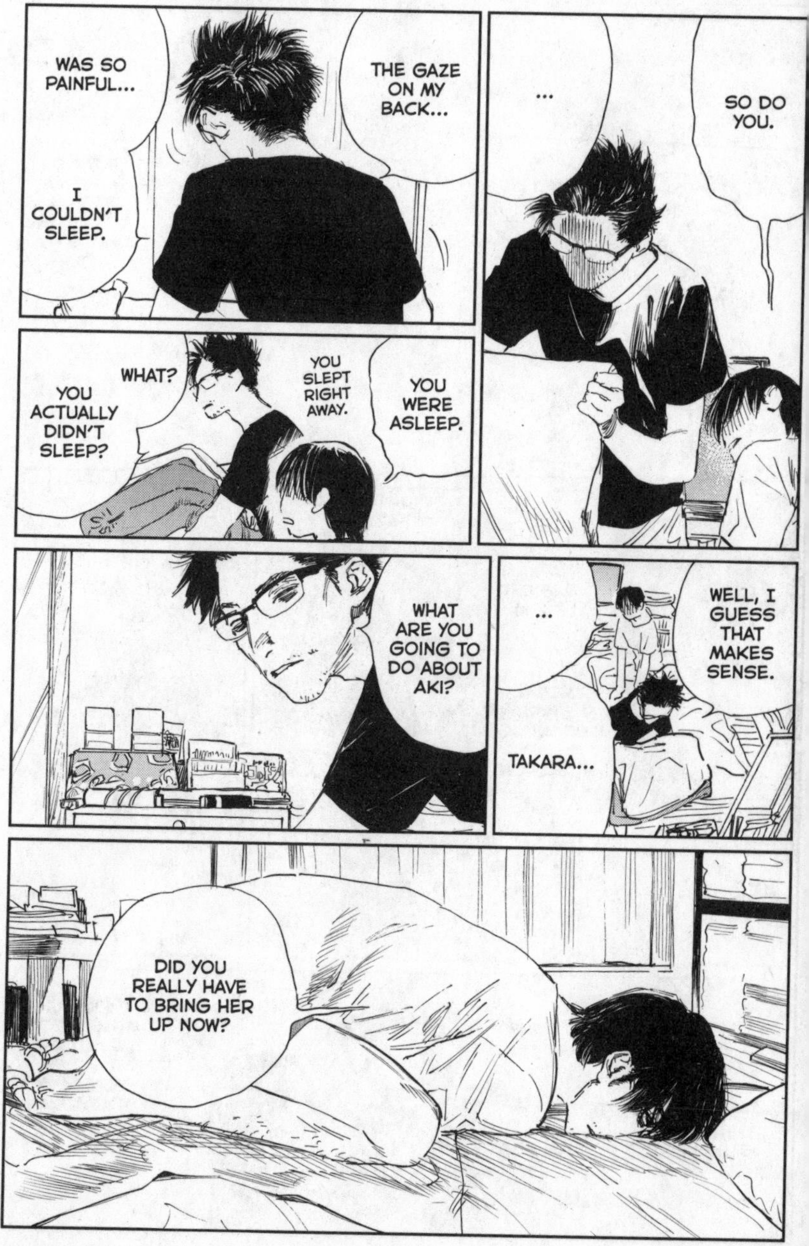
SO DO YOU.
...
THE GAZE ON MY BACK...
WAS SO PAINFUL...
I COULDN'T SLEEP.
YOU WERE ASLEEP.
YOU SLEPT RIGHT AWAY.
WHAT?
YOU ACTUALLY DIDN'T SLEEP?
WELL, I GUESS THAT MAKES SENSE.
...
TAKARA...
WHAT ARE YOU GOING TO DO ABOUT AKI?
DID YOU REALLY HAVE TO BRING HER UP NOW?

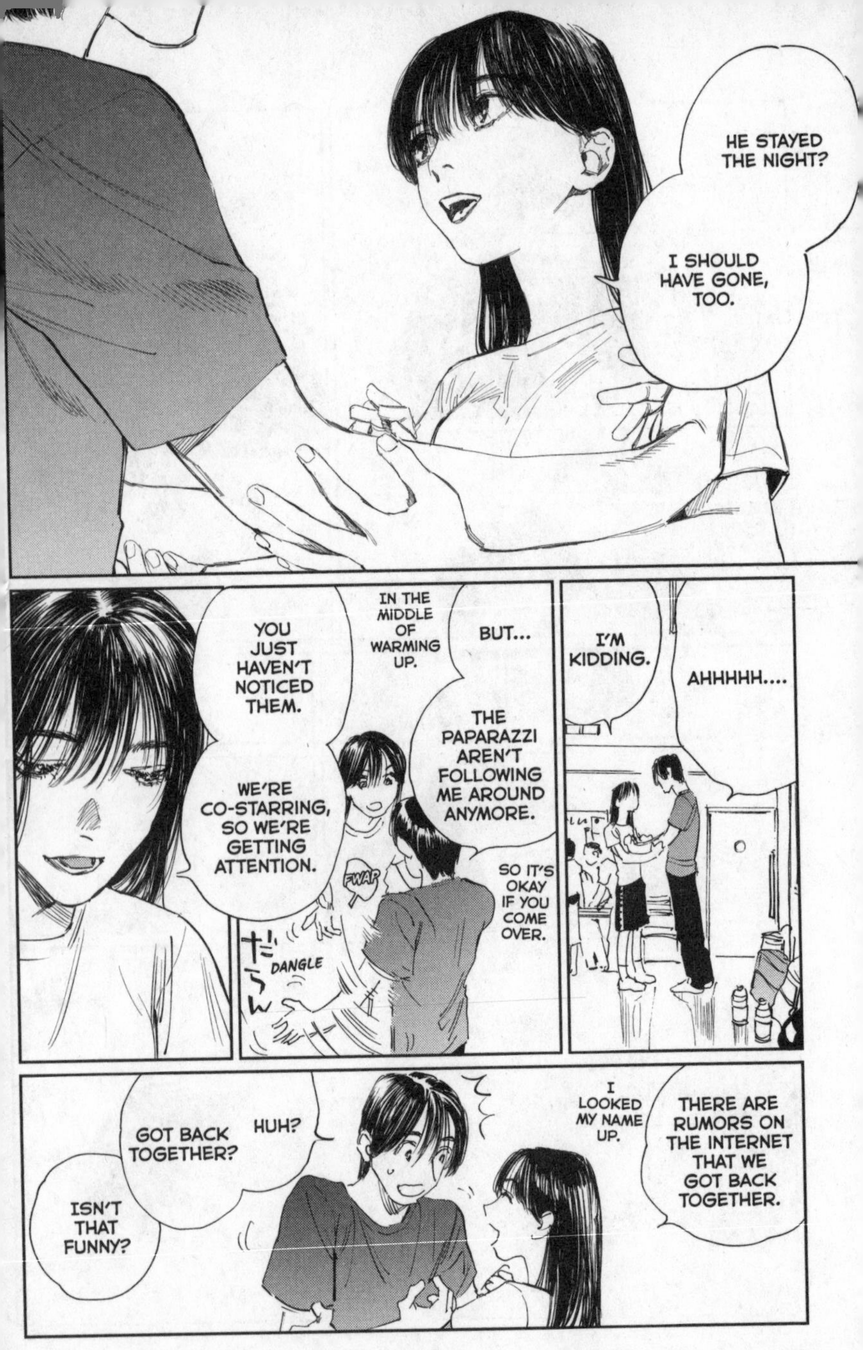
HE STAYED THE NIGHT?
I SHOULD HAVE GONE, TOO.
AHHHHH....
I'M KIDDING.
BUT...
IN THE MIDDLE OF WARMING UP.
THE PAPARAZZI AREN'T FOLLOWING ME AROUND ANYMORE.
SO IT'S OKAY IF YOU COME OVER.
FWAP
だらん
DANGLE
YOU JUST HAVEN'T NOTICED THEM.
WE'RE CO-STARRING, SO WE'RE GETTING ATTENTION.
THERE ARE RUMORS ON THE INTERNET THAT WE GOT BACK TOGETHER.
I LOOKED MY NAME UP.
HUH?
GOT BACK TOGETHER?
ISN'T THAT FUNNY?

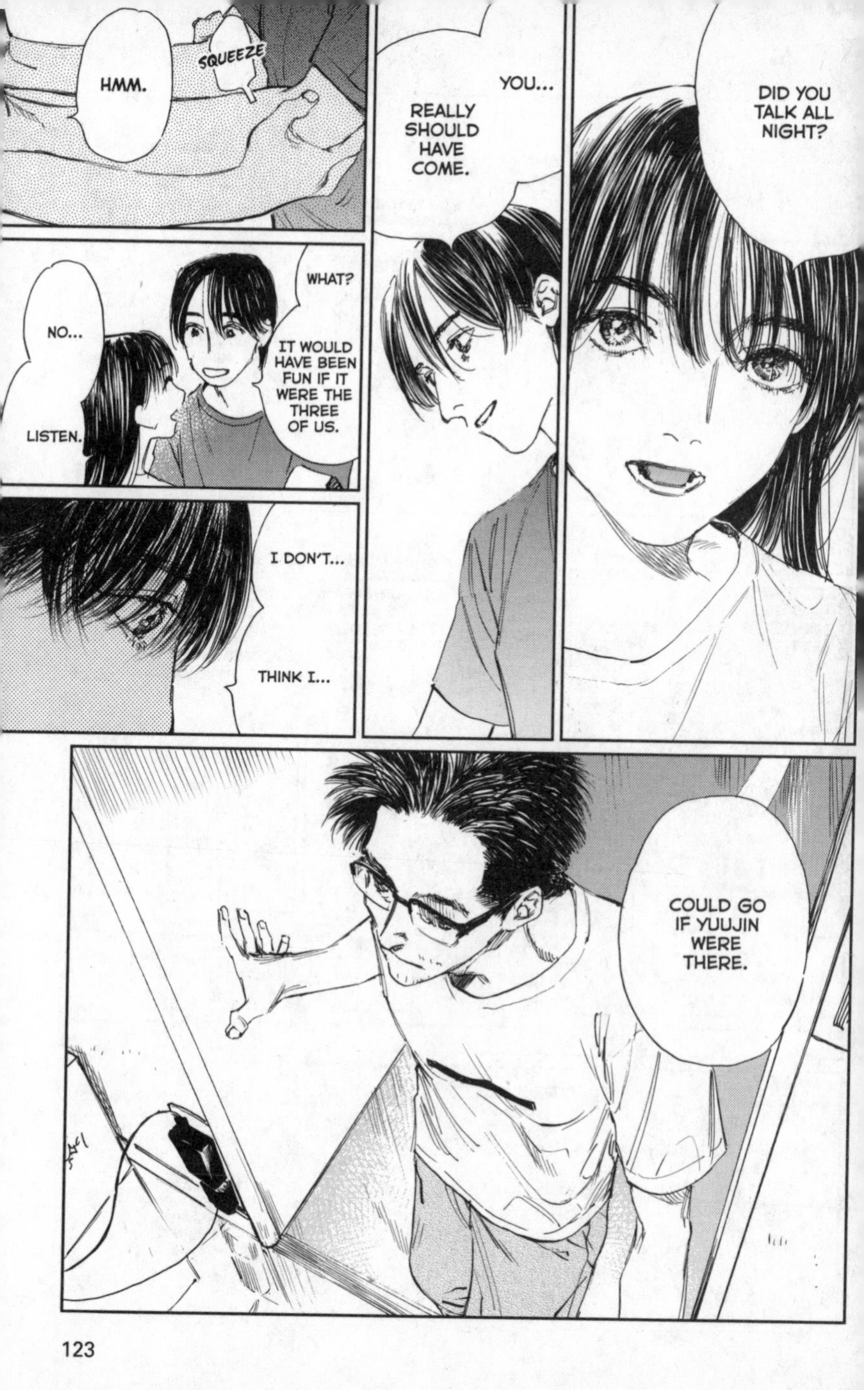
DID YOU TALK ALL NIGHT?
YOU...
REALLY SHOULD HAVE COME.
SQUEEZE
HMM.
WHAT?
IT WOULD HAVE BEEN FUN IF IT WERE THE THREE OF US.
NO...
LISTEN.
I DON'T...
THINK I...
COULD GO IF YUUJIN WERE THERE.

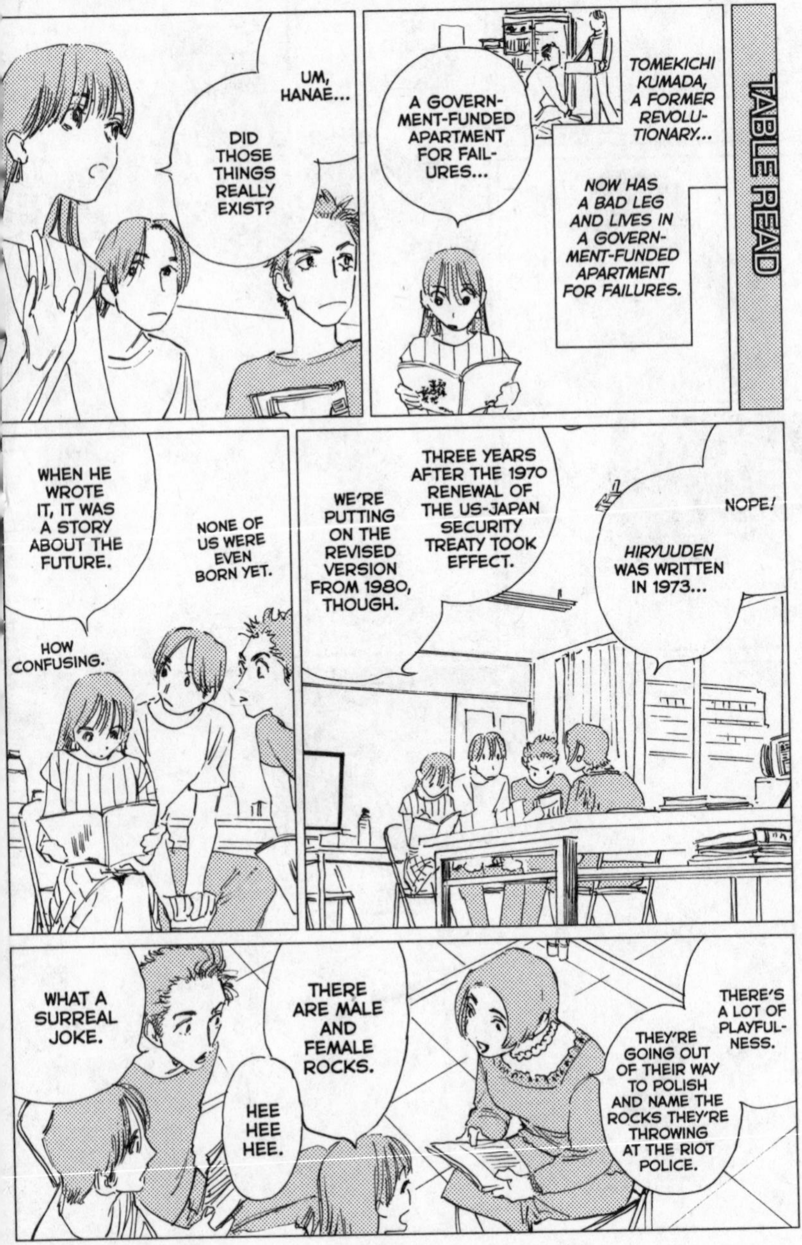
TABLE READ
TOMEKICHI KUMADA, A FORMER REVOLUTIONARY...
NOW HAS A BAD LEG AND LIVES IN A GOVERNMENT-FUNDED APARTMENT FOR FAILURES.
A GOVERNMENT-FUNDED APARTMENT FOR FAILURES...
UM, HANAE...
DID THOSE THINGS REALLY EXIST?
NOPE!
HIRYUUDEN WAS WRITTEN IN 1973...
THREE YEARS AFTER THE 1970 RENEWAL OF THE US-JAPAN SECURITY TREATY TOOK EFFECT.
WE'RE PUTTING ON THE REVISED VERSION FROM 1980, THOUGH.
NONE OF US WERE EVEN BORN YET.
WHEN HE WROTE IT, IT WAS A STORY ABOUT THE FUTURE.
HOW CONFUSING.
THERE'S A LOT OF PLAYFULNESS.
THEY'RE GOING OUT OF THEIR WAY TO POLISH AND NAME THE ROCKS THEY'RE THROWING AT THE RIOT POLICE.
THERE ARE MALE AND FEMALE ROCKS.
HEE HEE HEE.
WHAT A SURREAL JOKE.

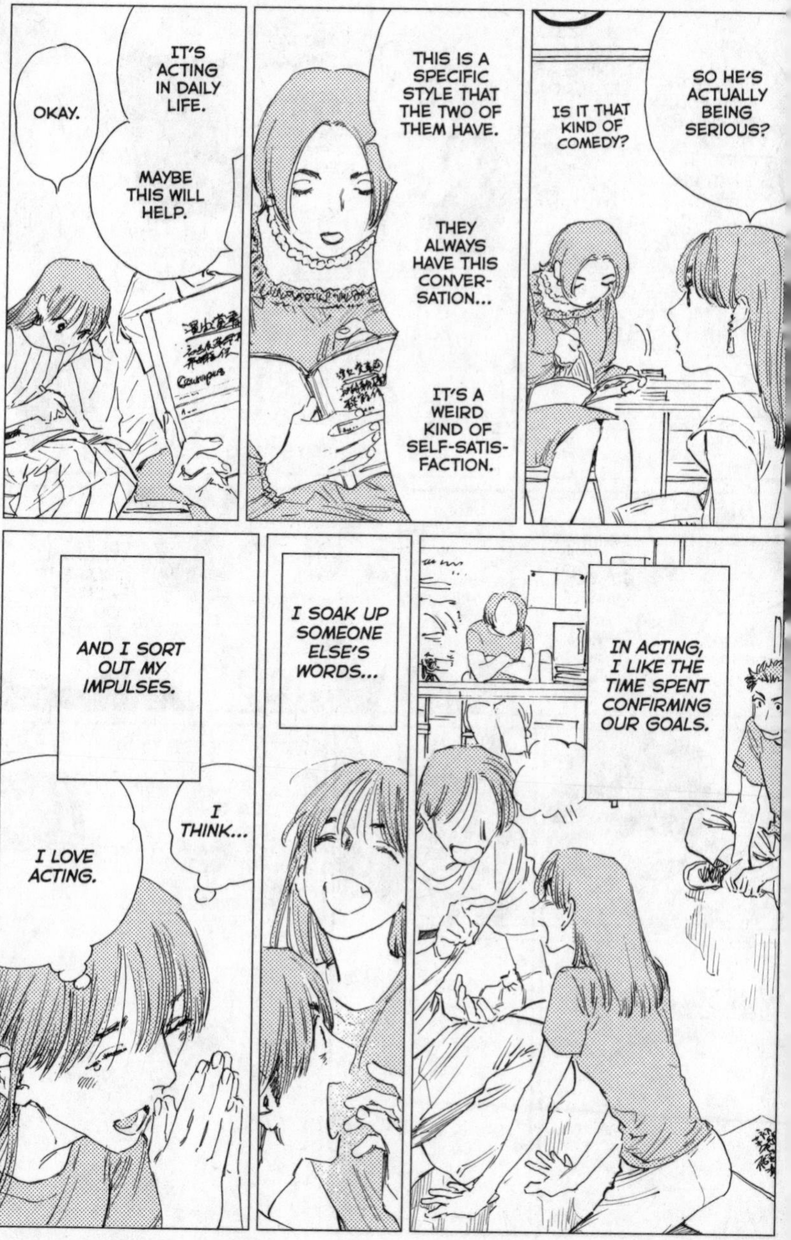
SO HE'S ACTUALLY BEING SERIOUS?
IS IT THAT KIND OF COMEDY?
THIS IS A SPECIFIC STYLE THAT THE TWO OF THEM HAVE.
THEY ALWAYS HAVE THIS CONVERSATION...
IT'S A WEIRD KIND OF SELF-SATISFACTION.
IT'S ACTING IN DAILY LIFE.
MAYBE THIS WILL HELP.
OKAY.
IN ACTING, I LIKE THE TIME SPENT CONFIRMING OUR GOALS.
I SOAK UP SOMEONE ELSE'S WORDS...
AND I SORT OUT MY IMPULSES.
I THINK...
I LOVE ACTING.

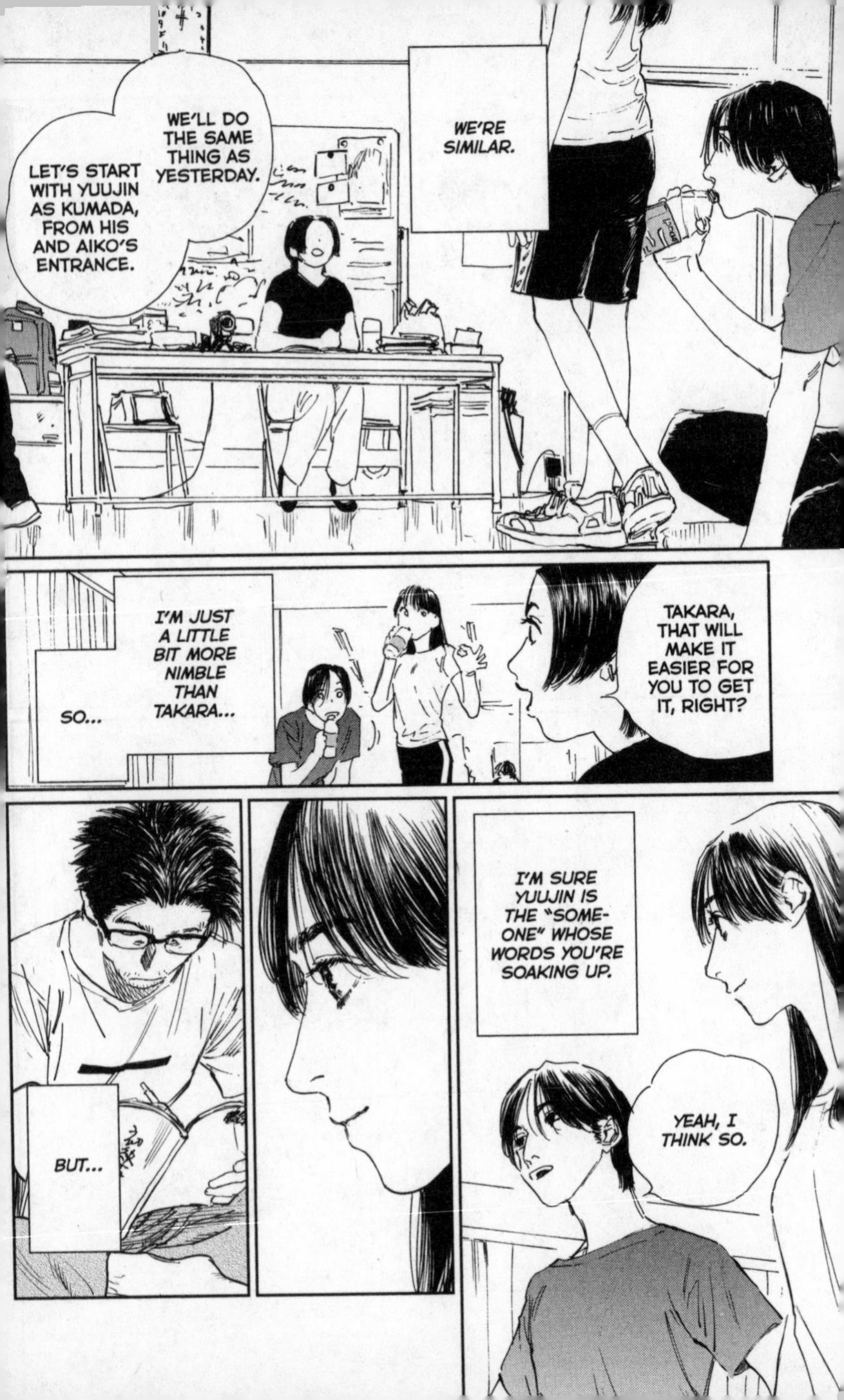
WE'RE SIMILAR.
WE'LL DO THE SAME THING AS YESTERDAY.
LET'S START WITH YUUJIN AS KUMADA, FROM HIS AND AIKO'S ENTRANCE.
TAKARA, THAT WILL MAKE IT EASIER FOR YOU TO GET IT, RIGHT?
I'M JUST A LITTLE BIT MORE NIMBLE THAN TAKARA...
SO...
I'M SURE YUUJIN IS THE "SOME-ONE" WHOSE WORDS YOU'RE SOAKING UP.
YEAH, I THINK SO.
BUT...

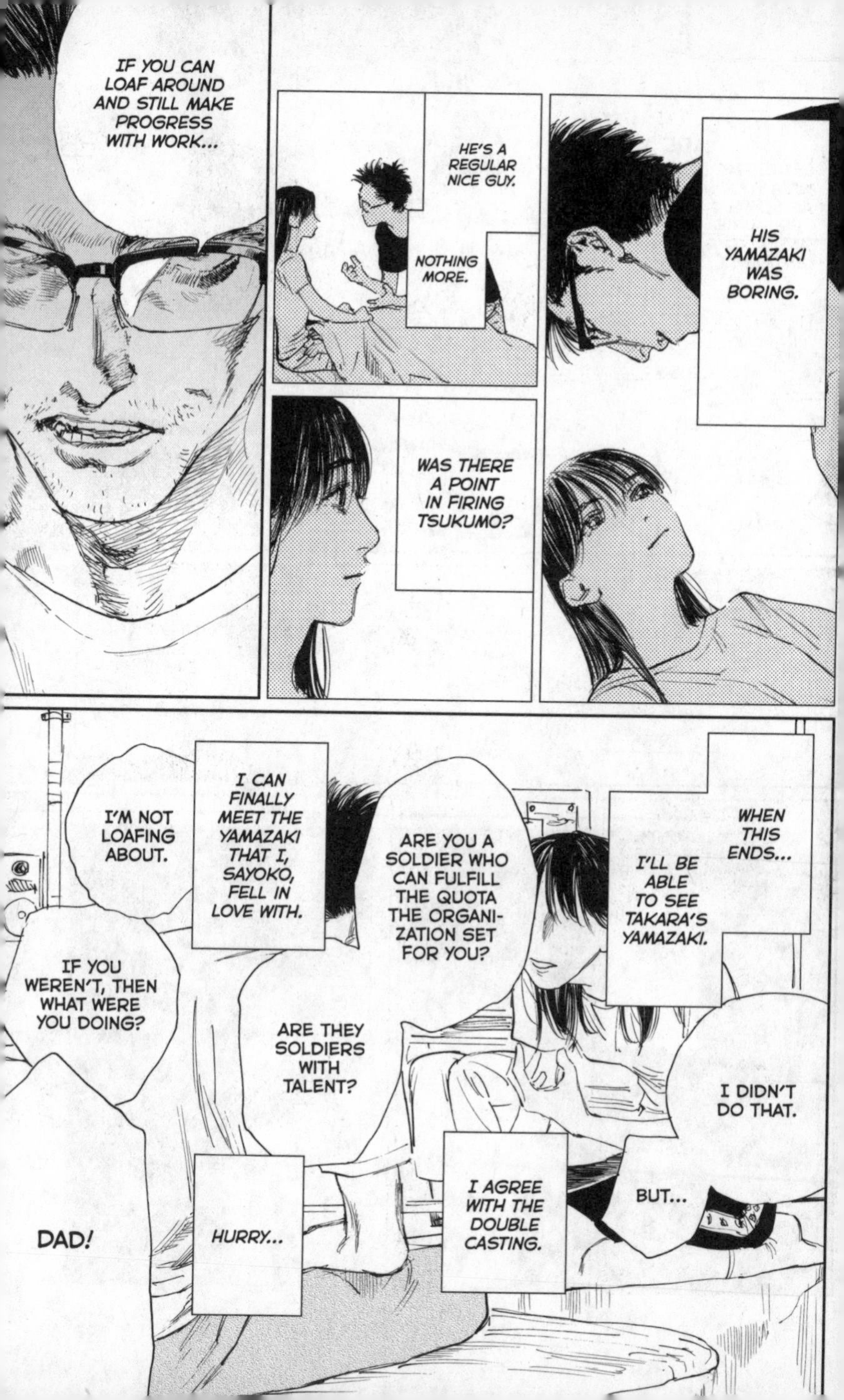
HIS YAMAZAKI WAS BORING.
HE'S A REGULAR NICE GUY.
NOTHING MORE.
WAS THERE A POINT IN FIRING TSUKUMO?
IF YOU CAN LOAF AROUND AND STILL MAKE PROGRESS WITH WORK...
WHEN THIS ENDS...
I'LL BE ABLE TO SEE TAKARA'S YAMAZAKI.
ARE YOU A SOLDIER WHO CAN FULFILL THE QUOTA THE ORGANI-ZATION SET FOR YOU?
I CAN FINALLY MEET THE YAMAZAKI THAT I, SAYOKO, FELL IN LOVE WITH.
I'M NOT LOAFING ABOUT.
I DIDN'T DO THAT.
IF YOU WEREN'T, THEN WHAT WERE YOU DOING?
ARE THEY SOLDIERS WITH TALENT?
BUT...
I AGREE WITH THE DOUBLE CASTING.
HURRY...
DAD!

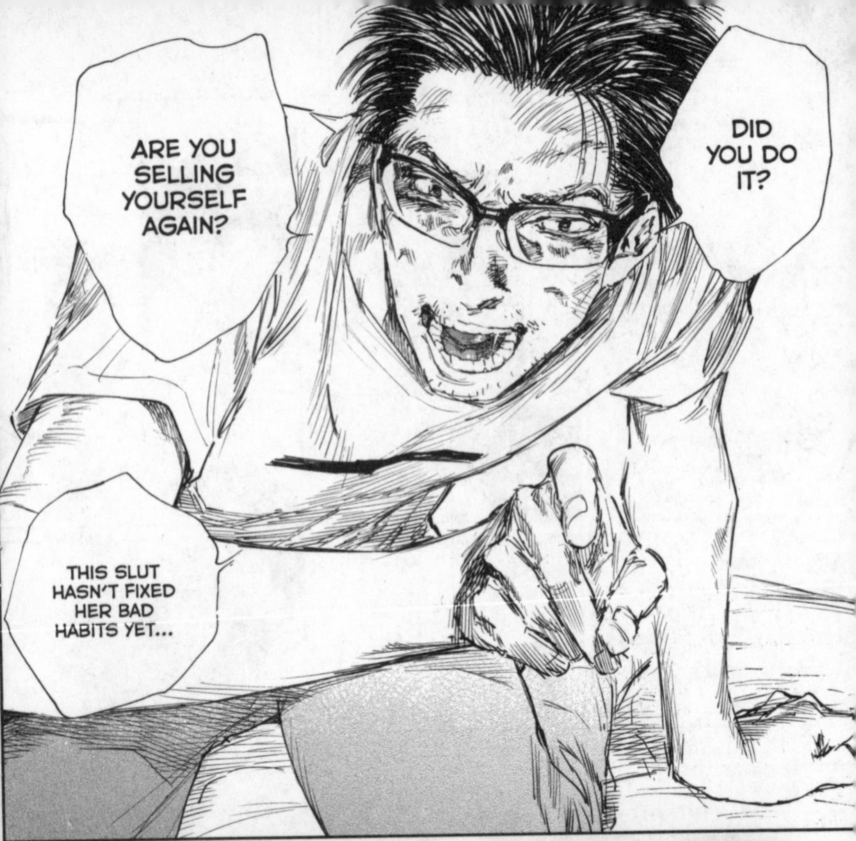
DID YOU DO IT?
ARE YOU SELLING YOURSELF AGAIN?
THIS SLUT HASN'T FIXED HER BAD HABITS YET...

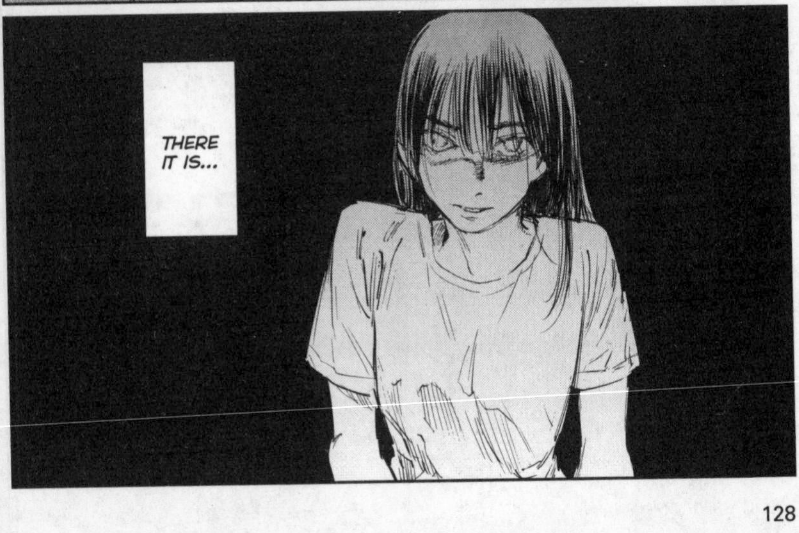
THERE IT IS...

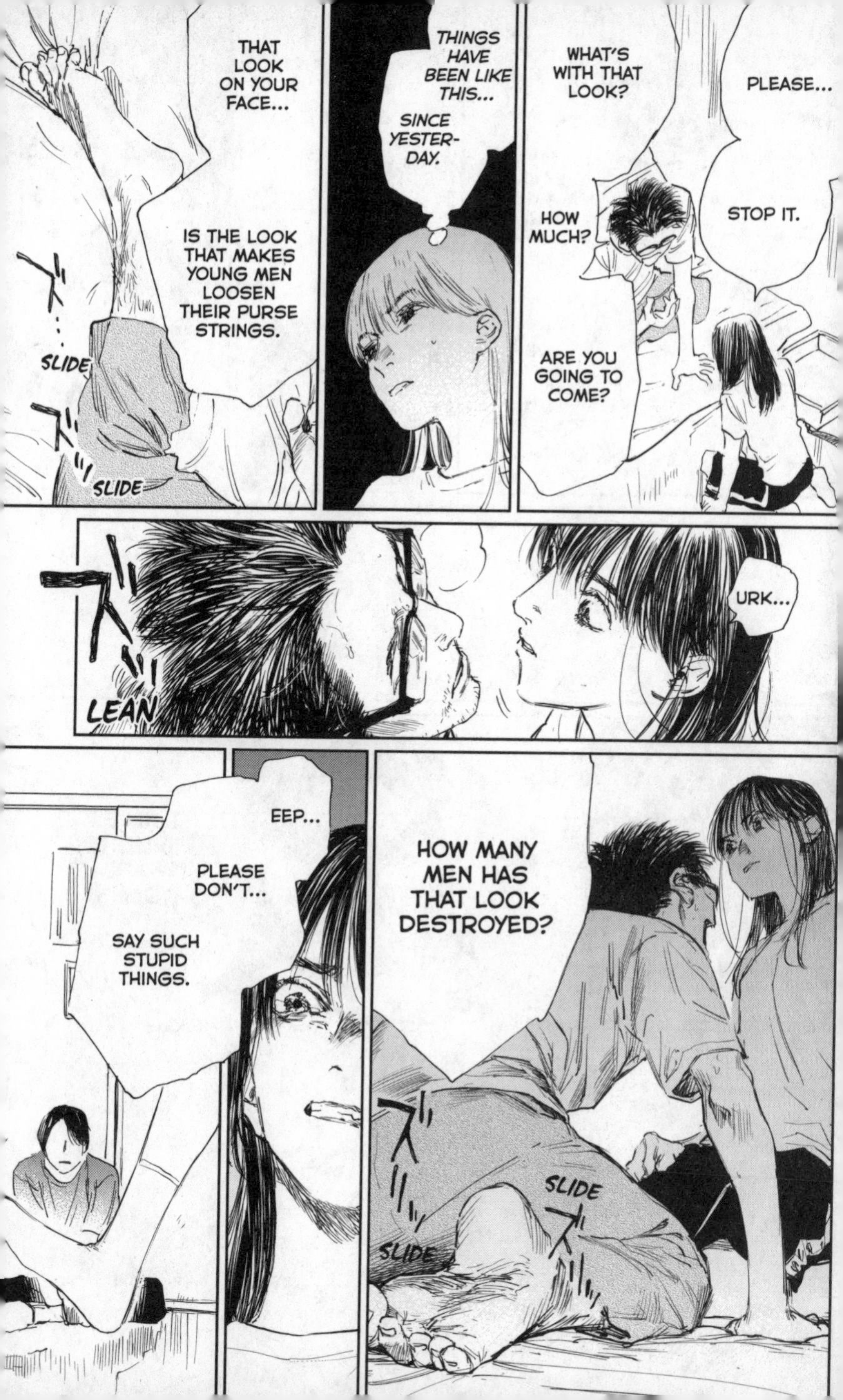
PLEASE...
STOP IT.
WHAT'S WITH THAT LOOK?
HOW MUCH?
ARE YOU GOING TO COME?
THINGS HAVE BEEN LIKE THIS...
SINCE YESTERDAY.
THAT LOOK ON YOUR FACE...
IS THE LOOK THAT MAKES YOUNG MEN LOOSEN THEIR PURSE STRINGS.
SLIDE
SLIDE
URK...
LEAN
HOW MANY MEN HAS THAT LOOK DESTROYED?
SLIDE
SLIDE
EEP...
PLEASE DON'T...
SAY SUCH STUPID THINGS.

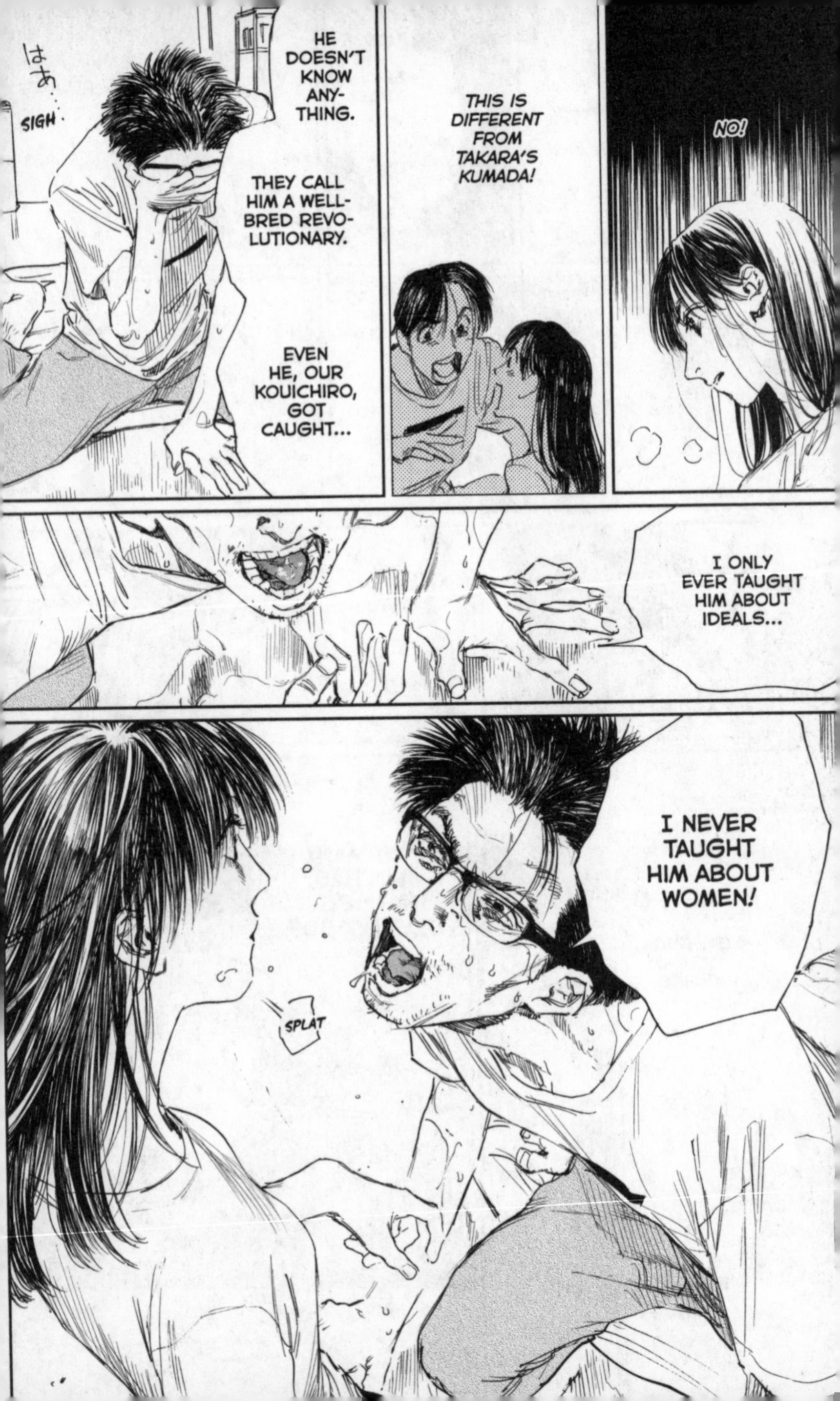
NO!
THIS IS DIFFERENT FROM TAKARA'S KUMADA!
HE DOESN'T KNOW ANYTHING.
はあ…
SIGH
THEY CALL HIM A WELL-BRED REVOLUTIONARY.
EVEN HE, OUR KOUICHIRO, GOT CAUGHT...
I ONLY EVER TAUGHT HIM ABOUT IDEALS...
I NEVER TAUGHT HIM ABOUT WOMEN!
SPLAT

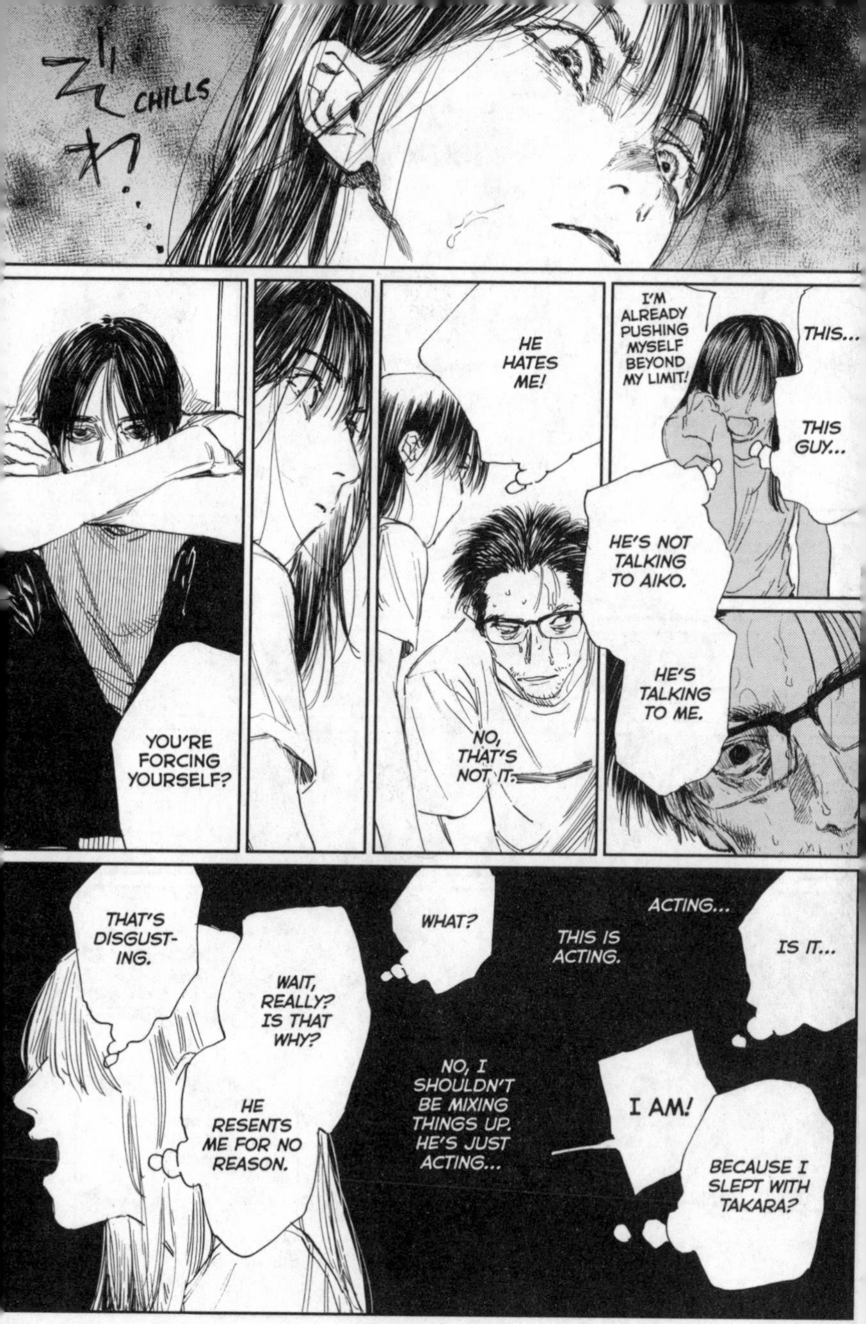

CHILLS
THIS...
THIS GUY...
I'M ALREADY PUSHING MYSELF BEYOND MY LIMIT!
HE'S NOT TALKING TO AIKO.
HE'S TALKING TO ME.
HE HATES ME!
NO, THAT'S NOT IT.
YOU'RE FORCING YOURSELF?
IS IT...
ACTING...
I AM!
BECAUSE I SLEPT WITH TAKARA?
THIS IS ACTING.
WHAT?
NO, I SHOULDN'T BE MIXING THINGS UP. HE'S JUST ACTING...
WAIT, REALLY? IS THAT WHY?
HE RESENTS ME FOR NO REASON.
THAT'S DISGUST-ING.

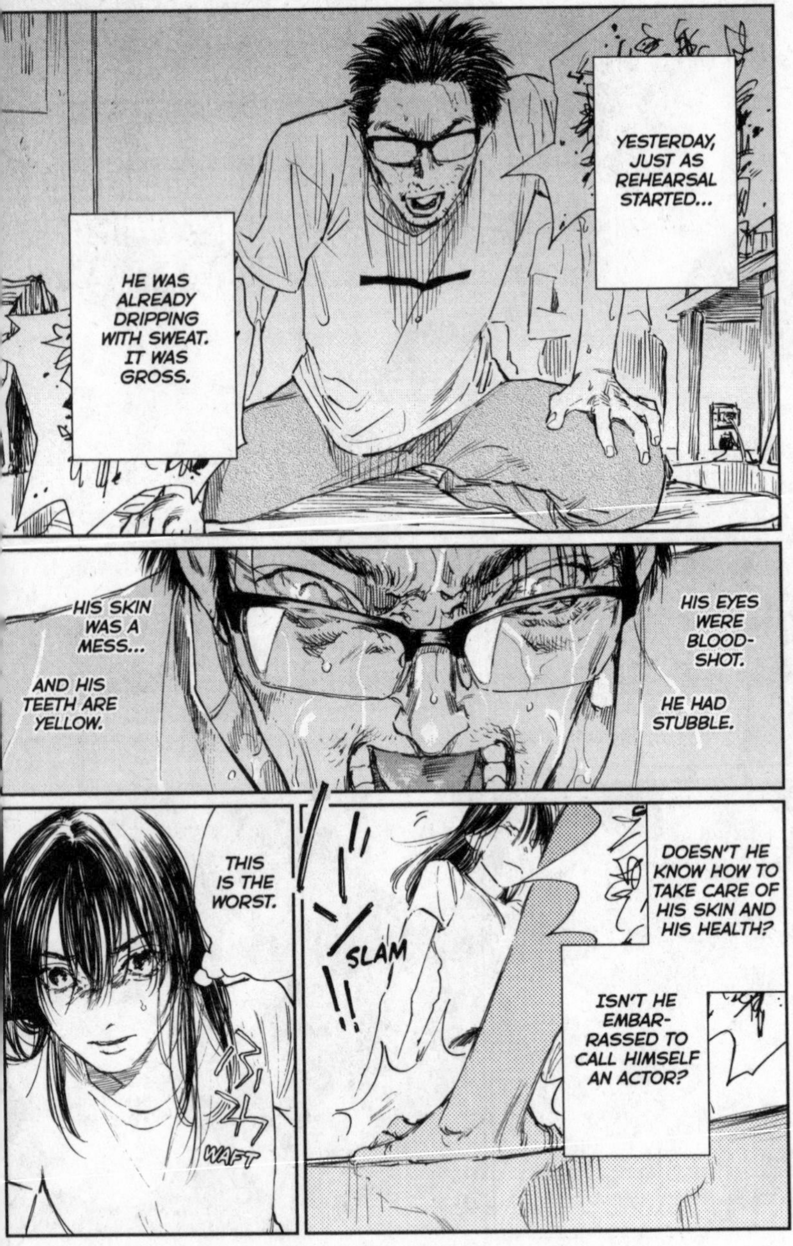
YESTERDAY, JUST AS REHEARSAL STARTED...
HE WAS ALREADY DRIPPING WITH SWEAT. IT WAS GROSS.
HIS EYES WERE BLOOD-SHOT.
HE HAD STUBBLE.
HIS SKIN WAS A MESS...
AND HIS TEETH ARE YELLOW.
DOESN'T HE KNOW HOW TO TAKE CARE OF HIS SKIN AND HIS HEALTH?
SLAM
ISN'T HE EMBAR-RASSED TO CALL HIMSELF AN ACTOR?
THIS IS THE WORST.
WAFT

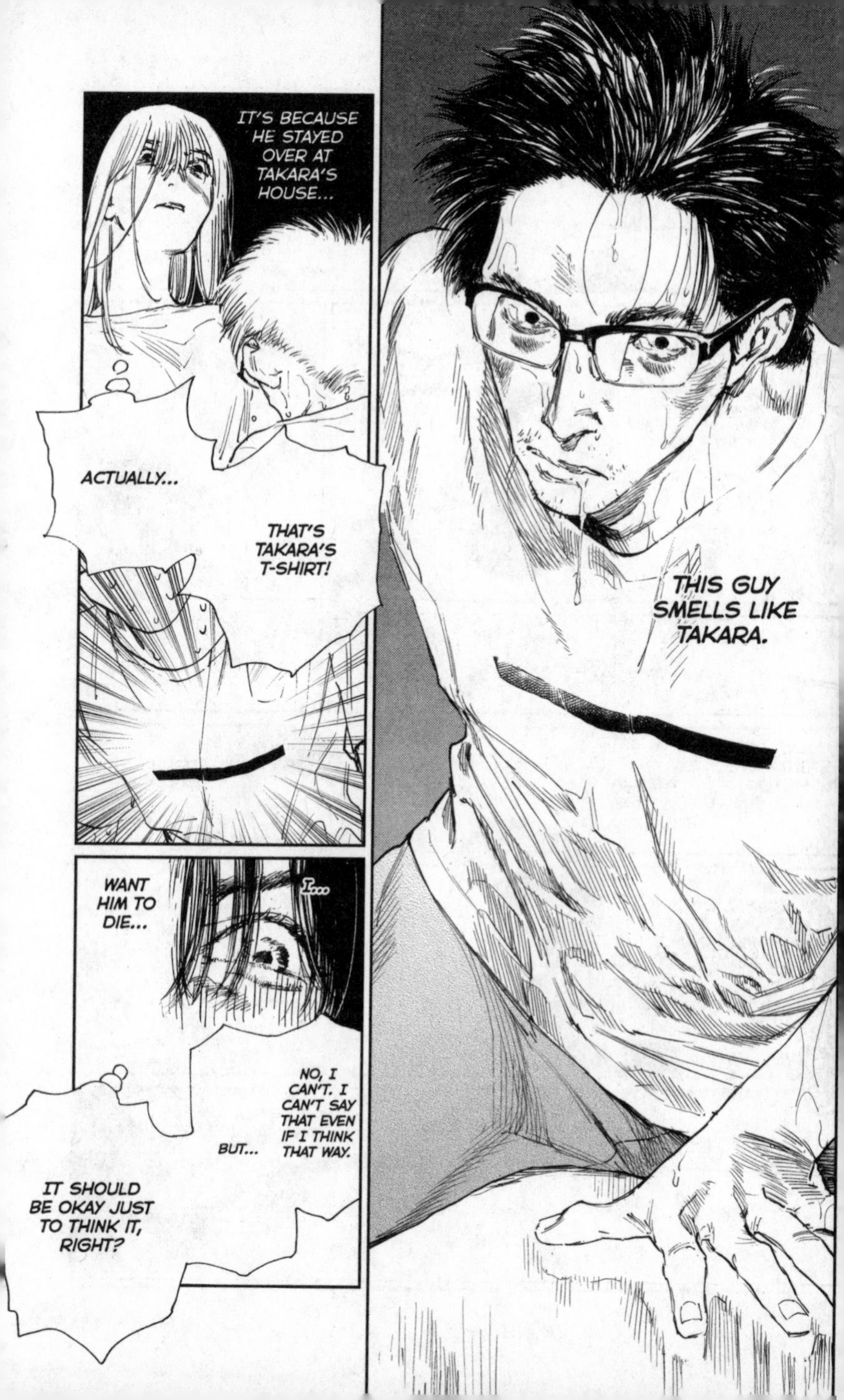
THIS GUY SMELLS LIKE TAKARA.
IT'S BECAUSE HE STAYED OVER AT TAKARA'S HOUSE...
ACTUALLY...
THAT'S TAKARA'S T-SHIRT!
I...
WANT HIM TO DIE...
NO, I CAN'T. I CAN'T SAY THAT EVEN IF I THINK THAT WAY.
BUT...
IT SHOULD BE OKAY JUST TO THINK IT, RIGHT?

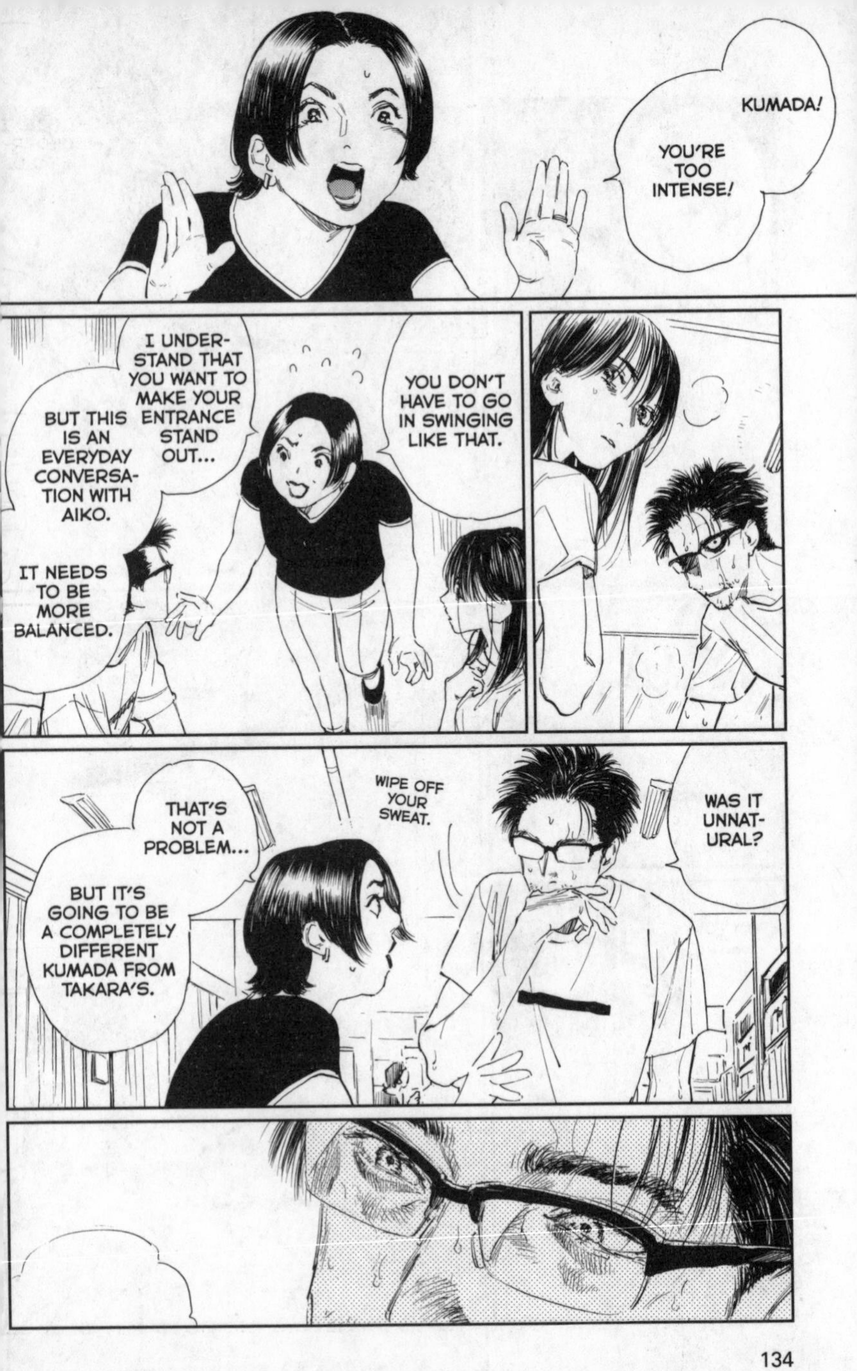
KUMADA!
YOU'RE TOO INTENSE!
YOU DON'T HAVE TO GO IN SWINGING LIKE THAT.
I UNDERSTAND THAT YOU WANT TO MAKE YOUR ENTRANCE STAND OUT...
BUT THIS IS AN EVERYDAY CONVERSATION WITH AIKO.
IT NEEDS TO BE MORE BALANCED.
WAS IT UNNATURAL?
WIPE OFF YOUR SWEAT.
THAT'S NOT A PROBLEM...
BUT IT'S GOING TO BE A COMPLETELY DIFFERENT KUMADA FROM TAKARA'S.

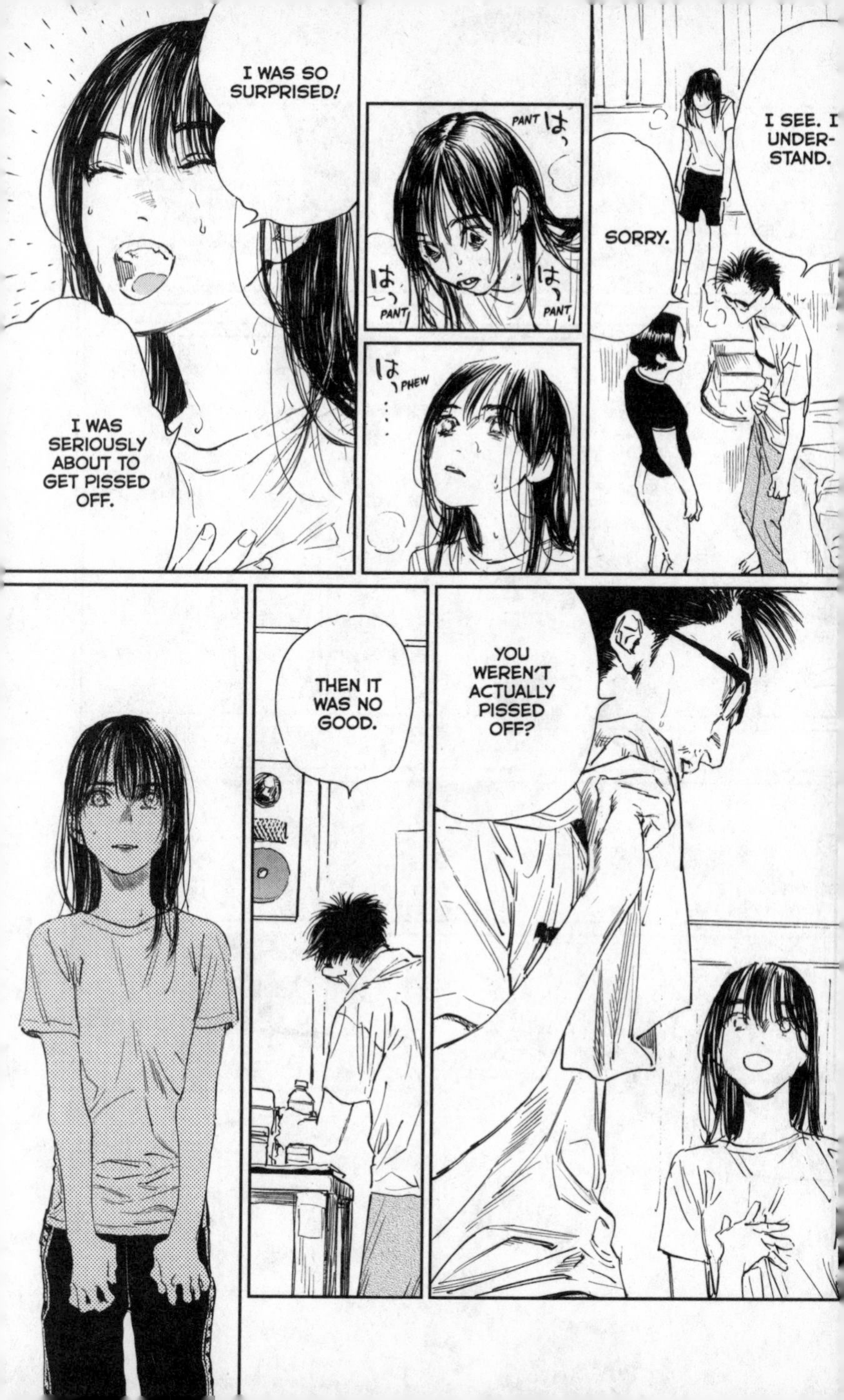
I SEE. I UNDER-STAND.
SORRY.
はっ PANT
はっ PANT
はっ PANT
はっ PHEW
...
I WAS SO SURPRISED!
I WAS SERIOUSLY ABOUT TO GET PISSED OFF.
YOU WEREN'T ACTUALLY PISSED OFF?
THEN IT WAS NO GOOD.

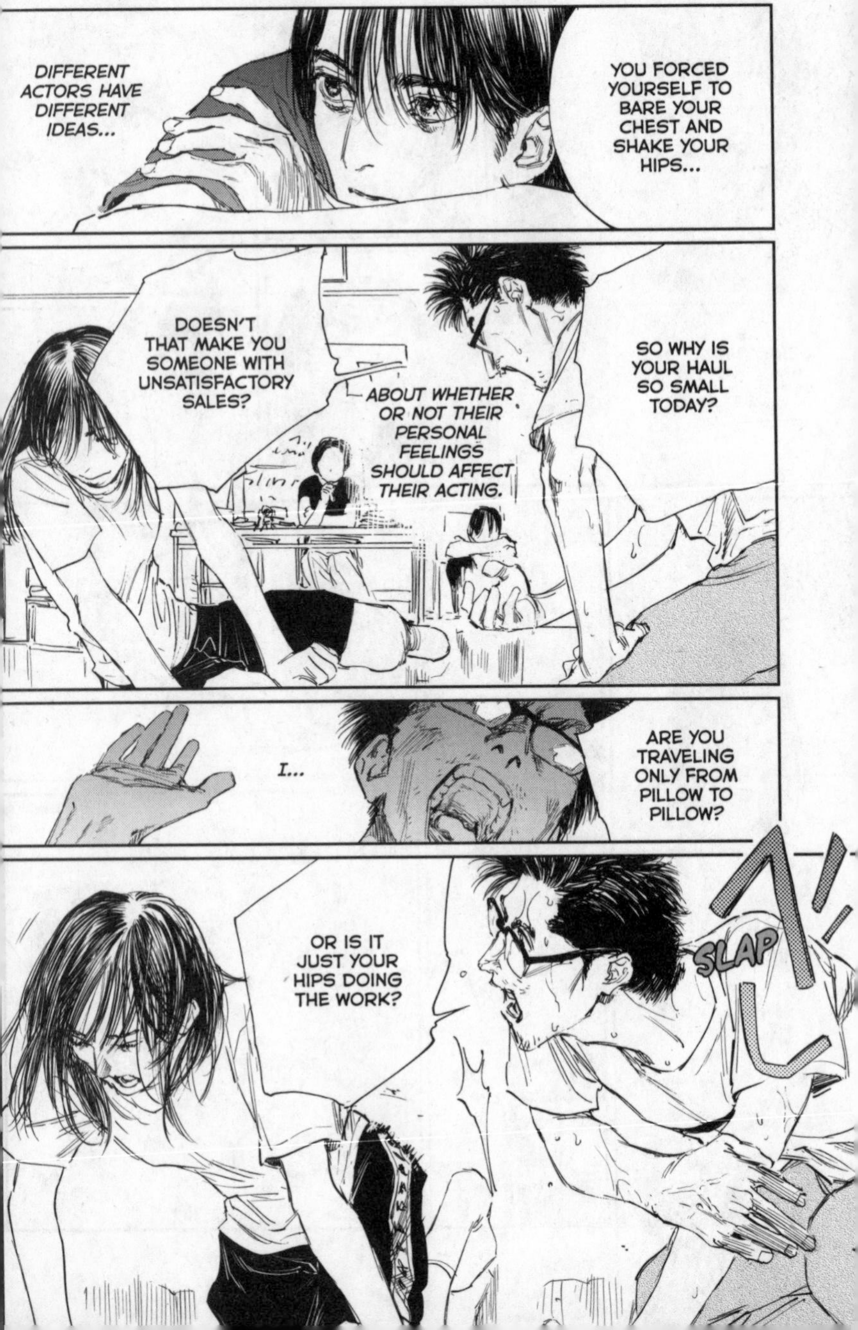
YOU FORCED YOURSELF TO BARE YOUR CHEST AND SHAKE YOUR HIPS...
DIFFERENT ACTORS HAVE DIFFERENT IDEAS...
SO WHY IS YOUR HAUL SO SMALL TODAY?
ABOUT WHETHER OR NOT THEIR PERSONAL FEELINGS SHOULD AFFECT THEIR ACTING.
DOESN'T THAT MAKE YOU SOMEONE WITH UNSATISFACTORY SALES?
ARE YOU TRAVELING ONLY FROM PILLOW TO PILLOW?
I...
SLAP
OR IS IT JUST YOUR HIPS DOING THE WORK?

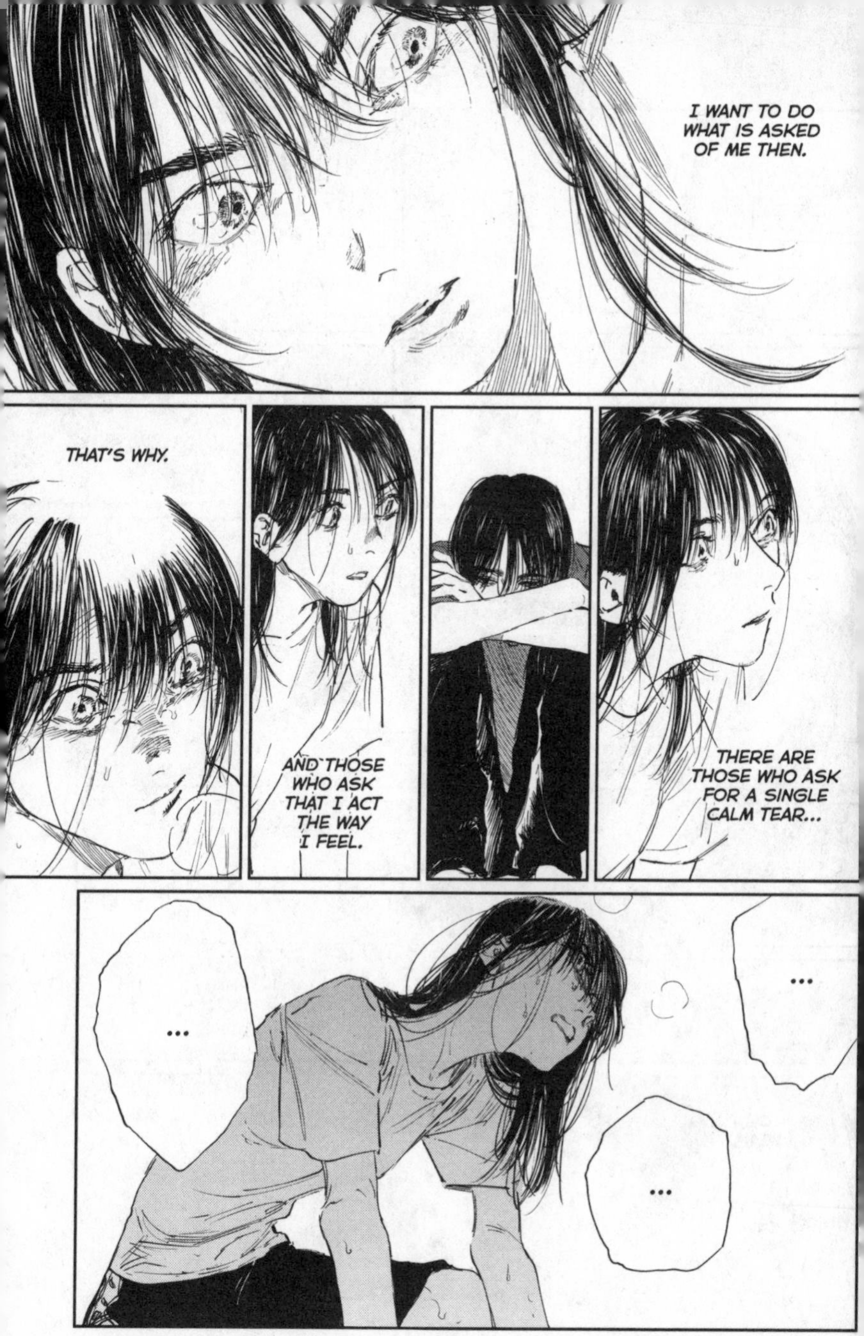

I WANT TO DO WHAT IS ASKED OF ME THEN.
THERE ARE THOSE WHO ASK FOR A SINGLE CALM TEAR...
AND THOSE WHO ASK THAT I ACT THE WAY I FEEL.
THAT'S WHY.
...
...
...

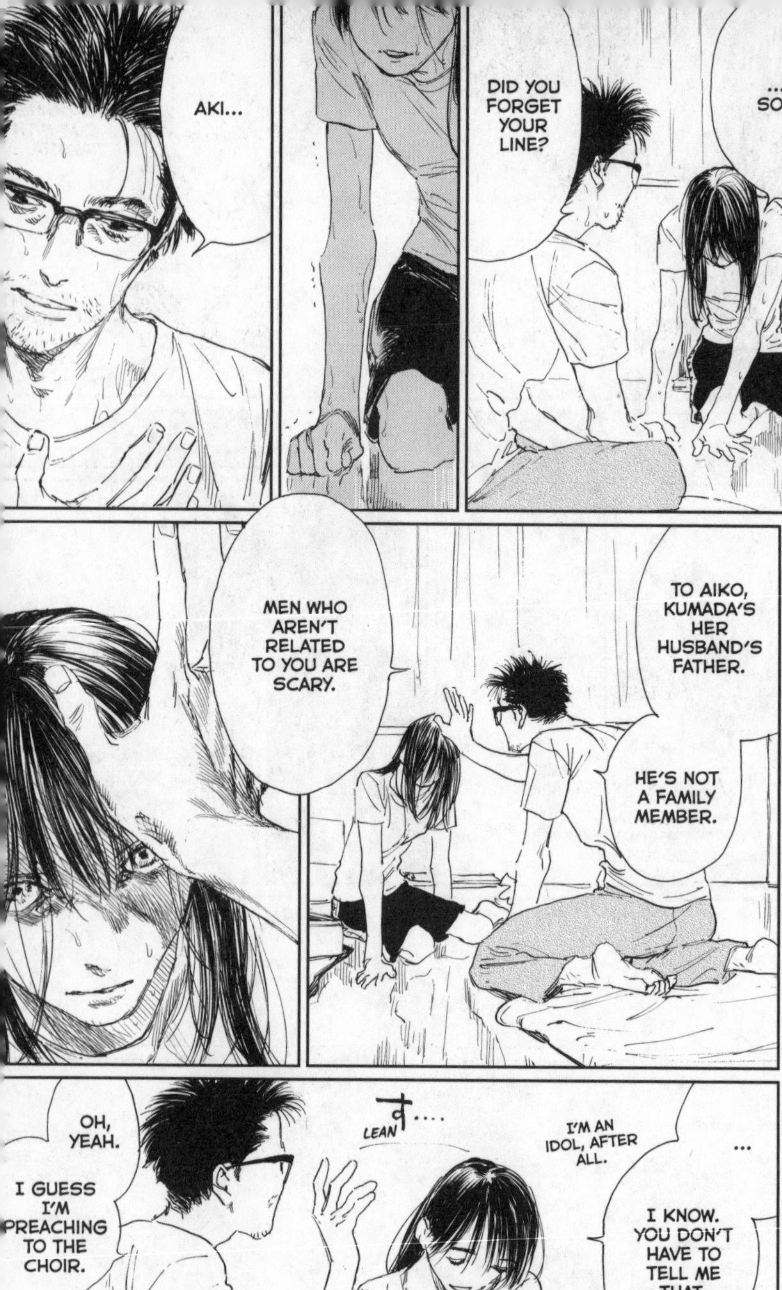

...I'M SORRY.
DID YOU FORGET YOUR LINE?
AKI...
TO AIKO, KUMADA'S HER HUSBAND'S FATHER.
HE'S NOT A FAMILY MEMBER.
MEN WHO AREN'T RELATED TO YOU ARE SCARY.
...
I KNOW. YOU DON'T HAVE TO TELL ME THAT.
I'M AN IDOL, AFTER ALL.
す....
LEAN
OH, YEAH.
I GUESS I'M PREACHING TO THE CHOIR.

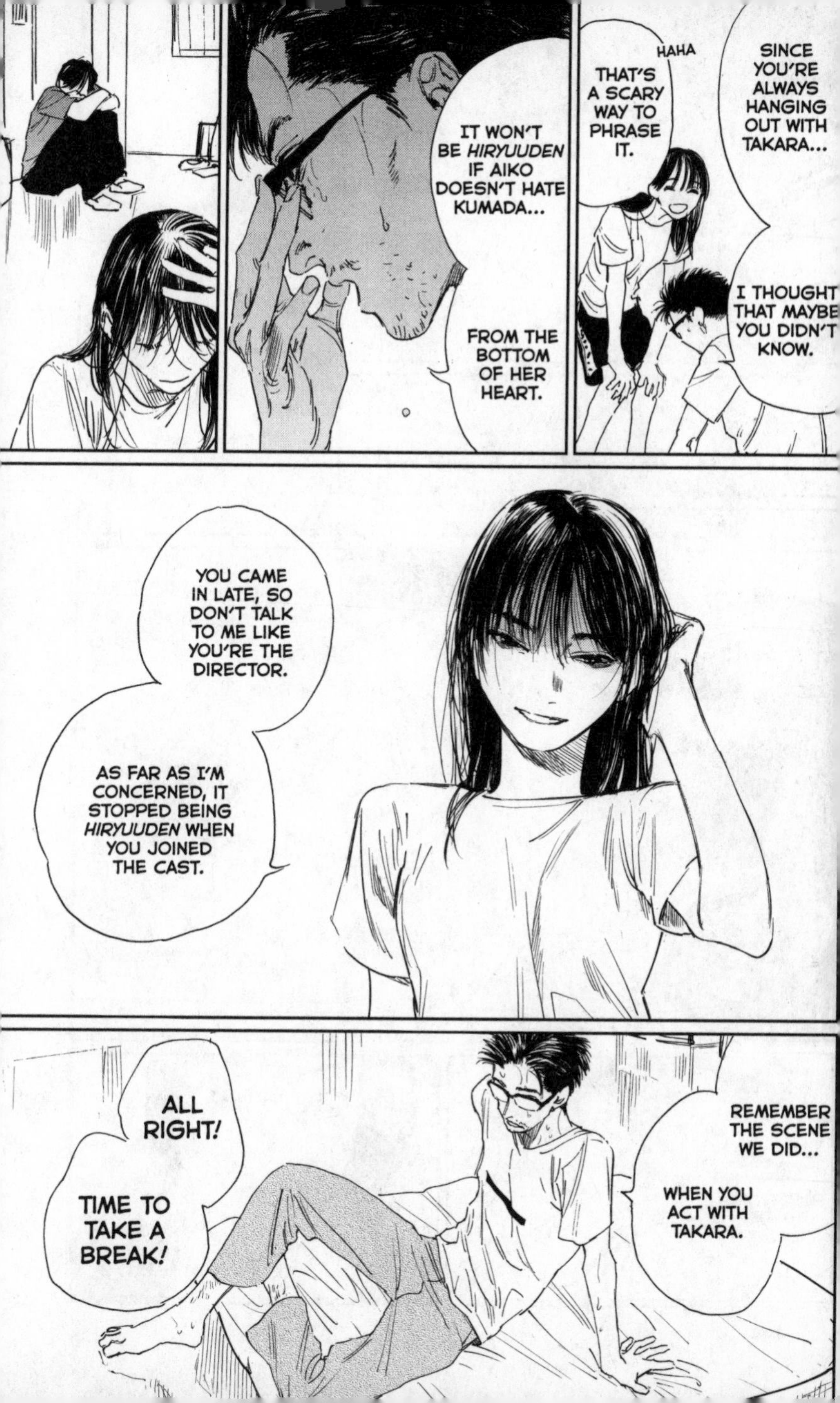
SINCE YOU'RE ALWAYS HANGING OUT WITH TAKARA...
HAHA
THAT'S A SCARY WAY TO PHRASE IT.
I THOUGHT THAT MAYBE YOU DIDN'T KNOW.
IT WON'T BE *HIRYUUDEN* IF AIKO DOESN'T HATE KUMADA...
FROM THE BOTTOM OF HER HEART.
YOU CAME IN LATE, SO DON'T TALK TO ME LIKE YOU'RE THE DIRECTOR.
AS FAR AS I'M CONCERNED, IT STOPPED BEING *HIRYUUDEN* WHEN YOU JOINED THE CAST.
REMEMBER THE SCENE WE DID...
WHEN YOU ACT WITH TAKARA.
ALL RIGHT!
TIME TO TAKE A BREAK!

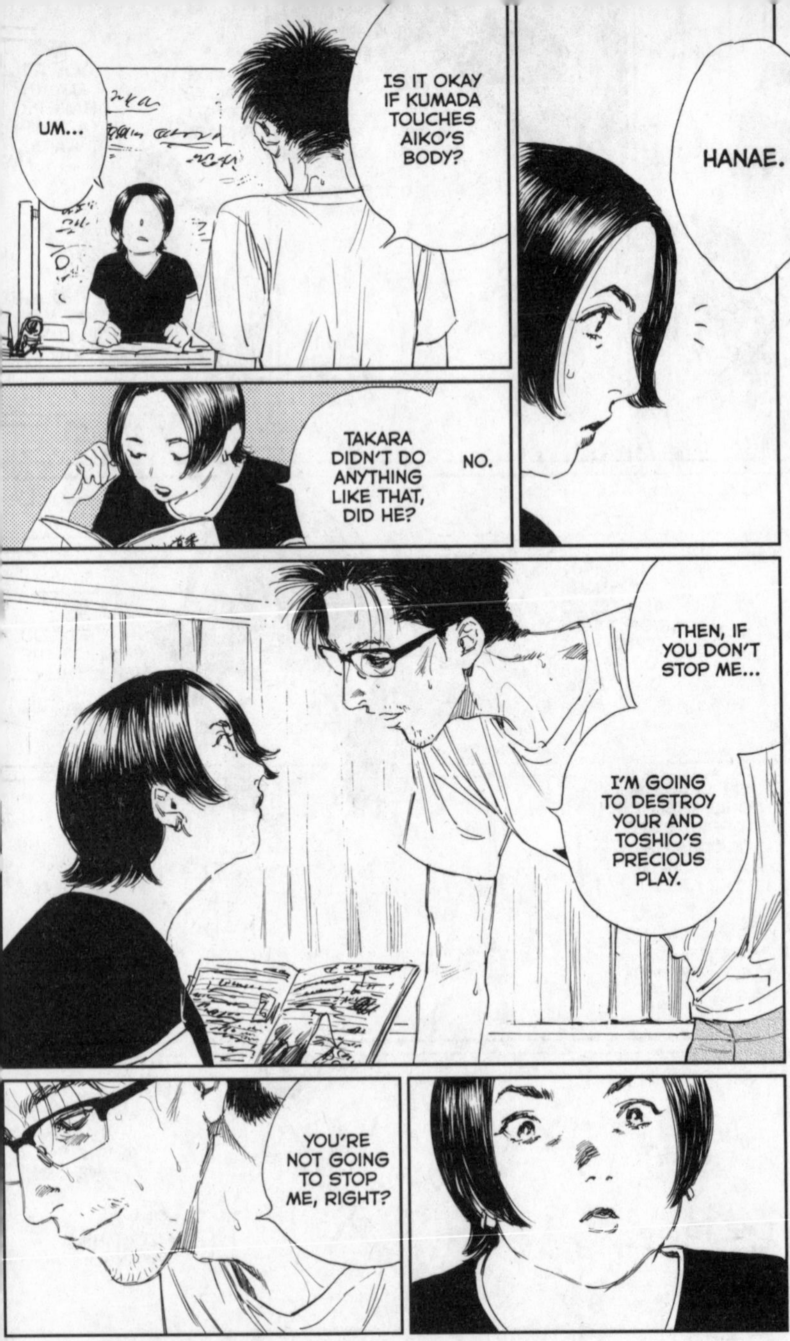
HANAE.
IS IT OKAY IF KUMADA TOUCHES AIKO'S BODY?
UM...
NO.
TAKARA DIDN'T DO ANYTHING LIKE THAT, DID HE?
THEN, IF YOU DON'T STOP ME...
I'M GOING TO DESTROY YOUR AND TOSHIO'S PRECIOUS PLAY.
YOU'RE NOT GOING TO STOP ME, RIGHT?

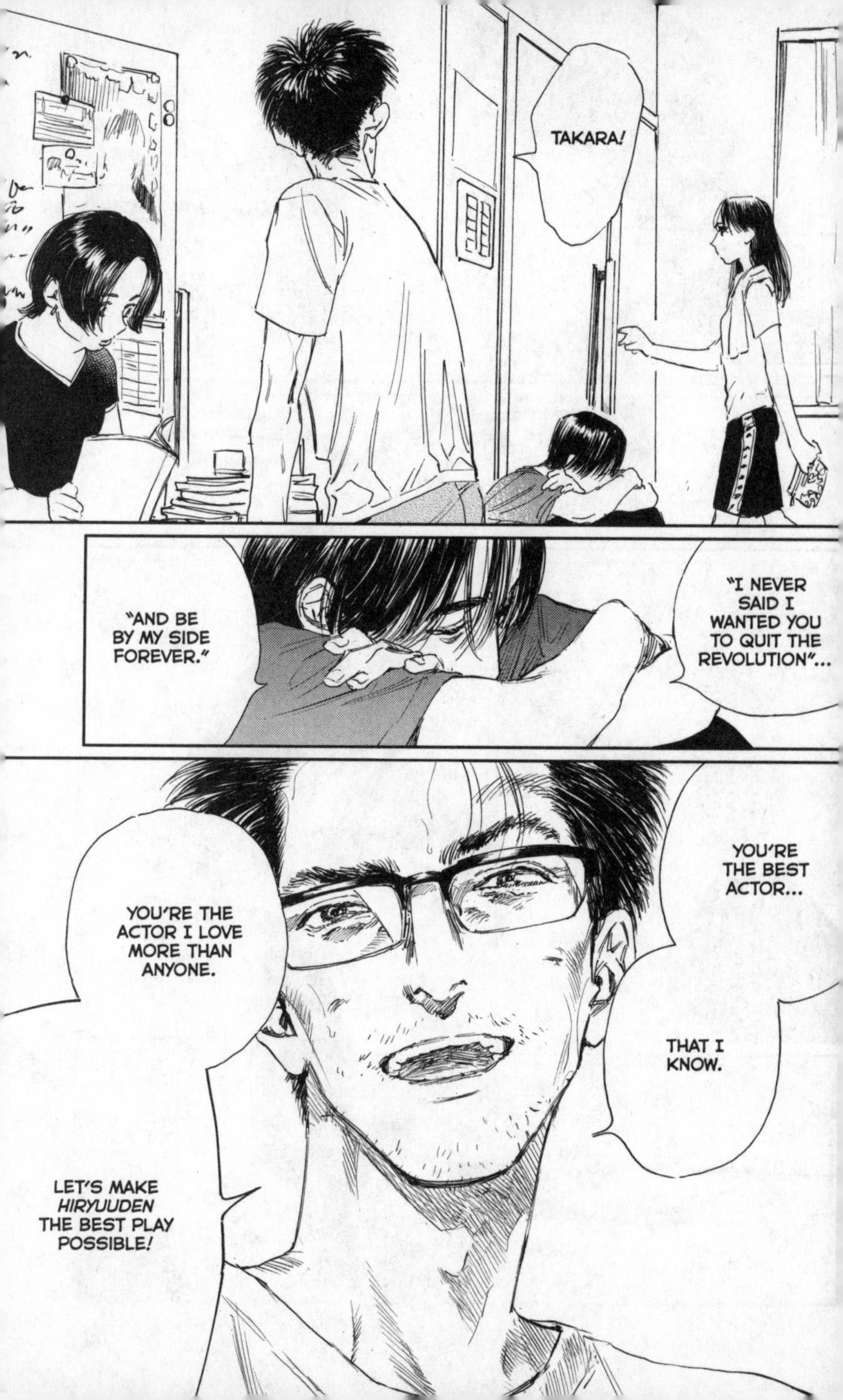
TAKARA!
"I NEVER SAID I WANTED YOU TO QUIT THE REVOLUTION"...
"AND BE BY MY SIDE FOREVER."
YOU'RE THE BEST ACTOR...
THAT I KNOW.
YOU'RE THE ACTOR I LOVE MORE THAN ANYONE.
LET'S MAKE *HIRYUUDEN* THE BEST PLAY POSSIBLE!

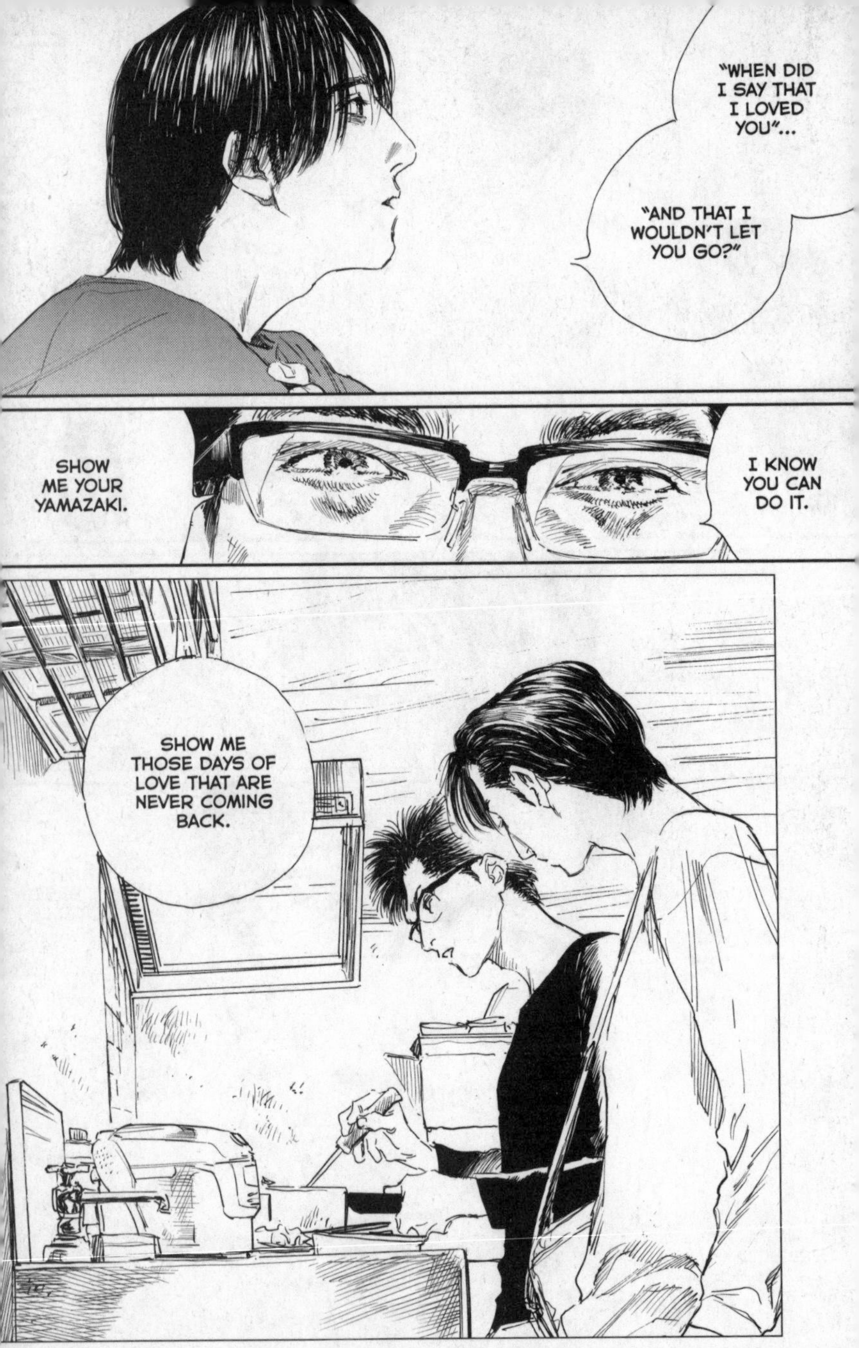
"WHEN DID I SAY THAT I LOVED YOU"...
"AND THAT I WOULDN'T LET YOU GO?"
I KNOW YOU CAN DO IT.
SHOW ME YOUR YAMAZAKI.
SHOW ME THOSE DAYS OF LOVE THAT ARE NEVER COMING BACK.

DOUBLE

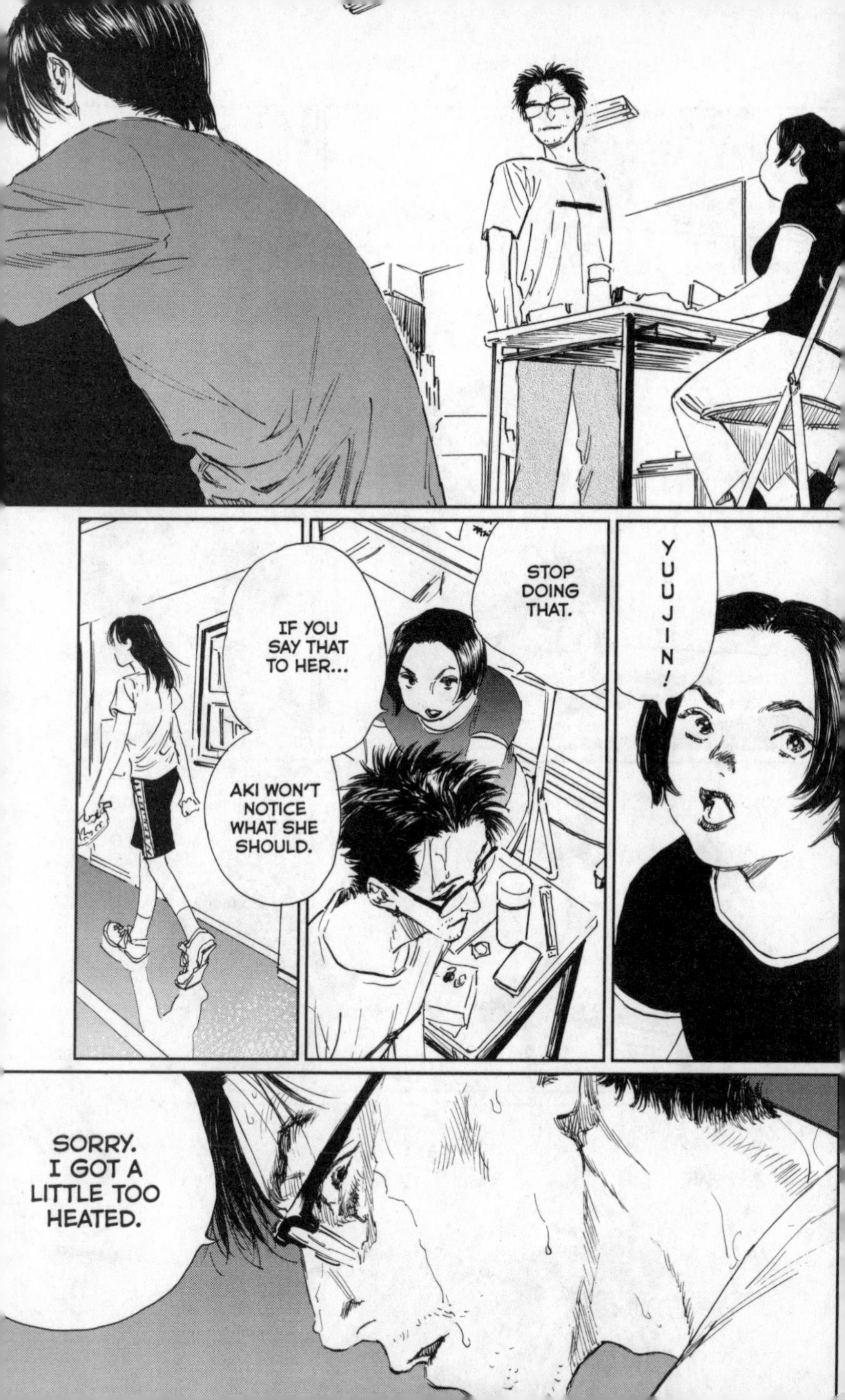
YUUJIN!
STOP DOING THAT.
IF YOU SAY THAT TO HER...
AKI WON'T NOTICE WHAT SHE SHOULD.
SORRY. I GOT A LITTLE TOO HEATED.

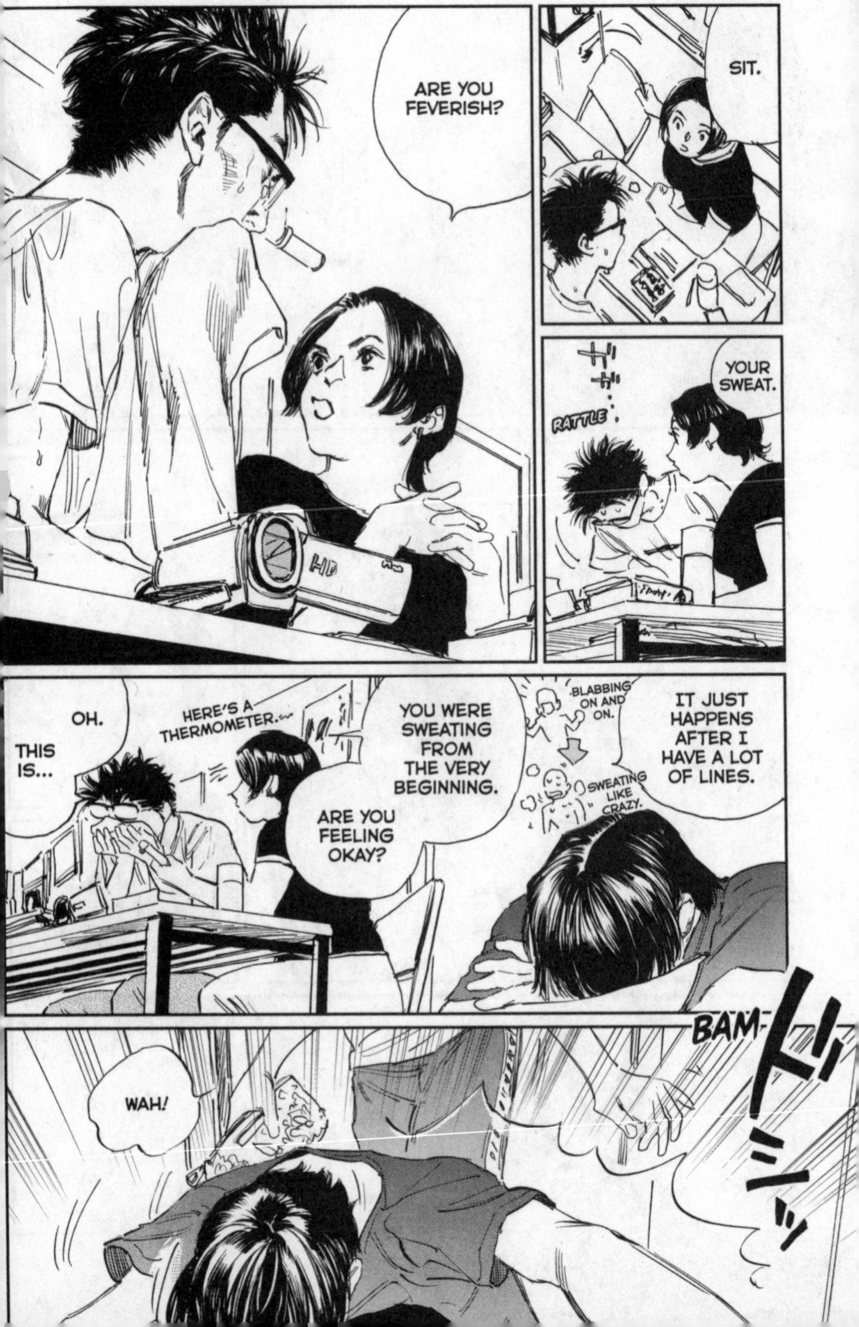
SIT.
YOUR SWEAT.
RATTLE
ARE YOU FEVERISH?
IT JUST HAPPENS AFTER I HAVE A LOT OF LINES.
BLABBING ON AND ON.
SWEATING LIKE CRAZY.
YOU WERE SWEATING FROM THE VERY BEGINNING.
ARE YOU FEELING OKAY?
HERE'S A THERMOMETER.
OH.
THIS IS...
BAM
WAH!

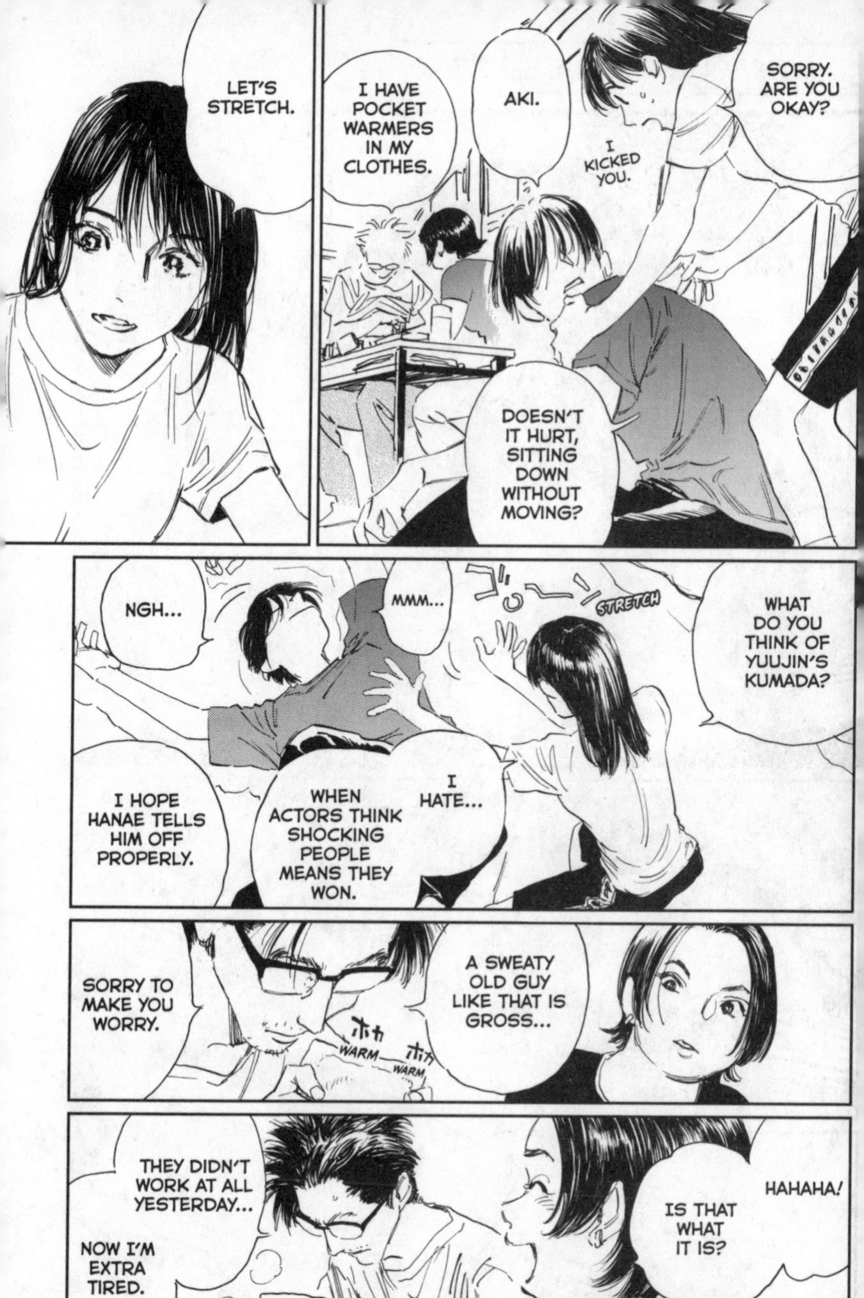
SORRY. ARE YOU OKAY?
I KICKED YOU.
AKI.
I HAVE POCKET WARMERS IN MY CLOTHES.
DOESN'T IT HURT, SITTING DOWN WITHOUT MOVING?
LET'S STRETCH.
WHAT DO YOU THINK OF YUUJIN'S KUMADA?
STRETCH
MMM...
NGH...
I HATE...
WHEN ACTORS THINK SHOCKING PEOPLE MEANS THEY WON.
I HOPE HANAE TELLS HIM OFF PROPERLY.
A SWEATY OLD GUY LIKE THAT IS GROSS...
WARM
WARM
SORRY TO MAKE YOU WORRY.
HAHAHA!
IS THAT WHAT IT IS?
THEY DIDN'T WORK AT ALL YESTERDAY...
NOW I'M EXTRA TIRED.

CHAPTER 25 | CYRANO DE BERGERAC

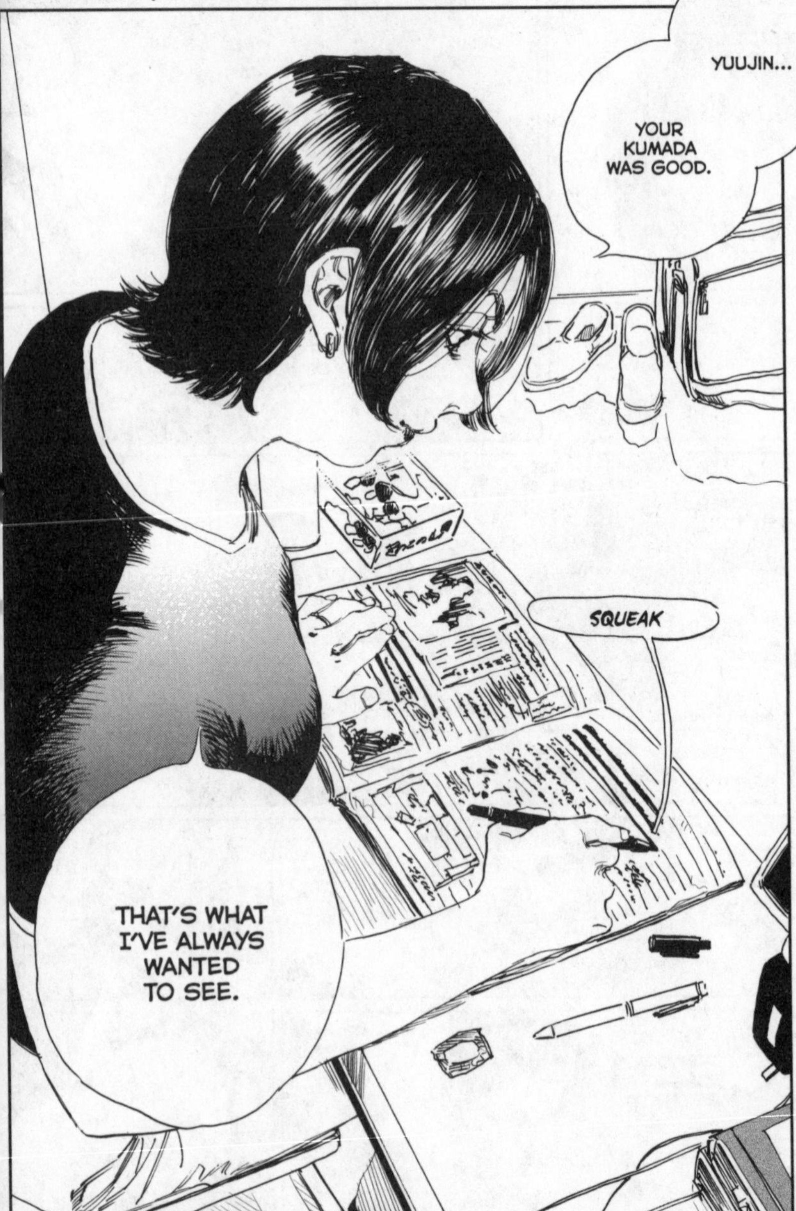

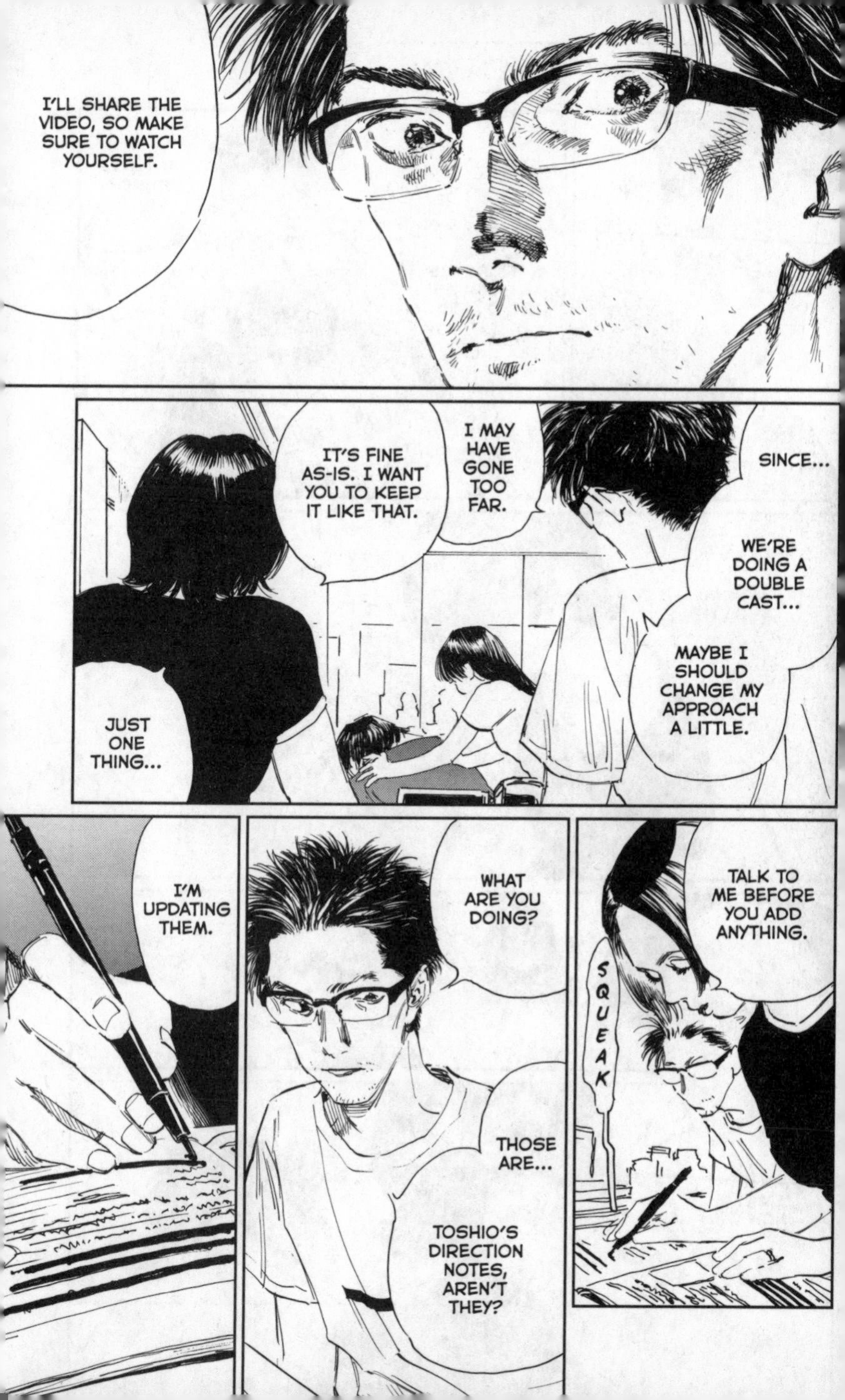
I'LL SHARE THE VIDEO, SO MAKE SURE TO WATCH YOURSELF.
SINCE...
WE'RE DOING A DOUBLE CAST...
MAYBE I SHOULD CHANGE MY APPROACH A LITTLE.
I MAY HAVE GONE TOO FAR.
IT'S FINE AS-IS. I WANT YOU TO KEEP IT LIKE THAT.
JUST ONE THING...
TALK TO ME BEFORE YOU ADD ANYTHING.
SQUEAK
WHAT ARE YOU DOING?
THOSE ARE...
TOSHIO'S DIRECTION NOTES, AREN'T THEY?
I'M UPDATING THEM.

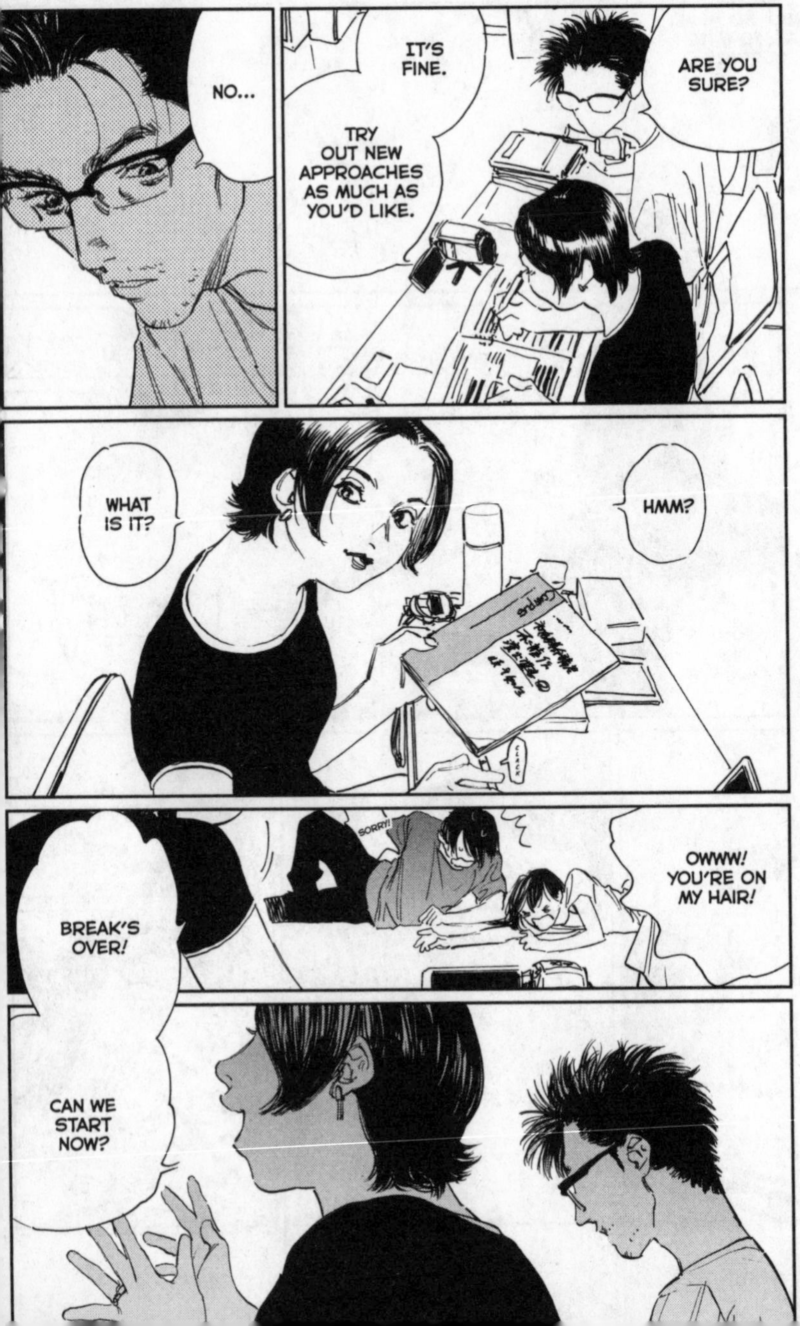
ARE YOU SURE?
IT'S FINE.
TRY OUT NEW APPROACHES AS MUCH AS YOU'D LIKE.
NO...
HMM?
WHAT IS IT?
OWWW! YOU'RE ON MY HAIR!
SORRY!
BREAK'S OVER!
CAN WE START NOW?

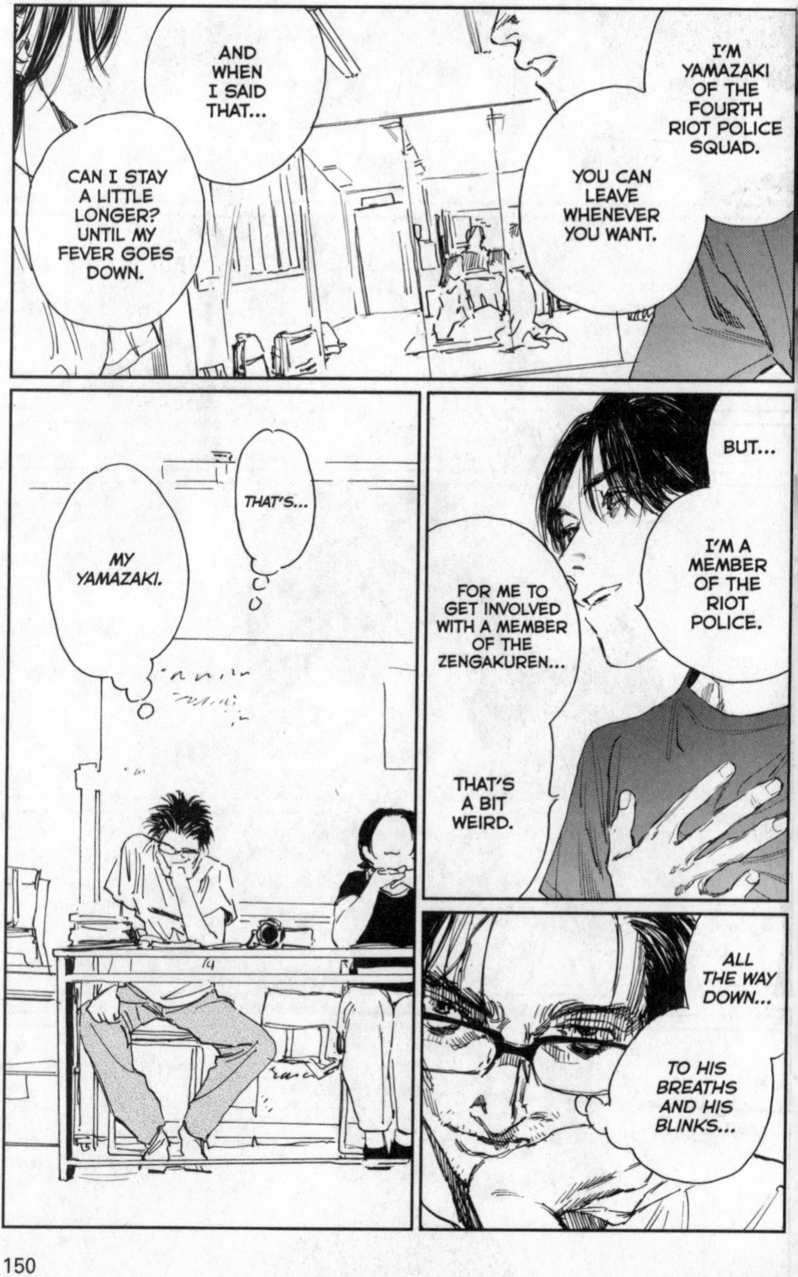
I'M YAMAZAKI OF THE FOURTH RIOT POLICE SQUAD.
YOU CAN LEAVE WHENEVER YOU WANT.
AND WHEN I SAID THAT...
CAN I STAY A LITTLE LONGER? UNTIL MY FEVER GOES DOWN.
BUT...
I'M A MEMBER OF THE RIOT POLICE.
FOR ME TO GET INVOLVED WITH A MEMBER OF THE ZENGAKUREN...
THAT'S A BIT WEIRD.
ALL THE WAY DOWN...
TO HIS BREATHS AND HIS BLINKS...
THAT'S...
MY YAMAZAKI.

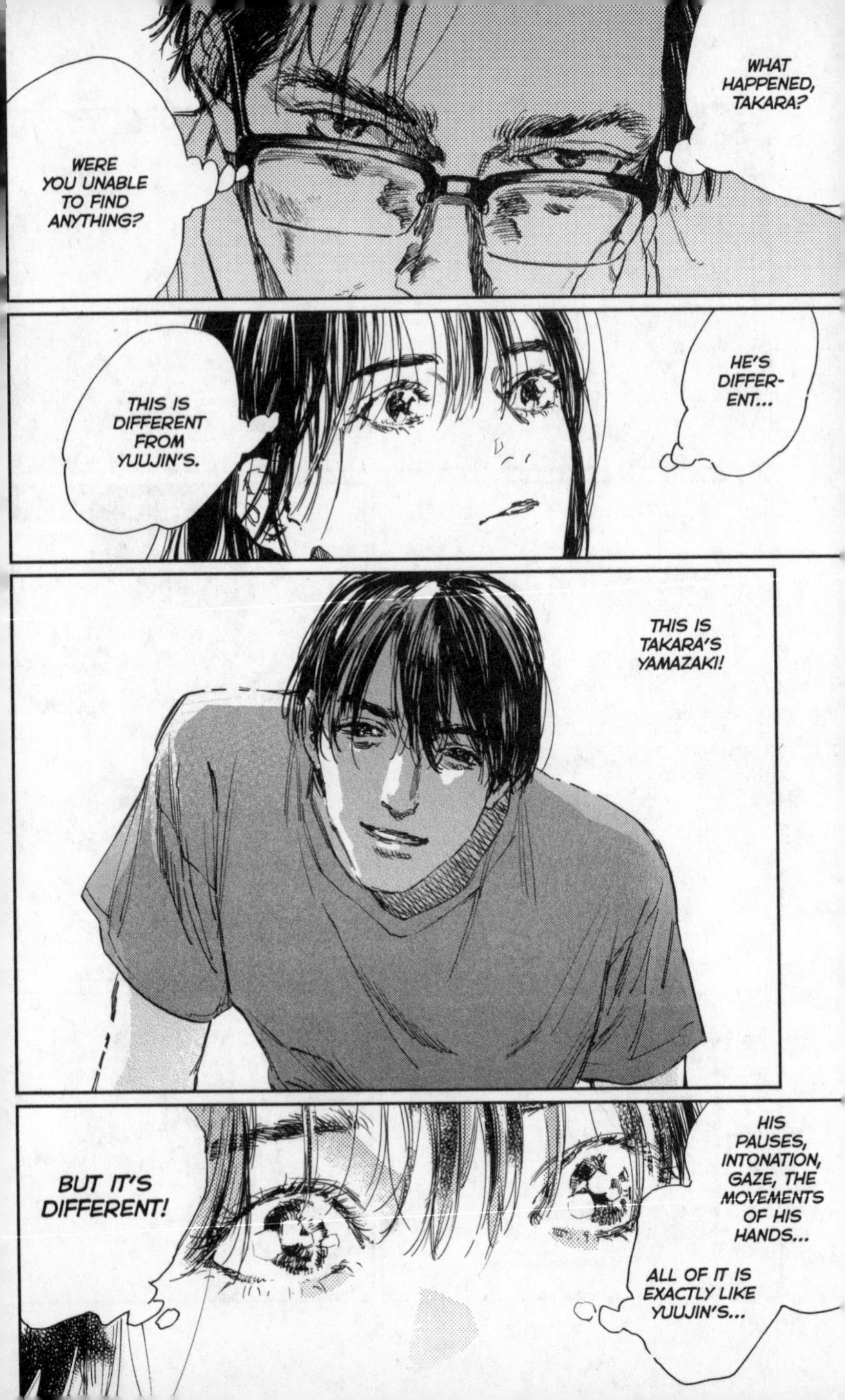
WHAT HAPPENED, TAKARA?
WERE YOU UNABLE TO FIND ANYTHING?
HE'S DIFFERENT...
THIS IS DIFFERENT FROM YUUJIN'S.
THIS IS TAKARA'S YAMAZAKI!
HIS PAUSES, INTONATION, GAZE, THE MOVEMENTS OF HIS HANDS...
ALL OF IT IS EXACTLY LIKE YUUJIN'S...
BUT IT'S DIFFERENT!

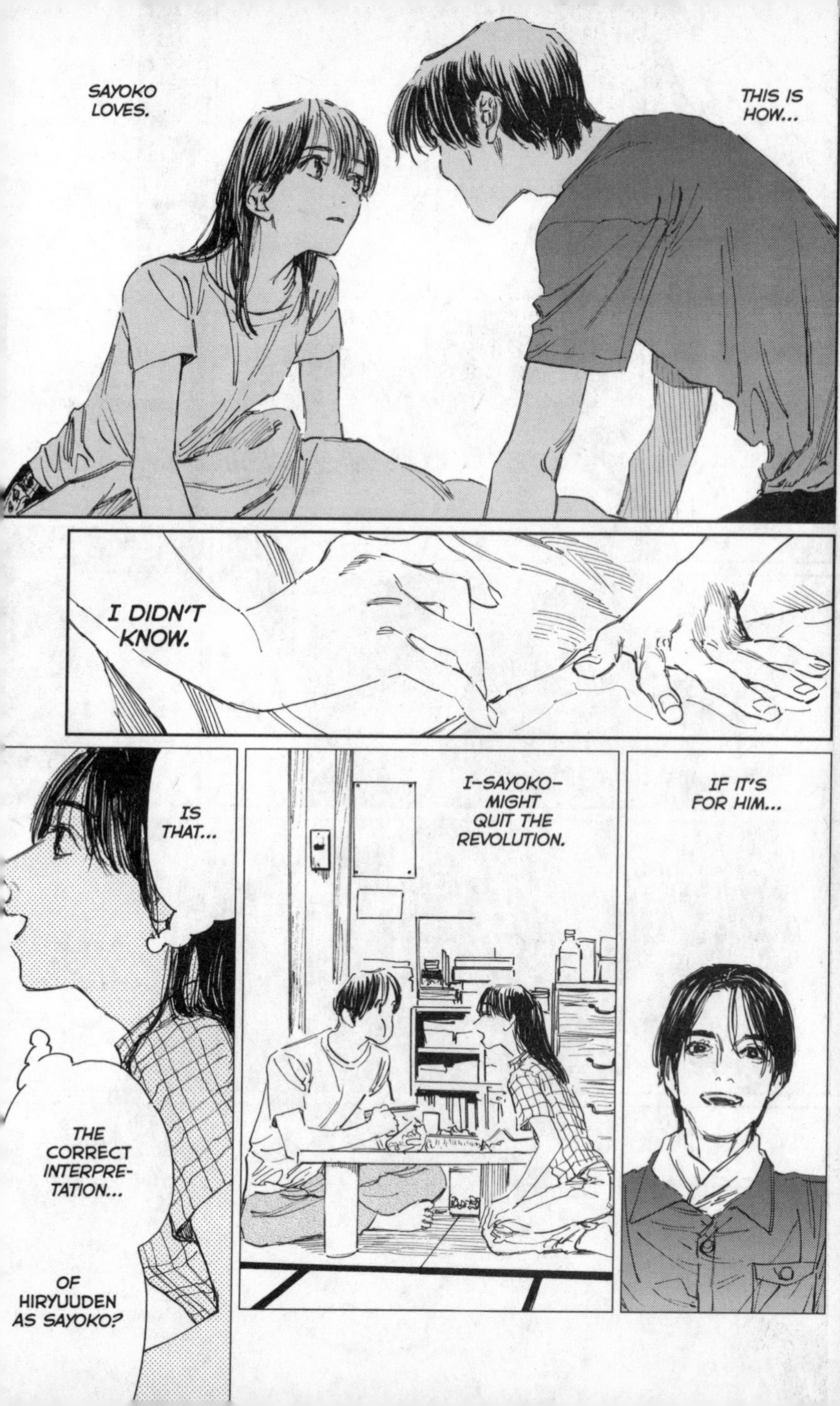
THIS IS HOW...
SAYOKO LOVES.
I DIDN'T KNOW.
IF IT'S FOR HIM...
I—SAYOKO—MIGHT QUIT THE REVOLUTION.
IS THAT...
THE CORRECT INTERPRETATION...
OF HIRYUUDEN AS SAYOKO?

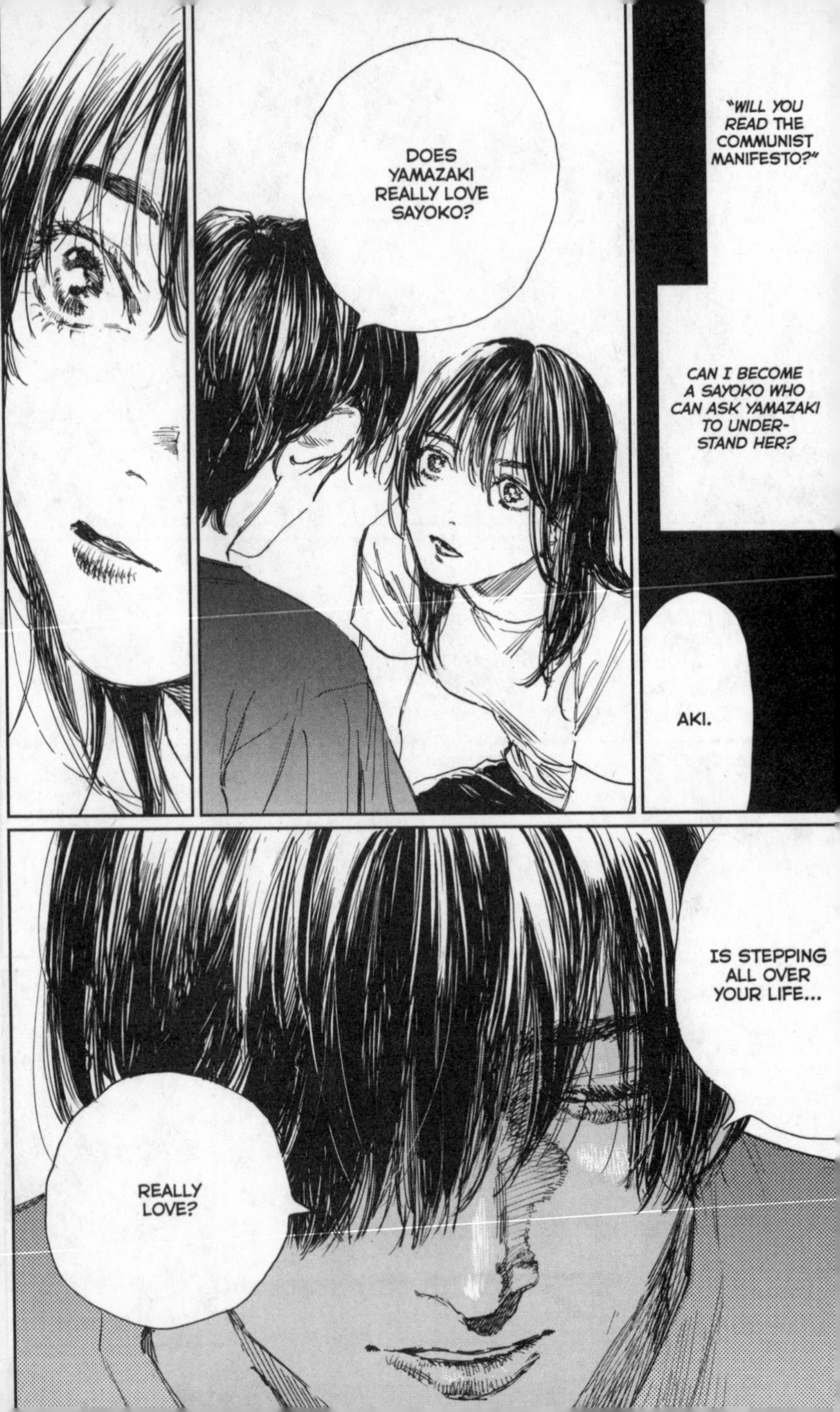
"WILL YOU READ THE COMMUNIST MANIFESTO?"
CAN I BECOME A SAYOKO WHO CAN ASK YAMAZAKI TO UNDER-STAND HER?
AKI.
DOES YAMAZAKI REALLY LOVE SAYOKO?
IS STEPPING ALL OVER YOUR LIFE...
REALLY LOVE?

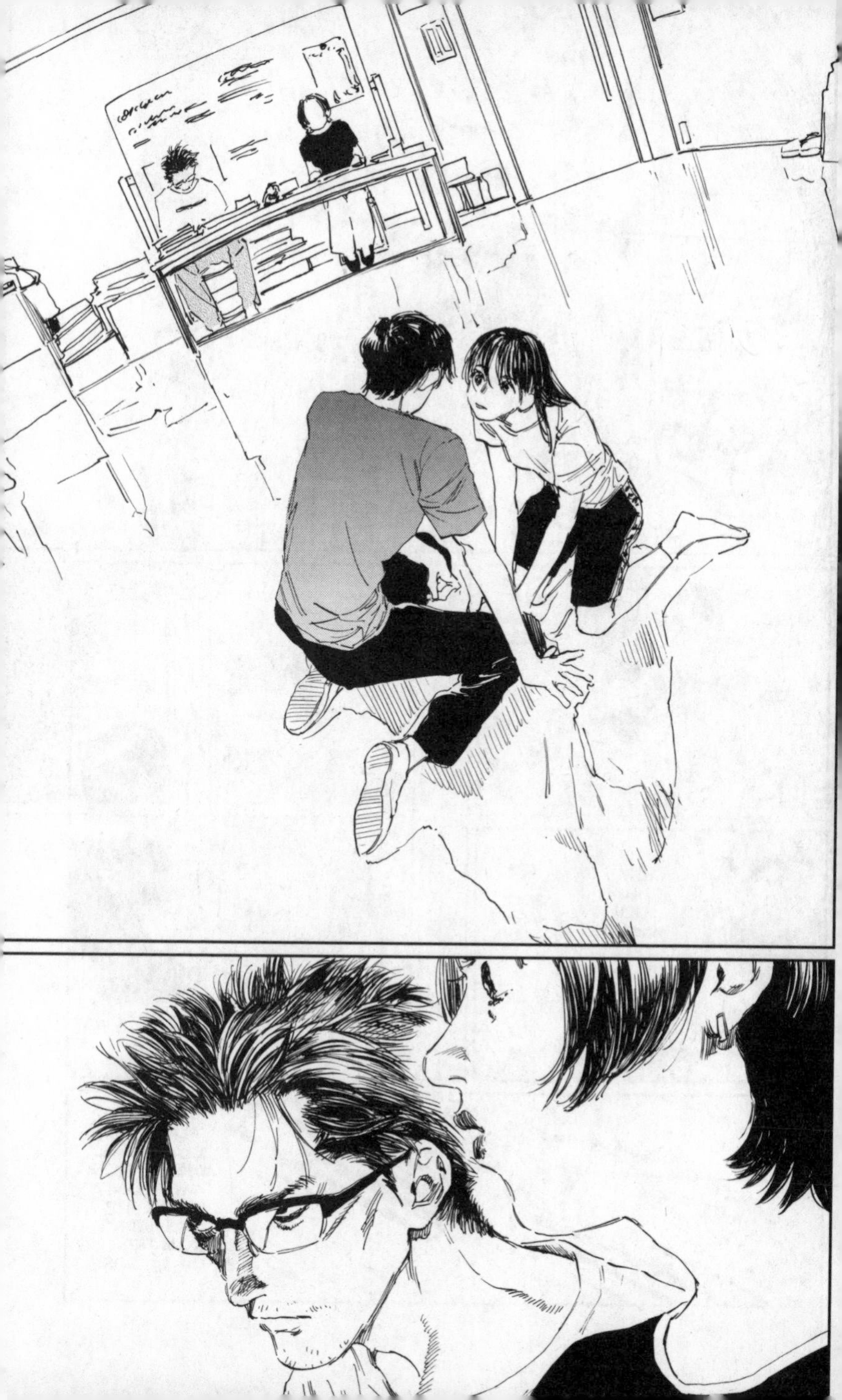

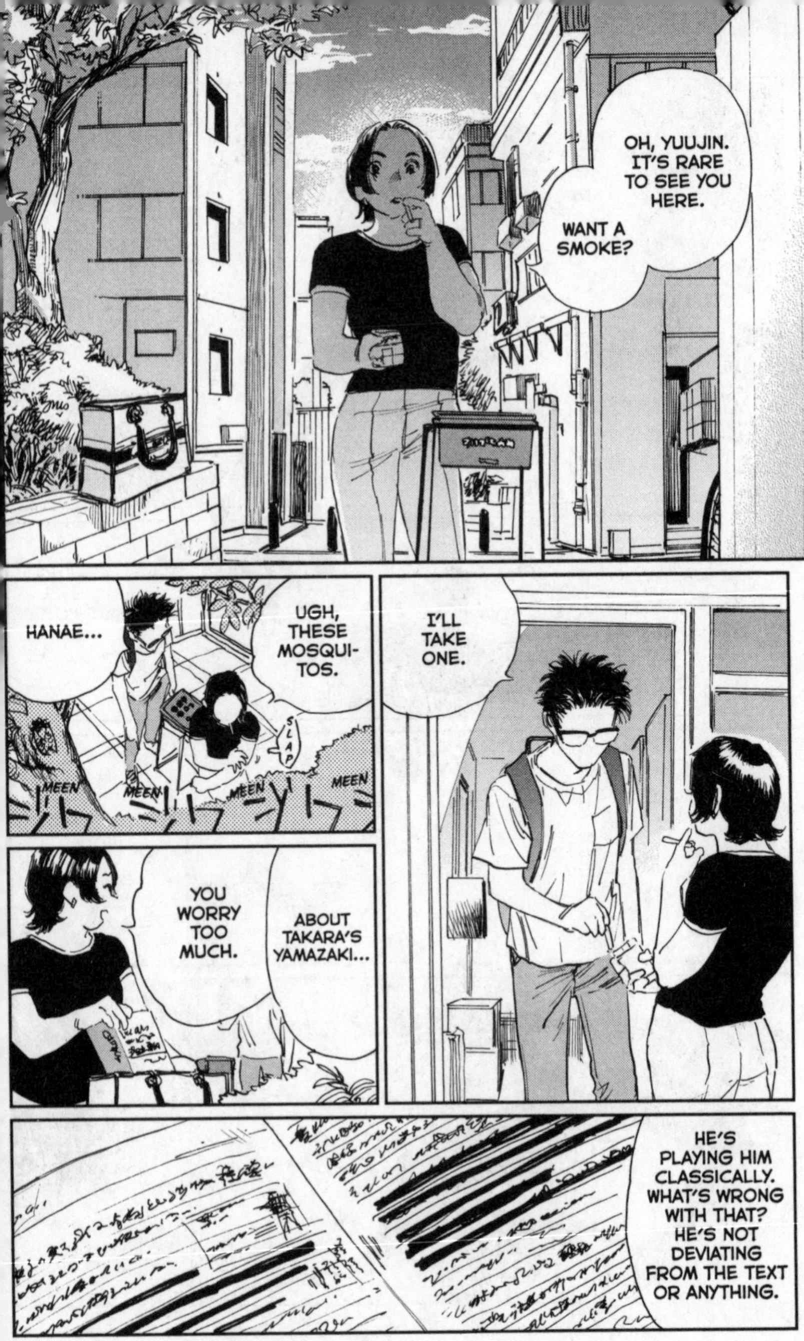
OH, YUUJIN. IT'S RARE TO SEE YOU HERE.
WANT A SMOKE?
I'LL TAKE ONE.
UGH, THESE MOSQUI-TOS.
SLAP
HANAE...
MEEN
MEEN
MEEN
MEEN
ABOUT TAKARA'S YAMAZAKI...
YOU WORRY TOO MUCH.
HE'S PLAYING HIM CLASSICALLY. WHAT'S WRONG WITH THAT? HE'S NOT DEVIATING FROM THE TEXT OR ANYTHING.

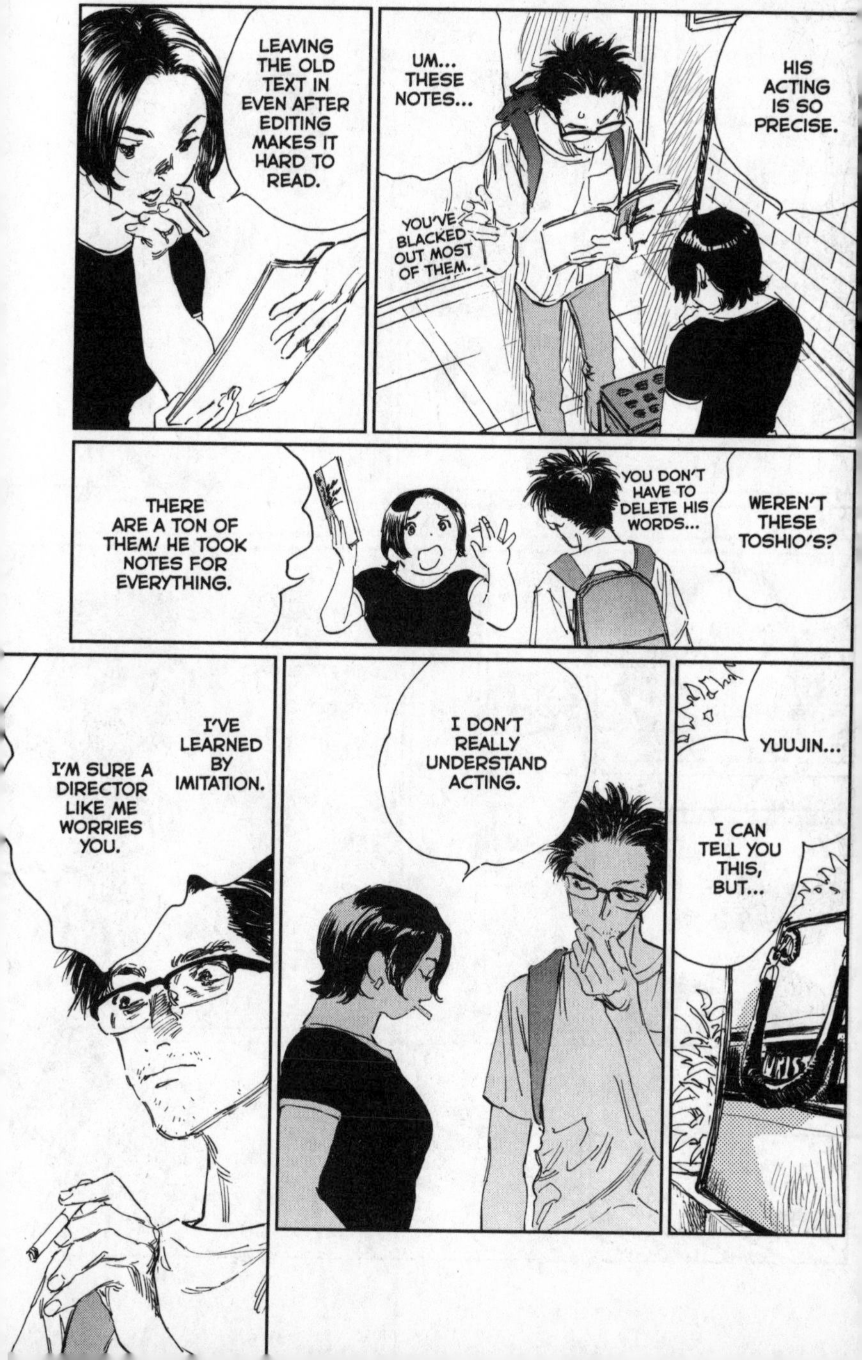
HIS ACTING IS SO PRECISE.
UM... THESE NOTES...
YOU'VE BLACKED OUT MOST OF THEM.
LEAVING THE OLD TEXT IN EVEN AFTER EDITING MAKES IT HARD TO READ.
WEREN'T THESE TOSHIO'S?
YOU DON'T HAVE TO DELETE HIS WORDS...
THERE ARE A TON OF THEM! HE TOOK NOTES FOR EVERYTHING.
YUUJIN...
I CAN TELL YOU THIS, BUT...
I DON'T REALLY UNDERSTAND ACTING.
I'VE LEARNED BY IMITATION.
I'M SURE A DIRECTOR LIKE ME WORRIES YOU.

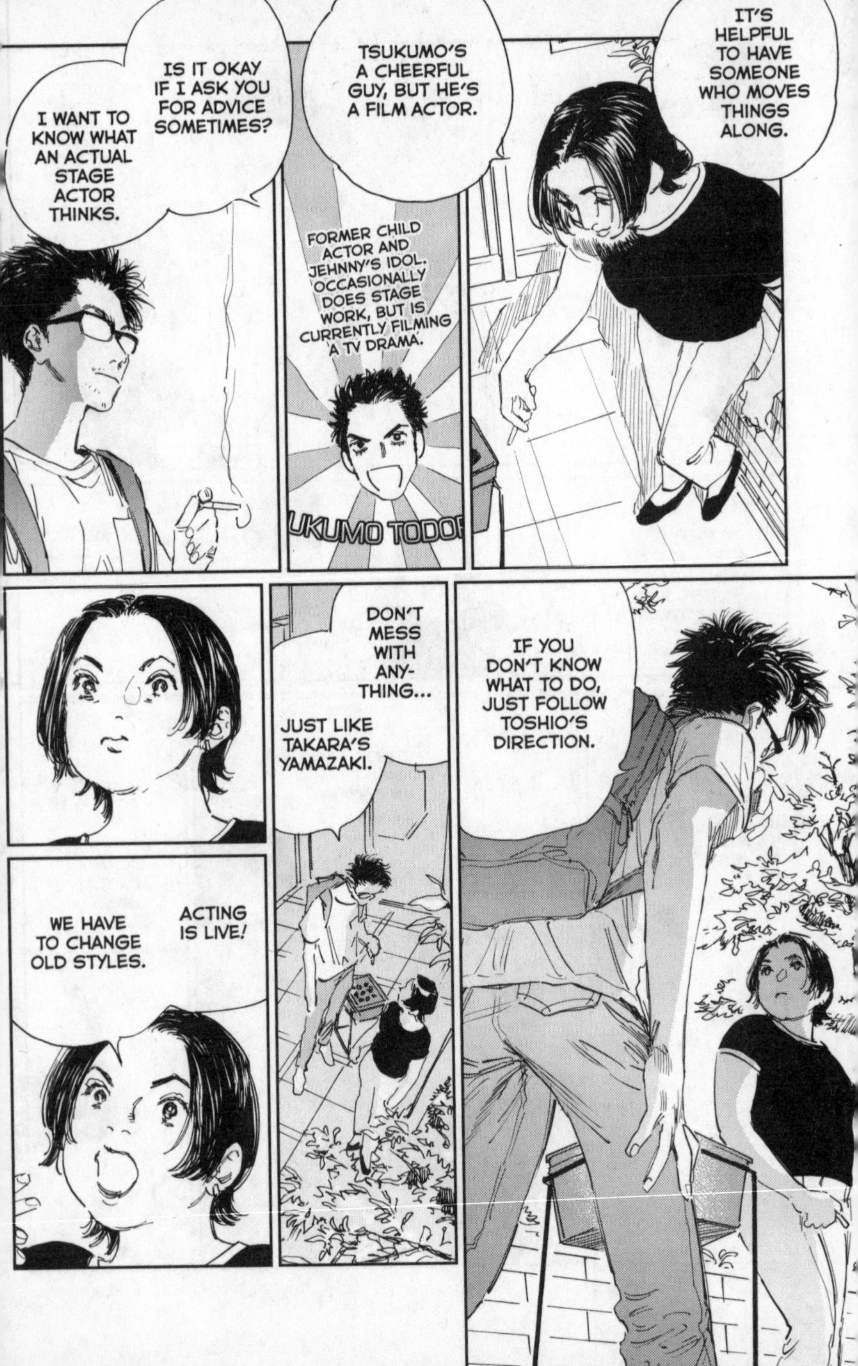
IT'S HELPFUL TO HAVE SOMEONE WHO MOVES THINGS ALONG.
TSUKUMO'S A CHEERFUL GUY, BUT HE'S A FILM ACTOR.
FORMER CHILD ACTOR AND JEHNNY'S IDOL. OCCASIONALLY DOES STAGE WORK, BUT IS CURRENTLY FILMING A TV DRAMA.
IS IT OKAY IF I ASK YOU FOR ADVICE SOMETIMES?
I WANT TO KNOW WHAT AN ACTUAL STAGE ACTOR THINKS.
IF YOU DON'T KNOW WHAT TO DO, JUST FOLLOW TOSHIO'S DIRECTION.
DON'T MESS WITH ANY-THING...
JUST LIKE TAKARA'S YAMAZAKI.
ACTING IS LIVE!
WE HAVE TO CHANGE OLD STYLES.

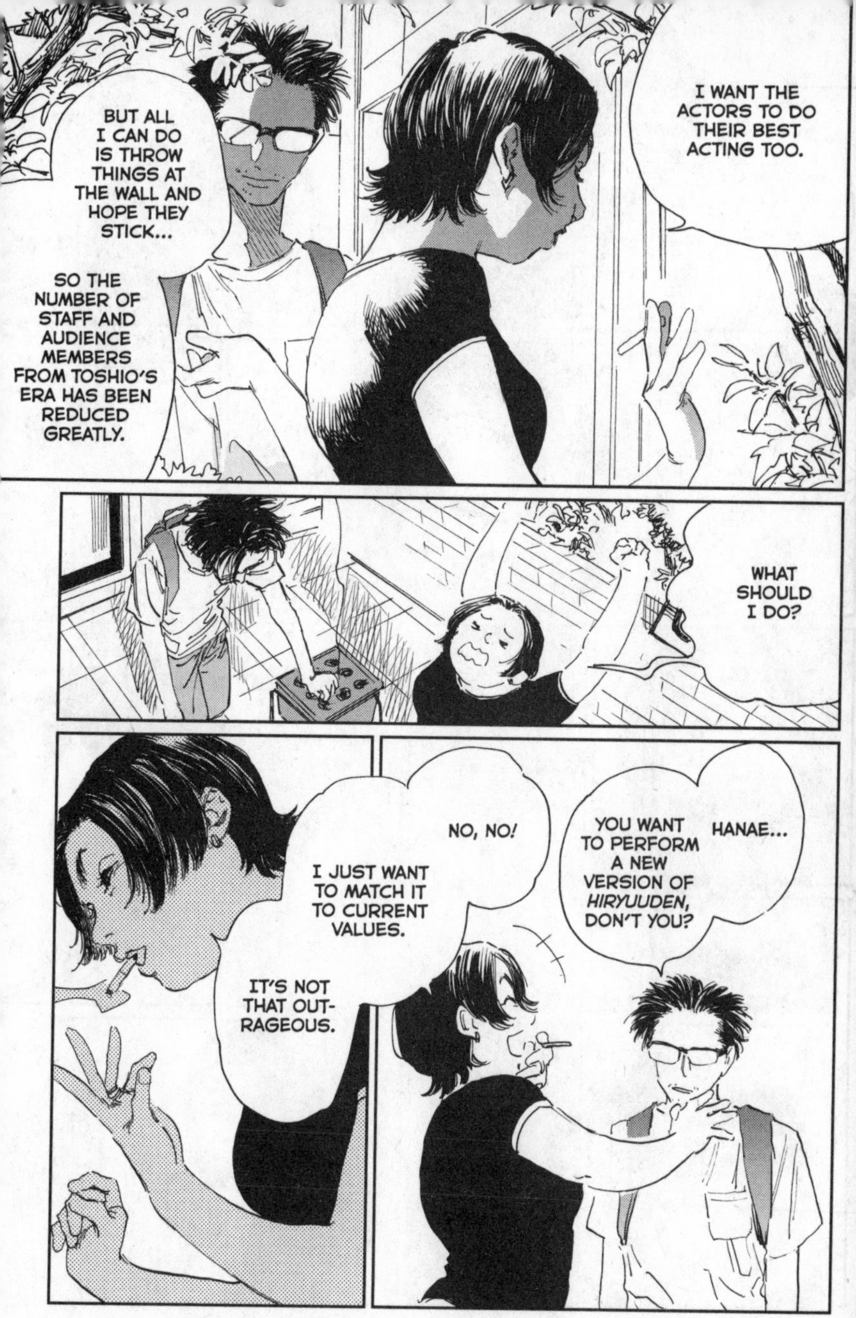
I WANT THE ACTORS TO DO THEIR BEST ACTING TOO.
BUT ALL I CAN DO IS THROW THINGS AT THE WALL AND HOPE THEY STICK...
SO THE NUMBER OF STAFF AND AUDIENCE MEMBERS FROM TOSHIO'S ERA HAS BEEN REDUCED GREATLY.
WHAT SHOULD I DO?
HANAE...
YOU WANT TO PERFORM A NEW VERSION OF *HIRYUUDEN*, DON'T YOU?
NO, NO!
I JUST WANT TO MATCH IT TO CURRENT VALUES.
IT'S NOT THAT OUT-RAGEOUS.

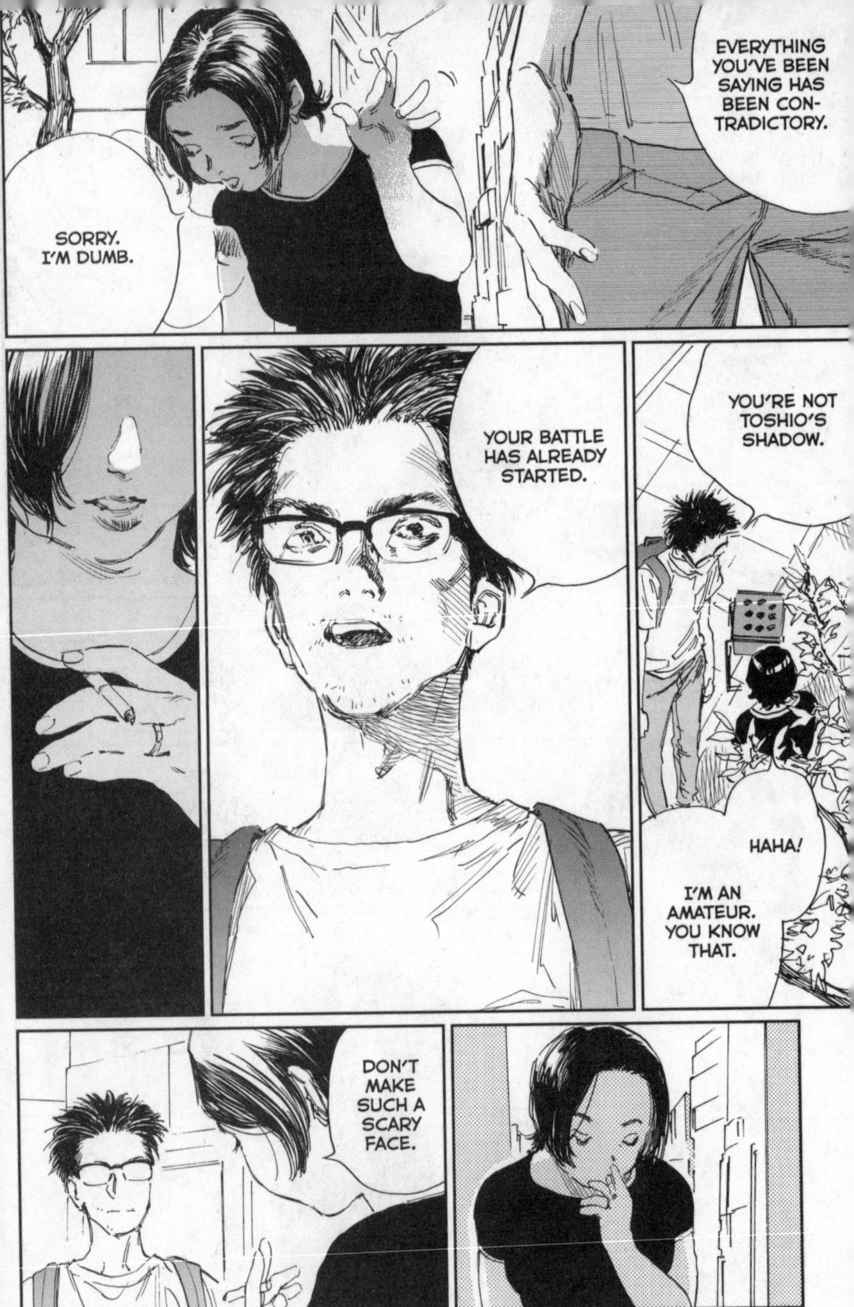

EVERYTHING YOU'VE BEEN SAYING HAS BEEN CONTRADICTORY.
SORRY. I'M DUMB.
YOU'RE NOT TOSHIO'S SHADOW.
HAHA!
I'M AN AMATEUR. YOU KNOW THAT.
YOUR BATTLE HAS ALREADY STARTED.
DON'T MAKE SUCH A SCARY FACE.

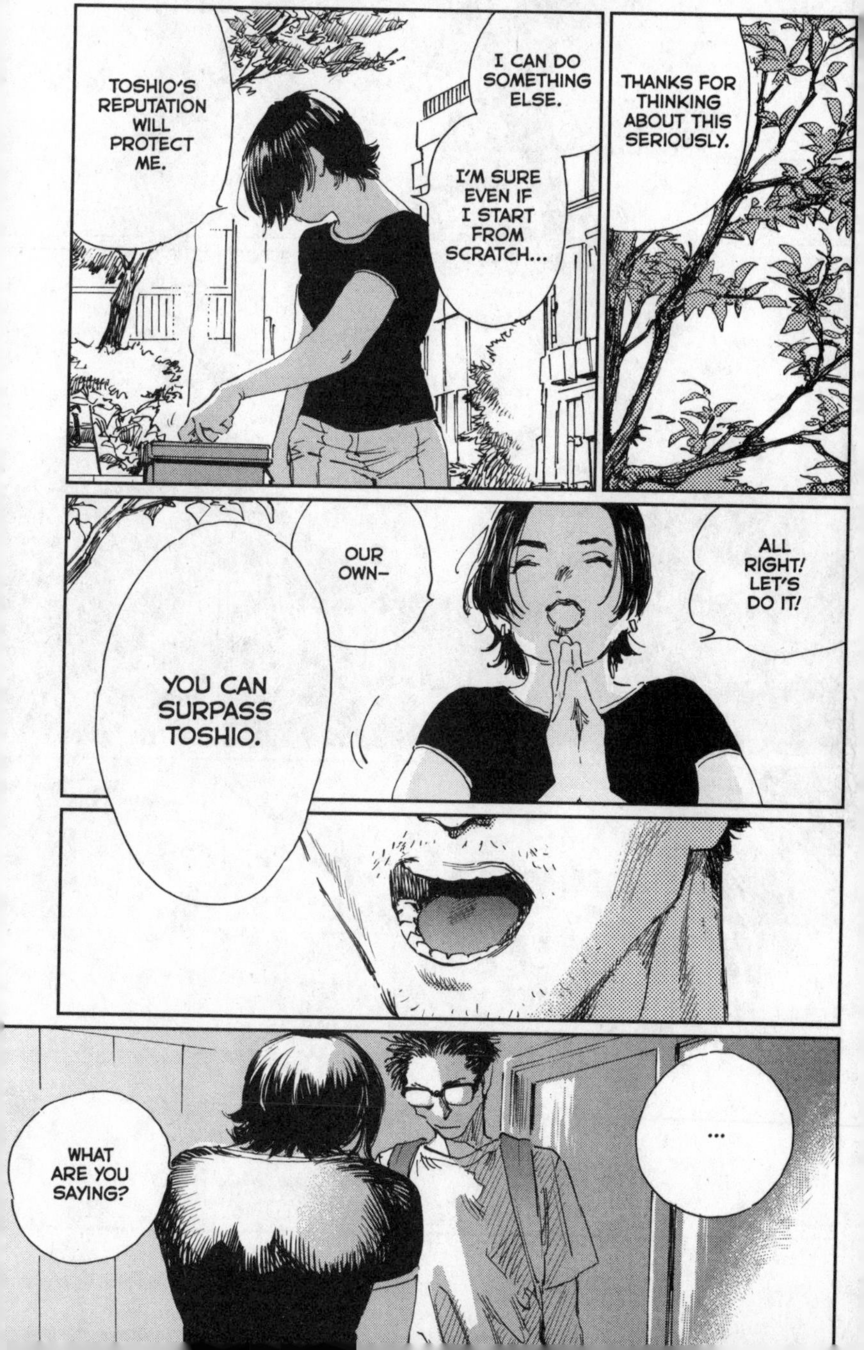
THANKS FOR THINKING ABOUT THIS SERIOUSLY.
I CAN DO SOMETHING ELSE.
TOSHIO'S REPUTATION WILL PROTECT ME.
I'M SURE EVEN IF I START FROM SCRATCH...
ALL RIGHT! LET'S DO IT!
OUR OWN-
YOU CAN SURPASS TOSHIO.
...
WHAT ARE YOU SAYING?

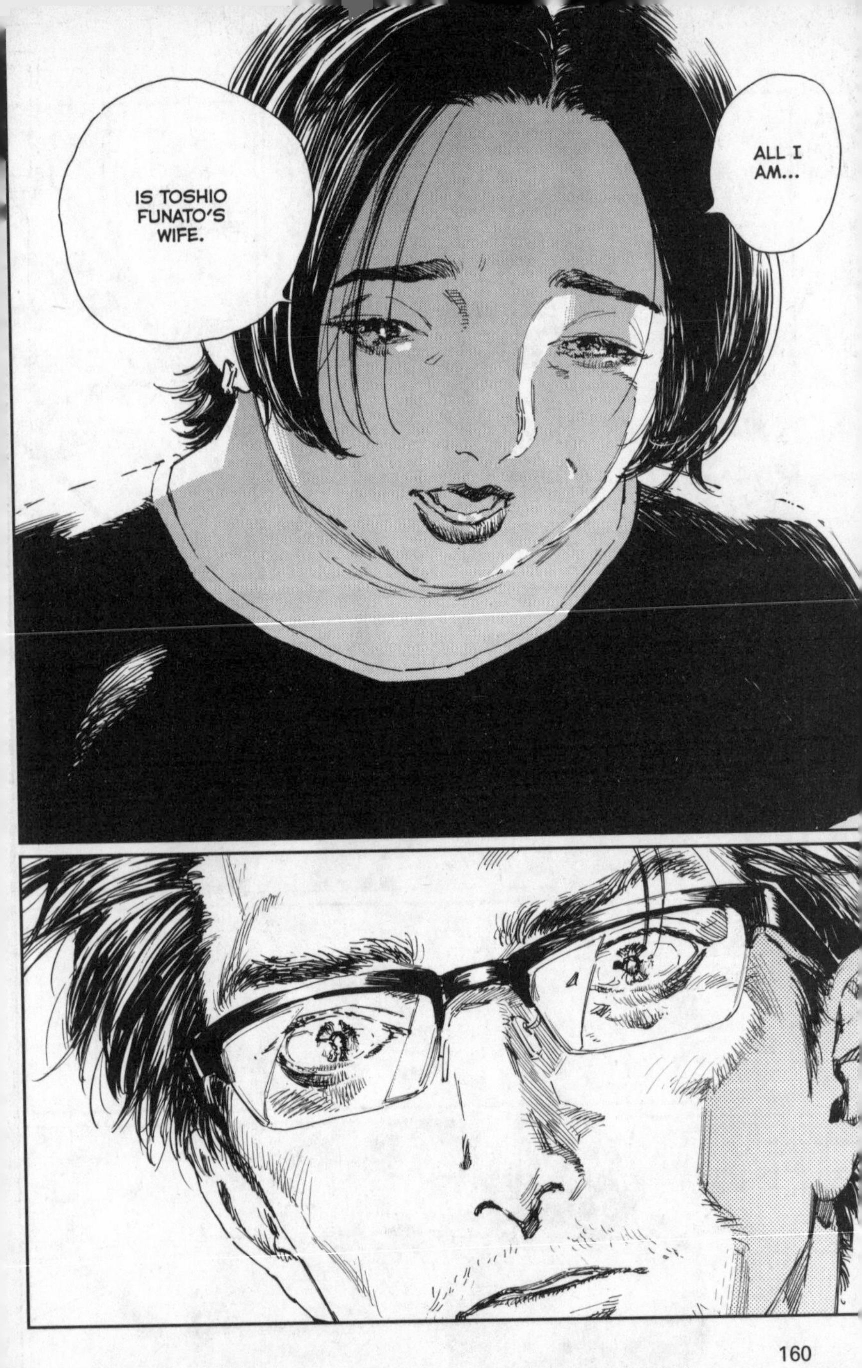
ALL I AM...
IS TOSHIO FUNATO'S WIFE.

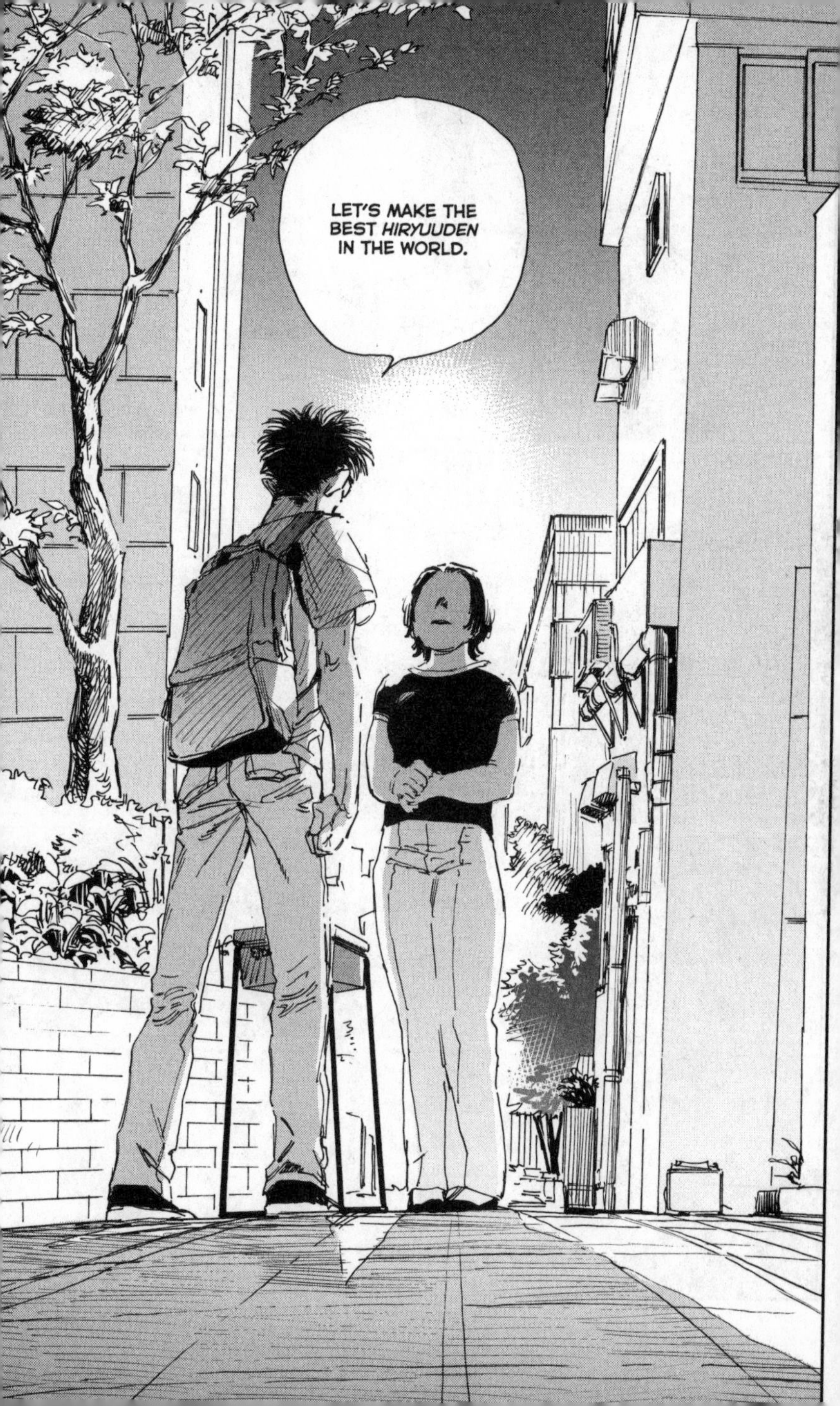
LET'S MAKE THE BEST *HIRYUUDEN* IN THE WORLD.

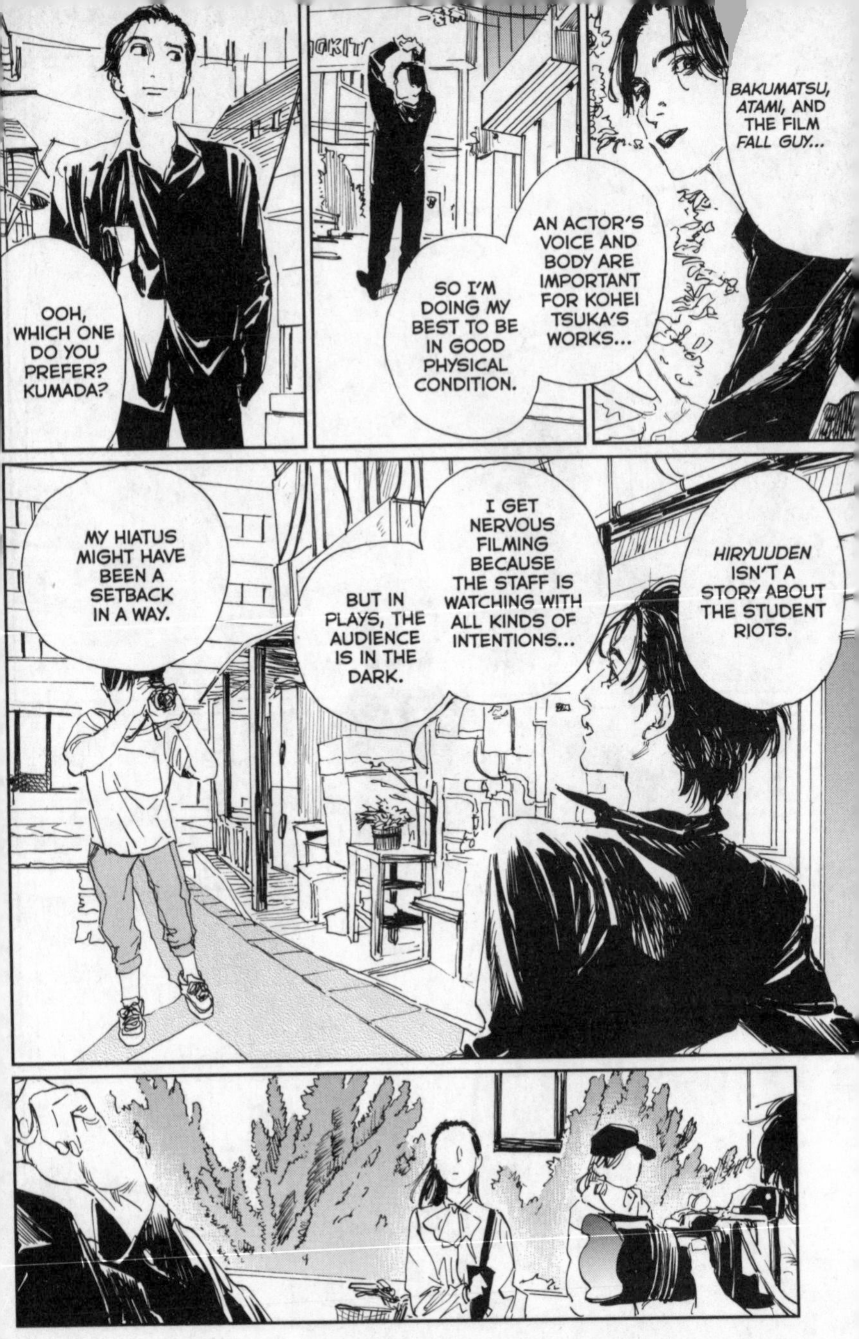
BAKUMATSU, ATAMI, AND THE FILM *FALL GUY*...
AN ACTOR'S VOICE AND BODY ARE IMPORTANT FOR KOHEI TSUKA'S WORKS...
SO I'M DOING MY BEST TO BE IN GOOD PHYSICAL CONDITION.
OOH, WHICH ONE DO YOU PREFER? KUMADA?
HIRYUUDEN ISN'T A STORY ABOUT THE STUDENT RIOTS.
I GET NERVOUS FILMING BECAUSE THE STAFF IS WATCHING WITH ALL KINDS OF INTENTIONS...
BUT IN PLAYS, THE AUDIENCE IS IN THE DARK.
MY HIATUS MIGHT HAVE BEEN A SETBACK IN A WAY.

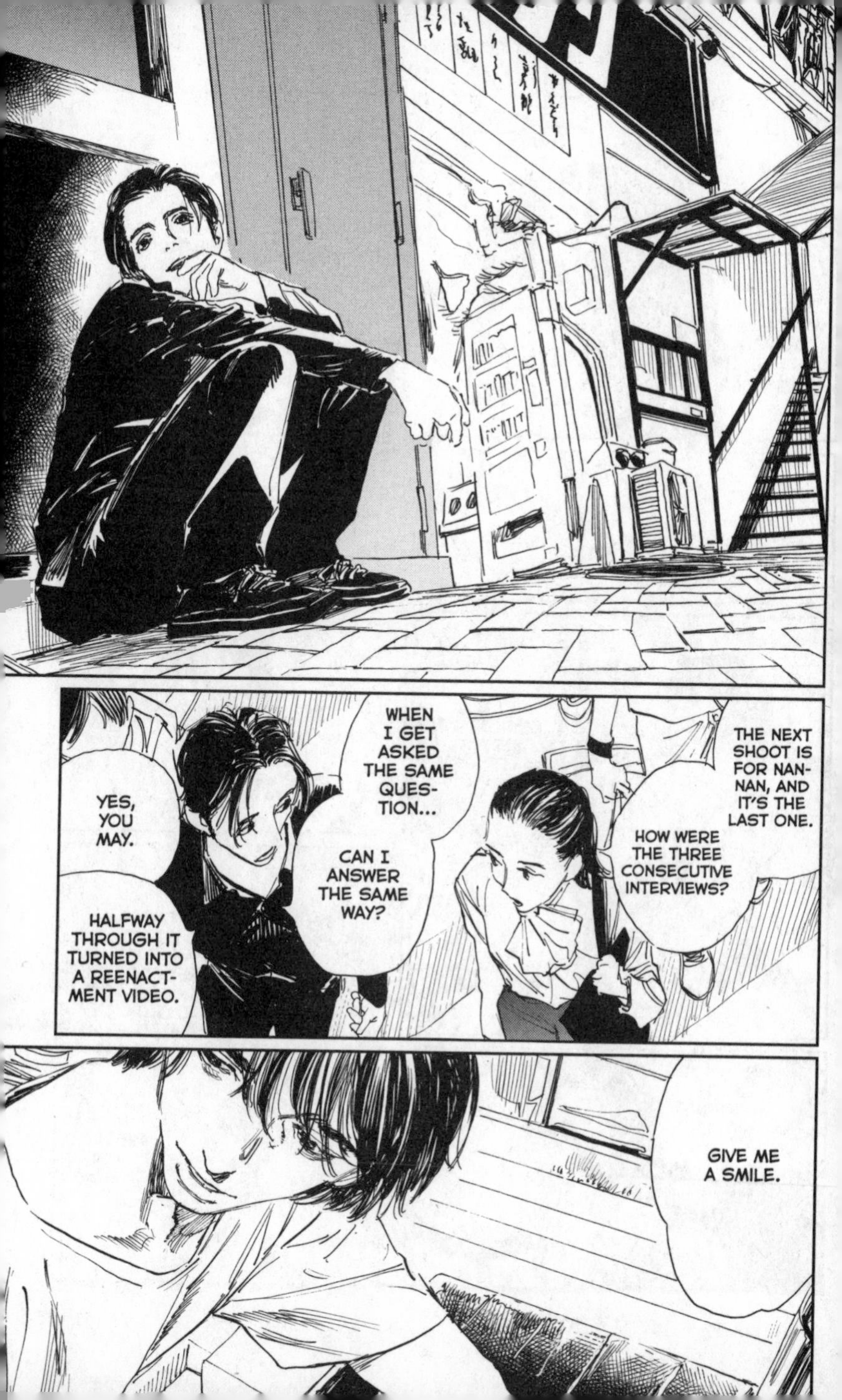
THE NEXT SHOOT IS FOR NAN-NAN, AND IT'S THE LAST ONE.
HOW WERE THE THREE CONSECUTIVE INTERVIEWS?
WHEN I GET ASKED THE SAME QUESTION...
CAN I ANSWER THE SAME WAY?
YES, YOU MAY.
HALFWAY THROUGH IT TURNED INTO A REENACTMENT VIDEO.
GIVE ME A SMILE.

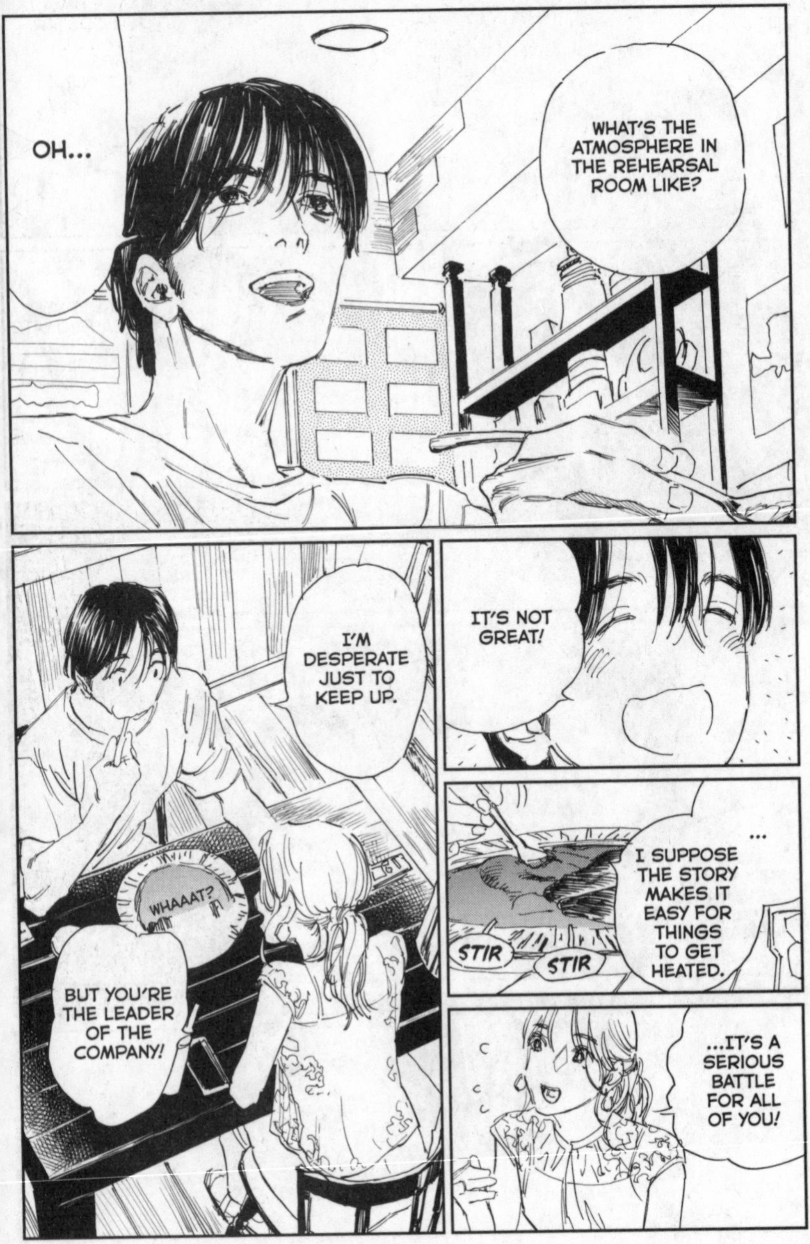
WHAT'S THE ATMOSPHERE IN THE REHEARSAL ROOM LIKE?
OH...
IT'S NOT GREAT!
... I SUPPOSE THE STORY MAKES IT EASY FOR THINGS TO GET HEATED.
STIR
STIR
...IT'S A SERIOUS BATTLE FOR ALL OF YOU!
I'M DESPERATE JUST TO KEEP UP.
WHAAAT?
BUT YOU'RE THE LEADER OF THE COMPANY!

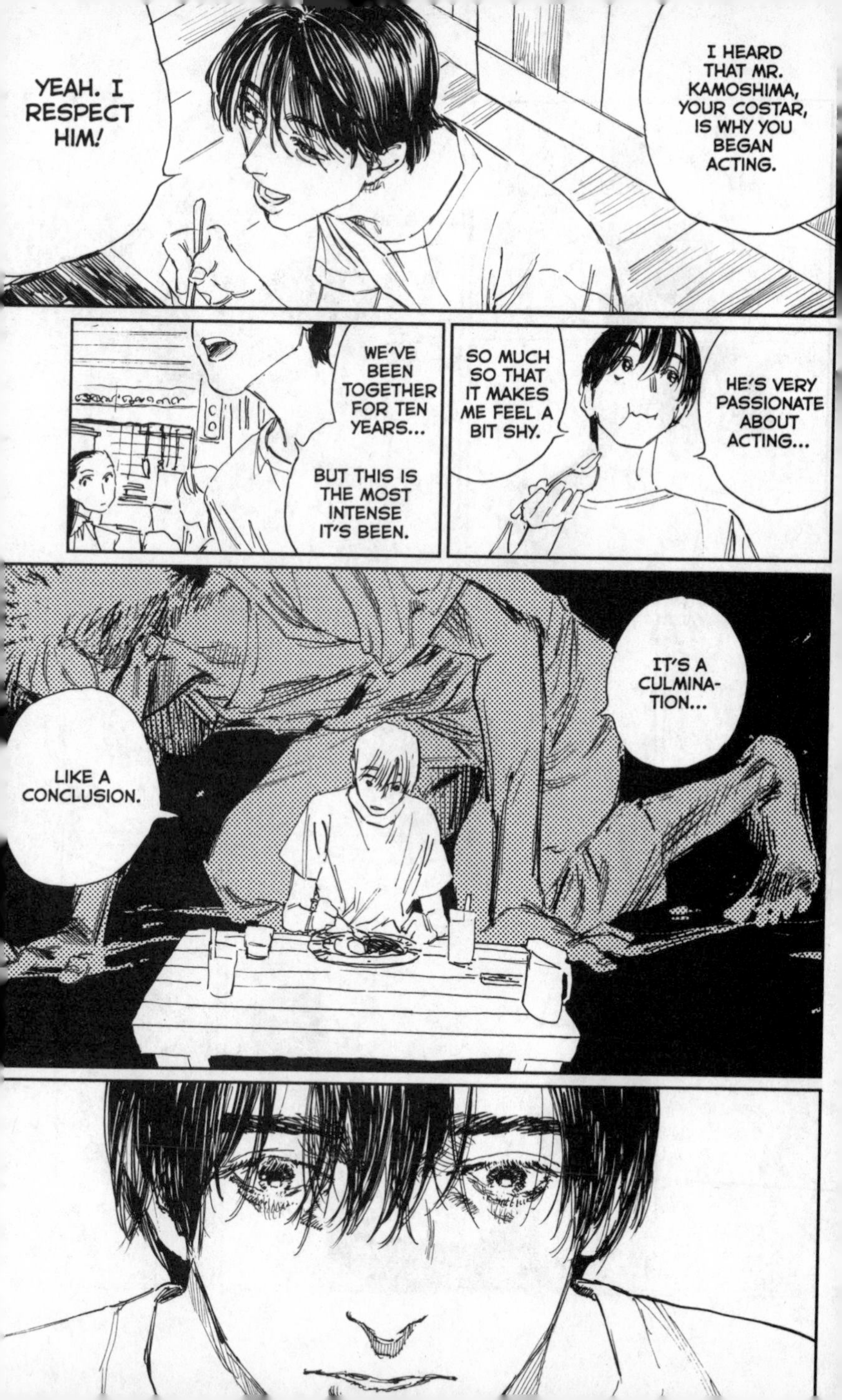
I HEARD THAT MR. KAMOSHIMA, YOUR COSTAR, IS WHY YOU BEGAN ACTING.
YEAH. I RESPECT HIM!
HE'S VERY PASSIONATE ABOUT ACTING...
SO MUCH SO THAT IT MAKES ME FEEL A BIT SHY.
WE'VE BEEN TOGETHER FOR TEN YEARS...
BUT THIS IS THE MOST INTENSE IT'S BEEN.
IT'S A CULMINATION...
LIKE A CONCLUSION.

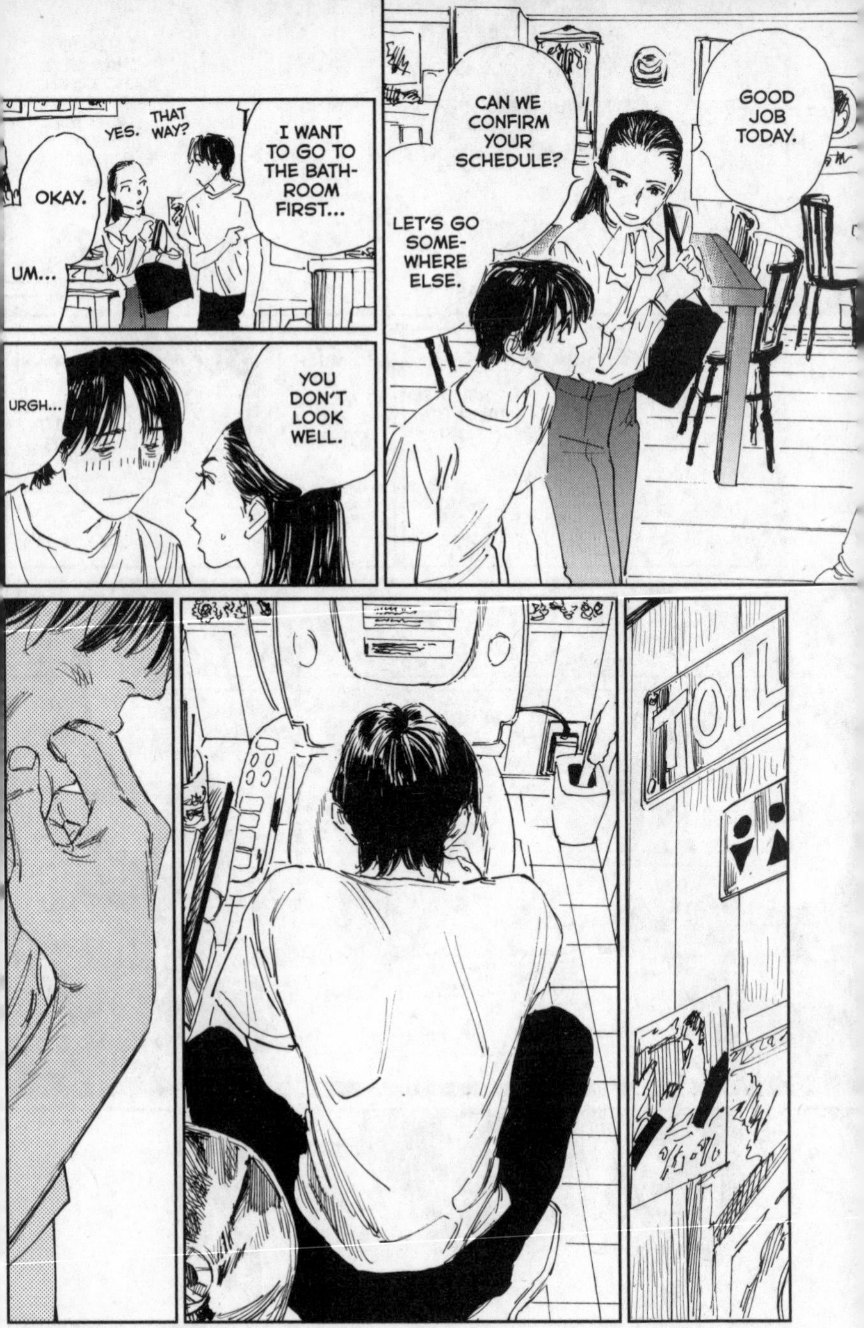
GOOD JOB TODAY.
CAN WE CONFIRM YOUR SCHEDULE?
LET'S GO SOME-WHERE ELSE.
I WANT TO GO TO THE BATH-ROOM FIRST...
THAT WAY?
YES.
OKAY.
UM...
YOU DON'T LOOK WELL.
URGH...
TOIL

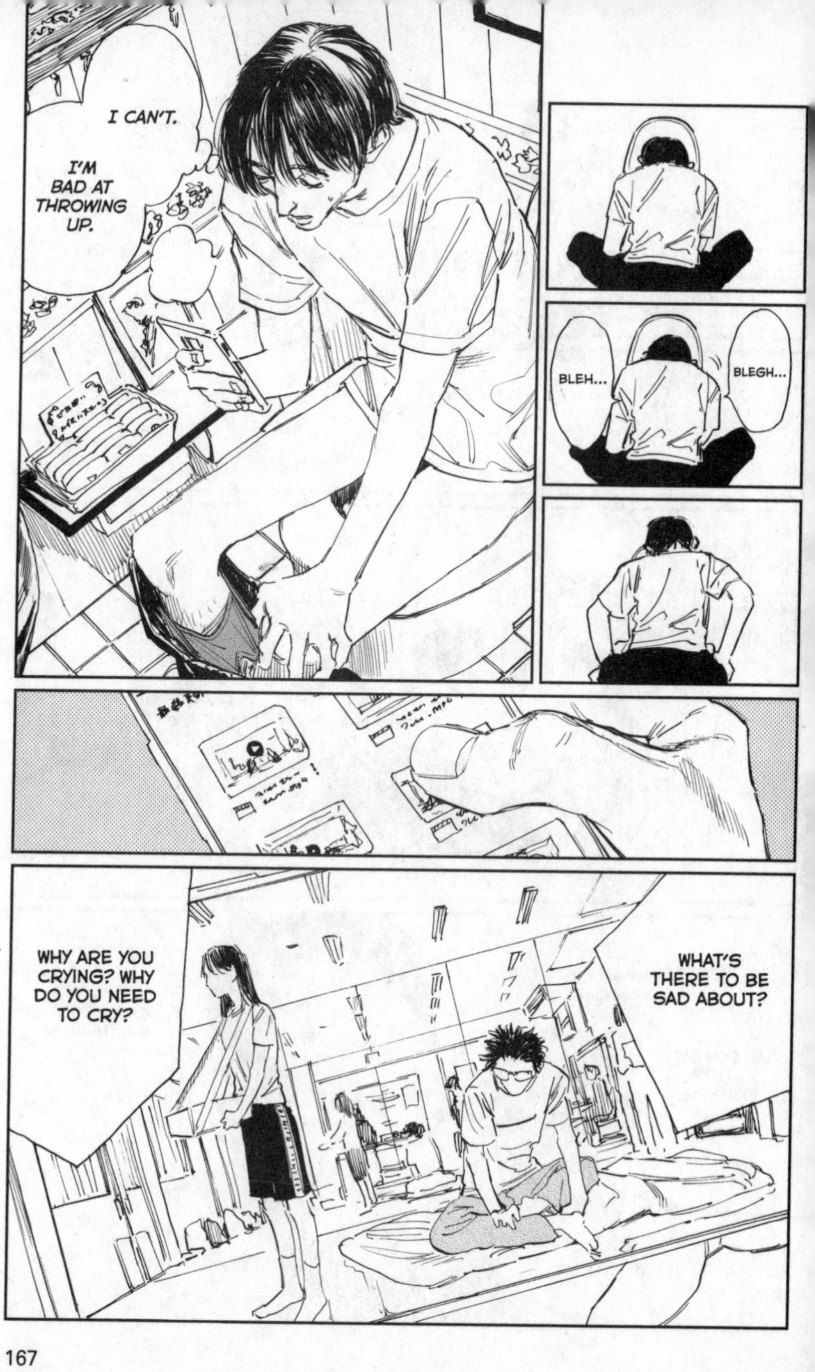
BLEGH...
BLEH...
I CAN'T.
I'M BAD AT THROWING UP.
WHAT'S THERE TO BE SAD ABOUT?
WHY ARE YOU CRYING? WHY DO YOU NEED TO CRY?

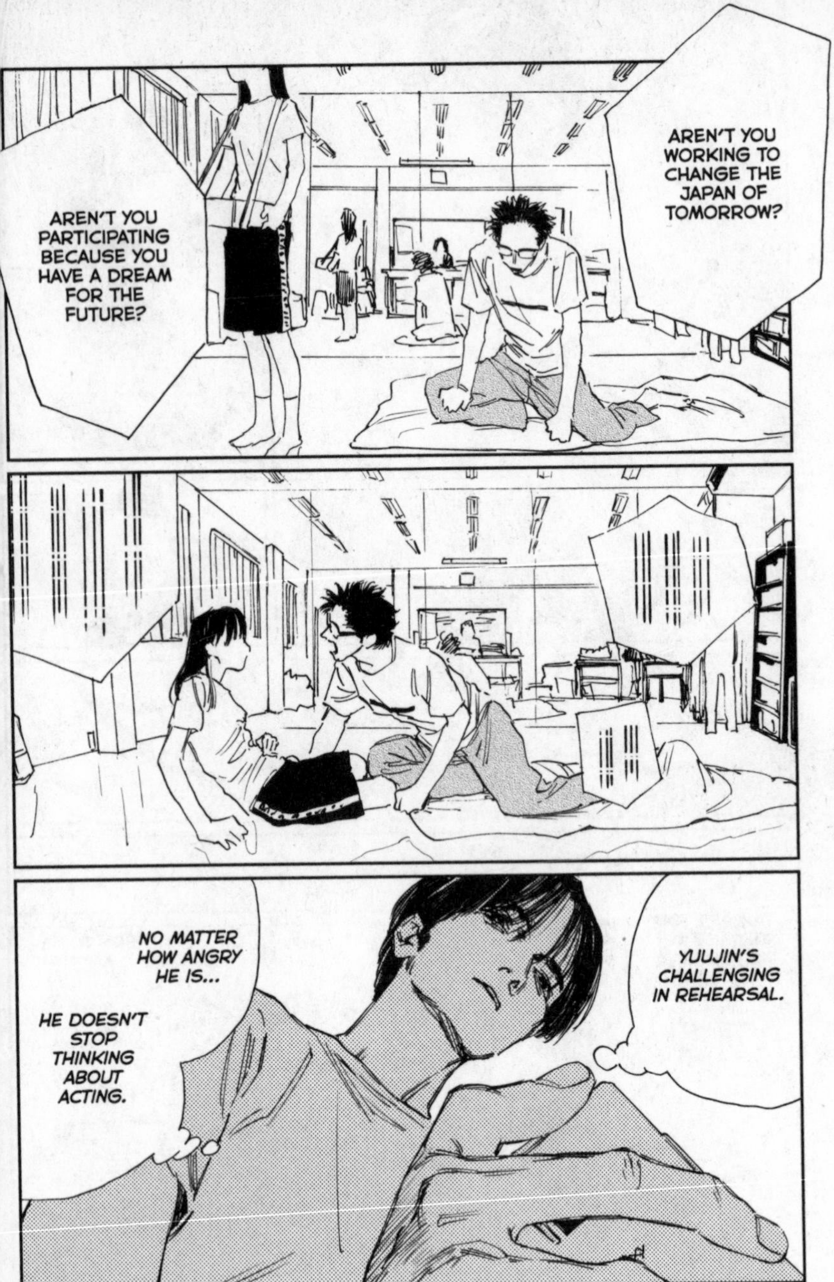
AREN'T YOU WORKING TO CHANGE THE JAPAN OF TOMORROW?
AREN'T YOU PARTICIPATING BECAUSE YOU HAVE A DREAM FOR THE FUTURE?
YUUJIN'S CHALLENGING IN REHEARSAL.
NO MATTER HOW ANGRY HE IS...
HE DOESN'T STOP THINKING ABOUT ACTING.

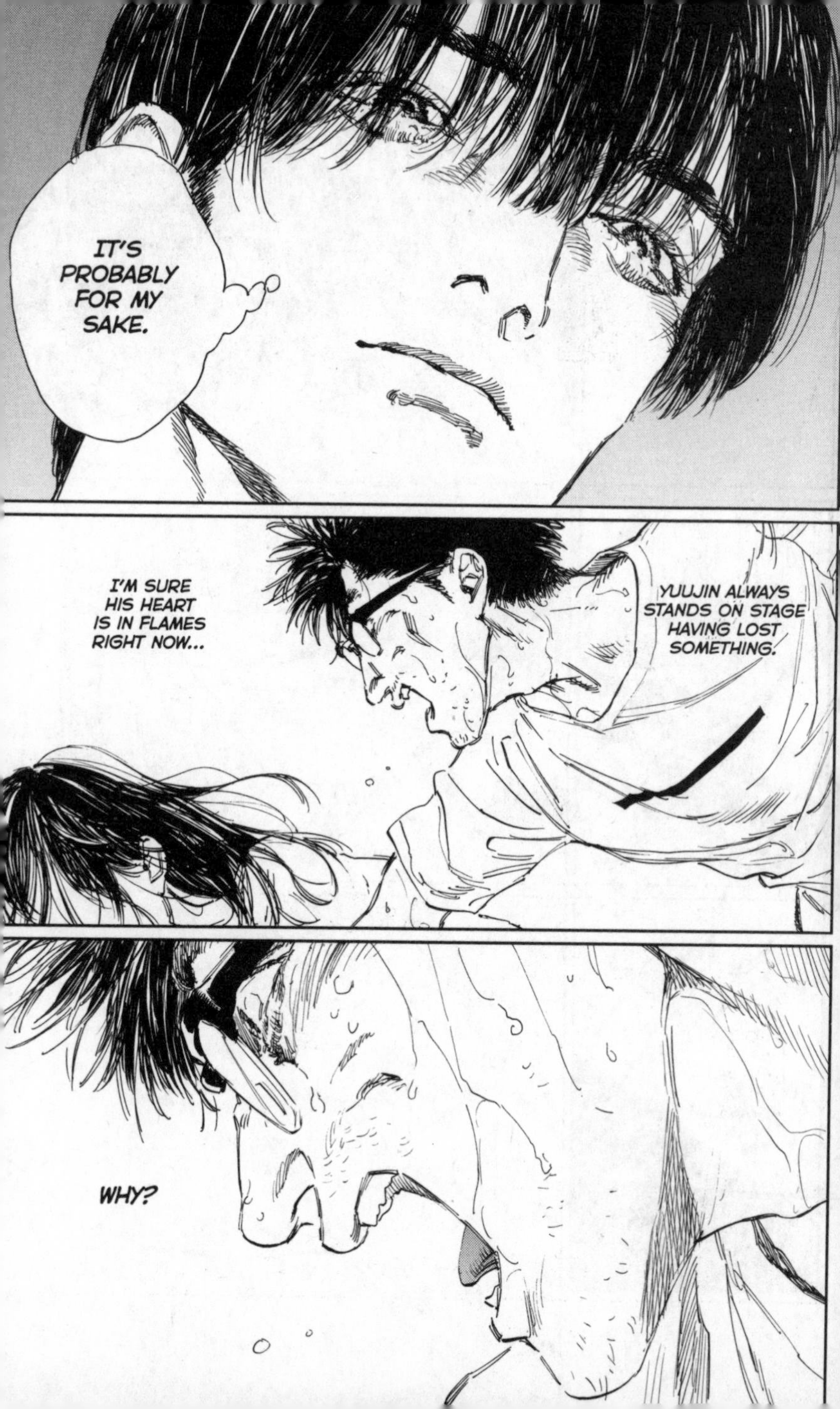
IT'S PROBABLY FOR MY SAKE.
YUUJIN ALWAYS STANDS ON STAGE HAVING LOST SOMETHING.
I'M SURE HIS HEART IS IN FLAMES RIGHT NOW...
WHY?

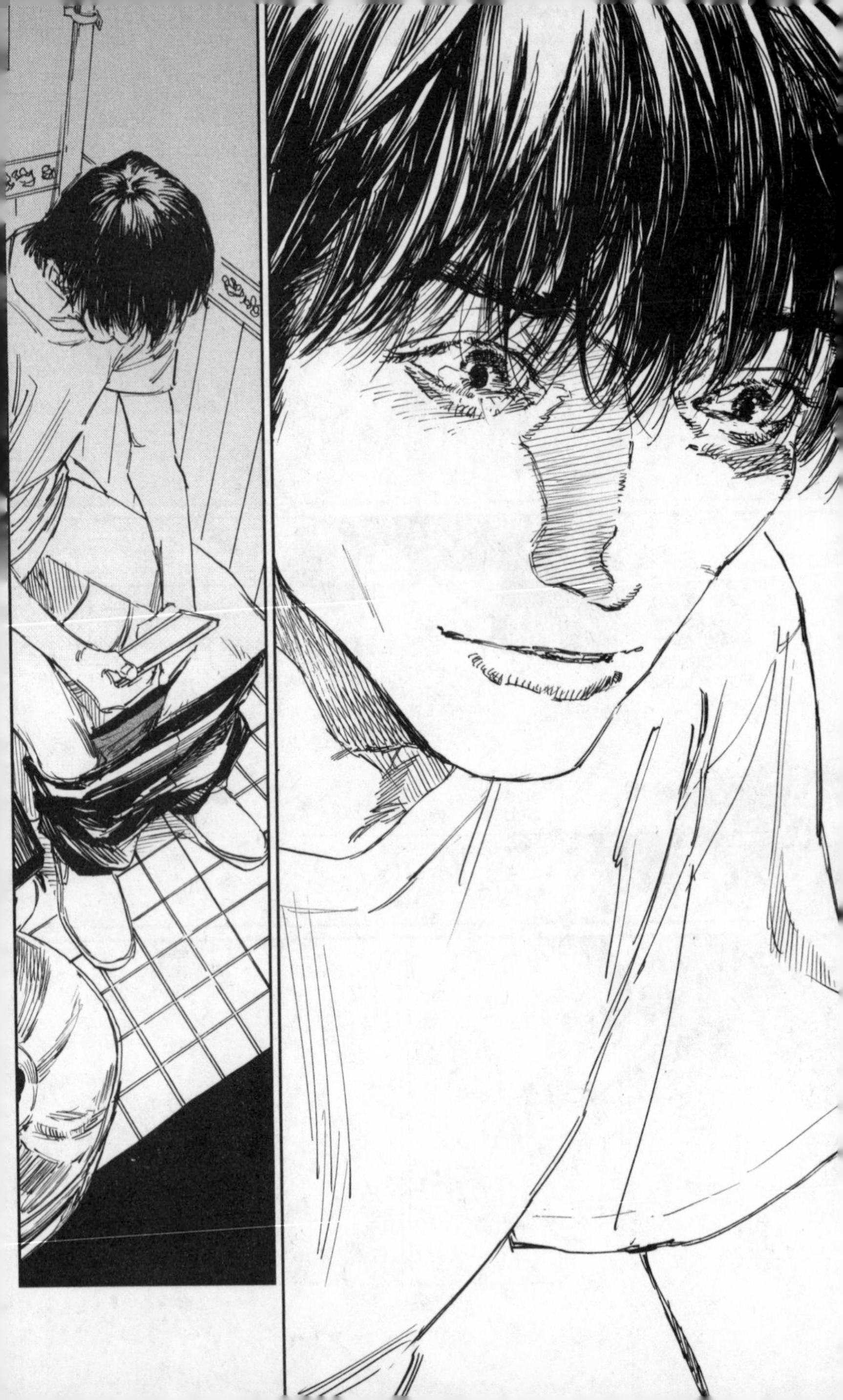

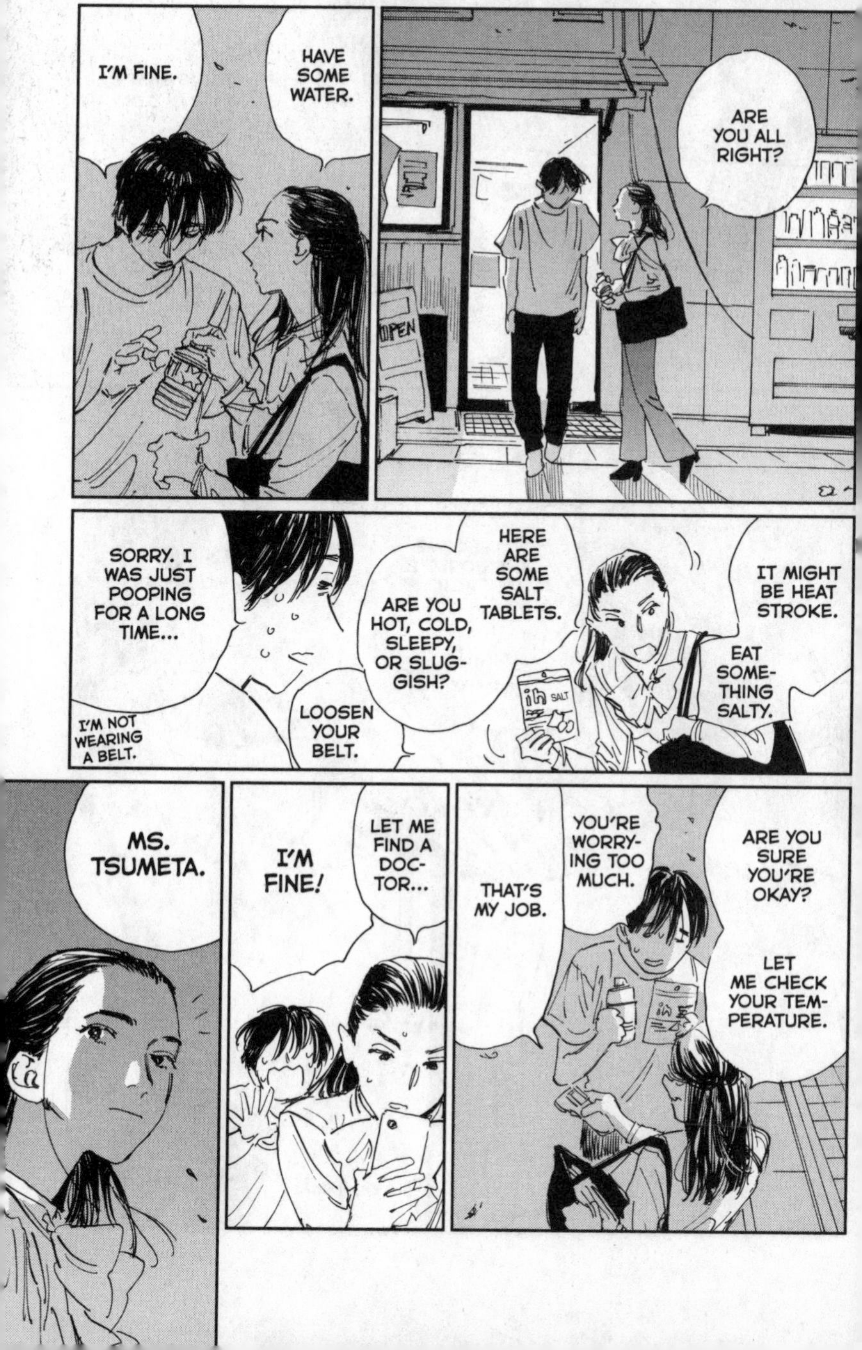
ARE YOU ALL RIGHT?
OPEN
HAVE SOME WATER.
I'M FINE.
IT MIGHT BE HEAT STROKE.
EAT SOMETHING SALTY.
HERE ARE SOME SALT TABLETS.
ih SALT
ARE YOU HOT, COLD, SLEEPY, OR SLUGGISH?
LOOSEN YOUR BELT.
SORRY. I WAS JUST POOPING FOR A LONG TIME...
I'M NOT WEARING A BELT.
ARE YOU SURE YOU'RE OKAY?
LET ME CHECK YOUR TEMPERATURE.
YOU'RE WORRYING TOO MUCH.
THAT'S MY JOB.
LET ME FIND A DOCTOR...
I'M FINE!
MS. TSUMETA.

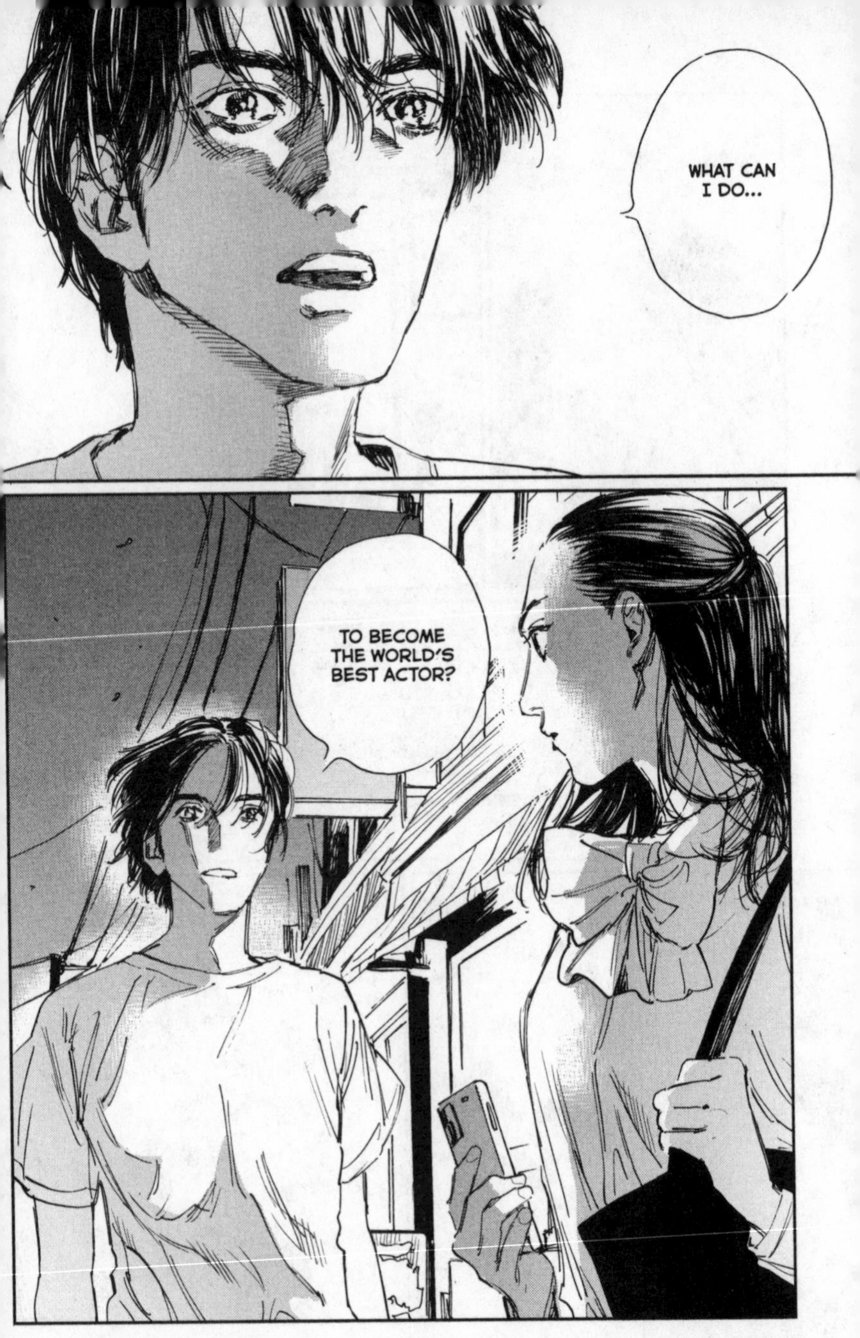
WHAT CAN I DO...
TO BECOME THE WORLD'S BEST ACTOR?

DOUBLE VOL. 4 COMPLETE

CONTINUED IN VOL. 5

ASSASSIN'S CREED DYNASTY, VOLUME 2

Xu Xianzhe, Zhang Xiao

ACTION ADVENTURE

In the 14th year of the Tianbao Era (CE 755) An Lushan, a military governor with ties to the Knights Templar, leads his elite corps to rebel against the Tang Dynasty, and the ill-prepared Tang empire falters under the threat. The two capitals Luoyang and Chang'an fall and China falls under the oppression of the cruel An Lushan. As the Tang dynasty starts to crumble, Li E, a shady Assassin trained by the Hidden Ones in the far West, teams up with Tang loyalists to turn the tide and save both the dynasty and the country from this crisis.

© 2021 Ubisoft Entertainment.

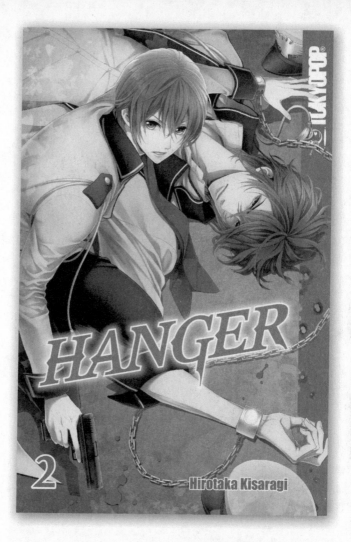

HANGER, VOL 2
Hirotaka Kisaragi

HANGER

2

Hirotaka Kisaragi

δLOVE·x·LOVEδ

TOKYOPOP

Afraid that Hajime could suffer the same tragic fate as his previous Keeper, Zeroichi intentionally widens the emotional distance between them for Hajime's own safety, leaving a frustrated and hurt Hajime doubting the kind of relationship they really have. Unfortunately, finding the time to sort out their feelings isn't a luxury either of them can afford— not with the mysterious group responsible for the death of Zeroichi's former Keeper suddenly terrorizing Neo-Tokyo once more.

© KISARAGI HIROTAKA/GENTOSHA COMICS INC.

OSSAN IDOL! VOLUME 4

Mochiko Mochida, Ichika Kino

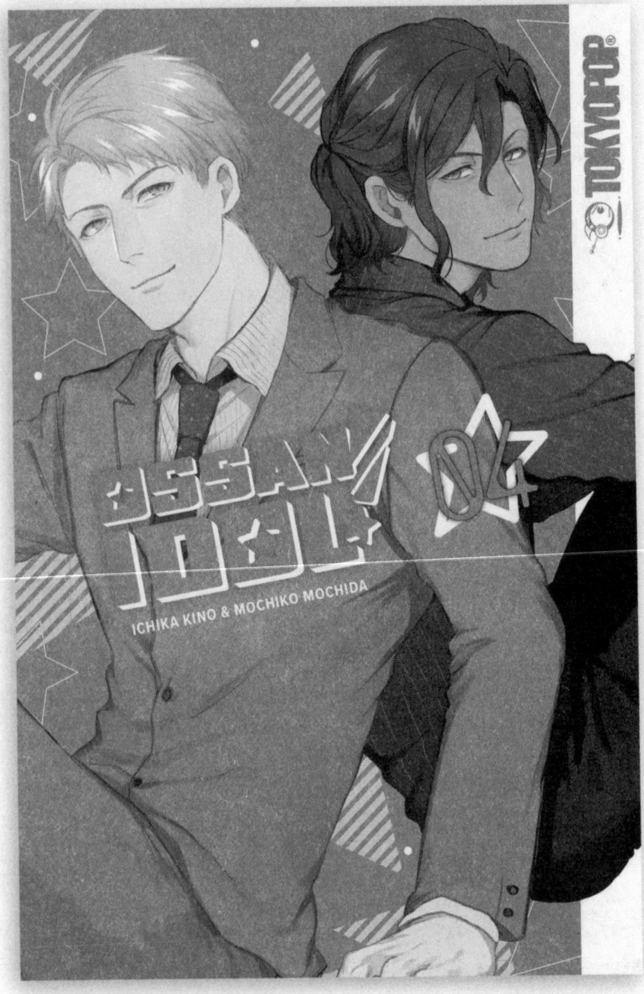
TOKYOPOP
OSSAN IDOL
04
ICHIKA KINO & MOCHIKO MOCHIDA

IDOL

A new friendship blossoms between Miroku and a fan, and MiYoShi's popularity blossoms both onstage and behind the scenes. Meanwhile, Fumi discovers Miroku was her mysterious hero, after all! Does this mean that a sweet romance between a brand-new idol and his manager is also about to bloom?

TOKYOPOP

A GENTLE NOBLE'S VACATION RECOMMENDATION, VOLUME 4
Momochi, Misaki

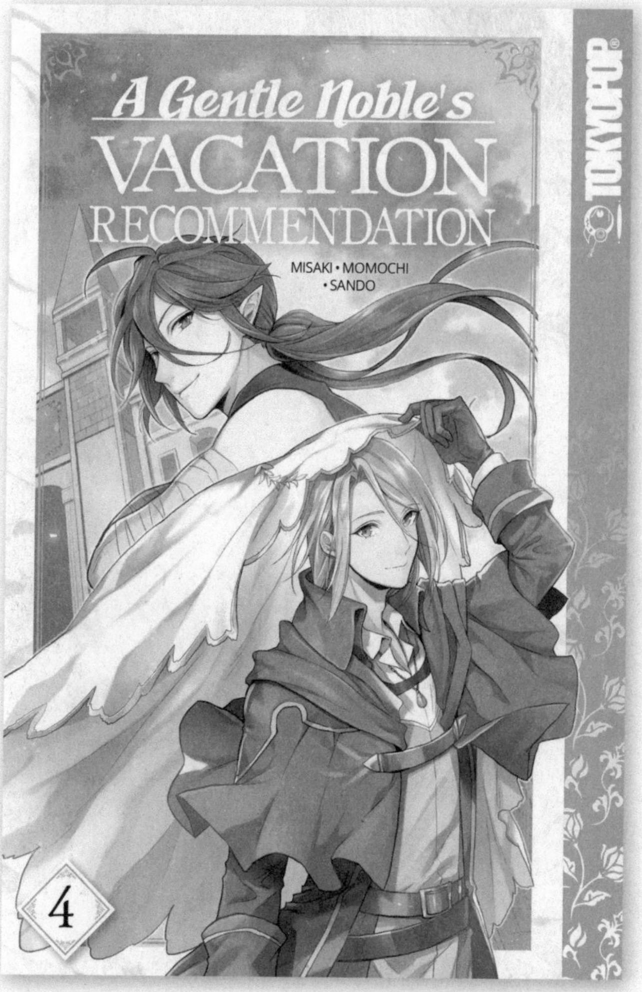
A Gentle Noble's
VACATION
RECOMMENDATION
MISAKI • MOMOCHI
• SANDO
4
TOKYOPOP

ISEKAI

TOKYOPOP

Lizel and Gil finally flush out their mysterious attacker and settle the score with him... but it seems the assailant isn't quite the threat they initially believed him to be.

Is it possible this former foe could actually be a new ally? Maybe so... but first he'll have to convince them to give him the chance he knows he deserves!

Karakarakemuri

LAUGHING UNDER THE CLOUDS, VOLUME 5

ACTION FANTASY

In the early Meiji era, against civil unrest and the end of the samurai way of life, Japan's crime rate skyrocketed. As prisons overflow, the government has no choice but to build a new, inescapable prison. This prison is Gokumonjo, located in the center of Lake Biwa, which means it relies on the three sons of the Kumo family to transport criminals to it. But is Gokumonjo truly just a prison for petty criminals...?

© KarakaraKemuri / MAG Garden

LAUGHING UNDER THE CLOUDS, VOLUME 6

KarakaraKemuri

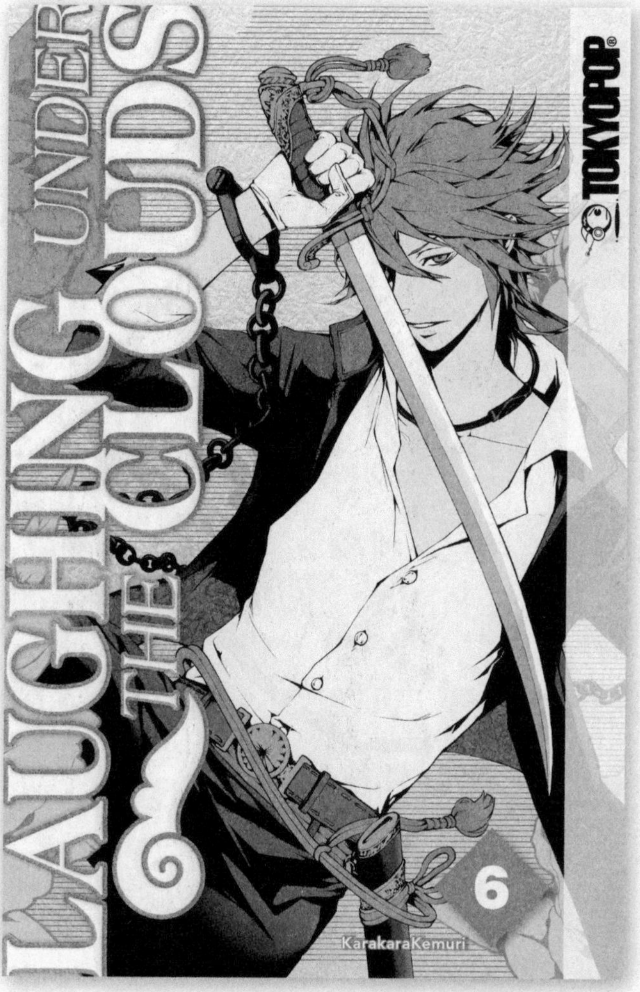

LAUGHING UNDER THE CLOUDS
TOKYOPOP
6
KarakaraKemuri

ACTION FANTASY

Under the curse of Orochi, the great demon serpent reborn every 300 years, Japan has been shrouded in clouds for as long as anyone can remember... The era of the samurai is at an end, and carrying swords has been outlawed. To combat the rising crime rates, an inescapable prison was built in the middle of Lake Biwa. When brothers Tenka, Soramaru and Chutaro Kumo are hired to capture and transport offenders to their final lodgings in this prison, they unexpectedly find themselves faced with a greater destiny than any of them could have imagined.

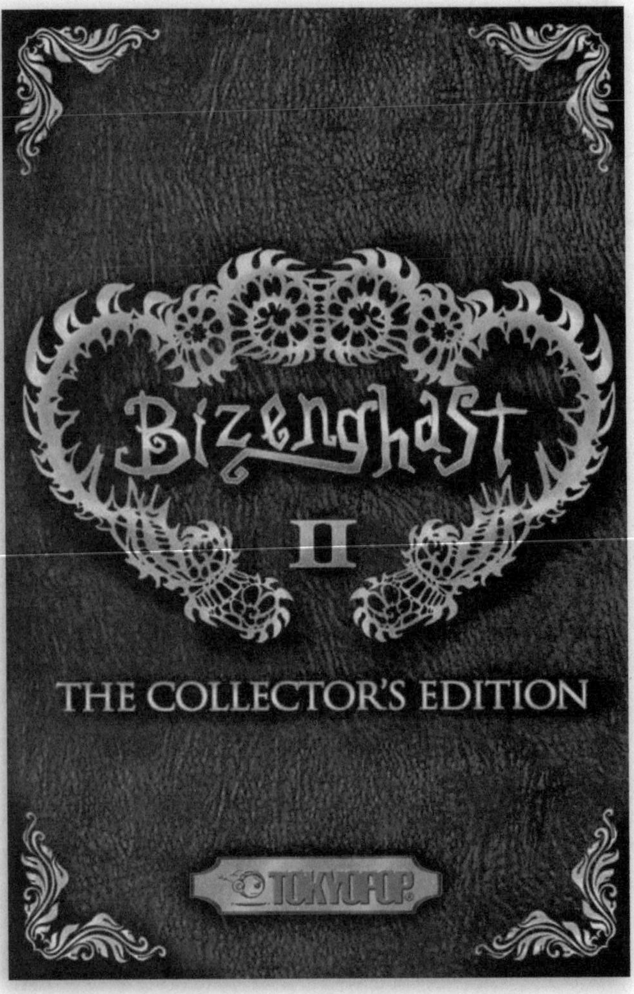
Bizenghast
II
THE COLLECTOR'S EDITION
TOKYOPOP

BIZENGHAST: THE COLLECTOR'S EDITION, VOLUME 2

M. Alice LeGrow

SUPERNATURAL

Adrift and in despair, Dinah will have to fight to keep her sanity, keep her life together and keep all hell from breaking loose in the Mausoleum! The town of Bizenghast holds many secrets, and Dinah will have to grow up and grow strong if she intends to seek out the truth. Hatred and murder underlie the very foundations of the town, and Dinah's struggle is only just beginning... This special collector's edition includes volumes 4, 5, and 6 of the best-selling original series plus bonus content!

TOKYOPOP

TAROT CAFE: THE COLLECTOR'S EDITION, VOLUME 2

Sang-Sun Park

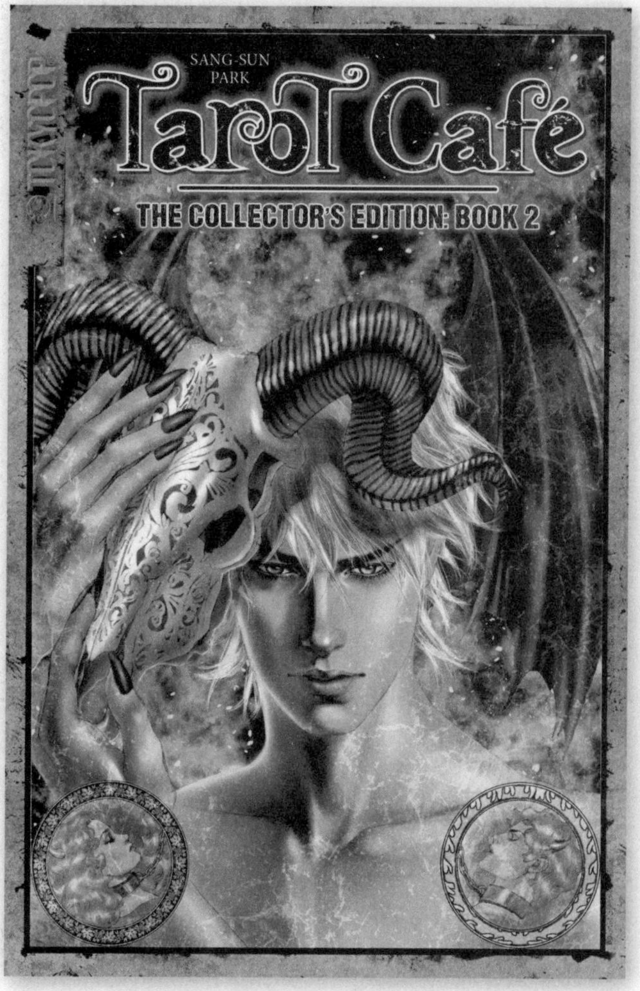
SANG-SUN PARK
Tarot Café
THE COLLECTOR'S EDITION: BOOK 2
TOKYOPOP

SUPERNATURAL

A Sultan who has fallen in love with a young slave... A poor student who drives away a lake fairy over doubt and jealousy... A dragon that seeks to avenge the death of a dear friend... These are just a few of the supernatural beings that Pamela, owner of The Tarot Café, welcomes through the doors of her mysterious establishment. But can she help them while dealing with a deep, dark secret of her own? Among the cries of lost love and unfinished business from visiting spirits, the mystery of her poignant past unfolds...

TOKYOPOP

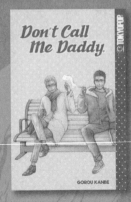

Check out *LOVExLOVE.info* for all kinds of romance!

LOVE × LOVE

TOKYOPOP believes all types of romances deserve to be celebrated. *LOVE x LOVE* was born from that idea and our commitment to representing a variety of stories and voices as diverse as our fans.

© 2021 Ataka © 2021 Sou Inaida © 2021 Hachipisu Wan / TO BOOKS, Inc.

TOKYOPOP®

YURI ♡ ESPOIR, VOLUME 1

Mai Naoi

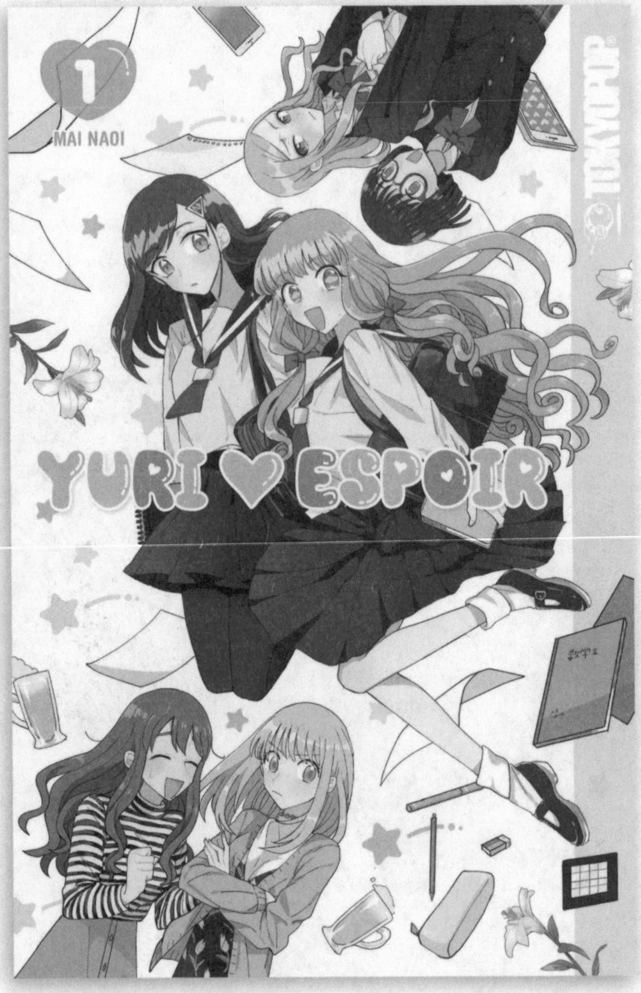
1
MAI NAOI
YURI ♡ ESPOIR
TOKYOPOP

♀LOVE-x-LOVE♀

After finding out she's to be forced into a marriage of convenience as soon as she graduates high school, Kokoro sees her life ending before her eyes at her father's wishes. And so, in her final year of high school, she decides to indulge in her love of other women — and create an incredible sketchbook of lesbian romance to leave behind as her legacy. As she observes the young women of her town, she learns more about their desires, their struggles, and the unpredictable whims of love.

TOKYOPOP

TOMORROW, MAKE ME YOURS

Koruko Miyama

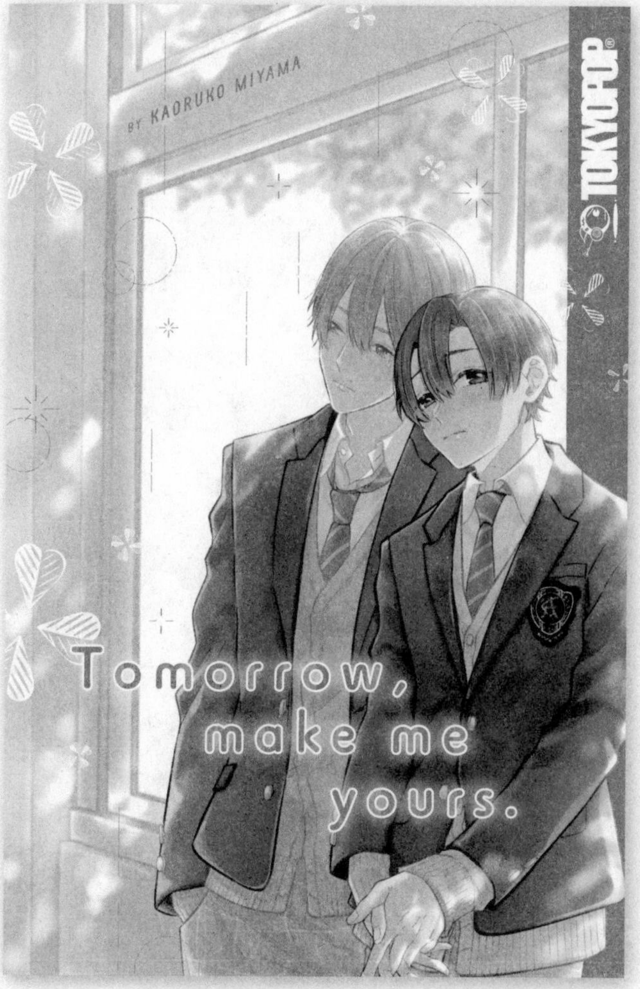

BY KAORUKO MIYAMA
TOKYOPOP
Tomorrow, make me yours.

MATURE 18+

LOVE x LOVE

Timid, shy Yuki is dreading the start of a new semester surrounded by unfamiliar faces. Sitting on the sidelines, he watches as the other students cluster around Hayato, the most popular boy in class — and his total opposite in every way. But when a chance conversation with Hayato draws Yuki out of his shell, he finds himself slowly opening up to the other boy's relentlessly cheerful and kind attentions.

TOKYOPOP

Shoko Rakuta

I'M LOOKING FOR SERIOUS LOVE!

I'M LOOKING FOR SERIOUS LOVE!

SHOKO RAKUTA

♂LOVE-x-LOVE♂   MATURE 18+

Born and raised in the countryside, Kyouhei immediately clashes with his next door neighbor, an outgoing playboy called Takara, when he moves to Tokyo. As someone who's always been teased for being a country bumpkin, he doesn't exactly have much in common with an extroverted city boy.But when Takara makes a move on him one day, Kyouhei can't get it out of his mind. Even though he can barely stand Takara, he can't help finding himself strangely drawn to him. But Kyouhei's not looking for a one night stand; he's looking for serious love!

TOKYOPOP

© 2019 Rakuta Shoko / OVERLAP, Inc.

OUR NOT-SO-LONELY PLANET TRAVEL GUIDE, VOLUME 2

Mone Sorai

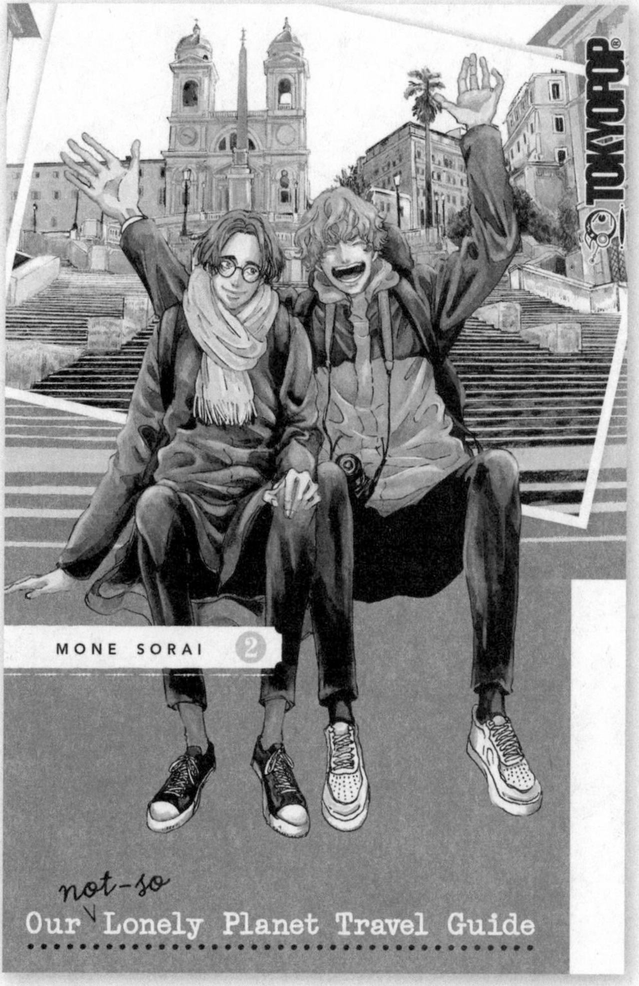
TOKYOPOP
MONE SORAI 2
Our not-so Lonely Planet Travel Guide

LOVE-x-LOVE

Super serious Asahi Suzumura and laidback, easygoing Mitsuki Sayama might seem like an odd couple, but they made a deal; they'll vacation around the world and when they get back to Japan, they'll get married. As they travel from country to country, the different people, cultures and cuisine they encounter begin to bring them closer together. After all they're not just learning about the world, but about themselves too.

TOKYOPOP

Double, Volume 4
Manga by Ayako Noda

Editor - Lena Atanassova
Translator - Massiel Gutierrez
Copy Editor - Tina Tseng
Proofreader - Katie Kimura
Quality Check - Daichi Nemoto
Marketing Associate - Kae Winters
Cover & Logo Designer - Sol DeLeo
Editorial Associate - Janae Young
Retouching and Lettering - Vibrraant Publishing Studio
Licensing Specialist - Arika Yanaka
Editor-in-Chief & Publisher - Stu Levy

A  Manga

TOKYOPOP and 🐾 are trademarks or registered trademarks of TOKYOPOP Inc.

TOKYOPOP Inc.
5200 W. Century Blvd. Suite 705
Los Angeles, 90045

E-mail: info@TOKYOPOP.com
Come visit us online at www.TOKYOPOP.com

f www.facebook.com/TOKYOPOP
🐦 www.twitter.com/TOKYOPOP
📷 www.instagram.com/TOKYOPOP

© 2022 TOKYOPOP   All rights reserved. No portion of this book may be
All Rights Reserved   reproduced or transmitted in any form or by any means
without written permission from the copyright holders.
This manga is a work of fiction. Any resemblance to
actual events or locales or persons, living or dead, is
entirely coincidental.

© Ayako Noda 2021   All Rights Reserved. Originally published by HERO'S INC.
HERO'S INC.

ISBN: 978-1-4278-6919-7
First TOKYOPOP Printing: May 2022
Printed in CANADA

STOP

THIS IS THE BACK OF THE BOOK!

How do you read manga-style? It's simple! Let's practice -- just start in the top right panel and follow the numbers below!

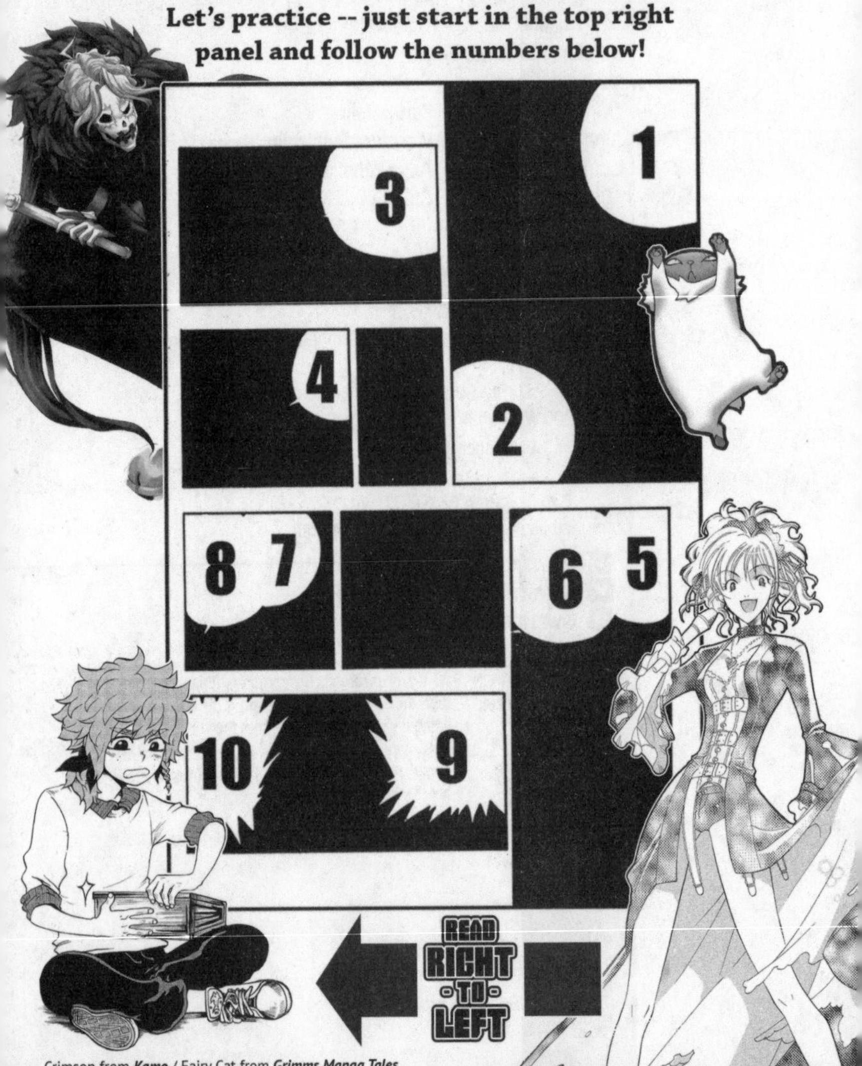

1
2
3
4
5
6
7
8
9
10
READ
RIGHT
-TO-
LEFT

Crimson from ***Kamo*** / Fairy Cat from ***Grimms Manga Tales***
Morrey from ***Goldfisch*** / Princess Ai from ***Princess Ai***